NO HELMETS
REQUIRED

Pitch Publishing Ltd
A2 Yeoman Gate
Yeoman Way
Durrington
BN13 3QZ

Email: info@pitchpublishing.co.uk
Web: www.pitchpublishing.co.uk

First published by Pitch Publishing 2013
Reprinted in paperback 2018
Text © 2013 Gavin Willacy

A CIP catalogue record for this book is available from the British Library.

13-digit ISBN: 9781785314025
Design and typesetting by Olner Pro Sport Media
Printed and bound in India by Replika Press

NO HELMETS REQUIRED

THE REMARKABLE STORY OF

THE AMERICAN ALL STARS

GAVIN WILLACY

INTRODUCTION

Since *No Helmets Required* finally made it onto bookshelves on Independence Day 2013, I have often been asked how I came about the American All Stars' crazy story. I can clearly remember reading Our Game magazine on a London train platform and becoming engrossed in a feature about a guy called Mike Dimitro and a bunch of college gridiron kids going down under. In a couple of pages, writer Tony Collins ignited a fascination in me that led to more than a decade spent creating *No Helmets Required*. Tony, this is all your fault!

In the winter of 2002/03, my wife Jo and I spent three months travelling around the States: many of our stops just happened to have connections with American rugby league! As we headed down the east coast from Cape Cod to Key West, I immersed myself in the scattergun history of the game in the States. In Floridian libraries I started reading newspaper reports online of the All Stars games posted by an Australian fan called 'Roopy'.

Now fascinated, once in California I decided to try to track down an All Star to interview. Starting with an obscure name, I discovered Gary Kerkorian had recently died but found phone numbers for his son, Paul, and widow, Joyce. The following evening we found ourselves in their house in Fresno! They welcomed us and enchanted me with tales of Gary's adventures in Australia and the NFL. Crucially, they also put me in touch with many of Gary's old rugby mates, for which I owe a great debt.

From that came many more breakthroughs: I borrowed our friend John Friend's vintage BMW sports car to drive from San Francisco around the Bay Area to meet the wonderful Al D. Kirkland and the fascinating Vince Jones. They put me together with Jack Bonetti. All three told me wonderful tales. I had to write their story.

In Australia I visited the grounds on which the All Stars had played in Sydney, Brisbane, Cairns and Townsville; to Auckland, Wellington, Christchurch and Greymouth in New Zealand; and several visits to France to see Carcassonne, Perpignan, Avignon and Albi.

I even joined Landon Exley on his golfing holiday in Ireland before heading back to California to visit old Trojans Al Abajian, Ed Demirjian and their mate Teddy Grossman. Up in Palo Alto, a bed-ridden Al Kirkland, recuperating from a major operation, sent his physical therapist away so he could talk me through the events of half a century before. "This guy's come further than you to see me," he said. Classic Al. I even got to dine with Tony Rappa at his seafood restaurant in Monterey's Fisherman's Wharf.

When I thought I had nearly finished writing the book, Michelle Dimitro, Mike's daughter. kindly sent me stacks of Mike's mementoes, cuttings and notes from his myriad of football, rugby and life adventures. Those boxes sent me back to the drawing board for another few years, but made the tale what it is now. They filled in a lot of gaps.

Mike Dimitro was just one of many people who has fought to promote rugby league in America. And he fought the longest. He failed, but not through lack of trying. Ironically, just as the story of his efforts was finally released, the USA played in the Rugby League World Cup for the first time. He would have loved that.

When sending off the completed manuscript, I checked the date: it was ten years to the day since I had turned up at the Kerkorians' front door. It was time their story was told.

Gavin Willacy, Bengeo, 2018

ACKNOWLEDGEMENTS

No Helmets Required was written mainly in Bengeo, Hertfordshire; but also in Sedbergh, Cumbria; Hallsands, Devon; Cisternino, Puglia; and Alghero, Sardinia.

I was privileged to meet and interview eight of the All Stars: the late great Big Al D. Kirkland, Al Abajian, Tony Rappa, Ed Demirjian, Vince Jones, Landon Exley, Ted Grossman and Jack Bonetti. I am also grateful to Erkie Cheldin, Don Lent, Pat Henry, Sam Grossman, Bob Buckley and Fran Mulcare for their wonderful written memories. You are all stars to me.

Many thanks to Michelle Dimitro, for sharing so many of her Dad's amazing mementoes.

The following friends all very kindly put us up in their homes while I followed in the All Stars' footsteps: Simon Hunt and Mathew Jones (in Sydney), John Friend (San Francisco), Sarah McGhee and Bill Taylor (Auckland), Barbara and the late Louis Guyomar (Wellington), Elizabeth and Guy Sancho (Fosse, near Perpignan) and Marie Toft (near Carcassonne).

I am especially grateful to the late Delpha Cadogan and her brother John for not only welcoming virtual strangers into their homes but coming to USC to support the launch - we had a ball!

Thanks also to all these good folk for their help, support and advice: RFL archivist Professor Tony Collins, Harry Edgar of Rugby League Journal, Keith Nutter, Roger Grime, Bill Abernethy, Steve Mascord, the guys at AMNRL and USARL, John Morgan and George Pelecanos.

Without Paul and Jane Camillin at Pitch Publishing *No Helmets Required* may never have made it out into the world, while designer Duncan Olner took my vision for the book and ran with it, creating a visual feast. What a talent! Duncan's design was quite rightly short-listed for the 2014 Bob Rushton Award for outstanding work that combines the arts with rugby league.

Also thank you to those who made the launch events at Stanford and USC, Cairns and Townsville so enjoyable.

I am especially grateful to my Mum and Dad: firstly for exposing me to the wonderful world of rugby league as a child, then showing parental enthusiasm for my *No Helmets* project throughout this century, and advancing some inheritance to ensure those trips to California and Queensland went ahead!

The praise *No Helmets* received from readers, sportswriters and broadcasters, who gave it such generous reviews, was considerable reward for the time and effort invested. It also helped pave the way for this paperback edition.

Most of all, thank you to my wonderful wife, Jo, for never once saying 'enough'! Her patience and support are astounding. I hope the magical experience of us taking *No Helmets* back to California was some consolation!

BIBLIOGRAPHY

'Atlantic Crossings' article by Tony Collins, *Our Game* magazine, Autumn 2000.
Rugby League Journal – numerous issues.
Huddling Up – Jeffrey Goodman, pub. Fitzhenry & Whiteside,1982.
The Pittsburgh Steelers – Abby Mendelson, pub. Taylor.
The Encyclopedia of Rugby League Players – Alan Whitacker and Glen Hudson, pub.
Gary Allen, 2002.
Being Eddie Waring – Tony Hannan, pub. Mainstream, 2008.
America's Game – Michael MacCambridge, pub. Anchor, 2005.
Going Long – Jeff Miller, pub. McGraw Hill, 2003.
Supercoach: The Life and Times of Jack Gibson – Andrew Webster, pub.
Allen & Unwin, 2011.
When The Colts Belonged To Baltimore – William Gildea, pub.
John Hopkins University Press, 1996.
The Great Grand Final Heist – Ian Heads, pub.
Stoke Hill Press, 2017.

Picture credit: *Rugby League Journal* – www.rugbyleaguejournal.net

Artefacts from Mike Dimitro's collection courtesy of Michelle Dimitro.
Photos from Paul Kerkorian, Don Lent, Al D. Kirkland, Landon Exley
and Pat Henry.

CONTENTS

PROLOGUE – FIVE MEN IN L.A.
LOS ANGELES, AUGUST 1950

Five men in the City of Angels: a Hollywood film star, an English broadcaster, an Australian hack, a Californian sportswriter and a Welsh rugby coach. They have nothing in common. Well, almost nothing.

Bob Hope is one of the world's biggest film stars. He part-owns LA Rams, the glamorous West Coast pro football franchise, which employs Mr Jane Russell at quarter back, has fans throughout Hollywood and a Beverley Hills HQ.

Eddie Waring is the voice of BBC radio sport in the north of England. A sporting svengali from Dewsbury in Yorkshire, he has a vision: seeing his beloved rugby league football beamed live into living rooms across Britain and around the world. He just wishes the BBC would share his faith in this new medium called television.

Harry Sunderland is a 60-year-old from Toowoomba, Australia. He has done pretty much everything in rugby league: first a journalist, then secretary of Queensland Rugby Football League in his early 20s, and Australia's national team manager at 40. At 50 he emigrated to manage English giants Wigan. Now

Cliff Evans, Harry Sunderland and B. Ward Nash

he is back writing, for the *Sunday Despatch*, commentating on BBC radio and living in Manchester. Sunderland is fearless, an expansionist, a promoter, a rugby league missionary. A stocky little fella, round glasses perched on his moon face. His nickname: The Little Dictator.

Cliff Evans is a former rugby league star. Man of the Match in the 1933 Challenge Cup Final, he was a top-class half-back for Salford, Leeds and his native Wales either side of the war. He had a spell as a parachute-jump instructor, quit playing and became coach at Leeds. After two years he gave it all up and left Yorkshire for California. In LA he set to work transferring his ample skills: within two years of arriving he had managed a theatre, a car wash and a restaurant at Venice Beach. He is still athletic, a dapper figure.

B. Ward Nash is a middle-aged, fair-haired, print salesman in downtown LA. He also writes about sport at the weekend and uses his printing business to publish sports books. He rarely leaves home without his Panama hat.

Sunderland and Waring were on their way home from Great Britain's Ashes tour. The team spent a month travelling to Australia by boat, played 27 games in less than three months there and took another month to come home. Ticket sales from so many games made it a cash bonanza for all concerned.

Both working journalists on the tour, filing copy back to England, Sunderland and Waring had followed the Australia leg and three weeks in New Zealand, with personal stop-overs in Fiji, Honolulu and San Francisco. There were visits to Dallas, Chicago and New York to come. Sunderland was in town to promote rugby league. Or perhaps more accurately, to promote Harry Sunderland and rugby league.

Waring was pretender to Sunderland's crown as 'Mr Rugby League'. Twenty years the younger, Waring had, like Sunderland, already been a club secretary, manager, author, newspaper columnist, BBC radio commentator, and expansionist. Waring knew Cliff Evans from their time at Leeds together, where Eddie was an up and coming manager.

Waring and Sunderland wrote for rival rugby league papers and were the only two press men at the formation of the Rugby League International Board two years earlier. They both knew more about overseas opportunities than most.

Sunderland had tried to launch the 13-man football code in Victoria, London, France, and, for the past 20 years, America. In 1932 he went to the LA Olympics and took the opportunity to visit some of football's major movers and shakers. He spent time with University of Southern California coach Howard Harding Jones, the legendary Pop Warner up at Stanford, and met players from NFL teams Portsmouth Spartans and Green Bay Packers.

Excited by the prospect of rugby league crossing over to the US, Harry aimed high. He wrote to Chicago Bears owner George Halas suggesting the Australia team play an exhibition rugby league game in Chicago en route to England the following year.

The legendary Halas was interested and proposed that they play the Bears in September 1933 as part of the World's Fair instead: one half of league, the other of American football. Neither happened, but little Harry would never give up.

On this trip, Sunderland went to see Bob Hope's LA Rams play the Washington Redskins at the Coliseum and was blown away by the spectacle. He was also a guest speaker at the influential Helms Foundation, giving a presentation on rugby league to a room of wealthy sports boosters.

Waring, who had been behind the mic for the BBC's first televised rugby league match – the 1949 Challenge Cup Final at Wembley – was more interested in how Americans consumed sport through the little box in the corner of the room. Stunned by the way televised games gripped the men watching in bars in every US city he visited, Waring was determined that rugby league should be broadcast nationwide on British TV – and that he would be the game's number one commentator.

He visited Hope on the set of his latest movie. Hope had been at the forefront of TV's breakthrough on the West Coast: he had hosted the first-ever show broadcast in California and was now beginning an illustrious TV career with NBC. Waring was impressed by Hope's knowledge of Australian rugby league, especially for a world-famous comic-actor from Somerset.

Waring suggested that they collaborate on a rugby league film with Hope's big

Eddie Waring and Bob Hope meet

screen side kick Bing Crosby and name it *On the Road to Wembley*. Hope encouraged Waring to jump on the television bandwagon – and before he left the City of Angels, Eddie guested on Californian TV, discussing the differences between rugby league and American football.

Needing another sympathetic ear in the LA press, Sunderland and Evans met up with Nash and told him about The Greatest Football Game he had never seen. He was hooked by the notion.

Across town, in South Central LA: Michael Machnov Dimitro was teaching social studies and coaching American football at Andrew Jackson High School in Boyle Heights. He was a long way from home. He would go a lot further.

CHAPTER 1
ONCE UPON A TIME IN AMERICA
WEST VIRGINIA, JULY 1922

As Ukrainians divided to fight on opposite sides in the First World War, Dimitro Machnov fled his home town of Zelinka for the land of the free. Carrying with him his life's belongings, he entered the United States through Ellis Island, where he was met by his nephew Alex, who had left Ukraine before him in search of the promised land. Together they made their way down through New York, Pennsylvania and Ohio before seeking work in the steel town of Weirton, West Virginia, 35 miles from Pittsburgh. Once settled, Dimitro called for his wife Mary and their three-year-old son John to follow him to the States. It was 1917.

Of the 20,000 citizens of Weirton, half worked at Weirton Steel. The mill was the town. The Machnovs were not total outsiders: the route they had taken had been travelled by enough of their people for there to be a Russian Orthodox Church in the town. If you have seen the Robert de Niro film *The Deer Hunter* then you have seen Weirton. It was shot there. It's where Dimitro Machnov lived, worked and died.

The Machnovs had eight children. Six survived childhood: John, Anne, Catherine, Harry, Michael and Joe. Michael Dimitro Machnov was born on 20 July 1922. Or 20 August 1923. Or 1924. Mike was never 100 per cent on that. It depended who was asking – and why. The US Census said it was 1922.

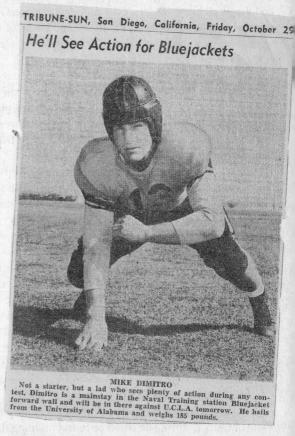

TRIBUNE-SUN, San Diego, California, Friday, October 29

He'll See Action for Bluejackets

MIKE DIMITRO

Not a starter, but a lad who sees plenty of action during any contest, Dimitro is a mainstay in the Naval Training station Bluejacket forward wall and will be in there against U.C.L.A. tomorrow. He hails from the University of Alabama and weighs 185 pounds.

They all lived in a two-bedroom house: Mum and Dad in one room, oldest son John slept in the living room. The other five kids shared the other bedroom: Anne and Catherine in one bed, Harry and Joe in the other, with Mike sleeping on a feather quilt on the floor. There was a kitchen, and the bathroom was in the basement.

Breakfast was coffee and toast. Lunch was a baloney sandwich with tea or water – no milk. Dinner was served in order of those who had worked: the youngest often ended up with just bread and butter and a mug of tea or coffee. Life was no picnic.

Michelle Dimitro: 'My father worked with his father at Weirton Steel in the open hearths. Dad was out there working from the age of five, picking up pop bottles, shovelling coal, anything which could help bring food home for the family.'

Mike's child labour was described as 'heavy chores': hauling coal to fill the bed in the basement from 6am to 7pm, all alone, wearing old pants with holes in the knees, no hat and cardboard shoes.

Like many mining and steel towns, Weirton was wrecked by alcohol. Mike's Dad – who played the accordion at Ukrainian weddings to raise a few bucks – was one of many immigrants who spent his meagre wages in Weirton's bars and staggered home in the dark of night. On payday, Mike would trail the bars to find his father and drag him home before all the money had gone. One perk of the drink culture was the number of bottle tops lying around for Mike to collect and cash in. He would also pick apples in summer to bring home to the family. The drink and the coal dust would cut his father's life short.

Michelle Dimitro: 'Dad realised at a young age that working in the open hearth of the steel mills was not how he wanted to spend the rest of his years, especially when he would listen to the Rose Bowl game being played on the radio and the temperature in LA was in the 70s while they were freezing in West Virginia. He knew he had to get out and he knew the way to do that was through education and playing sports.'

Mike was something of a sporting protégé. At Weirton High School in the late 1930s, he starred at baseball, football, boxing, and wrestling. In 1939 he was voted the top football player in the high schools of northern West Virginia and in 1940 played for the West Virginia All Stars when they beat the Ohio All Stars at Wheeling Island Stadium. Mike was the only kid to play the full game: at guard in defense and full-back on offence. He was already The Man, in Weirton.

He won Golden Gloves boxing titles in three states at three different weights. The precocious teenager lifted the light heavyweight crown in Boston – among his opponents was Tony Musto, who would lose a world title bout to Joe Louis a year later. En route he caught wanderlust, the travelling bug.

Soon, Mike was packing his bags. He had managed to combine sporting excellence with passing his exams and doing shifts in the mill. In the summer of 1941, he left home – and his brothers and sisters to care for their bed-ridden father – and fled 600 miles south-west to Tuscaloosa to take up a football scholarship at the University of Alabama.

There he continued his sporting journey: first he played guard for the freshmen football team. In spring he could be found minding third base for the Baby Tide baseball team. By September 1942, Mike, now a sophomore, was on the Alabama football roster. Under legendary coach Frank Thomas, the Crimson Tide roared into the ten-game season with five straight wins, conceding just one touchdown. They secured an invite to the Orange Bowl in Miami and on New Year's Day 1943, Mike and the Crimson Tide beat Boston College 37-21. He was voted on to the Southern Conference All Star team. He also showed signs of being a leader, opening a boxing school at the university – Dimitro's Athletic Club – where he coached Golden Glove fighters.

It was at Alabama that Dimitro met two major figures in his life: fellow jock Ray Terry and Evelyn Woodall. 'Woody' would become his first wife, Terry his sidekick on his greatest adventure.

Mike was living the American dream and needed an American name, not a Russian one. He dropped Machnov and became just plain Mike Dimitro. With thick dark hair, black eyes and brooding eyebrows, he looked every inch the Italian-American stallion. That was better than being 'a Ruski' in the south as the US joined the Second World War.

Dimitro signed up, and with a glowing reference from the Crimson Tide, was assigned to the US Navy. As he turned 21 in July 1943 he left his new wife Woody behind in Tuscaloosa and headed 2,000 miles south-west to the Naval Training Station in San Diego.

As Squadron Leader Dimitro awaited his first Pacific posting, his football flourished. The Training Station football team was filled with elite college players and former pros. They faced the best of California's college football in the Pacific Coast Conference. Three months after arriving, Dimitro was playing guard as the Bluejackets, coached by former New York Giants Bo Malenda and Mac McLinda, thrashed hapless UCLA 28-0 at Hull Field, in front of 6,000 exhilarated Navy personnel. He was at left tackle when the Bluejackets stunned the previously invincible USC in 'the greatest athletic achievement in NTS history'. Dimitro could see at first hand the allure of such prestigious football schools – and they could see his talent up close.

Mike was transferred to the US Naval Training Center at Bainbridge in Maryland. While on the banks of the Susquehanna River, Mike heard news from Europe: his little brother Joe had been seriously wounded in action in Italy and was now in an Allies hospital in north Africa. He never recovered, dying there, aged just 17.

In the freezing early months of 1944, Mike's passion burned even stronger. He needed revenge. He was thrilled to be finally sent to war: Dimitro headed for the South West Pacific Theater.

Mike was stationed in Port Moresby, the manic capital of New Guinea, an Australian territory defended by the American amphibious force. From there he flew north-east to the Caroline Islands, where the Allies destroyed a Japanese base in Operation Hailstone on two devastating February days. Dimitro later claimed he was 'wounded by a burst of shrapnel over the landing craft' as he arrived in the Carolines. It can't have been too serious. He might have been more hurt by the 'Dear John' letter Woody sent him: she was divorcing him already.

In the steaming heat of the Pacific theater, Dimitro was still getting his sporting fix. He boxed in the Carolines and played football for the Hawaiian Island All Star Team. Between all the boxing, football, baseball and wrestling, Dimitro claimed to have served in the Philippines, Guam, Japan, Tarawa (where the Japanese were massacred on 20 November 1943), Saipan (where the US forces ousted the Japanese in July 1944) and Okinawa (where the battle in 1945 was arguably the worst in the Pacific). He just happened to have been at four of the major US successes of the whole war. Dimitro liked to tell a tall tale. He just could not help himself. Much of it, however unlikely, was true. But the truth was never enough.

It was during two days' leave that a seed planted in Dimitro's mind that would change his life. He cadged a lift aboard a Royal Australian Air Force cargo plane to Sydney. The pilot, an Aussie named 'Bluey', was a rugby league player. He took Dimitro to see a game at the Sydney Cricket Ground. As a kid, he had seen immigrant Welsh miners playing rugby union on the slag heaps in Weirton between shifts down the pit, and US troops had played rugby in Guam in their down time. But this was something different. The West Virginian was blown away by the speed, the passing and the ball control. He had seen the future.

Mike Dimitro

CHAPTER 2
BECOMING A BRUIN

WAR IS OVER - BACK TO SCHOOL

Dimitro was discharged on 28 December 1945. He had continued his degree at Alabama by correspondence but, having tasted San Diego, nothing would tempt him back to the Deep South or West Virginia's coal fields. It was sunshine and surf for him.

In the summer of 1946, Dimitro returned to Southern Cal to get his teaching certificate, enrolling on a PE, History and Education degree at the University of California in Los Angeles: UCLA. But he was really there to play football. The swarthy, stocky, powerful Dimitro was a wanted man. He went straight in to Bert LaBrucherie's highly-rated Bruins squad at left guard. Dimitro wore 27. Number 26 was left tackle Xavier Mena, a towering 19-year-old kid from San Diego. Don Paul was the giant centre, Jerry Shipkey the full-back who had transferred from USC.

Dimitro excelled as the Bruins saw off Stanford, Cal and Oregon amid their first eight straight victories. In the winner-takes-all clash with city rivals USC at the Coliseum in late November 1946, the Bruins came through 13-6 to win the Pacific Coast Conference and an invite to the annual Rose Bowl Game: the biggest day in college football. And therefore the biggest day in US sports.

They finished the regular season by beating Nebraska 18-0. They had played ten, won ten.

Then, in front of 90,000 mainly-Bruins fans in Pasadena, Dimitro and Co were humiliated by Illinois, 45-14. It was a New Year's Day nightmare.

1947 It was supposed to have been Big Mike's perfect ending. Going into that game, Dimitro had planned to quit college for a career in pro football. In December 1946, he and three other Bruins were drafted by Bob Hope's Los Angeles Rams in the 11th round. The Rams had only been in town a year, having moved from Cleveland as reigning NFL champions, opening up the West Coast to pro sport and making the National Football League what it claimed to be. But they were still struggling financially, losing a couple of thousand bucks a week.

Dimitro was also wanted by the Rams' more affluent rivals:

LH-AL HOISCH
5:7-150 lbs.
Senior

the LA Dons, of the All American Football Conference. The AAFC was a post-war success. It briefly challenged the NFL and temporarily succeeded in becoming more attractive to players and fans than the established pro competition. Outbidding the NFL to sign the best available players, the AAFC soon

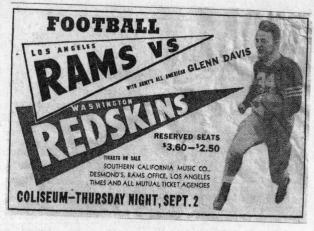

became known as a superior league and its crowds dwarfed those in the NFL. The flamboyant Dons were owned by a syndicate of millionaires: actor Don Ameche, MGM Studios head Louis B. Mayer and horse racing magnate Benjamin Lindheimer. They were getting bigger by the year. But still the Dons and Rams were fighting over second place in the press and the fans' hearts: college football remained king in LA.

The Dons bid for Dimitro, also in the 11th round, of the AAFC draft along with four other Bruins. In February 1947, the 210lbs guard withdrew from UCLA, his future all planned out.

When his father died in August after a long illness, Mike headed home to Weirton. There he realised a teaching qualification would offer him far more security than jacking it all in for what could be a few months as a pro football player. He returned to UCLA to complete his degree.

Dimitro had an outstanding season for the Bruins in 1947. Bursting out of the blocks in defence, he was a tackling machine, snuffling out danger all over the Coliseum field. In an extraordinary few minutes against Southern Methodist, he tackled All-American Doak Walker four times in a row on the Bruins' two-yard line. On the offensive line he blocked everything defences could throw at him to protect his quarterback. He was a colossus of the Coliseum.

LG-MIKE DIMITRO
5:10–210 lbs.
Junior

MIKE DIMITRO

HE'S A ROUGH, TOUGH GENTLEMAN FROM WEST VIRGINIA, ONE OF UCLA'S MOST AGGRESSIVE LINEMEN.

15 NOVEMBER 1947
Los Angeles Daily News

MIKE DIMITRO
NEED WE SAY MORE

PERHAPS THE BEST IN THE NATION. RATED AS SUCH IN A RECENT RADIO-NEWSPAPER POLL. BRILLIANT IN ALL PHASES OF PLAY.

17 NOVEMBER 1947
Californian Daily Bruin

RE-
BILL
CLEMENTS
6:0–200 lbs.
Junior

18 NOVEMBER 1947

BEST GUARD IN US – DIMITRO

Californian Daily Bruin

'While all the local experts who pick the All Star teams were watching the glamour boys, a stocky little lineman snuck in the back door and became the first man from the Pacific coast to be named for national honors: UCLA's scrappy guard Mike Dimitro…never a rahrah boy, never flashy but always there fighting, plugging holes.'

'Granite Dimitro' was an All-American. Chosen by New York sportswriters as the outstanding player in his position, Dimitro was invited to leave LA straight after the game with USC to fly to the Big Apple for the presentation dinner at the Waldorf Astoria. He could take any girl he chose: he picked a UCLA queen Juanita Breneman, who the papers claimed was his fiancée, and her twin sister Juana. After a week in the Big Apple, the bizarre love triangle moved on to Weirton, where 'Punchy' took the girls to meet his family at 305 Engle Street.

Dimitro was getting all the wraps ahead of the big game against USC Trojans. The Bruins' number 27 was at the heart of it all, protecting quarter back Benny Reiges from left-guard, playing both ways – defence and attack.

He was delivering the goods - and with them came stardom, in LA at least. He was getting used to the headlines, the photos, the girls. He kept every paper: ten copies if it was a good one.

MIKE DI MITRO

FRENCH GOVT FALLS IN CRISIS

BIG MIKE

COACH BERT LABRUCHERIE TABS MIKE DIMITRO AS HIS MOST VALUABLE MAN

LA Evening Herald-Express, back page

He was already in the big time. In Chicago to play North Western, the Bruins shared the front page of the *Daily Tribune* sports section with the all-New York 'Subway' World Series.

The Notre Dame-USC game took $10m at the bookies in Southern California alone. The front page of the *LA Daily News* had Bruins team news above Mao Tsetung's communists withdrawal into Manchuria:

'LINEUPS FOR BRUINS, STANFORD

– Expect 100,000 at big UCLA-Indians grid tilt'

'BIG RED RETREAT BEGUN IN CHINA'

The Bruins shoved the Jake LaMotta fight fix story into the round-up. A whole page of photos in the *LA Times* showed the players relaxing before the USC clash. The *Herald-Express* ran a Hollywood vox-pop: Betty Grable said the Trojans would win. Rita Hayworth said the Trojans by two touchdowns. Lana Turner picked UCLA.

It was boiling up.

PRINCESS ELIZABETH'S WEDDING DAY WILL BE LIVE ON ALL FOUR MAJOR RADIO NETWORKS

22 NOVEMBER 1947

LOS ANGELES COLISEUM (OLYMPIC STADIUM), LOS ANGELES, CALIFORNIA

102,938 squeezed into the Coliseum, just 265 short of the all-time record. They saw the Trojans snatch a 6-0 win. It was a grudge game with not an inch given. Everything was on the line and Dimitro's men lost it. There would be no return to the Rose Bowl game.

Despondent, Dimitro went AWOL. He failed to complete a physical exam and was told in January 1948 he was being expelled by UCLA. Only a frantic appeal allowed him to be restored within a week.

1948

That off-season, Dimitro took up rugby 'as a sort of summer training'. Rugby union was the only code played in California. The big schools used it primarily in the spring and summer for their athletes to keep fit and active, and middle-class students indulged

Mike meets Dorothy Lamour

in its social reputation. Several of the Bruins football team gave rugby a go.

While the offers from the Dons and the Rams remained, Dimitro decided again to stay at UCLA to complete his degree. He got married for a second time – to fellow student and trainee high school teacher Patricia Dodds – and changed his name again too, to Michael Mitchell Dimitro. It was his third, but far from final, identity.

He headed home to Weirton and took part in Olympic boxing trials, winning three heavyweight bouts to qualify for the final round in Boston, but had to return to UCLA's pre-season camp instead.

Dimitro also spent some of the summer of 1948 working in the post department at a Hollywood film studio. The *Hollywood Citizen* showed him delivering parcels to sarong-wearing sex symbol Dorothy Lamour, the straight girl to Bing Crosby and Bob Hope in the *Road to...* films. Mike was warming to the showbiz world, empowered by the buzz.

There was another medium making waves. KLAC-TV launched in LA to rival Bob Hope's KTLA and sent two cameras to every Trojans and Bruins game, beaming pictures to homes throughout California. Dimitro should have been the star. Instead, he was rarely seen.

The 1948 season started badly and finished worse. The Bruins got nilled by Northwestern in the opening game, Dimitro was injured and failed to get his starting position back. Strutting the Coliseum sideline in October, he would have seen a classy young quarterback leading Stanford's freshmen in the curtain-raiser against the UCLA 'Frosh': Gary Kerkorian would stick in his mind.

By November, with the Bruins out of Bowl contention again, Dimitro chucked his toys out of the pram. The 'UCLA Fireplug' turned Cry Baby. The UCLA campus became a gigantic crèche.

7 HOME GAMES
7 FOOTBALL COACHES
7 IMPORTANT DATES TO REMEMBER

BRUIN ROOTERS' LUCKY YEAR !

See the BRUIN ELEVEN IN ACTION
Collegiate Football in the Coliseum

Dimitro had been used off the bench against Nebraska Cornhuskers, played 40 minutes, and was on the field every time the Bruins scored. But that was enough for him to go on strike and spout off: 'Unless I can start, I won't play the last three games.'

4 NOVEMBER 1948

DIMITRO DROPPED FROM SQUAD
DIMITRO LEAVES TEAM – WILL FOLLOW PROFESSIONAL BOXING

UCLA Daily Bruin

DIMITRO'S OWN STORY OF FOOTBALL ROW AT UCLA

MIKE BLAMES COACHES, LISTS MEN WHO QUIT

The Mirror

Back page lead: *'Dimitro last night walked into the Mirror office, asked for a typewriter and wrote his own version of the argument.'*

BRUINS DROP MIKE

LA Times Green

It's a two page story. Big news.

He claims other players, including reserve George Kauffman, pulled out of the team because of LaBrucherie. The coach says Kauffman was never good enough to play anyway. The gloves are off.

LA BRUCHERIE SAYS MIKE NEVER EARNED TOP SPOT

Then:

COACH BERT LABRUCHERIE SAYS:

MIKE CAN COME BACK IF APOLOGISES

GUARD MIKE DIMITRO RETORTS:

I WON'T PLAY UNLESS I CAN START

On the eve of the game, Dimitro was back in. According to the *Evening Herald and Express*, he had 'smoked the pipe of peace' with LaBrucherie when a few choice remarks from two assistant coaches 'poured salt on old wounds'. 'Dimitro walked off in a huff and this time turned in his suit, once and for all.' 'I got sore and walked off,' Dimitro told the *Express*. 'I'm not going to take anything from those two.'

Bottom line, Dimitro's college career was ending in bitter acrimony. It would not be the last time he would put his ego ahead of loyalty. Come Christmas, LaBrucherie would be gone too.

In December, Mike was invited to try out with San Francisco 49ers. He withdrew, once more, from UCLA and headed to Honolulu to play for the Pac Coast All Stars in the Hula Bowl. It sated his wanderlust for another winter.

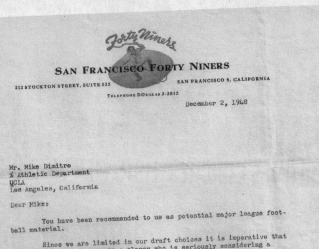

Forty Niners

SAN FRANCISCO FORTY NINERS

212 STOCKTON STREET, SUITE 322   SAN FRANCISCO 8, CALIFORNIA
TELEPHONE DOUglas 2-3812

December 2, 1948

Mr. Mike Dimitro
% Athletic Department
UCLA
Los Angeles, California

Dear Mike:

You have been recommended to us as potential major league football material.

Since we are limited in our draft choices it is imperative that each choice made represents a player who is seriously considering a professional career.

We would, therefore, deeply appreciate an expression from you as to whether or not you are considering playing professionally when you have completed your college eligibility and, if so, whether or not you would be interested in playing in San Francisco with the Forty Niners, provided a mutually satisfactory contract can be agreed upon.

We are enclosing a roster of the Forty Niners and we shall be glad to answer any questions you may have in mind regarding our organization.

We are enclosing a questionnaire and a self addressed stamped return envelope for your convenience. We would appreciate your checking the questionnaire and returning same to us at your earliest convenience.

Thanking you in advance for your cooperation in this matter and with best wishes for a successful season, I am

Sincerely,

L. T. "Buck" Shaw

L. T. "Buck" Shaw

ALL · AMERICA · FOOTBALL · CONFERENCE
BALTIMORE · BROOKLYN · BUFFALO · CHICAGO · CLEVELAND · LOS ANGELES · NEW YORK · SAN FRANCISCO

1949

Dimitro – now living at 2524 Prosser Ave – soon changed his mind again and finally finished his degree at UCLA. He accepted an all-expenses paid three-week trip to Chicago in August courtesy of the *Tribune* to play for the college's All Stars against the NFL champions, Philadelphia Eagles, at Soldier Field in the traditional season opener. Despite being 27, he was listed as being 24 years old. A year earlier UCLA had him down as 25. Curious.

The $150 game fee would take his little brother Harry three weeks to earn at Weirton Mill. And when Mike was offered $5,500 a year by LA Dons – plus a $250 bonus if he makes the team – he snubbed the LA Rams' latest offer and signed for the AAFC team.

On 1 June 1949, Dimitro finally turned professional. In mid-July he joined five other rookies at practice in Long Beach. Overwhelmed by dollar signs, Mike went out and bought a brand new, all-optionals, two-door Styleline Dix from a Chevrolet dealership on Santa Monica Boulevard. The Chevy cost him $2,000. Not a cent of his AAFC contract was guaranteed: all the Dons were committed to paying was his bed and board in training camp and a one-way ticket home if they released him. In mid-August, that's exactly what Dons coach Jim Phelan did. Mike flew to New York to try out with their new franchise, the Bulldogs. They didn't want him either. And they were awful, winning just one game of their opening NFL season, eventually evolving into Baltimore Colts.

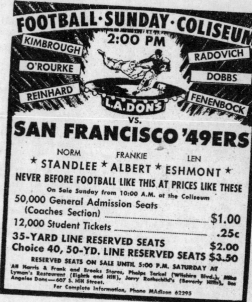

Devastated by his rejection by pro football, Dimitro enrolled across town at USC to do a Masters degree in education. But by October he had applied to transfer back to the University of Alabama. He was pin-balling from pillar to post.

He saw sense and stayed with Patty at their Stewart St home in Santa Monica. His Masters thesis was based on analysis of the 1947 SMU-UCLA game film in which he'd had a stormer. His football mates said Patty must have written it. They were probably right.

Dimitro mixed with USC's football players on campus but, as a twice-married 27-year-old war vet, he was almost a decade older than some of the kids arriving straight from high school. He was not one of them, never could be. His time had been and gone.

Leaving USC in 1950, he took up a post at Palo Verde Junior College. He would be paid $3,500 a year to teach and work as line coach during the football season, then take the college baseball team in the spring. When he went home to Weirton for the holidays, he came back having signed almost a whole football team from Ohio for the next season. But Dimitro would not return to Palo Verde with them. Desperate to make the most of his athletic ability, he started to hunt a pro football deal again.

The demise of the AAFC that year left only 12 pro teams and about 500 players in the States. So, in the summer of 1951, Mike headed up to Canada to try out for Edmonton Eskimos instead. They didn't sign him either. He could go back to West Virginia and play 'dirt-lot' semi-pro football in the mud and sludge. No thanks. LA was home now. All of his brothers and sisters were in Southern California now, too. The sunshine of LA proved irresistible. He moved in to a small detached house on Ceilhunt Avenue with Patty and got a teaching job at Andrew Jackson School in Boyle Heights.

His dream of being a football star was over.

All-America Football Conference

Contract Between

The Los Angeles Dons, ~~Inc.~~

herein called Club, and _Mike Dimitro_

of _2524 Prosser Ave, Los Angeles 34, Calif._ , herein called Player.

The Club is a member of the All-America Football Conference, herein called the Conference. The Constitution and Rules of the Conference define the relationship between Club and Player and vest in a Commissioner (herein called the Commissioner) powers of control and discipline and of decision in case of disputes.

In consideration of those facts and of the mutual promises and the promises of each to the other hereinafter set forth, Club and Player agree as follows:

1. Club hereby employs Player to render skilled services as a football player during the year(s) 19 _49_, including Club's training season, exhibition games, Conference games and post-season championship games in said year(s).

2. For performance of Player's services and agreements hereunder, Club will pay Player the sum of $ _5,500.00_ per year, which shall be payable in semi-monthly instalments commencing with the first and ending with the last regularly scheduled Conference game of Club.

In addition Player shall be entitled to all amounts allocated to him by the Commissioner or the Conference Rules for post-season play-offs and championship games.

3. Player agrees to perform his services hereunder diligently and faithfully and to conform to high standards of personal conduct, fair play and good sportsmanship and to Conference Rules and Club regulations respecting player conduct.

4. Player agrees that until June 2 of the year following the last year stipulated in paragraph 1, he will not play, or contract to play, football otherwise than for Club, except with the approval in writing of the Commissioner and Club.

5. Player represents and agrees that he has exceptional and unique skill and ability as a football player, that his services to be rendered hereunder are of a special, unusual, extraordinary and intellectual character which gives them peculiar value which cannot be reasonably or adequately compensated for in damages at law, and that Player's breach of this contract will cause Club great and irreparable injury and damage. Player agrees that, in addition to other remedies, Club shall be entitled to injunctive and other equitable relief to prevent a breach of this contract by Player. Player represents that he has no physical or mental defects, known to him, which would prevent or impair performance of his services.

6. Club and Player agree to accept and comply with all provisions of the Conference Constitution and Rules and all decisions of the Commissioner thereunder. Club and Player accept as part of this contract the Regulations printed on the reverse hereof. A copy of the Conference Constitution and Rules shall be available at Club's office during its regular business hours for inspection by Player.

7. Club may terminate this contract by written notice to Player if Player shall at any time (a) fail, refuse or neglect to render his services hereunder; or (b) fail, in the opinion of Club's coach, to have or exhibit sufficient skill or competitive ability to qualify or continue as a member of Club's team; or (c) in any other manner materially breach this contract, including the Regulations. If this contract is terminated by Club by reason of Player's failure to render his services hereunder due to disability resulting directly from injury sustained in the performance of his services hereunder and written notice of such injury is given by the Player as provided in Regulation 6, Club agrees to pay Player at the rate stipulated in paragraph 2, for the balance of the season in which the injury was sustained. In all other cases, if this contract is terminated by Club during its regular Conference schedule, Player shall receive as his full compensation such proportion of the sum stipulated in paragraph 2 as the number of days of his service during such Conference schedule up to such termination bears to the total number of days in such Conference schedule. If this contract is terminated during the training season, payment by Club of Player's expenses and his transportation as provided in the Regulations, shall be full compensation for Player's services during the training season and Club shall not be obligated to pay any part of the sum stipulated in paragraph 2.

8. Player agrees that he may be fined or suspended from payment and play by the Commissioner or the Club for violation of this contract, provided that any termination of this contract or fine or suspension by Club shall be appealable to the Commissioner in accordance with the Conference Rules.

9. Player agrees to cooperate with Club in any and all of its promotional activities and agrees that Club shall have the right to use his name, portrait, picture, likeness and performance in all exhibitions, descriptions and representations of the football games of Club on the field or by radio broadcasting, television, motion pictures, photography or other media and in connection with any and all promotional, advertising or trade purposes of Club and the Conference. Player recognizes that Club has an insurable interest in Player and Player agrees to cooperate with Club in all matters pertaining to that interest and its protection by Club.

10. Player agrees that on or before June 1 of the year next following the last year stipulated in paragraph 1, by written notice to Player, Club may renew this contract for said following year on the same terms, including the terms of payment, as those stipulated in the other paragraphs hereof, unless Player and Club agree upon a higher or lower payment to Player. Such option of renewal and the promise of Player not to play otherwise than for Club have been taken into consideration in determining the amount stipulated in paragraph 2.

11. This contract, including said option, may be assigned by Club to any other Club in the Conference, and Player agrees to report to the assignee promptly, as provided in the Regulations, upon notice of such assignment. Upon and after such assignment, all rights and obligations of the assignor hereunder shall become and be rights and obligations of the assignee and the assignee shall become liable to Player for his salary and the assignor shall not be liable therefor. The Conference may, under conditions prescribed in the Conference Constitution, become an assignee of this contract with the same effect as if the contract had been assigned to Conference by Club. All references in this contract to Club shall be deemed to mean and include any assignee of this contract.

12. Any dispute between Player and Club shall be referred to the Commissioner as an arbitrator and the Commissioner's decision shall be accepted by all parties as final. Club and Player agree that any claim by either party against the other shall be deemed waived and released unless presented in writing to the Commissioner within 90 days from the date it arose.

13. This contract sets forth the entire agreement between the parties. No verbal agreements or understandings between Club and Player shall be valid or binding.

14. A copy of this contract shall be filed with the Commissioner by Club within 10 days after its execution. This contract shall have no force or effect if disapproved by the Commissioner within 10 days after such filing.

SIGNED in triplicate this _26_ day of _April_, 19 _49_

THE LOS ANGELES DONS, ~~Inc.~~

WITNESSES:

Player to Rec. $250.00
Bonus if he makes the
team at training camp.

By _Tony M. Cellia_
(Club)

Mike M. Dimitro
(Player)

305 Engle St. Weirton,
(Home address of Player)

(PLAYER'S COPY)

CHAPTER 3
THE SHOW OF ALL SHOWS

Dimitro was a flitter. A chameleon. He changed jobs, homes, cities, sports, names, wives. But he could not contemplate never playing competitive sports again. A life of watching. A life without smashing someone legally. A life of never running with that leather oval under your arm again. Or stiff-arming an opponent. Or celebrating under the posts. No more cheers. No more victory songs. No locker room laughs. No back page headlines. No cheerleaders or nights out after a game.

Dimitro panicked. He could not live without such joys, yet. He was still a young man. He started to plot.

What if he built his own team? Then he could play when he liked. He had so many former team-mates from Alabama, the Navy, UCLA, USC, LA Dons, and the college All Star teams, not to mention the guys he had played against. Most of them were in a similar boat. Some were playing pro football, most were wondering what to do next with their lives. What if he got a team together and played exhibition games? The All Star games he had played in Honolulu and Chicago had been a blast – and the huge crowds must have made the promoters a fortune.

He wanted some of that. The football season was over in January. Fans were desperate for football by the summer. There was a gap in the market and Dimitro planned to fill it. The NCAA and NFL would never let them play even exhibition games in spring or summer. But he knew a team of college all stars could draw a crowd in Canada or Hawaii. Or both. He would get a squad of his old pals together and they would go abroad to play. They would be called the American All Stars.

Football in Canada had a few differences from American gridiron – 12 players, not 11; three downs, not four. But it was easy for American players to adjust. Canadian football teams were still called 'rugby football clubs'; they had semi-pro leagues in the Interprovincial Rugby Football Union and the Western Interprovincial Football Union. But it was still football with helmets, pads, blocking, downs and forward passes. The evolution from rugby was almost complete.

But football was expensive: you needed dozens of players, loads of equipment, a myriad of coaching staff and medical teams. Better have a Plan B. What about the game he had seen that afternoon in Sydney during the war? Rugby league football. Maybe they could go to Australia and play that game, too. Dimitro convinced himself that high quality American football players could adjust and play the 13-man code. He knew plenty of boys who had played a bit of rugby union in college, like he had at UCLA. He could get enough guys interested to play again. How hard could it be?

Rugby was not on the American sporting landscape. The football codes had diverged in the first half of the century. There were just as many differences as similarities between gridiron and rugby. Both codes had backs that ran with the ball and created attacks. They both had wide men who finished off those attacks, who plucked the ball from the sky to score. Both codes had big men up front who tackled and fought. They both had expert kickers. Only the names for each role were different. But football players were covered in pads and a helmet. Rugby was played relatively naked: it was raw football.

The only rugby being played in California was rugby union: 15-a-side, line-outs, mauls and a lot of scrums. Top schools Stanford and Cal were major forces in college rugby, Cal hosting tour games against New Zealand All Blacks, Australia's Wallabies and Oxford and Cambridge Universities. When they graduated, some of their players continued with this foreign football at clubs such as Palo Alto Ramblers and the Olympic Club in San Francisco. There were enough 'ruggers' around LA for the horror movie star Boris Karloff to have launched the Southern Cal Rugby Football Union before the war – and for Dimitro to find men who could tackle, pass and catch an oval ball.

The Californian boys would seem glamorous and exotic to post-war Australians. They could pack stadiums and Dimitro's back pocket. It was win-win. The more he thought about it, the more he convinced himself that rugby league could go down a storm with American college players facing life without football. And Australia sounded fun. Rugby league was massive on the east coast there.

Mike got in touch with his old mate from the Bruins, Xavier Mena. They had played together in 1946. He had told 'X' all about the rugby he had seen in Sydney. Mena had graduated as a teacher but was now working as an architect in LA. He liked the sound of this latest adventure.

Little did Dimitro know that elsewhere in LA, Ward Nash was working with Aussie impresario Harry Sunderland on their own plan to break rugby league in the States.

FEBRUARY Dimitro wrote to the Australian Rugby Football League Board of Control in Sydney, selling them the idea of the All Stars tour. He thought it was a done deal. He penned press releases for the Australian papers under a new alter ego – Rig Rigby – and sent them out via the Pacific News Service in Wilshire Boulevard to the sports desk of every major paper down under: the *Daily Mirror, Morning Herald* and *Daily Telegraph* in Sydney; the *Age* and *Evening Herald* in Melbourne; the *West Australian* in Perth.

His release read: 'We are forming a team from the cream of American rugby-football players for a tour of Australia. Our squad should be able to hold its own with the best in Australia. Our club will be a star-studded outfit made up of the finest players in the United States. Some of the most famous names ever to grace American football fields already have signified their willingness to make the long trip. We'll have the greatest galaxy of US football players ever to perform in a foreign country.'

Dimitro claimed the whole venture would be backed by a millionaire Californian sportsman-turned-citrus-grower named Ang Alexander. They would take 35 players to Australia to play 15-minute exhibition games of American

football followed by a rugby game. The plan included a trip to Japan to play in front of the United States Armed Forces.

English magazine *Rugby League Review* reported that the Australian Board of Control had 'invited an American All Stars team to tour the following year'. They had not. Not yet anyway.

Winnipeg Rugby Football Club

Canadian Champions
1935 - 1939 - 1941

FOUNDED 1930
WINNIPEG BLUE BOMBERS

Western Canada Champions
1933 5 - 7 - 8 - 9 - 40 - 1 - 2 - 5 - 6 - 7 - 50

Winnipeg   Manitoba

March 6th, 1952.

R. S. MISENER
IMMED. PAST PRES.

W. CULVER RILEY
PRESIDENT

FRED J. CAINE
JOHN DE B. PAYNE
K. G. SLOCOMB
A. H. WARWICK
VICE-PRESIDENTS

J. F. MYERS
TREASURER

K. F. WINTEMUTE
SECRETARY

EXECUTIVE
DR. W. ALEXANDER
S. M. ALLMAN
J. HILLINKOFF
F. BOOTHROYD
B. BRACKEN
DR. D. BRACKEN
T. J. CAINE
JOHN COYAL
L. L. DESJARDINS
R. G. B. DICKSON
R. B. DONALDSON
DR. N. L. ELVIN
DR. JOHN FARR
J. A. FRANCE
W. R. GALBRAITH
PERCY GENSER
G. C. GOODRICH
R. D. GUY, JR.
G. B. HALTER, Q.C.
DR. C. HOLLENBERG
L. W. HOUSTON
E. L. ISARD

Mr. Mike Dimitro,
American-All-Stars,
2713 Ceilhunt Avenue,
Los Angeles 64, California .
U.S.A.

Dear Mike:

　　　　　Your letter to the President of the Ball Club, as well as to myself, on hand and we are giving it due consideration.

　　　　　What ball players have you on your Roster, or who consists of your ball club that you are considering bringing up here and where are you going to play whom and when? The ball players you bring are very important, due to publicity purposes and how much money do you expect?

　　　　　You understand, we start our season on August 23rd and we have already arranged a trip East.

HONORARY PRESIDENT
HON. J. S. McDIARMID

HON. VICE-PRESIDENTS
MAYOR G. COULTER
DR. W. F. ABBOTT
W. E. BROWN
E. A. POWELL

CHAIRMAN
HONORARY COUNCIL
H. E. SELLERS

HONORARY COUNCIL
F. S. AUGER
J. H. BORGER
C. G. CARTER
W. H. CARTER
A. U. CHIPMAN
ERNEST CHOLAKIS
W. R. CLUBB
S. C. COOK
HORACE EVERETT
ROY FLANIGAN
L. D. FRASER
F. J. HANNIBAL
J. HARRIS
JAMES JACKSON
JOHN JACKSON
H. JOHNSON
WALTER KANE
BRUCE LAWRIE
F. G. MATHERS
R. J. McCORDICK
DR. A. C. McINNES
MAYOR GEO. McLEAN
W. C. McNAMARA

George C. Trafton

MARCH Attacking on two fronts, Dimitro also wrote to Canadian pro football teams Ottawa Roughriders, Edmonton Eskimos, Hamilton Tiger-Cats and Winnipeg Blue Bombers proposing to bring an American All-Stars team north to play exhibition football games in early August. Before they had the chance to reply, he sent out a press release to the US media: the All Stars would be playing the Blue Bombers, Eskimos and Roughriders in August 1953.

Within days, each club turned down his offer, apart from Ottawa. Winnipeg head coach George Trafton was dubious: 'What ball players have you? Who consists of your ball club?' He was right to be suspicious. There was no such thing as the American All-Stars. Yet.

APRIL Dimitro sent the Australian RFL a tour proposal. The Board of Control replied almost immediately. They were 'keenly interested' in the All Stars touring from May to July. They would 'create great interest here', they agreed.

Australian Rugby Football League Board of Control

165 PHILLIP STREET, SYDNEY
'PHONE BW 8565

Cable Address:
"RUGLEAGUE"

Please address all

Letters to

Box 4415, G.P.O.,

Sydney, Australia

12th April, 1952.

HRM/JB

M. Dimitro Esq.,
American - All - Stars,
2713 Ceilhunt Avenue,
Los Angeles 64,
CALIFORNIA, U.S.A.

Dear Sir,

Further to our letter of the 1st instant, we desire to advise that your proposal was given consideration at the Annual Meeting of the Board held last evening, when I was directed to advise you that we are keenly interested in your proposal for Season 1953.

I am also directed to point out that the best financial period for matches of an International character is from the last Saturday in May until approximately the second Saturday in July, fixtures would include those played in New South Wales and Queensland.

We have no doubt that a visit of your team would create great interest here, and we would be pleased to have further details from you at your convenience.

Expressing the wish that some good will result from your suggestions, and with kind regards.

Yours faithfully,

HON. SECRETARY.

MAY The Board of Control sent Dimitro copies of the rugby league rule book and the financial breakdown of France's recent Australian tour. Mike liked what he saw.

JUNE Dimitro told ARFL secretary Harold Matthews 'the terms are fine by us'. Matthews, the distinguished elder statesman of the game, fond of wearing a white trilby, would put the detailed proposal to the Queensland and New South Wales RFL boards.

JULY AND AUGUST Iron Mike revived his pro football dream. He hit the try-out circuit again: first to Canada and then to the Cleveland Browns' training camp. Nobody wanted him.

SEPTEMBER Dimitro was back at Jackson High, teaching English and social studies to rough boys in a tough neighbourhood of East LA. He did not plan being there for long. Never did.

OCTOBER Dimitro wrote to Harold Matthews: 'Our head scout spent the summer in the east and has signed up some outstanding stars.' The lies just kept on coming.

Then:
NOVEMBER Matthews to Dimitro. The amber light.

ARFL Board of Control
165 Phillip Street, Sydney

3rd November 1952

'Dear Sir,

'We desire to advise you that your proposal to bring a team to Australia next year was again considered at length at our Brisbane sitting of the Board last week. It was resolved that the International Board, which will be meeting at Blackpool, England, commencing on Sunday 9th instant, consider ways and means of propagating and developing our Code in America.

'We have no doubt here that an American team would be a magnificent draw, but it is felt that it would be most necessary to embrace some Rugby Union players who play our Code in the University of California. We have written to Mr R.J. Stull, Director of Hospitals, University of California, soliciting his co-operation in this matter. You might also contact Mr Stull and inquire as to what progress he has made as we are still awaiting a report from him.'

J.E. Knowling, secretary of the New Zealand RFL, wanted the Americans to play in New Zealand too and the Kiwi leader had 'very kindly consented, whilst passing through America on business, to interview you, along with various sporting personalities and a Mr W.B. Nash of 818 Santee Street, Los Angeles between 21-23 November. Trusting that the outcome of Mr Knowling's visit will be for the ultimate good of our Code in your parts.'

Knowling wrote to Dimitro from the Imperial Hotel, a gothic pile in London's Russell Square: 'At the International Conference of Rugby League Nations held in England (Blackpool), the writer was appointed and empowered to explain to you the interest which is resulting in your evidence that a touring team may travel from your country.'

Knowling was desperate to impress: he did not yet know he was dealing with a fantasist son of a miner from Ohio. Once Dimitro had translated the letter into plain English, he knew he had a goer. Knowling wanted to meet him in LA on his way back to New Zealand – and finally put Dimitro, Nash and Sunderland together.

Santee St, downtown LA.

Sunderland wrote to Dimitro from his home in Manchester. He wanted to meet up and help with the tour. He also suggested the USA enter the inaugural Rugby League World Cup in France in 1954.

DECEMBER Knowling arrived in LA on his way home from Europe. Dimitro met him downtown at Clark Hotel on Hill Street. They started to plan. He took Knowling on a tour of the City of Angels. They headed south across downtown among the sweatshops, taco houses, tax offices and rag trade towers of Santee St to meet up with Nash in his office. Nash and Dimitro both wanted the same thing: to break rugby league in the US. It took a man from Auckland to bring them together.

Over the weekend, the trio went to a couple of football games. Knowling was blown away. The Kiwi supremo took Dimitro and Nash's tour proposal away to show the Australians. They loved it. The American All Stars were born.

The green light:
Australian RFL Board of Control meeting, 11 December 1952: 'Following a visit of J. Knowling of the New Zealand RFL, it was agreed to extend an invite to the All American side in season 1953 at 60% cut of match profits.' The costs were predicted to be £20,000 but 'expenditure would be met.' Matthews proposed a 17-game schedule. 'Glamour will surround your country's first visit,' he promised. He was not wrong.

Dimitro agreed with Board of Control proposals: the full playing schedule, a game in Sydney on Queen Elizabeth's Coronation Day and a Test match against Australia to end the tour 'if your team does well'. There would be no substitutes allowed. *The New York Times* ran the story. Within days, Harvard University's coach was recommending east coast college rugby union players to Harold Matthews.

Knowling wrote to Dimitro offering them 50 per cent of the gate receipts in New Zealand, where the press were already positive and Knowling was confident 'the American team would have great drawing power'.

Knowling also wrote to Nash, telling him that the English RL had already reiterated how they want rugby league to start in America and benefit from exchange visits once the team proves itself in Australia: 'International football will be wide open for your organisation to take advantage of.'

1953 JANUARY

The hype had started in Sydney. The ARFL were already dishing out promotional stickers.

The Daily Telegraph ran features. The Board of Control would spend lavishly on a reception at the City Hall. Guests would include the Governor General of Australia, the American Consul, politicians and noted citizens. Great rugby league players of the past would also be there to welcome Dimitro and his team of pioneers. Harry Flegg, president of the Board of Control and doyen of the Sydney rugby league scene, claimed: 'We have the money to ensure the Americans get a great welcome. We will have the prettiest girls in town there, too. This will be the show of all shows.'

Dimitro could get to like this fella.

Harry Sunderland, still on tour with the Kangaroos in France, laid his head on his pillow in his Lyon hotel room and saw dollar signs on the inside of his eyelids. He met up with French Federation president Paul Barriere about the planned World Cup tournament, slated for 16–31 May 1954, and reported back to Dimitro: 'France is to invite Australia and New Zealand and your team to fly over with Britain and France also competing. The invitation will be a party of 17 players, two managers and a referee. All expenses will be guaranteed and any profits above estimated takings of £48,000 (about $114,000) will be divided.'

The US had no team, had played no games and yet already had an invite looming to the first ever Rugby League Football World Cup!

Sunderland also told Ward Nash what a money-spinner Australia's trip to Europe had been for the ARFL, their cut of the profits less damaged by transport costs: the Kangaroos spent weeks sailing back rather than flying home.

The Board of Control sent Dimitro the figures from the last two incoming tours: in 1951, France played 21 games and took home nearly £40,000. In 1952, New Zealand played only 13 games and returned across the Tasman with less than £17,000. It gave him a ballpark figure: 18 games in Australia should clear more than £30,000 for Tiger Mike. A tidy profit.

Dimitro was advised by the Board of Control that he would need at least 28 players for a tour of this length. With flights from LA to Sydney at $560 each, that would cost around $15,000.

All he had to do now was find the money and a couple of dozen athletes willing and able to spend their summer playing rugby league on the other side of the world. And do it against some of the best players on earth.

SEE **AMERICA** at **RUGBY LEAGUE**
SYDNEY
MAY 30, JUNE 2, JULY 25, 29,
BRISBANE
JUNE 20, JULY 8,
"The Greatest Game of All"

Crawford ran through the All Stars' provisional schedule and claimed Dimitro had 'spent seven years converting sufficient gridiron men and university rugby union players in America to league to undertake the tour – the most important venture in rugby league history. And Australia holds the key to its success or otherwise. If America catches on, with rugby league the future of the code in international sport is assured.'

According to 'aggressive, thick-set' Dimitro: 'This is the greatest football game. It is a game that would appeal to Americans. It would provide a chance for American youth to prove itself on the international field.'

Bill Fallowfield, secretary of the RFL – in American terms, commissioner of England's governing body – wrote to Ward Nash at his Manhattan Beach home, asking if any American players would like to spend a few weeks with the Doncaster club to help prepare for the Australian tour. It would cost them nothing but the airfare to England. This gift horse was looked straight in the mouth.

62 SUNDAY TELEGRAPH, FEBRUARY 22, 1953

Wealthy sport body to back League U.S. tourists

By GEORGE CRAWFORD

The Helms Athletic Foundation is backing the American Rugby League team's tour of Australia this year.

The Helms Athletic Foundation is a powerful and authoritative organisation of world-wide repute.

With a backing of millions of dollars, it interests itself mainly | is the greatest football game. "It is a game that would appeal to Americans. | a few newly formed clubs in the north of Italy. France is teaching the game to newly formed

The All Stars' fixture schedule was set, the hotels were booked – even the Kiwi leg, following on straight after Australia, was planned to precision by Knowling.

Dimitro also needed a coach. Preferably one who knew what he was doing.

In deepest France, Sunderland was stirring up the hype until a queue of illustrious characters put their names forward. Successful former Australia player and coach Vic Hey, a former team-mate of Cliff Evans at Leeds, was linked with the job. Ex Queensland and Australia half-back Henry Thomson threw his hat in the ring. Sydney and New South Wales Country coach Ray

Stehr even wrote to Nash, volunteering to go to California to prepare the All Stars, and told Dimitro that the Board of Control thought it would be an insult to give them an Australian coach – unless Mike requested one.

But having Stehr in charge would be like putting Herod in charge of a kindergarten. He was the only man to be sent off twice in Test matches – in the same three-game series! Stehr worked as an unofficial player agent too, arranging moves for Aussie players to the UK, and had his own rugby league radio show on 2UE every Friday evening. It could be used to whip up interest in the tour, but was not the role model the Board intended hoisting upon the innocent Americans.

Crawford recommended Stehr's fellow former Kangaroo international Ross McKinnon as he was known for 'taking on bum teams and repeatedly lifting them to the top within a season'. These were big names. But nothing compared to the keenest of the lot: Clive Churchill. The Little Master. Captain of South Sydney, New South Wales and Australia, Churchill was about to play his 50th consecutive representative game. He was a megastar of the code, Mr Sydney Rugby League. But the sport paid so poorly he could still be found selling his endorsed footballs in Anthony Hordern's department store during the week! Captaining the Kangaroos in France, Churchill wrote to Dimitro from his hotel in Roanne, via Port Said, desperate to help: 'It would be a great pleasure to help your team in any way.'

The excitement even led to two Aussie support staff from the US Davis Cup tennis team offering their services. One of them, Bill 'Husky' Moore, got the masseur's gig at the same £3 a day rate he got as trainer for South Sydney.

The Board of Control took control and handed the coaching reins to their main man: Norman 'Latchem' Robinson. On his way back from France, where he had led Australia to 33 wins on their 40-game tour of Europe, Robinson was the cream of the crop. He had helped Balmain to four successive Sydney Premiership finals. He was no mug.

Robinson was given the title of 'advisory coach' but a thrilled Dimitro knew who needed to run the training ground show. Mike requested Latchem take two-a-day practices in Sydney to prepare his men: morning sessions together and afternoon sessions alongside and against experienced Aussie players. Now Dimitro just had to find 28 good men for Latchem to work with.

He got together with his old Alabama pal Ray Terry. After the war, Terry became a pro football player with San Diego Bombers in the AAFC and when that blew out, headed west to California to work as a bookie's manager on LA's race courses. Terry could look after the money – and play if he had to.

Mike drew up a hit-list of potential players. All were once Bruins team-mates, football guys he had met at USC, opponents from Stanford, pros he'd tried out with, acquaintances or their friends.

From UCLA: Roy Jensen; Sol Naumu; Xavier Mena; Jerry Shipkey; Bill Chambers; Bob Waterfield; Robert Bland; Sam Miller; John Roesch; Vic Schwenk; Harry Thompson; Guy Way; Ted Narleski.

From USC: Tony Linehan; Jim Psaltis; Lou Welsh; Bob Bastian.

From Stanford: Gary Kerkorian; Vince Jones; Dick Borda.

From Pepperdine: Terry Bell; Bo Williams.

Tél. 48-82 - 48-83
ROANNE

LE GRAND HOTEL

L. Viennet, Propriétaire

C/O P & O Mooltan
English Coaling Co.
Port Said.

Mr Mike Dimitro.
American All Stars
California,

Dear Sir,

First I had better introduce myself as Clive Churchill, Captain Australian Rugby League Team now touring England & France. I heard that an American Rugby Team may tour Australia in the next few month & that you were in charge of them on there visit. If there is anything that I can possibly do for yourself or the team to me it would be a great pleasure. anything in the way of coaching or Rules that may help you & your team in anyway. I have coached Australian sides for a while now & have Captain Australia in fifteen test against England, France & New Zealand & I have some knowledge of the game. By the time you receive this letter we will have completed the tour & on our way home to Australia. Hoping that your team has ample success in Australia & once again anything in the way of Coaching that may help them I would be only to pleased to assist.

Your faithfully
Clive Churchill

SON RESTAURANT "Le Gambetta"
Même Maison : HOTEL DE FRANCE, ROANNE

AMERICAN ALL STARS

2713 CEILHUNT AVENUE
LOS ANGELES 64, CALIFORNIA
TELEPHONE ARIZONA 8-3187
March 4, 1953

MIKE DIMITRO
MANAGER-COACH

PAT DODDS
SECRETARY-TREASURER

Congratulations!

You have been selected to be on the American All-Star Rugby Football Team that is to tour Australia, New Zealand, the Fiji Islands, and Hawaii this summer.

You will be housed in the finest hotels available and all your expenses will be paid. In addition you will receive a beautiful sport coat and a weekly allowance to pay for incidentals on the trip. At the end of the tour, each player will receive a bonus.

Our gracious hosts are planning many interesting side trips for us. In Australia we will visit Canberra, Bondi Beach, Botony Bay, the Great Barrier Reef, and the Jenolan Caves. In New Zealand we will see Wellington, the Waitomo Caves, the Glowworm Grotto and the world-famous Totorna Spa where the fascinating Maoris live.

The tour will end about August 27th. On the way back to the U.S. we will visit the Fiji Islands and those who wish may relax for a few days in the Hawaiian Islands before coming home.

I will tell you more about our plans at the meeting to be held Sunday, March 8th at 2:00 on Spaulding Field at U.C.L.A.

If you are interested in making the tour please call AR-83187 Friday or Saturday evening.

Mike Dimitro

Mike and Mena also wrote to some of the fellas he had met in NFL training camps: star kicker Lou Groza, Abe Gibron and old Bruins mate Narleski at Cleveland Browns; Gerry Cowhig and Dan Towler at the Rams, Bud Copperson up in Canada.

Most of the old Bruins boys were free agents and open targets: Shipkey had been drafted to the LA Dons with Mike in 1947 but after five years in the NFL with Pittsburgh he was out of contract. So too was Cowhig. Five years as a running back in the NFL had made him prime meat for rugby league.

Dimitro was nothing if not bold. He also went after the biggest name in LA sports: Waterfield. After graduating from UCLA before Dimitro arrived, Waterfield was the NFL's Most Valuable Player as a championship-winning rookie in 1945 and led the Rams to the title again in 1951. His devastatingly effective use of the forward pass made it become a staple of gridiron, changing it forever from the short-passing and handling game that had evolved from rugby.

But as quarter back, defensive back and kicker for the Rams, Waterfield had all the ingredients of the ideal rugby league player: in attack he was quick with mind and feet, creative, with a good pass and eye for the gap; in defence he was tenacious and willing to muck in; and he could kick goals. No league coach could ask for more: and he was a free agent having just quit the NFL, aged 32.

Mike had crossed Waterfield's path on the football scene and in Hollywood, where they had both appeared in movies: Dimitro as an extra in an Alan Ladd vehicle, Waterfield as a co-star in some Sam Katzman productions. Katzman loved having ex-UCLA jocks in his films.

Dimitro knew that if he got Waterfield on board, he could sell his rugby league dream to America: the press would lap it up. Not only was he one of the biggest names in pro football, but he just happened to be married to screen siren Jane Russell. Russell would be starring in *Gentlemen Prefer Blondes* with Marilyn Monroe in movie theatres across the land when the All Stars were due to be trooping around the tropics. Monroe was dating baseball star Joe DiMaggio.

If Waterfield had gone, and been visited on tour by Russell, Monroe and DiMaggio, the media circus around Australia would have been absurd. But rather than touring the outback, Waterfield opted to spend his summer with his wife and two newly-adopted babies – and mixing in Monroe and DiMaggio's social circle.

Dimitro's hot ticket was in shreds.

CHAPTER 4
IRON MIKE IN THE CITY OF ANGELS

LOS ANGELES, SPRING 1953

Dimitro had two months
to put together a squad to
take on the best players in
the world at rugby league.
No one on the West Coast
knew what that was.
Dimitro had no intention
of telling them either.

ARIZONA 8-3187

AMERICAN ALL STARS

MIKE DIMITRO
MANAGER-COACH

2713 CEILHUNT AVE.
LOS ANGELES, CALIF.

The pro players and
old pals could not be
tempted. Time for Plan
B. He would sweep the
campuses of California's top football schools
in the hope of finding adventurous athletes who had some experience of
rugby union or at least the attributes of a rugby player. They needed to be
strong, quick or big (preferably both), know how to catch an oval ball, and
stop a man in his tracks. He had enough talent to plunder on his doorstep:
USC Trojans were the champions of the Pacific Coast Conference and Red
Sanders's UCLA Bruins were no slouches either.

He started at UCLA. Only two football lettermen from there signed up.
One was his old team-mate, Xavier Mena, a San Diego guy with a trigger-
happy grin. 'X' had played left tackle alongside Dimitro and returned in
1950 but now needed to take a three-month sabbatical from his architects
firm – and give up $50 a day – to tour. He brought along Fran Mandulay, an
olive-skinned tight end, like Mike from Ohio. Mandulay had played against
Dimitro for Nebraska in 1947 before transferring to UCLA and was now 27.
Mena and Mandulay were tall, heavy and strong – and enthusiastic. They
could make rugby league forwards.

Dimitro also got commitments from three other Bruins: at 6ft 3in,
Steve Drakulvich would be a giant among Australians, while 26-year-old
George Kauffman and Syd Walker had both played rugby union for UCLA.
Kauffman, a 6ft 2in business student from Glendale, was Dimitro's team-
mate during spring rugby in 1948 but when he took Mike's side in his bitter
war of words with LaBrucherie in the football season, the fourth-choice full-
back was easily discarded.

ALL U.S.C. MAFIA

Dimitro also started recruiting back down the new Santa Monica Freeway, stalking the USC campus where he had done his Masters, hunting for prey. Again he aimed high, talking to the stars of the Trojans' triumphant Rose Bowl team. Despite losing the city's biggest game to their arch rival Bruins, Jess Hill's USC team had clinched the Pac Coast title thanks to the nine game winning streak that started their season. Ranked fifth in the country, they took the Pac Coast's place in America's biggest game in front of the usual 100,000 fans in Pasadena. Wisconsin's awesome running back Alan 'The Horse' Ameche got little change out of an awesome USC defence as the Trojans sneaked a 7-0 win.

Dimitro wanted big names to grab back page headlines and unearth backers for the tour: he invited star quarter back Dean Schneider; shot-putting defensive back Jim Psaltis; Frank Gifford's successor at full-back – the Canadian Leon Sellers; defensive end Bob Van Doren and centre Lou Welsh, the Rose Bowl co-captains. None took up the offer. But Cal quarter back Ray Willsey who, having graduated in Berkeley, was trying out with pro teams back in his native Canada, and USC second-year letterman Bob Buckley, were keen.

Bob Buckley: 'I first met Mike when he was attending USC for his Masters. He introduced himself to me – I'd heard of him from UCLA when they were recruiting me from Santa Ana Junior College. We talked SC and UCLA football when he brought up the subject of going to Australia to play rugby. Even though I was a junior at the time, I said "count me in". After a few get-togethers he asked me if I could recommend any USC players who would do good on this trip. I suggested Ed Demirjian, Al Abajian, Harold Han, Sol Naumu, and Ted Grossman from C.O.P.'

Dimitro would be mighty glad he did. Boys from the Armenian community in SoCal were making a big impression on the college football scene. Albert Abajian was a body-builder and keen football player but was not in the SC Varsity squad, while Ed Demirjian was Schneider's back-up at quarter back, having been a huge success in junior college.

Al Abajian: 'I didn't know Dimitro then as he was a number of years ahead of me. He was working on a Masters and he recruited me while I was a senior, after I'd completed my football eligibility. I'd never played rugby before. I knew very little about league or union at the early stages.'

Being a rugby virgin was the least of Abajian's worries.

Abajian: 'I never should have gone to Australia. I just had one of the worst injuries I ever had. This was a scrimmage at school, in spring

Al Abajian.

practice. I got a bruised kidney and broken rib but I kept playing. When I came in for a shower and went to the bathroom it was all blood. I was in hospital for a week. We were so conditioned that if you were hurt you didn't say anything to the coach, you kept playing, which was stupid. I knew I was hurt. I played that year but when you have that kind of injury you get kinda timid – I wasn't the same. The head of the PE department called me in and said: "You ought to quit football 'cos your injury's so serious." But I went to Australia anyhow. I'm glad I did but I wonder what it did for my health.'

Sol Naumu and Harold Han were high school team-mates from Pearl City, Hawaii. Naumu had moved to LA in 1948 to study at Compton College in South Central, close to his cousin Johnny Naumu, a star football player. Sol turned heads for Compton Tartars, and soon stepped up to the Trojans, the Coliseum and all that. Tall, lean, craggy, he did it with aplomb: he was punt return leader on the 1950 Trojan team. Having graduated as a qualified teacher, he was looking for one last football thrill.

Han – short, dark and moon-faced – had already led a remarkable life. Born on the leper colony of Molokai, both his parents were lepers. He left at a young age for the island of Oahu. A few years later he was playing centre on SC's Rose Bowl team. Han, though, had another year at university and a season of college football ahead.

Han and Naumu would be the only brown faces in the All Stars team photos. There were two islanders and no black players in the squad. That said little about Dimitro but everything about football in the States in 1953. Recruiting from Californian colleges almost certainly meant there would be no black players. Dimitro had just one black team-mate on the 1947 Bruins roster. The All Stars emerged from a divided LA, a divided United States. Blacks and whites had their own streets, their own schools, their own bars, their own shops, their own communities.

And the twain rarely mixed. When they did, it was not often a comfortable meeting. It was no different for football players. There were very few black players in the top colleges: the majority were recruited by black schools such as Grambling or Howard. They, of course, had outstanding football teams. The pro game was almost a closed shop in the spring of 1953. No black player had ever thrown a pass from quarter back in the NFL.

Ed Demirjian: 'We called Sol "Pineapple #1" and Han "Pineapple #2"! We were all finished up with football and had played our final year but Buck and Han were younger than us and still had another year to go. Jess Hill said to them: "Don't go. You'll be getting paid so you'll count as pros and be ineligible for our senior year, or you'll get injured."'

Han and Buckley were getting pulled one way by Dimitro and the other by USC's athletic department. They could not commit. And they certainly couldn't leave in May as they still had exams to take.

Demirjian and Buckley had a mate at the College of Pacific in nearby Stockton, who was a real talent. Teddy Grossman, blond Teddy Boy quiff on a wiry frame, had starred at quarter back against SoCal's major schools and could kick goals too. Having thrown the winning touchdown pass and kicked the field goal against Stanford, he was gaining quite a reputation in the LA press. A jack in the box bundle of fun from Beverley Hills, Grossman had naturally gone into show-business, appearing as an extra and a stunt double in a series of Hollywood movies to help pay for college.

Letters went out to the players: practice would finally begin on Sunday 15 March at Spaulding Field, the Bruins' football facility on campus, two weeks later than advertised. It would not be every day and there would not be 45 players trying out. Dimitro hardly knew 45 players. He mentioned eight names but was desperate for more.

He tried Harvard in Boston and the University of British Columbia in Vancouver but got polite rejections. He did snare one more Trojan. And what a player he was. Alvin Earl Kirkland, a squat, tough flier from the Rose Bowl team. A talented all-round sportsman, PE student Kirkland had come to LA from Bakersfield in the heart of California, and by his third year at SC was established running deep and hard from half-back.

Dimitro can't have been spending much time preparing lessons at Andrew Jackson High. As well as trying to figure out who was going to pay for this fantasy football tour, he was enrolling on a course at LA State College and looking after his little brother who had moved in with Mike and Pat on Ceilhunt Avenue.

His next brainwave was to plan football games in Hawaii en route home. If the All Stars were going to spend a few days there, they may as well play an exhibition game, like the ones he had been in himself in the 1940s. He got on to his Honolulu contact: Mackay Yanagisawa. Mike suggested two games and wanted $15,000 per game. Mackay offered $6,000.

"Hawaii is no longer the goldmine it was during the war," he warned. He had sponsors offering a $5,000 guarantee. Mike reduced his demands to $7,500 a game, so he could pay his players 100 bucks each. The games would be football exhibitions. He made no mention of rugby. Nor how he would kit out a team in football gear after three months playing rugby league.

The line between codes was blurred in Dimitro's world. A deal was done. Dates were pencilled in for 28 and 30 August. They would discuss it when he was in Honolulu en route to Sydney. It was all coming together.

CHAPTER 5
WANTED: THE TRUTH

Two months before the tour was due to start, Dimitro found himself stuck in a newspaper war: 10,000 miles away. George Crawford at the *Sydney Telegraph* was right behind it. But the *Sunday Sun* smelt a rat.

29 MARCH 1953

COMING – READY OR NOT!
MR. DIMITRO AND HIS U.S. RUGBY LEAGUERS

Rugby League authorities in Australia seem thoroughly prepared for a visit by an American League team in May. They have even worked out a schedule of matches – including Test matches. But here in Los Angeles, the American team, and the organisation of the trip, are as vague as the possibility of the US players knowing the basic principles of Rugby League.

The Sunday Sun & Guardian

LOS ANGELES, SATURDAY

Dimitro had been caught on the hop. He originally quoted the whole trip would cost $54,000. Now he was claiming $75,000 – 34,000 Australian dollars – but 'the money doesn't worry us' because 'Pat Dodds, an Idaho farmer, is paying for our tickets to Australia'.

That may have come as some surprise to Patty Dodds, Dimitro's wife!

The Sun pointed out that they would need government permission to take money out of Australia but Mike wasn't concerned. Neither was he bothered that no player was contracted to tour, admitting: 'It's all verbal.' Asked which of the original squad he had named three weeks earlier were still touring, he ruled out Guy Way, Dean Schneider, Bill Chambers, Tony Lenahine and Roy Jensen. 'Who wrote that Jensen could throw 60 yards? He can't even run 60 yards!' he joked. 'A lot of fellows are drifting into town. I'm getting hold of some of them.' It was worryingly vague.

Cliff Evans was no longer going to prepare the team in LA. Dimitro would do that himself with a little help from one Frank Clark, who had played rugby union in Canada. Dimitro claimed they would play warm-ups against UCLA, a team called Spoilers and a two-game series with the University of British Columbia before flying to Australia. Publicist Ward Nash was also frozen out. Xavier Mena would cover PR.

Dimitro knew he could guarantee column inches – all the Sydney paper clippings were being sent to him in L.A. by Harold Matthews or his inside man Crawford, but not all news was good news.

The Board of Control in Phillip Street were not amused. They tried to phone Dimitro. No answer.

They sent a cable:

Western Union Telegram 1953 MAR 31
LA047 SYA047
BOARD MOST PERTURBED CONTENTS SYDNEY SUN ARTICLE MARCH 29 ALLEGING INTERVIEW WITH YOU BY LOS ANGELES CORRESPONDENT IN WHICH YOU STATE YOU HAVE ONLY FIVE PROSPECTIVE PLAYERS AND YOUR CASUAL ATTITUDE TOWARDS THE TOUR GENERALLY STOP IMPRESSION GAINED HERE MAY BE DOUBT ABOUT TOUR TAKING PLACE STOP OUR GOVERNMENT STATE DOLLARS WILL NOT BE PROVIDED TO COVER YOUR EARNINGS AND CONSEQUENTLY ARE NOT PREPARED TO ALLOW AN ADVANCE AGAINST SAME TO ENABLE TWO WAY TICKETS BEING PURCHASED THIS END IN AUSTRALIA CURRENCY OR PERMIT PROFITS TO BE TAKEN OUT OF COUNTRY STOP BOARD DESIRE TO COOPERATE TO FULLEST EXTENT AND ARE PREPARED TO PAY THIS END YOUR FARES HOME VIA NEW ZEALAND BUT DES RE ASSURANCES BY CABLE IMMEDIATELY THAT NOTHING HAS HAPPENED THAT WILL PRECLUDE TOUR TAKEN PLACE REGARDS = MATTHEWS =

On the same day Knowling sent a telegram from Auckland:
ALARMING REPORTS IN AUS NEWSPAPERS OF LACK OF PLAYERS AND FINANCE PLEASE ASSURE OF CORRECT POSITION

They were right to panic. Both Australia and New Zealand had laws in place to stop money being taken out of the country as it tried to recover from the war. All the money Dimitro had been told the All Stars would make from ticket sales – and Dimitro had agreed a 60 per cent cut – would be used to pay for hotels, internal flights, trains, cars, medical bills, laundry, newspapers and anything else he could spend it on. It was not going home with him. The majority would be used to buy one-way tickets home to the States.

The Board of Control were lobbying the Australian Government at the highest level to make an exception but with Knowling confirming that the NZRL could only pay half of the fares by law – the returns from New Zealand – Dimitro needed about $20,000. Without it he could not get the players across the Pacific in the first place.

Dimitro responded as requested. The Board of Control made sure *The Telegraph* was there to respond to *The Sun*:

U.S. LEAGUE TOUR TO GO ON
ASSURANCE TO BOARD

American Rugby League team organiser Mike Dimitro yesterday confirmed arrangement for the Australian tour.

He said in a radio-telephone talk that the team would arrive in Sydney on May 20. Dimitro for 10 minutes discussed tour arrangement with NSW members of the ARFL Board of Control. Chairman Mr H Flegg said after the talk with Dimitro: "I'll confess I've had a number of sleepless nights worrying about the tour. I'll sleep tonight because the Yanks are coming. I was 75 years old on Monday. Mr Dimitro's message of assurance was my best birthday present." Dimitro said to Board of Control secretary Harold Matthews: "I'm surprised that Australian administrators have doubts about the tour. It has been well-organised from this end. The 22 players will be efficient athletes, well coached in Rugby League."

The Sun

Matthews wrote to Dimitro requesting that he 'refrain from giving any interviews' to the LA correspondent of *The Sun*. *The Sun* dug again:

RUGBY LEAGUE FARCE OF THE DIMITRO TEAM FROM OUR SPECIAL REPRESENTATIVE

The Sun

The Sun suspected the ARFL would end up footing the £25,000 bill. Dimitro – 'a teacher of physical jerks in the Los Angeles area' – told *The Sun* that he had 'lost his angel, Pat Dodds, an Idaho potato farmer'. Dodds would have paid the fares to Australia at a cost of £6,139. When asked if he could interview Dodds, *The Sun's* man in LA was told: 'Dodds is moving around all the time and I can't tell you where to get him.' She was probably at home on Ceilhunt Avenue, oblivious to it all.

When challenged as to how the tour would be paid for, Mike said: 'I've got $12,000 and my wife's got $20,000', but that they did not have to pay for the fares until the day they departed.

Pan-Am had threatened to cancel the booking unless payment came. A cable from Sydney to Pan-Am confirmed that Dimitro would be able to pay their return fares from the gate money. That left $13,000 to pay in cash by 17 April: a month before they flew.

Dimitro also admitted his team had not had a single practice together: 'I have only six boys here at present. A lot of the boys are still in school.'

Mrs Dimitro – the hack had no idea it was Pat Dodds – then called the man from *The Sun* and said: 'It doesn't help anyone and it is no business of the Australian public to have our financial affairs front-paged down there. Mike can get all the money he wants for the tour. But you can't expect people to pay out money they can't get back. We've got to get the okay from the Australian Government to pay the fares there. We don't need any publicity down there. We shall have jammed stadiums at every game, anyway.'

Dimitro had to start spinning. He and Patty became 'Rig Rigby' again and got to work.

A month before the All Stars were due to leave, the whole tour was in trouble and the Aussies could sense it. In the *Sydney Sunday Herald,* a string of rugby league personalities poured doubt over the Americans' ability to learn the game from coaching books in a few weeks.

More Rig Rigby fantasies:

AMERICAN ALL STARS PREPARE FOR TOUR OF AUSTRALIA AND NEW ZEALAND

Players from 15 states reported to coach Mike Dimitro on the University of California campus. Forty-five top United States rugby football stars were selected for the try-outs but only 22 will be selected to represent the United States on tour.

U.S. TEAM HARD AT WORK

The All Stars met for the third day of practice at Joe E Brown Field. Practice sessions have been scheduled for five days a week. To date, competition has been extremely keen.

Coach Dimitro stressed that he wanted fast, agile players, not over-weight, slow obstructionists. To this reporter, he looks as if he has all three – speed, agility and weight.

He had playing uniforms made up: white socks, royal blue long football pants with red and white 'go faster' stripes, royal blue jerseys with white shoulders dotted by red stars. Neat.

He got Xavier, Al E. Kirkland, Sol Naumu, Harold Han, Van Doren and Bob Movilhill togged up and snapped in front of a Pan Am Strata Clipper that would

fly them down under and rushed out a press release: 'Contrary to Australian press speculation, the All Stars uniforms would not be steel armour or Indian feathers but their jerseys would be arm length, trousers knee length and skin tight and helmets will not be worn.' They would wear large squad numbers on their chests and backs.

Even the provincial districts away from Sydney hoping to host a money-spinner started to fear they had been sold a dud. Reputations, jobs and lifestyles were on the line. Newcastle, a rugby league-obsessed mining town 100 miles north of Sydney, was getting edgy.

16 APRIL 1953

US RUGBY LEAGUE TOUR COULD CAUSE STORM

The visit by an American Rugby League team to Australia could result in the biggest internal storm the game here has known. If the tour fails the League would find itself with a heavy financial responsibility. Club officials would place full blame on the Australian Board of Control, with reorganisation of its personnel inevitable. If the tour succeeded, the board, of course, would be men of business acumen assured their positions. A large section of the Rugby League officials feel they have been held in ignorance of happenings over the tour. They can't make up their minds whether it is to take place or not. Many will be wrathful with the board if the tour isn't a success.

Newcastle Sun

They were right to be worried. After all, the US team did not yet exist. The Board of Control were relying on one man's word that the tourists would be capable of giving the hosts a decent game, one man whose reputation and financial health was inextricably dependent on the All Stars team. Dimitro was hardly an independent analyst.

At a New South Wales RFL meeting, a Mr L. Moses, the Western Suburbs delegate, not only questioned whether the tour would happen but also 'whether the League knew whether the Americans were conversant with the code'. Chairman Harry Flegg informed the delegation that Dimitro had assured the board 'that the game had been played in America for the past three years'. Not only that but he had turned down the Australians' offer of a coach, claiming they did not need one as they had Cliff Evans, who had been coaching the team for some time now. Flegg said the Board had investigated Dimitro and 'it was satisfied he was a competent tour manager'. He would need to be. The lies kept coming.

A week later, *The Sun* continued its role as prophet of doom:

23 APRIL 1953

AIRLINE CANCELS SEATS FOR AMERICAN LEAGUE SIDE

Los Angeles, Mon. (O.S.R.): Pan-American Airways announced that tentative reservations for a Rugby League team to fly to Australia on May 17 had been cancelled.

The airline announced today that the reservations had been cancelled because promoter Mike Dimitro had failed to meet his obligations in completing payment of fares for his team.

Newcastle Sun

But Dimitro was adamant. 'We are leaving on 17 May with 22 good, fast boys and we are going to show them wide-open rugby like the French did in 1951,' he told the press agency.

That was some claim. The unheralded French had gone down under two years earlier and beaten Australia on their own patch, winning the series 2-1. That was a huge shock. The fact that they had done so playing a style of rugby unseen anywhere in the world before that – fast, expansive and full of magical tricks from their backs, led by the irrepressible Puig-Aubert – made them even more lauded, and generally accepted to be the best rugby team on earth, in either code. And all this just seven years after the fascist Vichy government had outlawed rugby league and seized its considerable assets, liquidating the whole sport. That success was the blueprint for Dimitro: if the French could get off their knees to do it, so could the Americans.

But the All Stars had about 20 days not 20 years to learn to play rugby league. Dimitro reported that 'we have selected boys with lots of speed, some with college football experience and a few professionals. The average age is 24, with the oldest man 29'. Dimitro himself was 30. Flegg backed the story and dismissed the negative rumours: 'The Americans will still be here next month – you can be definite about that. The tour has caused many problems and great bitterness but I am certain it will eventuate.'

The bitterness was all down to money. The trip was going to cost a fortune and no one wanted to pay for it up front. Noone knew whether the Americans would compete. No one knew if the Australian public would come out and watch them.

The Newcastle RFL were fretting that they would lose money by hosting a game, with the cost of a reception dinner, insurance, a new kit, and ground staff and referees' fees leaving them empty handed once the Americans had taken their 65 per cent of the gate, the local city council 12.5 per cent and the ARFL board five per cent. 'Unless the Americans learn quickly... Newcastle's chance of a good gate will depend on the novelty of their mixture of Gridiron and League football,' claimed the *Morning Herald*.

24 APRIL 1953
Telegram from Matthews to Dimitro:
PAN-AM LA SAY YOUVE BOOKED 27 SEATS 17 MAY LA – HONOLULU – SYDNEY 20 MAY AND ASKED PAN-AM SYDNEY TO WIRE $12375. SYDNEY OFFICE NO – NOT PERMITTED. CABLE IMMEDIATELY EXACT POSITION SO AS TO PREVENT CONTINUOUS ADVERSE PRESS CRITICISM THIS END.

25 APRIL 1953
U.S. LEAGUE SIDE VISIT "CERTAIN"

The American Rugby League team was due in Sydney on May 20, the secretary of the Australian board of control, Mr. H. Matthews, said to-day.

Mr. Matthews said the board had received a cable from Mike Dimitro, manager of the American All Stars. Mr. Dimitro, in the cable, said he had switched the plane reservations to Canadian Pacific airlines and was scheduled to leave the United States on May 16.

Mr. Matthews said it now appeared certain the tour would take place.

Newcastle Morning Herald

SYDNEY, THURSDAY
Queensland RL officials were 'pretty certain the tour won't come off'. They had got the inside track from an LA informer – gossip that only three players had committed to the trip, that Dimitro knew many of his named 18 were heading to pro football summer camps instead, and that university rugby union players had turned down the invitation because of exams. Most of the players 'are used to the gridiron game but there are some who have played Rugby Union at the University of California', claimed *Rugby League Review* newspaper.

Back in Sydney, the *Sunday Sun and Guardian* let rip in a furious, anonymous, editorial:

26 APRIL 1953

THE DIMITRO DOLLAR MYSTERY
A SHOESTRING PROMOTER CAN'T PAY HIS FARES

Two pertinent questions may be asked about the proposed Rugby League tour by Mike Dimitro's team of Americans.

Has Mr Flegg any reason for hoping that he can induce monetary control to allot Dimitro's circus dollars which are urgently needed to buy equipment for the development of Australia's national resources?

Is some political pressure being brought to bear to allow the Dimitro circus to take dollars out of the country?

Dimitro is a shoestring promoter of wrestling matches and of a team of alleged footballers which, after six weeks still does not exist.

Why has he cozened the Australian Rugby League into inviting a team of muscle-men, selected only by Dimitro, to visit Australia?

Dimitro is a professional. He is trying to induce professional wrestlers and small-time gridironers to join his team.

He failed last week in an effort to induce the Californian University Rugby Union players to join him.

They are amateur sportsmen.

Being a pro, Dimitro is motivated by the chance of making a fast dollar. He isn't trying to get to Australia for sheer love of sport or of Mr Jersey Flegg and his associates, on none of whom he has ever set eyes, anyway.

Dimitro is after dollars. Australian pounds are no good to him because you can't buy anything with them in America. Dimitro wants dollars. His professional muscle-men want to be paid in dollars not, as Flegg naively suggests, in boomerangs and athletic singlets.

Dimitro expects that any profits will be sent to America in dollars. He had Australian Rugby League officials dangling like puppets. He is a man of straw and a liar when it suits him to be.

This is far more certain than that he is a competent Rugby League player and coach, wrestler and bit-time movie player – all of which he claims.

In the Sunday Sun's attempts to stop the ARL making fools of themselves over this tour, Dimitro says he has never been interviewed about the tour on behalf of the Australian press. This is a lying answer. The Sunday Sun staff man on the West Coast several times has interviewed Dimitro. He has also interviewed Mrs Dimitro.

Our Los Angeles man was invited to attend a practice of the Dimitro squad at the University of Southern California on a certain day. He attended but there was no sign of Dimitro or any squad. Nor did anyone know anything about this alleged practice session. Dimitro later explained that it was vacation time and he hadn't been able to get the players together.

The only 'American All Stars' players our representative was able to find were three or four being photographed in football attire at an airport. These pictures constitute the advance publicity.

So far, Dimitro has given out 36 names as members of his touring party of 22.

He spoke of a backer Pat Dodds, who has "disappeared".

Coach Cliff Evans has "withdrawn". It is difficult to find any truth in anything Dimitro has said. At present he is running around trying to lay his hands on enough dollars to pay the fares of himself and his band of performers. This is the sorry record of the man in whom Australian Rugby League officials place so much confidence. Despite the fact that they are dealing with a stranger whose ability is proved very questionable, to put it mildly, League officials still stick stubbornly to this brave front that all is well.

This Flegg's Follies tour is the most haphazard sporting adventure of all time. It could make Rugby League look silly and, which is infinitely more serious, make Australia look silly.

Sunday Sun and Guardian

It was a slaughter. An annihilation. A character assassination. And much of it was fair. Much of it true.

The 45-man, daily practice sessions at UCLA were a total fabrication.

Abajian: 'We did have some practice sessions in LA. Dimitro ran them at a field adjacent to Dorsey High School. I remember one other practice at UCLA, too. They were poorly structured and loosely organised and did little to prepare us for rugby league. His instructions were so poor. Mike tried to coach us but he didn't know what he was doing. We were playing rugby union! It's so funny. All we were doing was keeping our legs in shape and running!'

Dorsey High was in South Central LA, plagued by racial violence in the early 1950s. A smart, 1930s-built low-rise with proud green detailing on its bright cream walls, among the single-storey houses and lock-ups. The school's football field backed on to Rancho Cienega Park. It was fitting that Dimitro should take his foreign football game there: Cienega was already home to LA's immigrant soccer teams. Folk strolling through would be used to seeing strange ball games being played by Scots, Hungarians and Germans. But the sight of a dozen or so young local men in sweats, tossing an oversized football backwards and trying not to block each other off the ball must still have raised eyebrows.

Dimitro had not got 25 players there, let alone 45. It was time to widen the net. He headed up Big Sur to the Bay Area in search of a few good men.

CHAPTER 6
INDIANS TO THE RESCUE

If it wasn't for the Stanford football team of 1951/52, there would be no American All Stars rugby league team.

In 1951, Stanford appointed Chuck Taylor as head coach at the age of just 31. Taylor instituted a two-platoon system, with defensive and offensive units, developed a short passing game, and moved players into positions they hadn't considered playing before. It worked a treat.

Gary Kerkorian

Dimitro targeted several starters from that Stanford line-up. There were two relative giants at 6ft 2in and 200lbs: 20-year-old right guard John 'Jack' Bonetti, and 21-year-old right tackle Alfred Dell Kirkland. The quarter back was another American-Armenian playmaker Gary Kerkorian, a 21-year-old from Inglewood, near Los Angeles airport.

Jack Bonetti: 'I had a basketball scholarship to Stanford in 1948 but I was unsure that I could cope with the academic requirements so I went to Santa Rosa Junior College instead. I was All Conference Football in Offense and Defense at Santa Rosa and I played baseball. I was a Catholic All-American, too.'

After a couple of years at Santa Rosa, Bonetti was offered another scholarship to Stanford: this time in football. A year later he was playing in the biggest game in America.

Gary Kerkorian had learned to play football in sandlots around Inglewood during the war. When he was only 12 he was playing against 16- and 17-year-old high school players at a small park on 5th Avenue. It was six to eight guys each side, no cleats, pads or helmets. Most boys wore tennis shoes or played bare foot. Kerkorian was fast, nimble, smart and tough. By the time he graduated from Inglewood High, he was offered a place at Stanford.

There he broke every passing record in the book and earned a place in the All-America first team in 1951 after leading the Indians to a 9-1 record, the Pacific Coast Championship and a trip to the Rose Bowl game. If his greatest game was the 27-20 victory over arch rivals SC in front of over 96,000 fans at the Coliseum, his greatest football disappointment, surely, was what happened in the Rose Bowl.

Jack Bonetti

TO-DA

On New Year's Day 1952, Stanford Indians and Illinois walked out on Pasadena's field for the annual extravaganza shown nationwide for the first time on the exciting new media of television.

Expectations were high and Kerkorian started well, plotting an 84-yard drive leading to a touchdown by fellow Armenian Harry Hugasian, and kicking the extra point to give Stanford a 7-6 lead. But it did not last.

Jack Bonetti: 'We were 7-6 up at half-time then Gary went off with broken ribs and we fell apart. We ended up losing 40-7!'

The Indians disintegrated, conceding 27 points in the final quarter. Watching his team's humiliation from the sidelines was a sad way to end a glorious college career. But Kerkorian's performances would earn him a place in the Stanford Hall of Fame.

Graduating with a bachelor's degree in economics, Gary was drafted by the NFL's Pittsburgh Steelers as back-up for quarter back Jim Finks. He played in the Coliseum again, this time in front of 90,000 Rams fans.

Vince Jones.

Along with Finks, the 1952 Steelers had more Hall of Famers in Ernie Stautner, Jack Butler and Elbie Nickel – but were still dismal. When they somehow thrashed New York Giants 63-7 in November, Steelers fans tore down the Forbes Field posts in delirium and celebrated with the players in the clubhouse. When the season mercifully ended, Kerkorian was cut after throwing one touchdown, kicking four field goals and 35 points in twelve appearances. The dream was over, in Pittsburgh anyway.

Kerkorian started playing amateur football and selling cars part-time. He needed a new challenge and found it: in a different country and a different sport. At the Steelers, Kerkorian had played QB, some defence and taken up kicking duties: all the components of a back in rugby league. Dimitro claimed Kerkorian had played two seasons of rugby union for Pittsburgh Athletic Club, but his family called that bunk. Other Stanford rugby players were among Mike's targets.

Al D. Kirkland: 'I had played three years of rugby (union) at Stanford and Jack had played two and Pat one or two. I was a USC freshman but I transferred to Stanford in the winter of 1950, so I lost a year. In football, I thought I was an end but Chuck Taylor made me into a defensive tackle. Bonetti had been defensive end but Chuck made him into an offensive guard. He made us think about football differently.'

Jack Bonetti: 'A lot of us had to get permission to leave in May and go back to school in September after the tour to re-do that final quarter. I had to ask the Marine Corps if I could postpone my induction until that fall.'

Al D. Kirkland: 'I didn't know Dimitro but the tour sounded like a lot of fun. Getting out of the country was tough because they thought I was going overseas to avoid the draft. I had to write letters to the Draft Board to say I wasn't and I

Al D. Kirkland

would join up when I got back if they wanted me.'

Pat Henry, from Rochester, NY, had already lived a life before he boarded the plane to Sydney. A former PT instructor in the Marines, he served at the infamous Ellis Island immigration camp, where Dimitro's father had entered the United States 30 years earlier. He was an all-round sportsman: he represented the Marines at football and played soccer against Argentina. After two years at Unity College in Vallejo he won a football scholarship to Stanford in 1952.

Henry missed the Rose Bowl game due to concussion and spent it on the sidelines as an unused reserve. But he still claimed he had been offered a $6,000 deal to turn pro. That off-season he took up rugby union at Stanford. By the spring of 1953 he was playing for California against Ireland at the Rose Bowl. Two weeks later he was on a plane to Australia.

They dragged in another guy from the Stanford rugby team: Vince Jones, from Long Beach, who was up there at Law School having done his degree at Dartmouth College in New Hampshire. A football star at Dartmouth, Jones was so bright he had won a Rhodes Scholarship to Oxford University and was expected in England in September. Surely he was too intelligent to put his body and reputation on the line for Dimitro's crazy scheme?

Vince Jones: 'I knew I had my scholarship to England when I got back so I had a break and took this opportunity to travel.'

To Vince – and many others – that's what it was. A chance to travel, an adventure.

Dimitro reduced the official squad size from 30 to 22 when he realised that only 13 men would be playing each game. And yet he was still struggling for players. He applied for visas for anyone and everyone – from a 38-year-old (Perry Schwarz) and a ham actor (Chuck Kicks) – to current players Trojan Leon Sellers and Rams reserve quarter back Don Klosterman. But none of them could come.

He wrote begging letters to colleges, clubs and players but none worked. Ray Willsey had trained with the All Stars since late April but Cal was not going to waive him.

Mike had 19 players confirmed. He needed one more guest at the party. And if you can't find another rugby player or football player, why not a track and field world champion and Olympic medallist?

William Everett Albans came seventh in the hop, skip and jump at the 1948 London Olympics; in 1949 he broke the shuttle hurdles relay world record; in 1950 he helped North Carolina to the NCAA track and field title thanks to becoming 220m hurdles champion himself; and when Dimitro was putting his plan to the Australian board, Bill Albans was winning bronze in the decathlon at the Gothenburg Olympics behind the legendary Bob Mathias.

He reckoned he never ran over 9.7 seconds for 100 yards and had done it in 9.5. His 100m personal best was 10.6. He high-jumped his own height and long-jumped 26 feet. A lightning-fast, blond, striking giant, once he was off and running, no one would catch him. At first they called him 'The Jet Winger'. Then 'Wild Bill'.

Albans, the 6ft 4in, 170lbs, Bayonne, New Jersey native was a relative veteran in the squad at 27, but a rugby novice.

Al D Kirkland: 'He had never played rugby before. He was a track man. Track men can run straight, so that's what he did, every time.'

Albans had at least seen rugby league played. Serving with the Marines in the Pacific during the war, he spent a few weeks in Australia and saw 'League Rugby' for the first time. 'It's the greatest of all football games,' he said. 'When Mike asked me if I would like to join his team in Australia I couldn't believe it.'

While Dimitro finally gathered the LA-based players together at Dorsey High, up in Palo Alto the Stanford contingent had no training whatsoever. They had not even heard of rugby league. They assumed they were going on a rugby union tour. No matter. Dimitro had devised a series of plays – 'Harry Truman or 40', 'Johnny Boy or 52', '72 or Joey Boy', '30 or Houston'. Unfortunately, they were based on eight-man scrums (rugby league scrums have six) and line-outs. Rugby league doesn't have line-outs.

Vince: 'Mike probably knew we were going there to play rugby league but didn't know there was much difference from the rugby we played. To us, rugby was rugby. Maybe he didn't tell us because we might have had second thoughts.'

Bonetti: 'We had 21 players, about a dozen of whom knew what they were doing! The others were Mike's friends. We didn't know each other until we got there.'

The *Sunday Sun's* un-named man in LA was still digging:

3 MAY 1953

DIMITRO 'CIRCUS' HAS NO VISAS

LOS ANGELES - Shoestring promoter Mike Dimitro and the ex-gridiron players and wrestlers he names as his Rugby League team to tour Australia have not yet applied for passport visas.
Sunday Sun

LOS ANGELES

The hack had quizzed travel agents, airline staff and the Australian Consul-General in San Francisco, determined to prove the tour was a doomed farce. He had tracked Dimitro's movements for weeks, and knew he had tried and failed to book flights with at least two agents and airlines. With only $2,000 to deposit, no one would trust him to come up with the other $12,000. Asked if he had the tickets yet, Mike fobbed him off: 'Sure I've got the tickets. Everything is under control.'

Asked if the entire squad have been together and practised as a team yet, he replied: 'Sure – they're all here except Van Doren.' The reporter did a ring round and found that at least eight were still at college up north and Van Doren had signed for the 49ers.

Dimitro panicked. The Foreign Service at the American Consulate in Sydney pulled some strings: permits were drafted, visas were stamped. The tour would go ahead.

Now Mike needed dollars. Lots of them. Fast. Ray Terry was the man. Secretary of the tote workers' union – the Parimutuel Employees Guild – Terry was managing over 1,000 staff at LA's racetracks. Terry knew bookies, Terry dealt with dollars, Terry knew people who knew people. He was mates with comedian Joe E Brown (of UCLA field fame) and crooner Bing Crosby: Terry gave Bing football tickets when he was a young player at San Diego. Bing returned the favour, teaching Ray to play golf. Crosby then gave Terry a job on the Del Mar racetrack, which he part-owned.

Terry had lived the good life, moving with the shakers. His body told the story: overweight, balding, but claiming to still be in his 20s. Ray's father, Dr A.J. Terry, was a wealthy chiropractor in Rosemead, CA. Dr Terry dug deep. Between them they came up with the cash to pay the airline.

Dimitro was digging his own hole. Luckily, not all the press were looking for the kill.

With a week before they arrived in Oz, Dimitro was talking up his squad.

Australian papers reported that ten of the All Stars had played in the Rose Bowl, watched by 105,000 in the stadium in Pasadena and 43m on TV: Dimitro (West Virginia), Mena (Texas), Van Doren (Cal), Naumu (Hawaii), Kerkorian (Nevada), Buckley (New York), Bonetti (Cal), Al E Kirkland (Arizona) and Demirjian (Illinois).

TALK OF THE TOWN

The American All Stars that will tour Australia and New Zealand have turned out to be one of the most colorful teams ever to be assembled. The team has created a new topic of conversation from Toots Shore's to the famed Sunset Strip.
Rugby League News

Some of these players had never even been to those States. Dimitro was trying to give the impression his players were from all over the US. He needn't have bothered. California was exciting, glamorous and new, and would do for the

Aussies. He told their press 'most of the players have been in numerous movies' – *Brute Force, Killer McCoy, That's My Boy, Sons of Iwo Jima,* and *All My Sons*.

Whatever his reasons, Dimitro couldn't help getting carried away with the truth. It would backfire more than once.

Each player received a letter from 'Pat Dodd, secretary of the American All Stars, 2713 Ceilhunt Avenue, Los Angeles 64'. Attached was a tour itinerary and a list of essential baggage.

They were advised to pack the items on Dimitro's list.

Dimitro could have added one large heart and one sense of humour. But no helmets required.

They were due to depart LA International Airport at 9.30am on 16 May 1953. 'Be there with your bags and ready to roll,' were Dodd's instructions.

A group of young American strangers were about to become a rugby league team.

AMERICAN ALL STAR RUGBY LEAGUE TOUR OF AUSTRALIA

The Team will depart from International Airport, MAY 16, 1953, at 9:30 A. M. Be there with your bags and baggage ready to roll. The following list covers the clothing that will be needed on the tour.

1 – Raincoat	3 – Sports shirts
1 – Suit	8 – T-Shirts
1 – Sports Jacket	8 – Underdrawers
3 – Pairs of Slacks	6 – Handkerchiefs
1 – Pair black shoes	2 – Pair pajamas
8 – Pair woolen socks	1 – Light sweater or jacket
2 – Pair evening socks	1 – Belt
2 – White shirts	3 – Neckties
	1 – Bathing trunks

In addition to the above list, do not forget your Tooth Brush, Tooth Paste, Hair Oil, Shaving Lotion, Razor and EXTRA MONEY.

PRACTICE EQUIPMENT THAT WILL BE NEEDED IS AS FOLLOWS:

Football shoes	Sweat Shirt (2)	2 Athletic Supporters
Sweat Pants	1 Pair Knee pads	

- -

SYDNEY HEADQUARTERS: – Oceanic Hotel, Coogee 'Phone FX8421

Monday	May 18	8:00 PM	Arrive Mascot Airport
Tuesday	May 19	9:30 AM	Training Coogee Oval
		2:30 PM	Inspection Sydney Cricket Ground
		8:00 PM	Attend Referees' Coaching Class
Wednesday	May 20	9:30 AM	Training Coogee Oval
		8:30 PM	Welcome N.S.W. Leagues' Club
Thursday	May 21	9:30 AM	Training Coogee Oval
		8:00 PM	Civic Reception by Mayor, Randwick Town Hall
Friday	May 22	11:00 AM	Reception City Tattersalls' Club
		2:30 PM	Training Sydney Cricket Ground
		6:45 PM	Broadcasting Station 2SM
Saturday	May 23	9:30 AM	Training Coogee Oval
		3:00 PM	Witness Fixture Queensland V,

CHAPTER 7
SYDNEY 1953

16 MAY 1953
0930

The 18-man party departed LA International Airport on board the Canadian Pacific Airlines flight to Hawaii. They were heading for the trip of a lifetime.

Al Kirkland: 'We met at LA airport one morning and flew to Honolulu, then to Fiji then Auckland then Sydney – it took about three days. It felt like we were going to another planet, let alone the other side of the world. We'd certainly gotten to know each other on the plane by the time we got to Sydney! The stewardess on the United flight from Hawaii was a girl I knew from Stanford. We were young kids, having a ball. It was so hot and humid in Fiji I had to take a shower. I drunk the water there and by the time we got to Sydney I had diarrhoea. It must have been the water in Fiji.'

The players had no idea what was coming their way, on the field, or off it. They had not seen the Australians play. They had not seen anyone play. And they certainly had not read the Australian press. While the American media were oblivious to it all, the Australian sports pages covered the story slavishly. The interest in a bunch of no-names who had never played the game was phenomenal.

That these outrageous chancers were from California made them even more attractive to an Aussie public still grateful to America for saving it from Japan. Less than eight years had passed since Anzac and US troops had fought together as the Japanese closed in on the North Queensland coast. Throw in the magic of Hollywood and a dose of international sport, and these Californian hunks were poster boy material. Australia's thirst for sporting success was being stoked by watching Americans dominate post-war sport.

THE YANKEES ARE HERE!

The curtain is up! The Big Show is on! Despite rumours to the contrary the Yankee Boys are here, see! They arrived at Mascot with their regalia, pantaloons 'n everything tucked away in their baggage... ready for action.
Daily Mirror

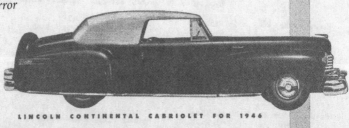

LINCOLN CONTINENTAL CABRIOLET FOR 1946

U.S. MEN MOBBED BY GIRLS

More than 500 people – many of them young girls – mobbed the American Rugby League team at Mascot last night. They broke through barriers to surge around the Americans. Eighteen-year-old Maree Morgan, Miss American Valentine 1953, kissed the captain, Vince Jones. "Boy, I'm all for this," he said.

A girl in a green skirt and tight sweater illegally entered the Customs room and waved her name and address on a card.

Police had to escort the Americans to a bus to save them from a swarm of autograph-hunting boys.

Many of the Americans wore brightly coloured floral shirts. All admitted they had never played Rugby League before.

Daily Telegraph

These Yanks were filling the role usually played by British, French or Kiwi rugby teams: they were there to entertain and excite the Australian public before departing across the sea, beaten and bowed. Not that they knew it. Yet.

Dimitro and Terry show a stewardess their wares

Hundreds greet the Americans' arrival

18 MAY 1953

The party touched down at Mascot Airport, in Botany Bay, southern Sydney. They were met by New South Wales RFL supremo Jersey Flegg and an hysterical crowd. Don't believe the hype: only the maverick Teddy Grossman had a Hawaiian print shirt on under his sports jacket. Half wore jackets and ties, others open necks and short-sleeved shirts.

Bonetti: 'When we got to Sydney there were about 25,000 at the airport to meet us!

We didn't know what was going on.'

U.S. LEAGUE TEAM HEAVIEST, TALLEST

Eight six-footers are included in the American Rugby League team. The huge men dwarfed the Australian stars who greeted them. The team is the biggest and heaviest ever to come to Australia, with only three forwards under 15st. and one under 14.7. The three wingers include the tallest man in the team, 6ft 4in Bill Albans.
The Daily Telegraph

The All Stars were front page news as well as back. *The Daily Telegraph* gave a whole page over to photos of the players arriving. Jack Bonetti, all 6ft 1in of blond athleticism, the dark-skinned Armenian Al Abajian, and the beanpole Olympian Bill Albans quickly changed into the star-studded playing uniforms to give the press a sneak preview of their game day outfits. With eight players weighing over 15 stones, these Americans were freakishly big by Aussie standards.

While Jersey Flegg tried to keep order, ringmaster Dimitro took control. He was the centre of the whirling mob, microphones, cameras and autograph books shoved under his chin from all directions, and loving every second of it. As Flegg pronounced he was going to speak to the throng, Mike answered every question fired his way 'like a conjurer pulling rabbits out of a top hat'.

Jim Mathers, *Mirror*: Where did the money for the fares come, Mike?

Dimitro: I guaranteed $20,000 personally.

Flegg: The Australian Rugby League didn't give a penny for the fares.

Airline man: The Rugby League has paid the return fares.

Mathers then claimed in the *Mirror*:

> ## 'DIMITRO HAS SUCH A FLOW OF READY WORDS HE COULD SELL THE SYDNEY HARBOUR BRIDGE TO THE COMMONWEALTH BANK.'

The players were cornered by the press pack asking if they had ever played this game before. 'Yes, sure, we've all played – eh? You call it rugby league? We call it football.' Mike Dimitro was on the spot: 'No, no! None of the boys has played rugby league before. They know something about rugby union. They are all good gridironers.'

U.S. TEAM OF "CONVERTS"

All members of the American Rugby League team which arrived in Sydney last night are converts from rugby union. None has yet match experience in League.

Team manager Mike Dimitro, immaculately dressed in a blue sports coat, answered questions with the rapidity of machine-gun fire: 'Stories you've read about the tour being in doubt are false. There was no trouble in getting the team away, and I had no finance difficulties. Sure I was slow in naming the members of my team. But that was only because I hand-picked the men I wanted and then had to persuade them to make the trip. I could have got 100 players but the men I have brought are the men I wanted.'

By George Crawford

The weary All Stars at Mascot Airport

Dimitro kept spouting BS: 'Every man in the team has had university experience in union rugby. Some have played gridiron as well. We've been training in league rugby since 15 March. Sure we haven't played a league rugby match yet but aren't league rugby and union rugby first cousins?'

The Aussies' administrators must have been reeling. Not only had they never played rugby league before, the manager did not even get its name right and some of the players sounded like they had never even heard of it. At least none of them knew Dimitro had been sketching out set plays from line-outs.

Iron Mike allayed their fears: 'All my guys are intelligent, university graduates. I figure they'll wise up to the slight difference in the two games in a matter of minutes. We hope to learn the league rules in the eight days before our first match. I'm not going to boast that we'll beat Australia yet! Only a fall guy would say that. But take it from me: my boys are big enough, tough enough and athletic enough to win quite a few games.'

Cheerful Xavier Mena, his 6ft 1in frame topped with thick black hair, told Crawford and the press pack that he and Mike had been planning the trip since 1946: 'Mike told me all about this league rugby game he had seen when he was on war service down in the South Pacific. It sounded pretty good to me. Ever since we've been working side by side, steadily organising this team.'

Al D. Kirkland's modern rimless glasses caused quite a stir. The flat-topped buzz-cut blond reckoned: 'Before Mike finished explaining I told him to put my name on the list.'

The message was clear: say anything, all news is good news, publicity is the oxygen we crave. One gesture won plenty of plaudits: most of the All Stars brought greetings from their pals to friends they had made in Sydney during the war.

★ ★ ★ ★ ★ ★ ★ ★ ★ ★ ★ ★ ★ ★ ★ ★

Some sportswriters saw the All Stars' arrival as the start of the next era for rugby league. They hoped they were seeing a new world order. 'Rugby league attitude here is that no matter whether the Americans are good, bad or indifferent, it is a start and can lead to a big future in the game between the two countries,' wrote one excited hack. Within minutes of touching down on Mascot's tarmac, Dimitro was telling the world that Australian and Kiwi teams would be invited to tour America and play in ten different states and that an organisation would be founded 'to control and expand rugby league' in the States. No mention that not a single rugby league team existed in the US.

In his 'Town Talk' gossip column in the *Mirror,* Robert Kennedy poured scorn on the *Sunday Sun's* sustained attacks: 'What was that mass arrival at Mascot last night – a mirage?' He also revealed that two nights earlier, someone purporting to be Dimitro had phoned Jersey Flegg at the Leagues Club in Phillip Street to tell him the team had arrived at the airport and were wondering where their meet and greet was. A flabbergasted Flegg rushed around, ordered a fleet of cabs and rounded up a welcoming committee when the phone rang again. An American voice told him it was a hoax.

The squad of greenhorns headed for their Sydney base: the Oceanic Hotel in the seaside suburb of Coogee. They may have been almost as far from home as physically possible but Coogee was a familiar setting for these Californian kids: a bay of golden sand, surfers, sunshine and 'sheilas'.

Al D. Kirkland: 'We were based at Coogee, a real surfers' paradise. It was probably my favourite place on the trip. I think Ted and Vince surfed out there. I didn't, but it's a beach town so it was good fun.'

It was late autumn in Australia though and the Pacific was colder than it would have been back home. Big Al D. was the only swimmer at Coogee some days.

Once training was over each lunchtime and evening, the Americans learned about the British Empire's drinking culture: and Australia's 'Six O'Clock Swill'.

Stringent rules and regulations designed to keep drinking to a minimum meant pubs were closed at 6pm every night. Only clubs and hotels could stay open later. Most Aussies clocked off work at 5pm and rushed to the nearest pub for an hour of speed drinking. Mayhem often followed.

Al D.: 'We went to get a beer the first night and the place was a madhouse! We said "My god!" I'd never

Sol Naumu (12), Mike Dimitro (27) and Al D. Kirkland.

seen anyone drink like that. They were pouring it down their necks and the place was rammed. We couldn't get in so we went away and came back a little later… and it was shut. "Ah, that explains it," we said.'

HIMALAYAN LEARNING CURVE

The following morning the bleary-eyed, jet-lagged crew had their first training session at Coogee Oval – a white picket-fenced sports field on the promenade – all captured by the Sydney paparazzi. They even got Teddy to blow the froth off a schooner of beer for the cameras. Not only were the press there but around 500 fans, about a hundred of them screaming girls, and a clutch of former international players who came to see what the fuss was all about. The Americans, used to such adulation in college football, tried their best to ignore the girls – their time would come. The Yanks had to concentrate on Latchem Robinson's crash course in rugby league.

Jack Bonetti: 'Whether Mike knew we were going to be playing rugby league not union, I don't know. We found out when we got there. Mr Robinson put us together, and taught us league.'

Al D.: 'We had no idea what rugby league was. Mike must have known that we were going there to play rugby league but just didn't tell us. Harold Han had never played rugby at all or even seen a game! Of course Kerkorian had never

Al D. Kirkland and Xavier Mena at Coogee Oval.

played rugby before either but Gary turned out to be a very good rugger.'

Jack: 'Gary had never played rugby. But he had a good throw – he could throw it 50 yards across the field. The Australian people went goofy when they saw that! The press couldn't believe it either.'

Joyce Kerkorian: '"Dad" said: "We went over there and didn't know what the hell we were doing! We didn't know which way to run or when to throw the ball. It was ridiculous, but wonderful."'

Jack: 'Mike may have played rugby himself but very little. To me, it wasn't a problem playing league rather than union because league was faster. The biggest difference was that we had to be in excellent condition… and some of us weren't! Mike's mates hadn't played football since they left college and they were out of shape.

'We had no problem with the no forward pass rule either because we did laterals in football. And playing offense and defense in football helped my rugby league, no question. If you'd played football, rugby league was not the least bit difficult. In rugby [league] there were always one v one situations and I liked league more than union because of that, and the speed.'

Al D.: 'Basically we had two weeks of rugby league lessons when we got there and then we had to play their top teams. There was no pressure on us, though – it wasn't stressful at all.'

Looking back it seems extraordinary that the Americans felt no pressure. Perhaps they didn't know what was to come.

The local aficionados were intrigued and quietly impressed.

YANKS SPECTACULAR IN COOGEE TRIAL
HANDLING SUPERB, SCRUM WORK WEAK

With their foundation of American gridiron football, the Yankees who gave their first training display this morning on Coogee Oval, look like eclipsing in their Rugby League tour of Australia the spectacular Rugby Union Fijians. If enthusiasm means anything, the Yankees are going to hit the high spots. They simply captured Coogee Oval today in their long sweat suits and swept the large crowd off its feet in a war–whooping training workout.
Daily Mirror
By Jim Mathers

The Fijians had made such an impact in Australia that some of them were recruited on reputation alone by English rugby league club Rochdale Hornets. *The Mirror* compared the backs' handling to the all-conquering French national team: 'Not the quick, snappy passes but lightly thrown ones and they handled them well after a shaky start with the bigger Australian ball. Interspersed in their training were frequent long spiralling passes which are part of their own gridiron game.' Asked if that type of pass would be incorporated in their game in Australia, Dimitro claimed: 'Well, there are some things I want to keep as a surprise.' The writer was left to wonder 'how these Yanks will work out as a League team. They have the size and speed required and excellent ball sense'.

Others were less generous – and used the press to throw muck at the Board of Control. Ross McKinnon, snubbed by the Board as the All Stars' prospective coach, wrote a stinging piece in *Sportsweek*:

YOU'LL NEED A MIRACLE, DIMITRO
LEAGUE TEAMS NOT FORMED IN A DAY

If Mike Dimitro's American football team can learn enough about Rugby League to give any team in Australia a reasonable match, it will be a miracle.
Sportsweek

Former Kangaroos skipper Len Smith wrote in another Sydney paper, slaughtering the All Stars' shambolic scrummaging technique – complete with accompanying labelled photograph – and pointed the finger at Phillip Street.

U.S. LEAGUERS VISIT PREMATURE

If this tour fails, the blame must fall on the Australian Board of Control for not having sent an official to America when the tour was first discussed. A man like North Sydney's coach Ross McKinnon could have put the Americans through the fundamentals and then the finer points of the game before the team left America.

Clive Churchill, Australian Rugby League star, shows American Johnny Kauffman the correct method of playing the ball during the visitors' training at Coogee Oval this week.

Sides were being taken. Dimitro's men were again pawns in a political row.

The first session at Coogee Oval was chaotic, as players were interrupted every few seconds by fans swarming the field. George Kauffman, practising his place kicking in his soft toed boots, had to stop mid-run-up to sign autographs. Dimitro discussed business with various officials while jogging around the Oval with his similarly unfit team.

Many had no idea how to pass a rugby ball backwards, all were clueless at the play the ball, and scrums were a mystery. But Latchem was pleased with their handling skills and boundless enthusiasm. After all, they had only had about seven hours' sleep after a 48-hour journey.

After lunch, coach Robinson took them for another session at the legendary Sydney Cricket Ground, where they would face Sydney's best just 11 days later: Coronation Day. Robinson drafted in six New South Wales players to help demonstrate play the balls, scrums and other tactics on the SCG's wide expanses beneath its towering colonial stands. Australia captain Clive Churchill demonstrated the art of kicking from hand to fellow full-back Kauffman, all while wearing his suit and street shoes. Churchill and former international Ray Norman offered again to help with coaching.

That night the Americans had a supposedly secret session across the city at North Sydney Oval: but word got round north of the Harbour Bridge and 200 fans still found a way in.

The All Stars were undoubtedly the week's big story: they even snatched a share of the back page of *The Sun* from the Australian cricket team's annihilation of MCC at Lords.

'Will Yanks Be Ready?' asked one newspaper. Beat writer Harry Jefferies was circumspect: 'The Yankee footballers… still have a long way to go to really understand the rules and method of play of the rugby league game as we know it. They have started to get the hang of it but I don't know how they are going to go against a strong country team… The players are speedy, can handle, take and throw a ball with accuracy, but time is against them learning the general set-up of the game. The Australian Board of Control, notwithstanding the cost, should have flown a man to America a month ago and started the training programme there.'

But Dimitro was being his usual bullish self, telling the *Telegraph* – which ran five All Stars stories on the first day – that all they needed to sort were the scrums and the play the balls!

'Don't worry, we'll be ok,' he told reporters. 'The boys are practically there now.' If 'there' meant understanding the basic rules and set pieces a few days before taking on world class opposition then he was certainly talking a good game. He even told the *Telegraph* he wanted the Australia and New Zealand national teams to make a 'barnstorming tour of the US' in their off-season.

But the ugly issue of money had already raised its unwelcome head.

LEAGUE BRIDGES A DOLLAR GAP

One paper claimed that the Board of Control had advanced the American team £100 because the All Stars were skint, already.

Dimitro claimed the players would be paid £12 a week each and yet they had arrived without a penny. Harold Matthews claimed the French had done the same the year before and he promised to give the Americans another large wad on Friday.

The itinerary for that first ten days was well planned. They trained every day at Coogee and had a team outing most days. On Tuesday night they had the first coaching class with leading referee Jack O'Brien. On Wednesday, after seeing what they were actually trying to do – by watching New South Wales train at the SCG – they headed off to Phillip Street, right in the heart of Sydney city centre, to the NSW Leagues Club. The highlight of the reception was Fran Mandalay's rendition of 'I'm in the Mood for Love', which 'had the girls sighing', according to *RL News*. Then, on Thursday night was the Mayor of Randwick's Civil Reception.

The All Stars admire Mr Alphabet's football cake.

"THANKS FOR THE WINE AND COOKIES.
NOW WHERE'S THE BROADS?"

Ted: 'At the first reception we went to, the Australian Rugby League guy gave a great welcoming speech. Then Dimitro stands up and says: "Thanks for the wine and cookies. Now where's the broads?" It was so embarrassing. We decided there and then that he couldn't speak for us. It had to be Vince instead.'

Abajian: 'We cringed every time Mike spoke. That comment about "broads" went out live over the radio!'

The next night saw another reception, this time at the City Tattersall's Club on Pitt St. The 'City Tatts' had a fine reputation in Sydney social circles, playing host to overseas sports stars on a regular basis, in the gym, dining room and bar. For this occasion, chef Martin Eykelenkamp – known as 'Mr Alphabet' – spent 70 hours producing an edible rugby field, complete with posts and

players, as the main decoration. All the top Tatts members were in attendance, along with NSWRL officials, movers and shakers from the city's ten District clubs, and the press.

There to meet the All Stars was Aussie league legend Dally Messenger – aka Dally M. Dally M was endorsing footballs, boots, headguards, leather ribbed shoulder pads and shin pads: all for sale at Mick Hammond's chain stores, among the rifles and shotguns.

Ted: 'I remember the meal at the Tattersall club for one moment. Dally Messenger was like the Babe Ruth of rugby league. He's sat there on the top table. He's eating away, then stops, does this 'urrrgggah' sound, pushes back from the table and hawks one between his legs. Unbelievable.'

Messenger's chunder blunder didn't stop the Tatts making the Americans and Dally M honorary members of their club! That night, Dimitro and his merry men had also made their first radio appearance on 2SM to start hyping the Sydney game.

If the All Stars were still thinking they could sneak under Sydney's radar until they were ready to face the public, they soon realised how wrong they were. With TV yet to reach Australia, there were several daily papers in Sydney and seven different radio stations had their own rugby league shows: 2SM, 2FC, 2UE, 2UW and 2GB had preview shows on Friday night, while 2CH and 2KY were among the choices on a Saturday morning. Everyone knew everything.

CHAPTER 8
THERE WILL BE FIREWORKS

After recovering in the early hours, on Saturday afternoon the players had a frightening sight: New South Wales v Queensland at the SCG. It was the second of a four game inter-state series. NSW Blues won 27-16 to go two up in the series but the Maroons gave it a good shot. Suddenly the Americans saw just what they were up against. Now they knew how good they would have to be just to avoid humiliation by the best Aussies. They had a week to arm themselves.

Vince Jones used his new Polaroid camera to take photos of the NSW moves: for the first time, the Blues were splitting their centres to the left and right sides of the field rather than working in tandem to one side of the ball. This was at the request of captain Bob Bartlett who had used that system when playing for Bramley and Leeds in England. The Polaroid's instant images were bewildering to the Australians. It was cutting-edge technology. Vince Lombardi was about to introduce Polaroids to the NFL: as the new coach of New York Giants, he took pictures of opposition's defensive line-ups from the press box at Yankee Stadium and got the prints lowered to the coaching staff down on the touchline inside a sock weighed down by a rock.

The Americans were winning the publicity game. During half-time of a curtain-raiser to the NSW-Queensland game, four of the All Stars entertained the SCG crowd by showing off their gridiron-style throwing technique. There were 'choruses of gasps at the distances the ball travelled' as the four 'gave an amazing exhibition of throwing': the 'spiral action' sent the ball 'practically 50 yards and the crowd of more than 40,000 at that time cheered the unusual display'. Dimitro also led his team on a lap of the ground behind the marching band. They were given a 'mighty reception' and waved to spectators on the hill.

Support was clearly not going to be a problem. Playing rugby league might be.

Mr P.M. Jarman, the American Ambassador to Australia, wrote in the tour brochure: 'While I am much afraid that, without the experience in rugby, you have slight prospects of victory over the experienced players of Australia, I hope and believe your play will afford the fine, athletically-minded people of Australia some idea of our football and sportsmanship.'

SUNDAY 24 MAY 1953

The team headed to the Bondi Icebergs Club, principally a winter swimming club but something of a magnet for any top athlete who found themselves in Sydney. Members at the Icebergs included many of the Australia national rugby league and rugby union teams, Olympic weightlifters, track and field stars and top personalities from Australian horse racing. They hosted Test match cricketers and Grand Slam tennis champs. Anyone who would draw a crowd and impress the members was welcome at the Icebergs. The Americans were perfect.

CHURCHILL "A HELLCAT ON WHEELS," WOULD BE BIG SUCCESS IN AMERICA

By MIKE DIMITRO, American Rugby League player-manager.

Your Rugby League full-back, Clive Churchill, would be a 10,000-dollars-a-year-man in American gridiron football.

He would rank among the highest-paid players in the game.

Back in the States I had heard a lot about this little guy.

Now that I've seen him in action I fully support all the fine reports that came to us before we started out on this tour of Australia.

Churchill is a hell-cat on wheels.

He's everywhere . . dynamite all the time.

They tell me Churchill is the best Rugby player in the world.

I have no doubt about that.

It would be impossible to get better material for any of the football codes in which handling, running, kicking, and positional play are the main factors.

I can well imagine how the big American gridiron promoters would flash their cheque-books if they saw this guy in action.

Churchill, in gridiron, would be a masterly quarterback and safety-man.

The Rugby League code is indeed fortunate that it has in its ranks such a gifted footballer.

I've seen Rugby League played before, but most of my team yesterday had their first observation of the game being played in real competitive spirit.

Let me tell you, we were all impressed.

I'm not here to tell you Rugby League-minded folk your business.

But I can already see improvements that could brighten the game.

It should be permissible to replace injured players, the American long pitch-pass would bring greater thrills, and spectators should learn to root for their teams.

Queensland yesterday suffered an unnecessary handicap when winger Flannery and front-rower Rooney were injured.

I figured it ruined Queensland's chances of victory.

They yell, they scream, they chant encouragement to their heroes out in the middle.

I really do think the Australian spectator would enjoy his football more if he let his head go.

There's no law against it, you know.

The standard of play yesterday looked pretty high-class to me.

But I reckon my American boys will be your equal when we play a few matches together.

From this match we learned a lot about positional play—the feature of Rugby League that has been worrying us most.

I will say now that we will have it over Australian's in the art of tackling.

Your tackling is pretty good, but it is not so potent as the gridiron art to which my boys are accustomed.

You will find that when my boys tackle, his man won't get up in a hurry.

I'll let you see that for yourselves next Saturday.

Scanning the Sunday papers must have made some uncomfortable reading for the All Stars who were already detecting Tiger Mike was liable to let his mouth run away from him.

Dimitro poured praise on Churchill, having seen him destroy Queensland: 'He's everywhere – dynamite all the time... the big American gridiron promoters would flash their cheque-books if they saw this guy in action. Churchill, in gridiron, would be a masterly quarter back and safety-man.'

He admitted that seeing the top talent at first hand was an eye-opener for his men, but then started suggesting improvements league could make to its code: substitutions for injured players and long passes from one side of the field to another. Then he slated the Sydney crowd for being 'too conservative – the Australian spectator would enjoy his football if he let his head go. There's no law against it, you know'.

Any fan still reading and not throwing Dimitro's words onto the fire would have seen his most inflammatory comments yet: 'I reckon my American boys will be your equal when we play a few matches together. We will have it over Australians in the art of tackling. Your tackling is pretty good, but it is not so potent as the gridiron art to which my boys are accustomed. You will find that when my boys tackle, his man won't get up in a hurry.'

Clive Churchill and Vince Jones.

Gridiron tackling was all smash and blast. Rugby technique was about grapple and twist. You can't smash a ghost – and some of these Aussies would be drifting passed untouched.

Dimitro told *Rugby League News*: 'Once we get the ball there will be fireworks and we won't be kicking it back to that Churchill to run all over the field with, that's for sure. Scoring tries is our aim and the way we work it out you can't score by kicking it away to the other side when you get it.'

At least Dimitro admitted he was worried about getting enough of the ball to do anything with it: he feared young Syd Walker would be out-hooked in the scrums. If he did, no one could blame him. The happy-go-lucky Walker had tried his hand at most sports: swimming, diving, shot-put, volleyball, golf, handball, ping-pong and badminton, and some rugby union at UCLA. The youngest All Star at just 21, broad-shouldered Syd would need to put his big blond flat-topped head in where it hurts and hope for the best. No wonder he brought out his leather ear protectors.

That afternoon, the All Stars headed to the historic Redfern Oval, home of the South Sydney Rabbitohs, one of Australia's grandest and finest clubs. There they played a practice game of touch with the Rabbitohs players, including five international stars, under the gaze of a sceptical press pack. Souths treasurer George Hansen told the papers: 'Centres Al Abajian and Al E. Kirkland are really top class players. There are few better in Australia. Their handling is outstanding and they can side-step off either foot. Many people are underestimating this team.'

The *Courier Mail* agreed that Al E. was the best American player 'who moves fast, is a beautiful tackler and already looks like a top class league player. There was a perfect illustration of the possibilities of their long gridiron passes when centre Kirkland ran towards one wing, pivoted and sent a 50-yard pass to the opposite wing where Bill Albans took it at his top, and ran 40 yards before being pulled down.'

After laying a wreath at the Cenotaph on Monday morning, the squad headed to a lunchtime civic reception by the Lord Mayor of Sydney. Then it was time to put what they had learned so far into action.

Dimitro had fixed up a 60-minute practice game against the Royal Australian Engineers at Casula: their first game of rugby league and the first game of any rugby in some of the players' lives. The All Stars wore their training gear: some in shorts, some in long football pants, others in sweat suits. Al Abajian had already broken his nose so wore an ear and nose protector, his face all strapped up like Frankenstein's monster.

About a thousand spectators turned up to watch this rag-bag bunch in the pouring rain, including several reporters.

26 MAY

YANKS BIG TRIAL WIN

Sydney (by teleprinter) – The American All Stars Rugby League team beat the Australian Army Engineers 41-10 in a trial game yesterday.

The match, which was not part of the official tour, was played to give the Americans experience in the code. The Americans scored nine tries with their unorthodox play to the Army's two. Centre Al. E. Kirkland scored three of the tries. There were 60 minutes play, 30 each way, with full tackling.

Although allowed some latitude by the referee, the Americans often showed brilliant form and threw the ball about in a manner which reminded many of the French team which toured in 1951.

The Army side was not of particularly high standard, but some of the Americans' tries would have been good in any company.

The All Stars coach, Norman Robinson, said; "The team handled beautifully and with more experience would have secured more tries."

The All Stars official tour will open with a match against Southern Districts at Canberra tomorrow.
Courier Mail

YANKS UNORTHODOX AND FAST

Harry Jefferies predicted the All Stars would pack the grounds on tour after kicking off the tour "unofficially and sensationally against a tough Army side – and did they turn it on!"

The Rugby League News: 'The backs are a particularly brilliant bunch and big centre Al Kirkland is outstanding. Although the Army team at Casula was naturally nothing like international standard it was good enough to show that the Yanks will not need much playing experience to become stars in rugby league.'

'Let their backs get the ball and they'll drive their opponents mad,' reckoned former Australia national team half-back 'Chimpy' Busch. 'Their handling is phenomenal. I've never seen such bewildering passing – some of their players took passes as if they were jugglers. The Yanks could prove greater showmen than the French team.'

Goalkickers Kerkorian and the long-faced Kauffman were 'not nearly as fussy as Australian kickers when placing the ball. They mostly stand the ball upright, take a few steps back and then kick the goal'.

Coach Robinson was delighted by Jack Bonetti, Al E., Vince Jones and Kauffman at full-back. 'The Americans threw the ball about as if it were a cricket ball,' he told the *Mirror*. 'They were unorthodox and retained much of the gridiron idea.' Maybe that was no bad thing. They were treated to steak for dinner in the army camp.

The Army game and the session with the Rabbitohs had been eye-openers. Tuesday's scheduled visit to a children's hospital and another referee's coaching class were postponed. The boys needed to run through what they'd learned so far before their first game on Wednesday.

Maybe this wasn't going to be a nightmare after all.

CHAPTER 9
KICK IT, PASS IT OR EAT IT

Buoyed by their debut success, the next morning the All Stars flew out of Sydney to the modern Australian capital, Canberra, to play their first official game. The opposition was the local select XIII representing Southern and Monaro Divisions. It was time for the pomp and ceremony to begin. They were taken around Parliament House by MP J.P. Fraser and the local press snapped away as Dimitro shared drinks with local League officials at a Civic Reception: it was Hospitality Central.

The tour brochure presented a message from Australia RFL Board of Control chairman Harry Flegg: 'This, to us, is another record in the progress of the game of Rugby League Football…our game is progressing right through every state in Australia, and it is a pity that the stay of the Americans in Australia could not be extended to enable the people in other states to see them in action, but we trust that their visit will be the forerunner of many interchanges.'

Flegg compared Dimitro's tour with that of Baskerville's All Golds, the groundbreaking New Zealand rugby players who travelled to the UK in 1908 and changed the world of rugby forever.

The brochure had a further welcome message from NSWRL secretary Harold Matthews: 'America is noted for showing Australia top-class sport in many spheres. We all know how popular the American Davis Cup tennis players have proved… the best boxers to come to Australia in recent times have all been Americans and we also have been thrilled by the performances of their swimmers, speedway riders and wrestlers. No overseas athletes draw bigger crowds than Americans and for this reason Australian football fans have been keenly awaiting the arrival of Mike Dimitro and his buddies.'

Kangaroos captain Clive Churchill continued: 'I feel sure that a visit such as this one must create greater interest in R.L. in America as well as increasing the international reputation of this great game of ours. I feel sure that all Australia will join me in extending to the Team the same hospitality that we endeavoured to give the members of the American fighting services here during the war years.'

Dimitro had told *Sunday Telegraph* hack George Crawford that his men would be out to 'win at any cost' because wins would get fans excited and swell the takings back in Sydney. He said: 'I've told my players to go in at Canberra and give it everything.' The All Stars themselves were not so sure this was a good idea.

Ed: 'At the first game in Canberra I saw these guys coming off the field – they had played the curtain-raiser before our game.'

Ted: 'They had no teeth and cauliflower ears. We were a bunch of fresh-faced college kids.'

Ed Demirjian: 'I said to an official there: "What game have they been playing?" "Same as you," he said. Holy cow!'

AMERICAN ALL STARS
VERSUS
SOUTHERN & MONARO DIVISIONS
Mankua Oval, Canberra, May 27, 1953

LINEUPS

American "All Stars"	Southern & Monaro Divs.
Full Back	**Full Back**
GEORGE KAUFFMAN	K. BEAZLEY (Wollongong)
Wing Three-quarters	**Wing Three-quarters**
ED. DEMIRJIAN	R FREEBODY (Captain's Flat)
BILLY ALBINS	G. WATTS (Berry)
Centre Three-quarters	**Centre Three-quarters**
GARY KERKORIAN	R. BARTLETT (Wollongong)
SOL NAUMU	H. WELLS (Wollongong)
Five Eight	**Five Eight**
AL. KIRKLAND	K. SULLIVAN (Goulburn)
Half Back	**Half Back**
TED GROSSMAN	R. BERCENE (Bombala)
Lock Forward	**Lock Forward**
AL. D. KIRKLAND	R. SMITH (Wollongong)
Second Row Forwards	**Second Row Forwards**
JACK BONETTI	H. MILLER (Gerringong)
FRAN MANDULAY	H. YARHAM (Picton)
Prop Forwards	**Prop Forwards**
XAVIER MENA	W. HODGES (Captain's Flat)
VINCE JONES	S. EDWARDS (Robertson)
Hooker	**Hooker**
SID WALKER	C. STEWART (Bega)
Reserve Back	Reserve Back: J. PLATER (Yass)
HAROLD HAN	Res. Forw'd: C. WILLIAMSON (G'lbn.)

Ted Grossman: 'One guy had his nose in his ear. If he'd sneezed he'd have blown his own brains out. They looked like dogs had been chewing on their knees.'

Southern Divisions was a bunch of talented players from local amateur clubs: Wollongong, Berry, Goulburn, Bombala, Gerringong, Picton and Captain's Flats. But they were no mugs.

Luckily for Dimitro and his men, both of their international centres were away with the New South Wales squad preparing for the game against Queensland: Bartlett, who had just been put in charge of the Kangaroos for their tour to New Zealand, and his Wollongong club-mate Harry Wells, who had won the Sydney Premiership with Souths two years earlier.

But they still fielded up and coming winger Roy Freebody and NSW state rep Gus Miller in the second row. Surely this was far too much to ask of the All Stars in their first real game? One press preview suggested the Board of Control lend the Americans a hooker to give them direction and on-field coaching from that specialist role at the front of the scrum.

If it all went horribly wrong, the whole car crash would be no secret: the game was going out live that Wednesday afternoon in Sydney on 2SM radio with star commentator Reg Grundy on the mic. It was even going to be repeated on primetime that night for those who went to the NSW v Queensland game instead and missed it first time round.

MP Fraser did the honours with the ceremonial kick off. Fifteen minutes in, 'Wild' Bill Albans was carried off after being kicked on the head and rushed to Canberra Hospital. Unlike college football, where a whole new team would come on at different stages in the game, no replacements at all were allowed in rugby league, even if that meant one team or other going down to 12, 11 or ten men. Dimitro had publicly agreed to play by those rules. The rest of the half was played with just 12 men as lock Jack left the scrum base to cover the wing.

Vince Jones: 'I remember the first game, when we had guys who'd never played rugby before. The crowd could tell and they went wild!'

Courier Mail: 'They appeared to spend the first half learning League and the second half playing it. In the early stages some players in possession of the ball gave the impression they did not know whether to kick it, pass it, run with it or eat it.'

Miraculously, the Americans trailed just 20-8 at the break. Southern, in their Kangaroo-style bottle green shirts with traditional yellow V, black shorts and green and yellow socks, were softening up the long-trousered Yankees for Sydney on Saturday.

Dimitro knew he had made a mistake bringing such a small roster for such a punishing schedule, especially when he realised that substitutions were not allowed. He pushed the Board of Control to allow the Americans to replace injured players in the first half of games. Thus, Al Abajian entered the fray in Canberra. And Al E. started to play. What a sweet tune it was.

R.L. ALL STARS 34-25 WIN SHOCKS EXPERTS
U.S. CENTRE PRAISED

Rugby League critics rated American Al E Kirkland one of the world's best centres after he scored four tries against Southern Districts. Kirkland's brilliance converted an American half-time deficit of 8-20 into a brilliant 34-25 win.

Kirkland's running marked him as a threat to any of the sides to play America. He rarely moves across the field. He straightens up play immediately he gets the ball and weaves through defences.

by George Crawford

The second half was a sensational 40 minutes. The American novices scored six tries to the Southerners' one. Al E., all explosive power and stocky strength, scored four and set up the last for the athletic Bonetti with a 40-yard run. On-looking first grade referee George Bishop, the former Australia Test hooker, admitted: 'It would have been a thriller on the Cricket Ground.' Bishop was so impressed he volunteered to help out Latchem with coaching.

The press box was buzzing with excitement. Had they really seen what they thought they had seen? A balding, blond, Californian 22-year-old with little rugby and no rugby league experience, tearing it up?

W.B. Corbett: 'Alvin E. Kirkland plays with the speed, anticipation and finesse of a League star of many years' experience. Second rower Jack Bonetti is one out of the box and Abajian will be a dazzler with more playing experience.'

Latchem Robinson: 'I did not see a better centre than Kirkland during my recent tour of England and France. I most certainly would have liked him in my Kangaroo team.'

Courier Mail: 'Kirkland had never played rugby until he arrived in Australia a week ago but enthusiasts thought he compared with any League centre seen in Australia since the war.'

But when Al E. spoke to the press, he told them they had not seen anything yet: 'Wait until you see Bob Buckley in action. He'll lift those fans off the seats every time he gets the ball because he's one of the fastest, strongest and trickiest runners we've ever seen in the States.'

The *Morning Herald* reporter did admit that referee O'Brien, who had travelled south-west with the squad from Sydney, had been lenient to the newcomers 'with the result that nearly all Americans were guilty of many minor breaches of the rules', but this resulted in an open and fast game. Five-eighth Kirkland 'was everywhere on the field when required and gave an untiring display'.

Big Al D., grabbed by commentator Reg Grundy as he left the field, told 2SM listeners: 'Gridiron is strictly for babies! This is a man's game!'

All the press agreed that Al E. Kirkland was magnificent. But each were

(Above) The "All Stars" showed in their first game in Australia, played in Canberra, that although they had much to learn about Rugby, they had potentialities, but . . .

also swooning over a different All Star: half-back Teddy Grossman, lock Bonetti and second-rower Fran Mandulay were all 'potential match-winners', their backing-up 'a revelation', while the *Morning Herald* liked the 6ft Pittsburgh product Kerkorian and lock Al D. Kirkland, all 6ft 3in and 215lbs of him.

'America scored a brilliant try 15 minutes after the game opened. It was a credit to any international side. Bonetti broke from the All Stars' 25 before feeding Al Kirkland who set out on a speedy swerving run to beat three men close to him. As he came to the Southern full-back Beazley, he tricked him with a change of pace and scored between the posts. Kerkorian kicked a goal. America 5-0.' Simple as that.

The record Canberra crowd of over 7,000 – crouching under the rope and standing four deep around the edge of the Oval – must have wondered how on earth a 'Yank' could produce skills like that having never seen the game let alone played it!

Record Crowd Saw U.S.A. Beat Southern Districts

U.S. RUGGERS WIN

L.A. Times – Bulletin

THE LARGEST CROWD EVER to attend a football match at Canberra saw the American Rugby League team defeat Southern Districts 34-25 at Manuka Oval on Wednesday. More than 6,000 paid about £950 at the gate. In this picture Hawaiian Sol Nanumu (12) dummies toward winger Ed Demirjian (9). A. Watts is on the extreme left and S. Edwards is in the background.

AMERICANS PLAYED SPECTACULAR AND ENTERTAINING FOOTBALL AT CANBERRA

By BILL FITZGIBBON

Navy Sank Them

FIRST DEFEAT FOR HARP

Queanbeyan Harp suffered its first defeat of the season in the A.C.T. Soccer competition when they went down 2-1 to H.M.A.S. Harman last Sunday. Halftime score was one goal each.

The sailors were the first to break through when Guest intercepted a pass by Harp's left back, Di Prinzio, and slammed the ball into the net with a sizzling shot which Goalie Albo could not hold.

Harp attacked strongly, trying to pierce the armourplate defence of the Harman backs, Goodall and Parks, but with little success.

Rangoni and Duncan had unsuccessful shots from all angles before Barzotta centred a beautiful ball for Woods, the right winger, to score the equaliser.

In the second half the fast and furious pace of the game continued unabated. Each team spearheaded attack after attack and it was Navy's centre forward, Guest, who shot the winning goal.

Queanbeyan were conducting a determined sortie into Navy territory when the final whistle blew.

Honors for the victory go to Navy's defence and the fine leadership of Goodall.

Harp players combined well, with centre-half Halford outstanding.

TO REPRESENT A.C.T.

At Tuesday's meeting of the Canberra Soccer Asociation, five members of Queanbeyan Harp Soccer Club were selected to represent the A.C.T. in a match against Manly (Sydney) on Northbourne Oval this Sunday.

They are Albo Franceschini (goalkeeper), Di Prinzio (left back), Halford (centre half), Duncan (centre forward) and Rangoni (left wing).

Morning Herald: 'Considering the team has only had eight days' training since arriving in Australia it played remarkably well as a combination and showed good football sense.'

Courier Mail: 'Their passing and much of their kicking was clean and confident – by the end of the tour they could be a strong Rugby League side.'

Jack: 'At first the Aussies helped us a lot – they even told us when to pass! But as we got better they stopped helping us and realised we were there to be beaten.'

The fans went berserk. Thousands launched themselves over the fences and invaded the field to mob the American players. Officials tried to escort the All Stars back to the dressing rooms – without success. It was mayhem.

Ted: 'I remember one guy leant over the fence and tried to tear Al Kirkland's shirt off him!'

The All Stars were also considered sporting for applauding their beaten opponents off the field in the time-honoured rugby style, and few children went away unhappy after the exotic visitors patiently signed hundreds of autograph books. This was a PR dream.

Ted: 'There was a girl in the crowd wearing a sweater she'd had knitted exactly the same as our All Stars jersey, with the stars and stripes. She had a sign hung on the zipper saying "Give me a Yank any time".'

The news even reached the States:

The result from Canberra came through on the wire to the NSWRL HQ at 165 Phillip Street, where Sydney RL officials were meeting to select the squad to play the All Stars. They decided to select the strongest team possible.

CHAPTER 10
GOOD NIGHT, AND GOOD LUCK

All had been plain sailing – so far. Even Wild Bill joined them on the train back to Sydney the next day after a head x-ray had given him the all-clear. Tiger Mike was on the front page of the *Queanbeyan Age* calling for an America v Australia showdown at the Rose Bowl in 1954.

Dimitro's schedule demanded that the Americans sank or swam. So far they were frolicking in the water. This was not only a pleasant surprise to one and all but also vital. If the All Stars had not despatched the amateurs of the Royal Engineers and the Southern Districts, then their third game would have been a disastrous non-starter. A week after seeing their first rugby league match, the Americans faced some of the best players in the world: Sydney at the SCG.

And there were plenty of obstacles to overcome before that giant challenge.

Dimitro sat in his Coogee hotel room fielding phone call after phone call. Most were from women inviting the players to this party or that.

Writing in his guest newspaper column, he admitted: 'It ain't the football that's getting them down, it's the receptions, parties and speeches, where the boys are on their feet all the time. Then you find some guy has asked a bunch of them out some place and no-one's around just when you're gonna practise! We could spend more time practising if folks here in Australia weren't so hospitable. They'll just kill us guys with kindness before this tour is through.'

Amid the two-a-day practice sessions, the players had little time to worry. Thursday night brought a reception by the New South Wales Premier at Hotel Australia. Friday breakfast saw them draw the NSW State Lottery winning tickets before heading on a harbour excursion and a trip to Taronga Park Zoo. They just had time to buy some new lightweight Australian-style football shoes with better studs to grip the hard ground. As they headed to bed in the Oceanic on Friday night, some fans were already sleeping by the turnstiles at the SCG, determined to get a prime spot on the hill.

30 MAY 1953

YANKS LOOK FORWARD TO TUESDAY

"There is only one real way to learn football and that is on the field in actual matches," says Dimitro. "We will put up a great show, have no fear of that, but at the same time you have to realise we are meeting a really world-class team for the first time. We saw the full strength of New South Wales against Queensland last Saturday and they sure are a sweet team."
Rugby League News

Most amateur rugby league players would never get to play against an international player in their lifetime. The All Stars, after two matches to learn the rules, were about to face SEVEN. The Metropolitan selectors, having seen how the All Stars shocked Canberra, were not prepared to risk any embarrassment, let alone a humiliation. They named their strongest possible Sydney City team.

At full-back was arguably the greatest player on earth: Australia captain Clive Churchill. Considered by many Australians to be the finest rugby league player their country has ever produced, Churchill had been controversially replaced as captain, then reinstated. And when most players in the Sydney first grade comp were getting just $7 a game, newly-formed English club Workington Town had offered Churchill £10,000 (US$36,000) a year to join them in a £12,500 transfer from South Sydney. That's how good 'The Little Master' was.

On the right wing was prodigious goal-kicker Noel Pidding, a high-profile star for Australia and NSW. The swarthy Pidding was the cutting edge for St George as they launched a dynasty in the Sydney first grade Premiership. Scrum-half Keith 'Yappy' Holman was already a league legend, leading Western Suburbs Magpies to glory and being an Australia stalwart. At stand-off was Norths' Bob Sullivan, on the verge of an Australia call-up.

Holman's Wests club-mate, lanky hooker Arthur Collinson, was considered the best in Australia and around him in the forward pack were three more internationals: ferocious Souths prop Les 'Chicka' Cowie, bald Manly behemoth Roy Bull, and former Wallaby Ken 'Killer' Kearney, talisman of St George. Kearney had captained English giants Leeds before heading back to Sydney and developing 'The Brick Wall' defence, built on his gigantic thighs and calves. The pack was completed by Lloyd Hudson, the Norths prop who had just made the NSW state team.

The three-quarters were young and exciting: Easts' new centre Ron Taylor on debut, Canterbury's prolific teenage wing Barry Stenhouse, and the Norths pair of New Zealander George Martin at right centre and in-form wing Ben Haslam.

This was a formidable team for any side in the world to face. Let alone a bunch of innocent college kids from California. If the All Stars weren't scared now, they should have been. They should have been terrified.

Iron Mike was getting all the papers delivered to his room every morning. He knew the All Stars story was hot. He wasn't going to throw cold water on the flames. As usual, he was going out all guns blazing: 'Scoring tries is our aim. Getting the ball is our big problem… and the way we work it out you can't score by kicking it away to the other side when you get it. We won't be kicking it back to Churchill to run all over the field with, that's for sure. I'll tell you one thing: once we get the ball there will be fireworks!'

He was not wrong.

The Americans were undoubtedly the biggest sports story on Australia's eastern seaboard. They were the front cover shot on *Rugby League News*.

The game dominated the back pages – even up in Queensland. *The Brisbane Telegraph's* Sydney stringer, Harry Jefferies, announced the team news: 'Willo-the-wisp centre Alvin Kirkland, who scored four superb tries against Canberra, will lead the American All Stars backline against Sydney in their first big match of the tour.'

The All Stars were doing their bit. An hour and a half of Saturday morning – game day – was spent touring the radio stations to promote the game: 2GB at 9.30am, then 2UW, then 2CH and finally 2KY at 11am. By that time, there were thousands of fans already in the ground. The first had arrived in Moore Park at 10pm on Friday night to line up outside the gates.

Everyone in Sydney would know about the game come 3pm. And everyone in the States too, if Dimitro's plan worked out. He had agreed with the Board of Control that Associated TV in Sydney could film it so long as the Board and the All Stars received a third of any profits. The inevitable great humbling – and every individual humiliation – would be beamed into more than 10m American homes. 'This is part of my plan to introduce rugby league to America,' he told the papers. 'The huge crowd and pattern of rugby league should make an ideal spectacle on TV. The novelty will grip Americans and I figure it will have a 50m TV audience.'

It was also Memorial Day, the day when America honours its dead.

★ ★ ★ ★ ★ ★ ★ ★ ★ ★ ★ ★ ★ ★ ★ ★

64,953
YANKS' LEAGUE LACKS
WINNING SKILL

The Sunday Sun & Guardian

From HARRY JEFFERIES

The match programme wrote: 'Australia becomes the first of the Rugby League nations to attempt to foster the code in America. Any new venture is fraught with a certain amount of worry and occasionally a few doubts. This tour has proceeded along those lines and each hurdle has been taken as it came.

'Now the ball is in the hands of Mike Dimitro and his fine band of young American athletes who have come here to learn the game. The Frenchmen said the same thing when they made their first appearance two years ago and wound up giving lessons instead of taking them.

'America, of course, has not had the Rugby League experience that was behind the French team. They realise they are under a severe handicap and are playing a combination which could be stacked against any in the world without being disgraced. But the Yanks think they can make the grade, not necessarily to win today, but to acquit themselves well.

'Sydney crowds are noted for the liberal way they support visiting teams and the Yanks can be assured that the majority on the Hill and in the stands will be hoping they do as well as they would wish themselves.

'All Rugby League fans throughout the world today will welcome America into big-time Rugby League and say, "Good Luck".'

Writer W.F. Corbett suggested fans would see 'a softening up process not previously used with such intensity in Australia… a bulldozer system'. But would that be enough?

Or would they be a laughing stock? Dimitro told the press that while the Americans would not wear padding, they would don 'knee-length pants in wet weather and shorts in fine weather'.

Average first grade crowds in the ten-team Sydney Premiership were 10,000. New South Wales games at the SCG would usually attract around 50,000, and about half that to see the Sydney rep team play. The record was over 70,000 to see NSW take on England three years before. Now one of the biggest crowds ever seen flooded across Moore Park to watch a group of untried Yanks put to the sword.

The players lined up to enter the field, Sydney in their royal blue and gold hooped rugby jerseys, the All Stars in their star-spangled gridiron shirts. A policeman led out Dimitro and all 18 of his team, and they were paraded around the packed arena. Every seat, every step, every foot of space was taken. The rooftops were lined with dozens of precariously-perched fans, hundreds more filled the staircases down the back of the concrete Showground stand high above the SCG, kids sat on window ledges, their feet dangling over a deathly-drop below.

If the All Stars were in any doubt before, they now knew: this was massive.

64,953 PACKED IN TO SEE THIS

The lad with the grizzly bear approach is Al. F. Kirkland, and his "victim" is Clive Churchill. (For the sequel see Page 28). This was one of the incidents at the Cricket Ground yesterday when Sydney beat the American All Stars League team 52-25. (Story, Page 28)

★ ★ ★ ★ ★ ★ ★ ★ ★ ★ ★ ★ ★ ★ ★

Police closed the gates while thousands were still forging to enter the ground. Many spectators collapsed in the crush before the game.

Police claimed that the gates were closed in the interests of public safety. More than 5,000 people were locked out.

Several thousand people, forced back by the police, went to the nearby Showground and paid an entrance fee to see a pet show.

But instead of seeing the animals, they swarmed into the back of the stands, clambering walls and fences to see the football.

Police removed between 40 and 60 men who had climbed from the Showground side on to the roof of a small stand on the Hill at the Cricket Ground where they played hide and seek with officers.

Hundreds of women and teenagers who had never seen a football match before were at the match.

Joan Taylor, of Mascot, said: "I'm not interested in football but I like those Americans."

A pretty Coogee blonde who had been out with one of the team said: "He gave me tickets for today: he sure is sweet."

Hundreds who had gained admission walked out of the Cricket Ground because they could not see the game. Many of them had waited hours in long queues to gain admission to the ground.

When these people came out of the gates hundreds of others tried to force their way in to take their places.

More than 12,000 cars were in the car park when the game started.

As early as noon, cars were bumper to bumper from the SCG back to Oxford St. Cleveland St was choked for half its length. The position was just as chaotic after the crowds emptied.

'Mr Harold Matthews, secretary of NSWRL, said: "Police took action in closing the gates without consulting Rugby League officials, but, of course the decision to do so is in the hands of the police. I keenly regret that so many people were turned away."
The Daily Mirror

A large army of spectators invaded what is known as Scotsman's Hill – the stairway at the back of the big grandstand next door to the Showground. Even the tin roof on the Pavilion of the other ground of the SCG was lined by spectators.

A crowd of 60,000 gave the American All Stars a grand welcome when they filed on to the field. The Americans raced behind the posts and loosened up with gym exercises and then returned to the dressing room. The band of the Eastern Command played both teams on to the field. The Americans looked imposing in their long royal blue pants tucked in at the knees.

There was an inspiring moment before the kick-off as both teams stood to attention while the national anthems of both countries were played.

CITY COVES' CLASSY CAVORTINGS: 52-25
64,953 FANS FLOCK TO SEE LEAGUE'S YANKEE DOODLE DANDIES

If anybody is daring enough to take the scores seriously then I would suggest that the only thing wrong with the mighty motion picture of the Circus entitled "The Greatest Show on Earth" is that the players of both teams were not in it. It was so brazenly one-sided that if a Royal Commission were set up to inquire into some of the tries scored by the Americans it would make a finding that yesterday's game was Gilbert and Sullivan's comic opera applied to football....

It was a sympathetic crowd. And the Americans earned all the sympathy in the world. They came to America to learn the game. They have made remarkable progress. But, through a stupid publicity campaign which wrongly told the public the American boys were giving "smashing replies" to the cruel critics, the public was in part misled into the mistaken belief it would see what we in Australia term a "fair dinkum" game. I say it kindly. The Americans are in the kindergarten of Rugby League. If they have been officially misled that they are not, then they must be told.

There are no man-eaters among them, no monsters of the deep, no world-beaters who should be in Australia's Test team as has been stupidly publicised.

… There were no gems, no peaches. It was just mother's steak and kidney pudding which indeed the crowd devoured but whether fans will come back on Tuesday for a second helping with such vast enthusiasm remains to be seen.

Truth
by Jim Mathers

★ ★ ★ ★ ★ ★ ★ ★ ★ ★ ★ ★ ★

Fullback George Kauffman kicks rarely, but nevertheless gains great distance.

56   A.M. for July 7, 1953

THE BRUTAL TRUTH
YANKS' LEAGUE LACKS WINNING SKILL

The visiting American All Stars Rugby League team took a beating in their first big match of the tour at the Sydney Cricket Ground, but as they left the field they were mobbed by hundreds of autograph hunters.
Brisbane Telegraph, by Harry Jefferies

PIDDING'S CRICKET SCORE OF 34 POINTS AGAINST AMERICA

International Rugby League winger Noel Pidding – "Football's Bradman" – piled up a cricket score, 34 points, against America yesterday.
Sunday Telegraph, by George Crawford

AMERICANS OUTCLASSED IN FIRST S.C.G. APPEARANCE

The American Rugby League team was right out of its class. The game was a financial success but it was a failure as a football match.
The Sunday Herald

STRONG OPPOSITION TOO EARLY ON TOUR

ALL STARS MAY BE GOOD TEAM LATER IN TOUR

The Americans should have been given several more games in the country before being matched against any team at the SCG.

★ ★ ★ ★ ★ ★ ★ ★ ★ ★ ★ ★ ★ ★ ★ ★ ★ ★ ★

AMERICANS FAIL IN SYDNEY
GOOD SHOWMEN, BUT NOVICES IN LEAGUE TACTICS

Beaten 52-25 by Sydney in their Rugby League debut at the SCG yesterday, the American All Stars showed they were novices in many phases of the game. But in showmanship, spectacular passing and handling and straight running – features of gridiron – the Americans thrilled the crowd. They frequently changed the trend of play with long passes but in every case lost yards by the move. Once the ball was handled by eight players and see-sawed across the field and back but five yards were lost in the movement. The pitch-passing failed because the man awaiting the long-pass was caught flat-footed.
The Sunday Sun & Guardian, by Geoff Allen

Al D. Kirkland and Jack Bonetti watch Al E.

Alan Hull, writing in *Sports Notebook*: 'Some League officials who were chorusing "I told you so" were rather silent after yesterday's football exhibition. The result – a flattering one to the Yanks – bore out our conversation that this tour was the most haphazard piece of sporting organisation of all time. Had the League sent an expert coach to the USA to give players a month's grounding in the game, they could have put up a fine show. Instead, they were expected to learn from a rule book, and ten days' coaching here… in scrimmaging and playing-the-ball they haven't a clue… making large patches of yesterday's picnic match very dreary.'

Although they had conceded 52 points, a huge amount in the days of three points for a try, how did they manage to score 25 of their own against one of the world's leading teams? Did Pidding, Churchill and Co simply let their guests waltz in for some gimmes? Or did they have some latent talent worth pursuing?

Jefferies: 'As a spectacle the Yanks' play fell far below the standard of the spectacular French Rugby League team. The visitors were certainly triers but badly lacked the understanding of our rules. It is quite obvious now that the Board of Control blundered when they didn't send a coach over to America earlier to instruct them in the laws of the game. The Yanks have the colour, speed, and enterprise, but under pressure they are completely astray against a well-combined League team. The big crowd left the ground uncertain whether they liked them or not.'

The media were trying to be even-handed, to give praise where it was due and not write the tour off as a mis-match. But the overall impression was disappointment, which was rather unfair considering the Americans trailed just

22-13 at half-time and 32-20 late in the game. Kicker Kerkorian was deemed merely to have done 'all right' having converted all nine attempts at goal. Jefferies claimed 'the Sydney team clearly eased up in the second half', however they still scored 20 unanswered points in the closing stages.

Al D. Kirkland: 'The first game against Sydney didn't go too well because we didn't know the game. We got beat up!'

America competed well in possession but were destroyed without it. And with hooker Syd Walker understandably clueless in a defeated scrum time and again – he lost 25 of the 39 scrums to Kearney – Sydney took the ball like candy from a baby.

'Once the ball went out to the Sydney wingers it was generally curtains as the Americans had no idea of cover defence,' concluded Jefferies. Pidding took the All Stars' defence apart, scoring a hat-trick of tries and kicking 11 goals. Half-back Holman and forward Hudson also excelled but Churchill 'had a quiet day, although he ran into some heavy tackles early'. Dimitro's tactics clearly worked to some extent.

There were highlights for the All Stars. Apart from the extraordinary experience of lining up for the national anthems in front of over 64,000 Australians, the long passes were appreciated by the crowd but openings went unfulfilled. The broken field running of experienced footballers was more effective.

'A spectacular 65-yard run by winger Demirjian had the crowd roaring. He beat three tacklers, including Churchill, as he tore upfield. He was finally brought down about 15 yards out and from a ruck front-rower Walker scored for Kerkorian to convert,' wrote one report. That narrowed the score to 15-11 and the All Stars were giving as good as they got.

'Full-back Kauffman killed a certain try when he came up brilliantly and shot through to leave the Sydney defence flat-footed but then instead of trying a simple pass to his inside support, went alone into a sandwich tackle.'

'American ace centre, Al Kirkland, made another of his penetrating zig-zag bursts downfield but it was purely individual. He did not worry about his supports and a chance of a try was lost.'

Another skill from gridiron that needed adapting to league was the shoulder-barge. Kauffman rammed his shoulder into Holman long after he had punted. Pidding kicked the penalty after Kauffman had been reprimanded, apologised and Holman treated. Referee O'Brien – who had split loyalties for this game – came in for praise despite keeping the penalty count suspiciously low, just 10-9 in favour of Sydney. 'O'Brien had a difficult job, but did it well,' claimed Jefferies, 'helping the Americans as much as possible.'

'The All Stars were rewarded with a try through the exciting Al E. Kirkland. With short quick steps, and moving side to side, he is hard to stop and he beat at least six men to score,' reported Jefferies. Sol Naumu, the always-grinning Hawaiian stand-off, strolled through some weak tackling to get a consolation late on but by that stage the Americans had folded.

Fans streamed on to the field at the final whistle, kids in patterned cardigans, wing collared shirts and billowing slacks, mobbing players for autographs.

Walker and Big Al had worn headgear, but Robinson told the press that the long pants were out from now on. Dimitro admitted they may be slowing them down.

Al Abajian: 'I tell you a funny story about the long pants. The Australian coaches said "you can't wear those", so we started wearing shorts. But Mike carried on wearing long pants and someone else – it might have been Mandulay – who was wearing long pants to cover some injury, hit someone with a dirty hit. The Australian only saw long pants and so he hit Mike as he was wearing them too – Mike was the innocent victim. Mike chased that guy all over the field! We had a big laugh about that.'

The new lightweight Aussie boots the team wore split the group: Dimitro reckoned the short studs were too slippy, livewire willo'the wisp Ted Grossman loved them.

Former Test forward Frank Bugge said the Americans tackled and handled brilliantly but reckoned the All Stars knew less about the game than 90% of local schoolboys. He said: 'I felt sorry for them up against the Sydney side after so little experience. But from a vaudeville point of view, it was worth watching.'

It was a circus but Dimitro had to make sure it did not become a pantomime.

Pat Henry: 'We were forced to improve – or get annihilated!'

The start and close indicators on all 39 of the SCG's turnstiles were noted by moneyman Ray Terry in his NSWRL-issue ledger. He knew who had come in and what they had paid. Having kept tabs on the biggest racetracks in Southern Cal, and at 29 the oldest All Star in the party, he was the right man for this job. The final crowd was 65,433, paying nearly £9,000. After tax, Dimitro was owed £4,215. Forget the result: this was a good day.

Word of this extraordinary event even got back to California.

POLICE CALLED AS CROWD THRONGS STAR RUGBY TILT

Police reinforcements had to be called out to the Sydney Cricket Ground when the visiting American All Stars team played there yesterday. Police closed the gates 55 minutes before the match started with more than 5,000 people outside. American put up a gallant fight before a crowd only 5,500 smaller than the SCG record football attendance – England v NSW three years ago.
LA Times

Later editions of the *Times* were headlined: 'Kerkorian Stars In Rugby Defeat'. It was worth a mention.

CHAPTER 11
FARCE, FIASCO, FANTASY

The players had little time to reflect on their shocking introduction to Sydney football. They had to be up early Sunday morning for a barbecue on board a boat leaving La Perouse Wharf for a cruise around the bay, all laid on by South Sydney District RLFC. It was a glorious day, with boomerang throwers, steaks and speeches. With no first grade club games in the city for a month because of the representative games, Souths could afford to concentrate on their guests.

The cruelty of the All Stars' schedule may have begun to sink in. After being thrown into the lions' den after just one full practice match, the California college kids had only two days to recover before doing it again. This time, against even bigger cats: New South Wales.

This was virtually an international fixture. New South Wales featured most of the full Australia team, and some of the best Queenslanders who had moved south to earn a bigger crust. Among them Pidding, described as 'now the world's greatest scoring machine'.

Just when they needed a week off to get over their baptism of fire at the SCG, the Americans had to return to the scene of the assault and do it all over again. The reason for this Tuesday afternoon event was 12,000 miles away: Queen Elizabeth, the sovereign of Australia, was being crowned in London and the colonies were going to mark the occasion in style.

What better way in Sydney than an 'international rugby league football fixture'? And that meant the Americans trying to bridge the gaping ravine in class, again.

But whose fault was it? Dimitro had time and time again assured the Board of Control that he had a squad of experienced rugby

players who were also the nation's top American football players. If that were true, they may have been able to adjust to league a little quicker, would have been able to compete in scrums and be comfortable passing the ball across the line instead of trying to make 'lateral' passes. Instead, only a handful of the squad knew what rugby was all about. They had been cruelly exposed in Sydney: lambs to the slaughter. Not once, but twice.

The schedule agreed by Dimitro with the ARFL had one aim: to make money. Dimitro told the press he had spent $27,000 on the tour so far, $20,000 of it in airfares. It was actually $14,000 on the airfares from LA to Sydney, via Honolulu and Auckland. Whatever, he wanted it back.

In the States, he could have sold the TV rights to the games. But while 20m Brits crowded around the few sets – most bought especially – to watch the Coronation, TV was still a year away from reaching Australian homes. Cinema was still the real king. There was no money there.

Instead, Dimitro had to make it on the gate. All ticket revenue would be split between the hosts, the local rugby league board, and the tourists. And to make the most dough, they had to play, play and play again. Touring teams played twice a week: big games on Saturdays, trips to minor parks to play local teams in midweek. The system worked. But you needed the numbers to do it.

Abajian: 'I played scrum-half and wing sometimes. I loved it because we didn't have that kind of contact in football. But one of the main mistakes Mike made was he didn't have enough athletes on his team. You've gotta have a lot of men to play that game, 18–25 games. You can't play with the number of men we had. We only had 14 decent players. The rest I would never have taken.'

Al D. Kirkland: 'Most international sides have 30 on their team, we had 15 or 16 really, plus a couple of Mike's mates. We had to stick with the best 13 players for big games and played the rest in the midweek games, just like they do on major rugby tours.'

That meant most players played every match if they were still walking come game time. That Tuesday in Sydney, most were not.

On Monday night, eight were stuck in bed with dysentery. Of the other ten, seven had to visit a military hospital to satisfy the Board's promo schedule. The remaining three had nowhere to train with volunteer coach, former Balmain player Gene Barakat. Kerkorian was limping badly but Dimitro insisted he would be fit to play. Iron Mike himself would make his tour debut in the second row.

Reinforcements were needed already. Four more players were due to arrive any moment: Dimitro's best mate from UCLA, Jerry Shipkey, and Canadian Ray Willsey, plus the juniors Harold Han and Bob Buckley straight out of the exam halls at USC.

But Shipkey got a call from Chicago Cardinals and Willsey headed home to play pro football with the Edmonton Eskimos. Han and Buckley, the two 20-year-old juniors, were also doubts. They were under big pressure from Trojans coach Jess Hill not to go.

Ed: 'I wrote to Buck telling him all about it and what a time we were having. He said: "Fuck it, I'm going"!'

When the moon-faced Han and crew-cut Buckley landed in Sydney on Monday night, the local paparazzi were there to greet them. 'Husko' Buckley caused a fashion scandal with his red, grey and green tartan cap – all the craze back home, he claimed – while Dimitro told the press pack that Han and Husko would be his centre-wing partnership at the SCG the next afternoon. They would devour *Winning Rugby Moves* by Arthur Hennessy until jet lag crashed in.

SYDNEY CRICKET GROUND		June 2nd, 1953 ——— 2.30 p.m.
N.S.W.		**AMERICA**
(Sky Blue)		(Blue, Red and White Stars and Stripes)
	Full-backs:	
1—C. CHURCHILL (Capt.)		Harold HAN—10
	Three-quarters:	
2—N. PIDDING		Bob BUCKLEY—22
3—R. BARTLETT		Al. E. KIRKLAND—1
4—H. WELLS		Sol NAUMU—12
5—B. CARLSON		Ed DEMIRJIAN—9
	Five-eighths:	
6—R. DUNCAN		Gary KERKORIAN—11
	Halves:	
7—K. HOLMAN		Ted GROSSMAN—2
	Forwards:	
8—K. SLATTERY		Jack BONETTI—4
9—D. SCHOFIELD		Al D. KIRKLAND—15
10—A. PAUL		Fran MANDULAY—21
11—C. GILL		Vince JONES—18
12—K. KEARNEY		Sydney WALKER—19
13—R. BULL		Xavier MENA—13
		Pat HENRY—7
		(One to be omitted)
	Reserves:	
14—J. SLADE		
15—A. COLLINSON		
Referee: J. O'BRIEN;	Touch Judges: J. Lowe (Red flag), F. Erickson (Blue flag)	

Buckley: 'We spent the night learning the rules and how to play the ball after the runner is downed. Let's just say we didn't have a lot of preparation for rugby league!'

Ted: 'We had to coach them how to play during the game! But we were just so happy to see them. We needed some fresh blood out there.'

To ensure there was less blood and fewer casualties, Mike splashed out $20 and sent Ray Terry to collect seven sets of shoulder pads and a dozen pairs of shin pads from a city centre store.

Buckley: 'The next day was coronation day for the Queen. There were over 130,000 people at the Sydney Cricket Ground to see the Americans play the Australian rugby league "Test" team. What an experience.'

It must have felt like 130,000 to a bleary-eyed Buck – and it may as well have been the full Kangaroos team he was facing on his shell-shocking debut, just 15 hours after touching down on Australian soil.

S.G. Ball, acting chair of the Board of Control while Harry Flegg was hospitalised through illness, wrote in the programme: 'Today we pay homage to Her Most Gracious Majesty Queen Elizabeth II and our minds turn to the Coronation events in Westminster Abbey and to the pageantry associated with this great and historic occasion.'

FIASCO AT S.C.G. DISGUSTS R.L. FOLLOWERS

Prominent Sydney League men yesterday said that the N.S.W.-American All Stars match at the S.C.G. was detrimental to both the tourists and the code. The N.S.W. team, which included ten Kangaroos, coasted to a 62-41 victory.
Sydney Morning Herald

N.S.W. PLAYERS HOLD OFF AS GAME FINISHES IN FARCE

By W. F. Corbett

Although at little more than half pressure, NSW beat America 62-41 in their Rugby League match on the SCG today. The football became a pantomime with NSW allowing tries by declining to tackle.

FULL-TIME

NSW	62
AMERICA	41

FIRST SCORERS

NSW: Pidding (try).

America: Han (try).

Bob Buckley, who joined the American League team only last night, run with the ball in today's game against NSW. Left is Alvin Kirkland and righ Alfred Kirkland.

The Americans exhibited improved idea of positional play. NSW speed and tricks overwhelmed the Americans.

American five-eighth Gary Kerkorian maintained his 100 pc goalkicking achievement with four goals.

America's star centre Alvin Kirkland scored three tries.

Pidding contributed 16 of NSW first half total with two tries and five goals.

A crowd of 32,654 cheered the teams on to the field.

The Americans today wore short white pants. They certainly looked more efficient and businesslike than the long leg covering gear they had worn previously in their games.

The Americans were led by their player-manager Mike Dimitro, who made his first playing appearance at the tour. He was in the second row.

The Americans went into a huddle before the match opened.

Accompanied by a band the onlookers rose and sang God Save Our Queen. It was a unique event for a big League match in Sydney.

NSW men were holding off in defence. Bonetti went among a cluster of NSW players, trapped the ball and fired it to Han, who crossed for the try, which Kerkorian converted from inside the 25.
America 5-nil.

Han arrived only last night. NSW scored shortly afterward when Pidding went down the flank with great ease and scored in the corner. Pidding missed the goal from the 25, a foot inside touch. **America 5-3.**

NSW scored again. Ryan got a breaking scrum. Ryan got the ball and swung it across to Schofield, who crossed for the try between the posts. Pidding tacking the goal. **NSW 8-5.**

The handling of the Americans was good and

they were displaying better knowledge of positional football.

America were in again when Kirkland raced for the corner, turning infield and pulling out of Churchill's tackle to score the try which Kerkorian converted.
America 10-8.

The Americans had not mastered the offside rule and a couple of times were penalised when they raced downfield to gain possession.

Ryan made a curving run, brushed off a tackle by Naumu and scored between the posts. Pidding goaled. **NSW 13-10.**

Dimitro fell on Slattery in a tackle at half-way.

Ryan ran infield to make the extra man and sent Wells across for a smooth try between the posts. Pidding kicked a simple goal. **NSW 18-10.**

With a bunch of NSW men flatfooted and looking on, Alvin Kirkland ripped through for an easy try. Kerkorian again goaled. **NSW 18-15.**

Bonetti, with two tries coming at him, was at his best, and was applauded for a flick pass back to Buckley. It was the first time the Americans had exhibited th trick.

LEAGUE FIASCO AT S.C.G.
NSW WEAK TACKLING AS AID TO AMERICANS

NSW almost reduced an otherwise entertaining Rugby League game to a fiasco. Poor tackling marred the game and frequently the Americans were allowed to run 30 and 40 yards without a hand being placed on them.
By Jim Mathers

---

3 JUNE 1953

CRICKET SCORE IN LEAGUE

The New South Wales Rugby League team today put on a cricket score in defeating the American All Stars 62 to 41 in what was regarded by the players as a picnic match. The scoring rate – 103 points in 80 minutes – was the highest ever in an international match.
Newcastle Sun

★ ★

There was no argument that this was a 'blow-out', a thrashing, an annihilation. Tommy Ryan, a last-minute replacement for Brian Carlson (who had bronchitis), supposedly struggled with flu throughout the game but still scored six tries and was called a spoilsport for it. His fellow St George winger Noel Pidding kicked ten goals and touched down twice. Pidding had scored 50 points in two games against the Americans by himself! But no media asked how NSW conceded 41 points against a team who, let's face it, did not know what they were doing.

One hundred points in a game was a farce. Since the war, the average score in an Australia Test match was 15-15. The Kangaroos had only ever conceded more

ALL STARS TROUNCED IN LEAGUE FIASCO
YANKS FLOP AGAINST NSW

The Americans flopped as a team, and the NSW players eased up to allow the Americans to score tries.

Of the 103 points scored, 41 were against the powerful NSW team, which would test any Rugby League team in the World.

With referee Jack O'Brien ignoring American rule breaches, and NSW players allowing the Americans to run freely.

The Americans have had little League experience, several were suffering from stomach disorders, and two players arrived from America only on Monday night.

Individually, some of the Americans played well, but their display yesterday was below first grade standard.

Courier Mail

GRAND HOTEL

"HAPPY JACK BOYLE"

ONLY BEST ALES AND SPIRITS STOCK

Only Dimitro's ally George Crawford was sympathetic.

FIRST CLASS ACCOMMODATION

384

U.S. TEAM OUTCLASSED
OVERMATCHED IN S.C.G. GAMES

The American Rugby League, composed almost entirely of sick players, yesterday slumped badly against New South Wales at Sydney Cricket Ground. Six players had not fully recovered from a stomach upset that kept them in bed on Monday. Another had an abscess under his arm and another a bruised groin.

Daily Telegraph

By George Crawford

★ ★ ★ ★ ★ ★ ★ ★ ★ ★ ★ ★ ★ ★ ★ ★ ★ ★

than 30 points twice and both were huge upsets in the two seasons before the Americans landed: a 49-25 humiliation by the Kiwis in Brisbane, and the equally shocking 35-14 defeat by France at the SCG.

Australia had only once ever scored 40 points themselves in a game. A half-century in an international game was unheard of, 60 obscene. Tour games were never as tight but for a group of rugby league greenhorns to score nine tries against a top-class team, something was up. Ten of this NSW team would play for the state against Queensland in Brisbane two weeks later.

S.G. Ball was adamant his NSWRL board had not told the players to take it easy on the Americans, but Churchill refused to deny it and kicked straight to Kauffman most times, while Pidding rarely reached top gear. And the Americans' replacement hooker Pat Henry somehow won 11 of the 23 scrums against the world's best hooker, Ken Kearney.

Al D. Kirkland: 'New South Wales had Churchill, Pidding and Holman – they were all pretty good! But we scored 40-odd points against one of the top teams in the world.'

It was an exhibition, a freak show – and the All Stars were the fall guys. It was no surprise that Han stood offside for most of the game. He must have missed that paragraph when reading the law book the night before.

Former Leeds and NSW forward Frank O'Rourke called it 'completely unnecessary to make a travesty of the game – NSW were obviously so half-hearted that it was embarrassing to witness'.

By the second half, the appearance of long-haired wrestler Johnny Moochey on the sidelines and a 'full-blooded bout of fisticuffs by a couple of insurgents' in front of the public grandstand was the centre of the crowd's attention until the police arrived to bring an end to the off-field entertainment.

According to the *Newcastle Morning Herald*, Buckley and Han both played well, scored a try each but tired towards the end. The swarthy Buckley, as broad as an ox, with thighs like hams, took some stopping. The *Herald* wrote: 'Alvin Kirkland again thrilled the crowd with his brilliant running… his crashing twisting runs were always dangerous'.

Al E managed to grab another hat-trick, something few players have ever managed against New South Wales. Even when they somehow excelled at something, someone wasn't satisfied.

The *Herald*: 'The Americans were superior in only two departments, backing up and passing. Whenever a man was tackled there always was an American behind him to take the ball.'

They should only have been superior at lying down and dying. The Australians resorted to show-boating towards the end, Churchill and others attempting to mimic the All Stars by throwing long passes across the field. It was not something to warm the Americans' hearts.

There was some consolation at hand, though. Four free days in Sydney. Twenty young sportsmen overseas. Carnage ensued.

They were getting fan mail at the Oceanic from all over the Pacific, including Papua New Guinea. Everyone wanted a piece of the All Stars. Autographs, photos, phone numbers, and more.

Jack: 'At the hotel all the telephone calls were from young girls wanting to meet us. We couldn't believe it.'

MEET THE

American All Stars Rugby League Team

★ **IN PERSON** ★

Famous U.S. Gridiron Stars direct from Hollywood.

THURSDAY, 4th JUNE AT THE TROCADERO

★ ★ ★

★ ★ ★ ★ *Come to the* ★ ★ ★

American Rugby League Ball

Auspices: American Ex-servicemens Memorial Club. MA2657

Admission £1/1/- per person.

Reservations: The Trocadero, MA 6431.

Opening Match: Sydney v. U.S.A., Cricket Ground, May 30th.

Manly Taxation Services

FOR EXPERT ADVICE

Proprietors are both ex-Taxation Department.

56 BELGRAVE STREET, MANLY

Phones: Day XU 1634 — Night XU 3334, XU 3707

A. H. JENSEN, Printer, 56 Spring Street, Bondi Junction

Abajian: 'Jack was very sought after by all the women, they loved him. He was a tall, blond, blue-eyed handsome boy. He had his full page picture in the Sunday papers and he had so many calls he had to hide.'

Ed: 'Ted did an interview on the radio. He said: "The place is great, the food is great, but the girls are ice cold." Well by the time we were back at the hotel the place was full of them! They were sitting around the hotel waiting.'

The first stop was the American All Stars Rugby League Ball at the Trocadero, the George Street dance hall which heaved with thousands of twentysomethings intent on fun... even before 20 football players from California arrived to provide it. The American Ex-Servicemen's Memorial Club put the Ball on. First the players were introduced on stage, then came the dancing girls, before Marie Morgan – Miss American Valentine – was presented to the crowd. There were cocktail pies, cocktail fish and Saratoga chips, all the eating, drinking and dancing accompanied by Colin Bergerson and his Trocadero Orchestra. Exhausted, the players trooped home in the early hours.

Another night took them to the Celebrity Club, a cabaret bar and nightclub where the beautiful people stayed drinking and partying late into Saturday night/ Sunday morning. Anyone who was anyone – or visiting anyone who was anyone in Sydney – went there. Sports stars, film stars, gangsters. It was owned by local face Joe Taylor – aka 'The Boss'. Taylor sponsored a Celebrity Club rugby league team in the Eastern Suburbs competition. They were the reigning A Grade champions, their main man a young prop called Jack Gibson, who just happened to work on the Celebrity's door at night. A visiting Ava Gardner took some interest in him one recent evening.

The hosts ensured the Americans met Sydney's finest models to 'prove Australian girls were not ice cold'. The paparazzi snapped Dimitro with his arms around a Sandra Legge and Pat Woodley in the *Truth*'s society pages. Jack Bonetti looks more at home with a harem than Al D. did. The papers lapped it up.

Rugby League News's editorial wrote: 'The Americans like Rugby League and the Sydney sporting public like the Americans.'

Abajian: 'We had a lot of fun. I had a beautiful girl. Her name was Maureen Cooley – she was Australian-Scottish and worked for a bank. A lovely girl. Her mother died while I was there.'

Jack: 'I was so taken by the way the Aussies treated us. I made lifelong friends on that trip – it was a truly great experience… although one thing I do remember is the girls didn't shave under their arms! We had to get us some foreign girls – we couldn't stand the smell!'

Ed: 'We'd pull back the drapes in the morning and there'd be girls looking into our room.'

Jack's nickname was 'Lover', Fran Mandulay became 'The Burlesque King' and Bob Buckley was 'Mr Gigolo'. After two weeks the Oceanic had had enough. They took Dimitro's $500 and sent them on their way along the coast.

Jack: 'There could well be some children of the All Stars in Australia now! We were enjoying it too much. We had to move hotels!'

Ed: 'They kicked us out. The paper headline said: "US turn hotel into brothel".'

Ted: 'They were about right.'

Abajian was the most relieved man in town: he no longer had to share a room with Wild Bill.

CHAPTER 12
HANGING ON

Dimitro had to work his magic again and soon secured a new base for the party. Ormond Hall, a private hotel along New South Head Road in Vaucluse, would take them in.

They trained every day at Coogee until Saturday, when they had the choice of a trip to a Premiership game or to be guests of the Sydney Turf Club at Rosehill races. The evening took them to the monthly dance at Easts' Leagues Club. Dimitro made a trip to the tailors to get blazers and slacks for the late arrivals, Han and Buckley, and their Australian coach and trainer Latchem and Husky Moore, so they would look the part on the bus down to Wollongong on Sunday morning.

They also made the delayed visit to the Margaret Reid Orthopaedic Hospital in St Ives, to visit the children there who had polio. The NSW Society for Crippled Children had written to Dimitro way back in March asking them to come. Dimitro and Ray Terry took along Teddy, Ed Demirjian, George Kauffman and Handsome Jack. They chatted to the kids in their iron lungs and callipers and signed autographs. It was a goodwill visit that would come back to haunt them.

En route to Wollongong, about 50 miles south of Sydney in the mining region of Illawarra, the All Stars stopped to admire the view at Sublime Point. There was little sublime about the rest of the day. When they arrived back in the city late that evening, there must have been some serious debate about the value of the tour.

The *Sydney Morning Herald* announced that 'COUNTRY SETS 100-0 TARGET ON ALL STARS'. Like New South Wales and Sydney, Country

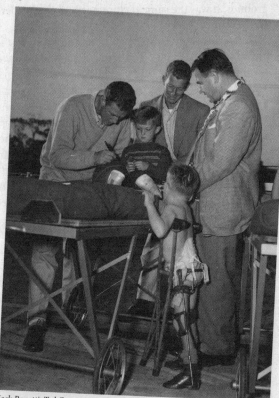

Jack Bonetti, Ted Grossman and Mike Dimitro visit kids with polio.

secretary Dudley Locke promised no let-up for the Americans. The Country players – those from outside the metropolitan city of Sydney but playing in the NSWRL – were fighting for places in the New South Wales squad and subsequently on Australia's tour to New Zealand.

A Combined Country side, coached by Ray Stehr – the firebrand former Kangaroo who had seen his offer to coach the All Stars snubbed by the Board of Control – had beaten Sydney by a point three weeks earlier in the annual City v Country clash. This was their last chance to secure a place in the NSW side that would fly north later that week to play two State games in Brisbane. Nine of them were holders of the New South Wales jerseys, six of them Australia internationals such as Bob Bartlett and Harry Wells.

The Telegraph's George Crawford, defending Dimitro and the gang again, said the Board of Control had given the Americans 'a ludicrous schedule' of four opening games against sides 'that would have shaken England at the opening of a tour'.

Wanting big games early in the tour to guarantee large crowds, naive Dimitro had been stitched up. Small-town teams in the maverick NSW and Queensland Country competitions could be almost as big a challenge as the city sides, with players earning more to play in the bush than in the first grade comp in Sydney. Crowds in the sticks were also similar in size to those at Sydney's suburban grounds. It was the same picture north of the border in Queensland. Bush footy was serious.

Not surprisingly, Country put the Americans to the sword in front of a record crowd nearing 12,000 – hundreds of whom had travelled down from Sydney – winning 35-9 in icy cold conditions. It was only eight more points than they scored against City and ten of them came in the final six minutes, but it was enough for one local paper to call it 'the greatest comedy of errors ever seen at Wollongong Showground'. The Americans were happy being a novelty and stared at, but they did not enjoy being a laughing stock. The best thing one journalist had to say about them was that the numbers on their starry shirts were bright.

The local press even mocked the All Stars' pre-match warm-up: 'The first act of the circus occurred when "Ringmaster" Mike Dimitro put his charges through a series of warming up exercises on the field some ten minutes before play commenced.'

The Australians did any preparations in the dressing rooms and just ran on to the field and kicked off.

The All Stars had already managed to upset the local officials by snubbing the now unwelcome pre-match welcome dinner, just as they had in Canberra. Ray Terry told the press they did not know about it. Truth was they were desperate to avoid getting stuffed off the pitch before the same happened on it.

Pat Henry: 'We kept having parades and luncheons and that kind of thing. It was really funny: they would serve us really rich food or lunch an hour before a game. They were trying to trick us. The Sun paper said we didn't want their lunches because we have special diets! We were just trying to give ourselves a chance in the games.'

Syd Walker and Al D. Kirkland on the chase against Country.

On arrival at the ground, Country lock Ron Battye was directed to the Americans' dressing room by an attendant because of his 'Yankee' outfit: he wore clothes more California than bush. Sadly he did not stay there.

The Americans had no answer to former Eastern Suburbs full-back Darcy Russell, who scored a try and seven goals. Russell was a class act, expected to be Clive Churchill's understudy for Australia in New Zealand.

The All Stars were not totally to blame for the one-sided nature of the game. Referee Darcy Lawler, trying to help them as much as he could, turned the crowd

'The All Stars played with two men having only their second game of League and one having his first game, yet held an almost New South Wales side to 9-20 till 15 minutes from time.

Newcastle Sun

Country, which included six 1952-53 Kangaroos, then added 15 points when the Americans became disorganised through injuries and were badly caught out of position.'

against himself and the touring side by handing out an unfeasible 18 penalties against Country – including the first nine of the game – and only two against the inexperienced Americans. 'Wipe the stars and stripes out of your eyes Lawler' cried the crowd angrily. Local referees had boycotted the game in protest at the appointment of a Sydney city ref for such a high-profile game and Lawler was cut no slack by the Illawarra faithful.

'Lawler did his utmost to aid the Americans, contributing largely to the farcical nature of the game by awarding free-kicks with great frequency for non-existent breaches of the rules,' said the local paper. It would not be the first time Lawler's judgement and equality was questioned. But with Lawler's help, the Americans had again remained in the game for over an hour.

Sports writers seemed divided over the merits of the Americans – and the tour itself. Local hacks took extreme positions: they were right behind Mike's men or went all guns ablazing against the Board of Control.

The *Newcastle Morning Herald* writer declared the display America's 'best performance of the tour', relishing the period midway through the second half 'when for 15 minutes the ball merely touched the ground as one side then the

other took it to within inches of the lines'. The Americans' 'spectacular exhibition' brought little reward though, as the Country side knew what to expect from their long passes and pulled off several interceptions.

Crawford wrote in the *Telegraph* that the Country team 'took a bashing from the Americans' and showed 'a 100 per cent improvement on their two farcical matches in Sydney – they became fiery for the first time on tour and referee Lawler three times cautioned the Americans for rough play'.

The All Stars were arming up: after breaking his nose against NSW, Abajian wore an aluminium nose-guard, and Syd Walker and Al D. wore head guards. If only they could put their pads and helmets on.

The Wollongong press rubbished Kerkorian for mis-kicking an attempt at goal under the crossbar, despite him converting three others and kicking 15 out of 17 in Sydney. They did like his two-step 'stab' technique though. The Americans' kicking tee was also seen as revolutionary: the Aussies were still kicking off a pile of earth.

Kauffman was praised for kicking long from full-back and the All Stars' play-the-balls were far better than a week or two earlier. Their long passes, often fired out from Ted Grossman at five-eighths, usually worked.

There was little argument over who starred for the Americans. Bill Albans 'on occasion made Country captain Bobby Bartlett look like a novice – Albans' mighty sidestep would have beaten any player in League' said the *Morning Herald*. There was also praise for new scrum-half Abajian, 'who captured the imagination of the crowd with his peculiar noseguard and penetrated the Country defences repeatedly but his passing let him down'.

Stehr, who liked a bit of biff, thought Country's 'robust football stirred the Americans and proved they can play when the rival team is prepared to play real football against it'. He dismissed the Sydney and NSW sides as playing 'cream puff football' that gave the All Stars no chance to show their ability.

There was at least something to build on.

★ ★ ★ ★ ★ ★ ★ ★ ★ ★ ★ ★ ★ ★ ★ ★ ★ ★

CHAPTER 13
A MILLION BRUISES

MONDAY 8 JUNE 1953

The battered All Stars took stock and considered what lay ahead. Their initial enthusiasm might have been threatened by three ultimately heavy defeats in a week. But a visit to the American War Memorial at the Rookwood Cemetery put everything into perspective. Their challenges were irrelevant, their problems miniscule.

On Tuesday they trained at Coogee and had the afternoon free before crashing out on the overnight sleeper train, heading out 400km north-west to Dubbo. It was the first time the All Stars had been out to the bush. It was a whole different Australia after two weeks in and around Sydney.

If they got any sleep on board, they were soon wide awake. The train pulled in at 8.30am to a show of pomp and ceremony befitting the Coliseum at a Bruins v Trojans clash. A cavalcade of cars swept by, music blared from speakers and a police escort ensured their short journey through the streets lined with waving crowds to the Club House Hotel was uninterrupted: all intersections were on green. The Yanks were in town.

But if the All Stars thought they could have a few hours' rest after breakfast to prepare for the afternoon game against Western Districts, they were mistaken. By 9.45am they were back out for a parade through the town to a civic reception at the Council Chambers.

An estimated 7,000 packed out the No 1 Oval to see Dubbo's first international rugby league visitors and they were not disappointed. They spent most of the second half on their feet with excitement as the two teams put on a cracker.

Leo Nosworthy had returned to player-coach at Narromine after starring for Balmain Tigers, and was selected for Western Division.

7000 SEE 'ALL STARS' IN HISTORIC MATCH WITH WEST

The All Stars led 10-0, then 14-8 and still 19-13 deep into the second half only to lose, agonisingly, 24-21. Kerkorian had kicked a penalty to square the game at 21-all but with five minutes left, Lumsden, of Coonabarabran, went over in the corner to break the All Stars' hearts.

"They had some real athletes but no idea of rugby league. We woke up to them and were up there belting them as soon as they caught the ball. They had one giant, well over 6ft 3, built like a rock. When he had the ball it took about four of us to knock him over. When he went off an even bigger bloke came on!"

WEDNESDAY 10 JUNE 1953

Again, the referee was Darcy Lawler. And again he did all he could to give the All Stars a chance, ignoring Ed Demirjian's blatant knock-on in the build-up to the opening try by stand-in captain Bonetti. He incensed the crowd by ignoring constant American offsides at scrums and other repeated offences went unpunished. The local country folk booed themselves hoarse. If Western hadn't won, Lawler could have been lynched. But the naive Americans were oblivious to the favours he was doing them.

Bob Buckley, a Rugby novice, quickly learnt the value of straight running.

Al D.: 'The refs may have helped us but we didn't know that at the time. We were playing to win – you've got to. In any game you want to play your best. I always enjoyed playing the games, however hard they were. I always looked forward to them. We never went into a game thinking we were going to lose, whoever we were playing. Winning was the most important thing. We had to give it our best shot or else we'd have got hurt. Someone would blindside you while you were looking at a pretty girl in the second row!'

The game was but a minor part of the excursion. That night's entertainment was a cocktail party at the Masonic Hall, followed by a ball at the Showground. Next morning they dragged their sore bodies and even sorer heads out of bed for a tour of Haddon Rig. By the time they boarded the 5pm train back to Sydney, they were shattered. And the injury list had got longer: Syd Walker broke his right foot, Drakulvich bruised his shoulder and Xavier did his collarbone.

The Yanks' display had certainly done enough to spread panic into the good folk of Newcastle, the next stop. First, a few days of R 'n' R back at Ormond Hall.

THURSDAY 11 JUNE
US LEAGUE TEAM IMPROVED; MAY TEST NEWCASTLE

There is a feeling among Rugby League people in Newcastle that the Americans are just about ready to enter the winning list again and that Newcastle's team will have to look out lest it be the victim. Against a strong centre like Newcastle this would be a remarkable feat for such newcomers, fine athletes though they be. But there isn't much doubt that their two more recent games in the country, at

Wollongong on Sunday and Dubbo yesterday, when the home side won only in the last two minutes, have really set the Americans on the way to playing the game the hard way.

Now after five matches, the American forwards are at last settling down to the tough, consistent play required. They have, apparently, "caught on" through hard experience, even though leniency by the referee has been necessary in such things as the play the ball and shepherding. Through this "nursing" technique by referees, all Sydney men appointed by the Board of Control, the stage seems to have been reached where the Americans, thanks also to their own efforts in picking up technique, are able to play on a more strictly competitive basis.

FRIDAY 12 JUNE
US FORWARDS TOUGH LOT

The six American forwards in the Rugby League game against Newcastle at the Sports Ground tomorrow will outweigh the Newcastle pack by an average of half a stone. It is because of their powerful forwards and the similarity of their gridiron game to League rucks that the Americans have been able to adjust themselves more quickly in that department and this is where they are likely to worry Newcastle. Constant pounding by young forwards weighing 15 and 16 stone – and the Americans use every ounce of their weight in the rucks – may well tell on the lighter Newcastle six whose main hope will be in keeping the ball away from the Americans.

Tomorrow's game could easily give them a break in their run of defeats.

SATURDAY 13 JUNE
GOOD SHOWING BY AMERICANS

The manager of the American Rugby League team Mike Dimitro said in Sydney last night he thought his team would make a good showing against Newcastle. "The boys are learning fast and have picked up new clues with each match," he said. Al Kirkland, the visiting team's star centre will play. Dimitro said Kirkland had not played for several matches due to an injury. He was now fit and Newcastle would see a brilliant centre in action.

The Sun wrote: 'The Newcastle team, though the best available, could get a rude shock from an improving American team, which showed at Wollongong on Sunday that it is quick to learn. The All Stars' strength is their fast, heavy, barging forwards who have picked up the game quickly and worry opposing teams with their gridiron barging and tackling. The backs are fast in attack and bring off unorthodox switches in play. Their main weakness is their inability to win scrums but once they gain possession of the ball they provide fireworks.'

Newcastle's press were preparing for a fall. They feared an upset but the All Stars, with only five or six games under their belts, should have been no match whatsoever for a Newcastle side that, although missing five New South Wales players, was one of the strongest districts in the country, playing invitation games against Sydney Premiership teams.

For the finest service all along the line...

"Fly TAA — the friendly way"

RESERVATIONS FROM TAA BOOKING OFFICE: Phillip House, 119 Phillip St., Sydney. Phone B 0526, and from all leading Travel Agencies
NP11194

Captain and full-back Darcy Russell was one of the best goal-kickers in the world and had destroyed the Americans at Wollongong a few days earlier; prop Henry Holloway was the next big forward on the verge of a major breakthrough; snowy-haired half-back Noel Hill had lifted the Sydney Premiership with St George in 1949 and captained NSW Country; Barry Levido and lock Anderson were wanted by the cream of Sydney. Surely this side was far too strong for the Californian college kids? They were greeted at the train station by Northern RL officials, thrilled to have such exotic visitors.

There was awe in the game-day programme for Albans' claim to have matched the Australian amateur sprint record of 100 yards in 9.5 seconds... on 14 occasions!

Kangaroos trainer 'Husky' Moore, who has effected a number of betting coups with pro sprinters in Victoria, said his mouth watered when he saw Albans stride out: 'Fancy being able to slip him in at Stawell off a reasonable mark.' It's surprising Albans didn't take the opportunity to clean up at a few athletics meetings, given his shady reputation.

The programme editor lauded Kerkorian's 'unique' kicking style and compared his accuracy with that of all-time great Jim Sullivan of Wigan, wondering if his style would be copied in Sydney. Kerkorian 'says there is nothing to kicking goals from short range provided you line up the kick correctly. He thinks the Australian and English idea of kicking the ball hard is unnecessary and leads to error.'

Pat Henry, who had deferred his exams at Stanford to come on tour, claimed he had brought his books with him but had not had time to open them. He even told the press that he intended studying the Australian education system, school sport and the famous sheep stations, where he wanted to 'follow the course of the wool from the sheep's back through the various processes until it is finally used in clothing'. A likely story.

Hawaiian high school swimming champ Sol Naumu said he planned to teach league at home and become a schoolteacher. Naumu was 'one of the trickiest players we have had in Australia... able to penetrate if he gets half a chance'.

The Americans were earning respect. They would have even more 80 minutes later.

US LEAGUE TEAM DESERVED VICTORY

The Americans richly deserved their victory at the Sports Ground on Saturday... the visitors proceeded systematically to give Newcastle a thorough beating... the All Stars showed much that was admirable. Big, agile men, they used their weight well, tackling splendidly and indulged in some lovely handling and amazingly accurate long passing... the crowd of 14,000 stayed on to see the Americans press home what from their angle was an encouraging and meritorious display. They are real Rugby League material, with many players who would soon be labelled great if they kept at the game.

Newcastle Sun
By R S Roulston

YANKS IN GOOD WIN

NEWCASTLE: The American All Stars downed Newcastle 19—10 before a crowd of 12,000 here today.

Kerkorian kicked five goals and scored a try for the Americans.

America scored first when Kerkorian kicked a penalty from the "25" line. Newcastle replied with a try by centre Pead, converted by Darcy Russell.

America led again when Kerkorian ran through a group of Newcastle forwards and scored a try wide out which he also converted.

Newcastle led 8—7 with a try by left winger Shanks. Russell missed the goal but then added a penalty goal.

America took the lead again when Han scored under the posts. Kerkorian kicked his third goal from three attempts.

Newcastle won the scrums 17—10 in the first half, and referee A. Oxford awarded America four penalties to Newcastle's two.

At half time it was America 12, Newcastle 10.

Playing with the strong wind America hemmed Newcastle in right from the start of the second half.

The American forwards were doing particularly well, and 20 minutes after the resumption America went further ahead as Han scored his second try under the posts after a tricky run. Kerkorian converted. America 17, Newcastle 10.

In the closing stages of the second half, the Americans stood right up on top of the Newcastle team and maintained their lead. Kerkorian kicked another penalty goal.

SAT, JUNE 13, 1953. **3**

LEAGUE LESSONS FROM AMERICANS

The American All Stars gave the Newcastle players lessons in handling, tackling and determination.
The Americans won because of the over-confidence of Newcastle... scenting a win, and under the guidance of their coach Latchem Robinson, the American forwards delved in and pounded Newcastle into errors of which the All Stars were very quick to take advantage... At least five of the Americans – Harold Han, who scored two tries, winger Bob Buckley, Gary Kerkorian who scored 11 of America's points from a try and four goals, Sol Naumu and Al Abajian – have the natural ability to win a place in any State Rugby League team.

Newcastle Morning Herald

Newcastle Sports Ground—2.45 p.m.

NEWCASTLE v. AMERICA

Newcastle	TOURING TEAM: AMERICAN	America
(Colours—Red, White Shorts)		(Colours—Blue, Red & White Stars & Stripes)

Full-back:
1—D. Russell

Three-quarters:
2—W. Shanks   L. Batey—5
3—W. Smith   B. Pead—4

Halves:
6—W. Foley   N. Hill—7

Forwards:
8—B. Levido
9—G. Harley   H. Holloway—10
11—D. Hawke   H. Pearson—13
12—K. McKiernan
14—W. Roberts   T. Anderson—15

TOURING TEAM: AMERICAN

8—Al Abajian
3—B. Albani
11—B. Buckley
9—E. Demirjian
2—T. Grossman
12—H. Han
20—G. Kaufmann
14—G. Kerkorian
1—Al E. Kirkland
10—Sol Naumu
6—R. Willsey
4—J. Bonetti
27—M. Dimitro
17—S. Brnkovich
7—P. Henry
18—V. Jones
15—Al D. Kirkland
21—F. Mandulay
19—R. Terry
19—S. Walker
5—Leon Eilers

Full-back:
10—Sol Naumu

Three-quarters:
1—Al E. Kirkland   Ed Demirjian—9
12—H. Han   B. Buckley—11

Halves:
14—G. Kerkorian   T. Grossman—2

Forwards:
4—J. Bonetti
15—Al D. Kirkland   M. Dimitro—27
21—F. Mandulay   P. Henry—7
18—V. Jones

Referee: A. Oxford.   Linesmen: E. Rowley (Red Flag); A. Wright (Blue Flag).

Local reporters were sympathetic to their mates in the Newcastle team. They claimed referee Aub Oxford from Sydney, whose appointment had been met with dismay by the Newcastle press, had 'ruined the second half as a spectacle' by favouring the tourists and ignoring their 'continual offside play'. Oxford was no mug. He had taken charge of the NSW v Queensland game at the SCG only two weeks earlier but headlines like 'Americans win but referee generous', and 'Yanks (and referee) humbled Newcastle' greeted his performance.

AMERICAN "ALL STARS"

RUGBY LEAGUE TOUR OF AUSTRALIA 1953

Souvenir Programme

The writer from *The Sun*, who 'even felt sorry for the frustrated Newcastle men towards the end' was not fooled: the All Stars were so impressive and Newcastle so 'inexcusably poor' that if Oxford had allowed the game 'to open up the Americans might still have won, perhaps even more easily. In the second half, Newcastle stood off and let the Americans run wild… many seemed to lose interest…. They were woefully weak.'

That afternoon, only one of the ten Sydney first grade teams matched the All Stars' haul of 19 points.

★ ★ ★ ★ ★ ★ ★ ★ ★ ★ ★

'The Americans showed they have now reached a stage where excessive referee protection of this type is actually against their best interests in learning the finer points and the rules as we know them. For most of the first half, Newcastle played like a team of champions in cotton wool, content to believe they could win when they wanted to. The big, hard tackling Americans dispelled the idea when Newcastle's forwards tried to redeem themselves early in the second half.'
Newcastle Sun

'The Americans made no mistakes in their passing and throughout the game only one instance of a pass being dropped was noticed… Questioned after the game on the standard of handling required in the gridiron game in America, Kerkorian said: "We handle with our fingers and it is required of a top gridiron player that if he can touch a ball with his fingers he must hold it." Something approaching this standard should be set in Rugby League. The Board's duty now is to tackle the job of establishing Rugby League in America, which would seem quite a task. If anything is to be done it will have to be founded on any lasting enthusiasm the present tourists may take home.'
Morning Herald

This was the headline-grabbing result the tour needed. Queensland Rugby League made plans for their game on 20 June to be filmed for American TV. Things were buzzing.

Abajian: 'That was the greatest victory we had in Australia. In fact, it was the greatest win we ever had.'

The tour party must have been one helluva night out. On the post-match itinerary was dinner at Winns' Shortland Room in the company of the Lord Mayor, followed by a dance at Newcastle City Hall. They must have made it swing. And Ray Terry slipped a cheque for $1,095 inside his blazer pocket. Another fine day.

It would have been a major challenge for the players to get up on Sunday morning for possibly the most bizarre event of the whole tour: a trip to the Richmond Main Colliery at Kurri Kurri club. Not the Kurri Kurri Curry Club. They dragged themselves from the back of a cavalcade of cars to pack into a cage and descend 800 feet in 30 seconds! The Kurri Club Ladies put on a lunch and, those who could still move, gave a display of gridiron passing before watching the match between Kurri Kurri and Maitland.

They eventually headed back to Newcastle and, at 11pm on Sunday night, pulled out of Broadmeadow station on the night train to Coffs Harbour.

The win in Newcastle sent shock waves as far as Leeds, West Riding. From his Chapeltown Road office, RFL Chief, Bill Fallowfield wrote to Dimitro in Sydney, raising the possibility of Great Britain playing in the States en route home from their tour down under in 1954. Bill

THE RUGBY FOOTBALL LEAGUE

FOUNDED 1895

PATRON: HER MAJESTY THE QUEEN

PRESIDENT THE RIGHT HONOURABLE THE EARL OF DERBY	180, CHAPELTOWN ROAD LEEDS 7	SECRETARY W. FALLOWFIELD, M.A. TELEPHONE 44637-8 TELEGRAMS "NORFU" LEEDS 7

Mr. Dimitro,
c/o The Australian Rugby Football
League Board of Control,
Box No.4415 G.P.O.
Sydney, AUSTRALIA.

WF/JBF.

17th June, 1953.

Dear Mr. Dimitro,

The English League are very interested in the performance of your team and on their behalf I would like to wish you a very successful Tour.

At the present moment preliminary preparations are being made for us to send a Touring Team to Australia and New Zealand in 1954. Normally we return to this country by ship leaving New Zealand sometime in mid-August and arriving home about the third week in September. If it were possible for us to play one or two games in America on our return journey we could then consider returning by air. This would, of course, involve extra expense which we would hope to recover from the gate receipts. At the moment these suggestions are purely tentative and have not been confirmed by my Committee but I want to evolve some practical proposition to put to them. If you have any suggestions to make I am sure they would be most helpful. Can you give any indication of whether games could be played, what would be the likely attendance and what financial terms you would be prepared to offer us? I am sure it will not be our expectations to show a profit on the venture although naturally we hope that this may be possible. We cannot, however, afford to indulge in any great extra expense because part of the profits from the Tour go to the players taking part.

Kindest regards,

Yours sincerely,

Secretary.

Recd.
2 4 JUN 1953

★ ★ ★ ★ ★ ★ ★ ★ ★ ★ ★

wanted to know what sort of crowd such a game would get, and whether ticket sales would cover the extra expense of travelling via the US and flying home rather than taking the boat. Tongues were wagging, brains ticking.

The All Stars had two much-needed days off and Coffs Harbour was as good a place as any to have them: a seaside resort more than 500km up the northern coast from Sydney, and a whole new ball game.

They checked in to the Coffs Harbour Hotel for three nights, full board. But this was no vacation. On their third day by the seaside, they would take on North Coast at the local Showgrounds. Their task: to prove the win at Newcastle was no fluke.

17 JUNE 1953
NORTH COAST V AMERICAN ALL STARS

Asked to play at full-back for the first time, Wild Bill was the last line of defence, the ultimate secondary. He would need to use his speed to get across and tackle breaking runners. He didn't exactly enjoy it.

He sulked when he was tackled. He threw a punch and was cautioned by the referee. Then, when brought down trying to run the ball clear from his own posts, he stuck an elbow in his tackler's face. Coach Robinson wanted to get him off the field at half-time and keep him off, but they had no replacements. The only sub had already come on for Buck, who was ill. Then Ed took a blow to the ribs and Mandulay ruptured his thigh.

Wild Bill was steaming now. With his head gone, he let two Norths plays romp over the line for tries untouched as the All Stars' 16-10 lead disintegrated. With a minute to go and the All Stars needing a try to win, Bill stood arguing with the referee while North Coast's lock strolled in for the match-clinching try.

When the final whistle blew, Bill stormed off towards the dressing rooms while the rest of his team stood to attention as the band played 'God Save The Queen'.

Al D. Kirkland: 'Bill Albans was a nutcase.'

Al Abajian: 'Bill was probably the most disliked person on tour. He had some strange ways. Some people thought he was crazy. We would have voted him off the team if we could.'

Another extremely competitive performance in a narrow defeat would have been honourable a few days earlier, but it undermined the All Stars' reputation in the eyes of the cynical footy fans awaiting them in Brisbane.

As their train crossed the border into Queensland for the next leg of the adventure, the Americans' pride was intact, if not their bodies.

The All Stars brought with them 11 skinned knees, nine skinned elbows, four torn muscles and a 'million bruises'. Forward Al D. Kirkland said at the time: 'Those NSW country grounds were sure hard. And your boys play hard.'

The All Stars must have wondered if they could match what the best of Queensland had to throw at them. They faced a daunting schedule in the north, with six games in 18 days. First up, the show game with Queensland in the state capital.

Pelaco

MANAGER and promoter of the American All Star football team, Mike Dimitro, sets tough training standards for his boys. Rugged, handsome Mike is married to a schoolteacher in Los Angeles.

FRONT-ROW FORWARD Xavier Mena (right) has a drink with a friend. Xavier is 24, tall, dark, and handsome. He paints landscapes and wants to meet pretty brunettes, preferably pianists.

U.S. footballers mostly bachelors

★ Eighteen of the 20 American All Star Rugby League team visiting Australia are bachelors. They told our staff reporter that they were interested in playing football, meeting some nice girls, and learning about Australia, in that order. After matches in Queensland and N.S.W. they will visit New Zealand.

WINGER Gary Kerkorian places the ball for a practice kick. He likes outdoor girls, but they must be pretty blondes, have good figures, and be about 5ft. 3in. in height. He doesn't like tall girls.

HANDSOMEST MEN in the team are fair, blue-eyed Jack Bonetti (left) and 6ft. 3in. Olympic athlete Bill Albans. Both of them are expert and enthusiastic dancers.

MOST CHARMING of the team are Rhodes Scholar Vince Jones (left) and scrum-half Ted Grossman. Both of them are unmarried. Vince is 25, has his pilot's licence, and will study law at Oxford University, England.

UNIFORMS of red-white-and-blue nylon are worn by the team. Mike Dimitro (left) is here seen with some of the team during a practice in Sydney. Majority of the men are university students or graduates. Two have their Master's degree in education. Pictures by staff photographer E. McQuillan.

MEDICAL STUDENT sandy-haired Sydney Walker, 21-year-old hooker, says he is a shy college boy who has just started at university. He doesn't like redheads.

SINGER and science graduate Francis Mandulay, of Los Angeles, sings "Don't take your love from me." A bachelor, he hopes to do some professional singing and meet some nice girls who like listening to popular songs.

THE AUSTRALIAN WOMEN'S WEEKLY — June 17, 1953.

Page 21

BRISBANE

Brisbane was different. It was growing and buzzing like Sydney, but provincial and gritty and in the grip of the Mother Country. The 23-strong American party were given a whole floor of the Albert Hotel in King George Square: a typical Brisbane town house with wrought iron balconies on its grand stone façade, right in the city centre.

The city's *Courier Mail* loved having the Americans in town. 'Yank Stars Rule Coffee Off Side' was one headline: the Americans had been converted to tea but were more interested in meeting a few local lasses. 'Australian girls seemed awful shy,' said Pat Henry. 'We're not big bad wolves. We're just plain average guys who like an occasional date. We see a lot of autograph hunters but they are all awful young.'

Women's Weekly magazine did its best to drum up interest. It ran a two-page photo feature on the hottest guys in town.

Friday morning and the All Stars trained at Woolloongabba, better known as The Gabba, the home of Brisbane cricket. Kerkorian showed off his 'spiralling gridiron pass' to the local snappers and Al E. Kirkland raced around the outfield with the ball in hand, his socks rolled down above his ankle-high boots and his shirt off. Queensland was still mild in mid-winter, just like home.

Things were looking good for chisel-jawed Jack Bonetti. He had received a telegram from the LA Rams offering him a professional contract when he got back to California. His performances in Australia must have been tempting a few local rugby league clubs to offer him a deal to stay, too. The Rams were one of the NFL's leading franchises: Hamp Pool's team had reached the 1952 play-offs and soon Jack could be lining up in the Coliseum with Norm Van Brocklin, Crazy Legs Hirsh and Night Train Lane.

There was some worrying news about George Bishop, the former Kangaroo-turned-top ref who had been helping Latchem with the coaching. Only a year earlier, Bishop was refereeing the NSW Grand Final between reigning champions South Sydney and Wests. Bishop ended up handing Wests the title on the back of a 15-4 penalty count and two hugely controversial and suspiciously wayward decisions. The spotlight was on him. He was known to be a big gambler on Sydney's horse tracks and in the illegal gambling dens frequented by gangsters, their molls, movers, shakers, hit men and the police.

Rumours swept South Sydney that the Rabbitohs had been deliberately robbed. Had Bishop been 'got at' by the fixers? Did he owe thousands to the racecourses or the card schools? And did he repay them by placing a fortune on Wests to upset the odds

Albert Hotel, Brisbane.

and made sure it happened? Rabbitohs' captain-coach Jack Rayner never spoke to Bishop again. Bishop quit: he never took charge of another game. He was a strange choice to accompany the Yanks.

As the Americans headed north, enough people objected to Bishop's employment that word came from Sydney that the ARFL Board of Control planned to axe Bishop and replace him with a tour liaison officer instead. Sensing a mutiny in the ranks if another font of league knowledge was lost to the tour party, Dimitro appealed.

The hurdles that lay ahead in Queensland were just as daunting as those south of the border – they were to play all three teams from the triangular Bulima Cup competition, Brisbane, Toowoomba and Ipswich. But first another almighty challenge: a Saturday afternoon clash with Queensland, the state side. Or what was left of it after eight Maroons had headed off to New Zealand with Australia. But they would still include Athol Smith, Neil Teys, Tom

The colourful American All Stars team trained solidly at the 'Gabba this morning for their Rugby League match against Que's'land tomorrow. Here are two of their stars in action. RIGHT: Five-eighth and goalkicker Gary Kerkorian illustrates the spiralling gridiron pass. LEFT: Hard-running centre Al E. Kirkland, bare-chested in the warm sun, gets into full stride after taking one of the passes

Tyquin, Bob Buckley, Norm Pope, Jack Veivers and Kel O'Shea. They were no mugs. It was a huge test and would be filmed for the All Stars' friends and family to see on American TV.

Yet the All Stars' improved form and results had captured Brisbane's imagination. The papers stoked the fire with reports of extra police on standby at The Gabba, the wide open cricket oval close to the city centre and the river. Special staff were lined up to control the expected huge crowds from 9am, two hours before the gates even opened.

The *Telegraph* had reminded fans to get in early to see the All Stars don their 'full gridiron

The **RUGBY LEAGUE** *News*

AMERICA v. QUEENSLAND

BRISBANE CRICKET GROUND

SATURDAY 20 JUNE 1953

6D

UNDER THE AUSPICES OF THE AUSTRALIAN RUGBY LEAGUE BOARD OF CONTROL

regalia of long, skin tight nylon pants and bright royal blue jerseys with red stars on the shoulders' and give an exhibition of American passing, 'spearing' the ball up for 50 yards, before carrying out their 'customary set of pre-match callisthenics'. They would return to the field in regulation rugby shorts.

The circus was coming to town. But these were no performing monkeys. They needed to be respected. Under-strength Queensland, captained by Denis Flannery, rested star half-back Cyril Connell to give Townsville's Max Short his debut and did not even have a training session together.

They were not exactly preparing for a tough test. They should have. As former Queensland star turned *Brisbane Courier Mail* sports editor Jack Reardon noted: 'It savoured of taking the Americans too cheaply and nearly proved disastrous.'

20 JUNE 1953

QUEENSLAND 39 AMERICAN ALL STARS 36

The press admitted that the All Stars benefited from the missing Kangaroo tourists and a helpful ref in Frank Ballard but pointed out that the man in black did nothing to influence the scoreline. The Americans also blamed the referee... for losing. They had played incredibly well.

AMERICANS CRITICISE REFEREE IN BRISBANE

American Rugby League players claimed that Brisbane referee Frank Ballard wrongly allowed Queensland winger Bob Buckley two tries, costing them a win. Dimitro said his players claimed that Buckley's third try resulted from a shepherd and he had been at least a yard offside when he received the ball to score his fourth try. "We should have won that match," Dimitro added. Former Test referee George Bishop said he would not have awarded Buckley either of the disputed tries.

★ ★ ★ ★ ★ ★ ★ ★ ★ ★ ★

AMERICANS "PIPPED ON THE POST"

Encouraged by raucous coaching from the sideline, the American All Stars led Queensland for 75 minutes. Team boss Mike Dimitro and coach "Latchem" Robinson coached the raw Americans throughout the game. The Americans, who have only been playing Rugby League for five weeks, were headed with five minutes to go. Dimitro was voluble for 70 minutes, jumping and clapping. But in the last ten minutes he sat biting his fingernails as Queensland's combination cut down the Americans' lead.

Daily Telegraph
From George Crawford

★ ★ ★ ★ ★ ★ ★ ★ ★ ★ ★

TRUE KICKING STAR

American forward A. D. Kirkland gets away in the League game at the Gabba.

Kerkorian's possible 9

By HARRY JEFFERIES

American five-eight and crack goal-kicker, Gary Kerkorian landed all his nine kicks for American All Stars, who went down 39-36 to Queensland in the Rugby League match at the Gabba today

Max Short (Qld.) fends off T. Grossman (U.S.A.) as he passes to O'Shea (Qld.) in the League game at the Gabba

Dimitro was a magnet for the press. One Brisbane paper ran a colour piece on his antics on the touchline. Their reporter sat beside Mike and Latchem and loved Dimitro's excitable, passionate encouragement to his team, and his exasperation as victory slipped through their fingers:

YANKS PLAY TO MIKE'S VOCAL RAZZLE-DAZZLE

It was bright open football. The spectacular Yanks attacked from the start and within six minutes had a 7-0 lead. Forward Al Kirkland smashed his way through a ruck and went 30 yards: "That baby's running!" Centre Al E. Kirkland threw a 30 yard torpedo pass to winger Buckley: "That's sparking!" Kerkorian kicked all nine attempts at goal: "Atta boy!" In the second half the All Stars miraculously led 29-16: "I'll eat my hat!" Minutes from time they were hanging on to a three point lead but couldn't match Queensland's clinical finishing in a thunderous climax: "Go chase yourselves!"

It had been frantic and thrilling but the Americans just missed out on a truly sensational scalp. Either way, they had pushed a team of high quality players to the limit – and it had not gone unnoticed. One paper reported fans calling it 'one of the mightiest games they had ever seen'.

Syd Walker and Ed Demirjian close down Queensland.

At the final whistle, hundreds of boys hurdled the picket fences and raced across the cricket outfield to reach their new heroes in stars and stripes. They swamped Teddy and Sol, Vince and Jack, wanting autographs, handshakes and smiles. And all of it was taped for TV viewers back in the States: surely this would leave them craving 13-man football?

The next day, the Brisbane papers were gushing:

"All Stars" gave Q'sland real test

By JACK REARDON

THESE American "All Stars" Rugby League players are no circus clowns— they're a bunch of hard running athletes and footballers and if ever the game becomes established over there it will be: "Look out Australia, England, France, and New Zealand."

Why have people in the South labelled them a circus? What have they got against the Yanks. The two Kirklands, Sol Naumu, Vince Jones, Syd Walker, and Jack Bonetti are names to remember.

Queensland won yesterday's game by 39 points to 36.

Americans will not beat class teams until they learn some cover defence.

But I am astounded at the improvement in their game. I saw the Americans in their first training run under coach Norm Robinson in Australia, the morning after they landed in Sydney.

Then I thought their task was hopeless. They were awkward, lost, and confused.

One week later I saw them in a practice match. The improvement was infinitesimal.

Entertaining

Now they have adapted themselves well to their new game, introduced some of their own "play" and the combination produced a fine entertaining game against Queensland yesterday.

The Americans' Australian coach, Norm Robinson, said after the match, it was their best performance of the tour.

Queensland's coach, Duncan Thompson, said the Americans won 75 per cent of the game, only lack of knowledge of covering defence cost them a win over Queensland.

Queensland seemed to take the Americans too cheaply in the first half. Their loose tackling around the shoulders deserved a worse fate than to be behind 29-16 at half-time.

The powerful Americans easily shook off the half-hearted tackles.

No long pants

The Americans introduced something new when they sent Gary Kerkorian, Bob Buckley, Al Albans and Al Kirkland out in "gridiron"

kit to give an exhibition of American passing. They speared the ball 50 yards at times.

Then the Yanks' team ran out and did their customary set of pre-match warming up calisthenics.

The American's team took the field in football shorts instead of the traditional long pants.

Queensland was led by Denis Flannery, the American by Sol Naumu.

The Queensland team was not at full strength. Besides the eight men chosen for New Zealand being rested, half-back Cyril Connell was also spelled to give Townsville half, Max Short, his first State game.

This Queensland team had not had a training run together. It savoured of taking the Americans too cheaply and nearly proved disastrous.

Early shocks

There was not much cohesion amongst the local team in the first half and they got an early shock when American Vince Jones gathered a high kick and crashed over for a try.

Kerkorian kicked two neat goals to put the Yanks in the lead, 7—0.

The Americans set about playing hard football from the start.

N They tackled solidly and the Queensland forwards had difficulty in handling their heavier opponents.

Queensland backs also had their troubles with centre Al E. Kirkland and Sol Naumu.

I have never seen a stronger runner than Naumu. He shakes off tacklers like a dog sheds water after a swim.

Kirkland feat

Kirkland is a different type. His footwork is unbelievably neat and fast, and he outpaced Queensland's defence often.

With those two players cutting down the centre, and five-eighth Gary Kerkorian switching play and sending his long accurate passes out to the wings, Queensland had to defend hard to keep them out.

There was one excellent movement by the Americans which brought a try.

Kerkorian took the ball from a scrum, shot a long pass to A. E. Kirkland on his own 25 line; Kirkland stepped around Blair, outdistanced cover defenders, and on reaching the fullback, Pope, passed to Grossman, who had backed

It was obvious, however, that once their line was broken the Americans had no idea of recovering.

Neil Teys scored when an American pitch pass misfired, then Smith scored after Short had wriggled through a breaking scrum.

The scores were 31-all after 30 minutes' play in the second half. Then Queensland took the lead when O'Shea backed up well to take a pass from Short.

A Flannery kick was gathered by Tom Tyquin for a try, and Queensland led 39-31.

The Americans seemed to have shot their bolt, but rallied well, and some crisscross running and passing sent winger Ran away for lock Bonetti to take the last pass and score.

Kerkorian kicked his ninth goal from nine attempts to make the final score 39-36.

Kerkorian's nine goals yesterday brought his total points for the tour to 93. He is accurate, but only seems to attempt goals from within 30 yards.

The All Stars, with their vastly superior weight, won scrums 17-14. Penalties also favoured them 7-5.

Referee Frank Ballard was lenient several times in the first half with the Americans. There was no direct benefit, however. In the second half he tightened up on them considerably.

Mission treat

The crowd of 25,000 was put in excellent humour by an amazing display of attacking football from Cherbourg All Blacks against Brisbane Reserves.

The aboriginals had the spectators continually on their feet with their juggling handling, tossing the ball over their heads, between their legs, but always with a man to take it.

Brisbane won the match 30 to 22 but the Cherbourg boys stole the show.

The Americans leave Brisbane by air this morning for Cairns, where they will play North Queensland on Wednesday.

Queensland captain, Ken McCaffery, was yesterday judged by the State selectors as the outstanding Queensland player of the interstate series.

He will receive the Jack Stephenson Memorial trophy for 1953.

First scorers

FIRST SCORERS: Naumu (Qld) and V. Jones (U.S.).

These American 'All Stars' Rugby League players are no circus clowns – they're a bunch of hard running athletes and footballers and if ever the game became established over there it will be: "Look out Australia, England, France and New Zealand."

Why have people in the South labelled them a circus? What have they got against the Yanks? The two Kirklands, Sol Naumu, Vince Jones, Syd Walker, and Jack Bonetti are names to remember.

Americans will not beat class teams until they learn some cover defence. But I am astounded at the improvement in their game. I saw the Americans in their first training run under coach

Norm Robinson in Australia, the morning after they landed in Sydney. Then I thought their task was hopeless. They were awkward, lost, and confused. One week later I saw them in a practice match. The improvement was infinitesimal. Now they have adapted themselves well to their own "play" and the combination produced a fine entertaining game against Queensland. Robinson said it was their best performance of the tour. Queensland's coach, Duncan Thompson, said the Americans won 75% of the game, only lack of knowledge of covering defence costing them a win.

Queensland seemed to take the Americans cheaply in the first half. Their loose tackling around the shoulders deserved a worse fate than to be behind 29-16 at half-time. The powerful Americans shook off the half-hearted tackles.

I have never seen a stronger runner than Naumu. He shakes off tacklers like a dog sheds water after a swim. Kirkland is a different type. His footwork is unbelievably neat and fast, and he outpaced Queensland's defence often. With those two players cutting down the centre and five-eighth Gary Kerkorian switching play and sending his long accurate passes out to the wings, Queensland had to defend hard to keep them out…. It was obvious, however, that once their line was broken the Americans had no idea of recovering.

Sunday 21 June
By Jack Reardon

Sunday's *TRUTH* tabloid gave the All Stars a whole page eulogy:

YANKEE ALL STARS ARE BIG LEAGUE STAYERS
'NOVICES' GAVE QLD. BIG FRIGHT

If these Americans ever take Rugby League seriously they'll lick the cockeyed world! And if English clubs ever get a look-see at such Yankee-Doodle dandy players as Alvin E. Kirkland, Sol Naumu and Jack Bonetti they'll leave the poaching of Aussies for dead.

Nigh 25,000 paid £900 to see this star-spangled band of football fledglings, after just four weeks of schooling in our game, almost shock the socks off a comparatively veteran Queensland team.

Almost, but Queensland got up in time to photo-finish the All Stars 39-36. Sure, we've got alibis. This was only a shadow of Queensland strength. And man, the elastic interpretation of the rules allowed the Yanks a latitude that too often achieved an unwarranted attacking longitude. What with the [Aboriginal team] Cherbourg All Blacks in the early game, mercurial as sunlight on dancing waters, and the Americans with their exhibition of spiral throwing and their wind-up gymnastic exercises before the main game, it was all Barnum and Bailey would have conjured up as ripe entertainment for the masses.

Here's their credit tally. They handled the ball like Cinquevallis. They throw mighty and accurate passes. They back up in attack and tackle like winged bulldozers. They have a goal-kicker of top-class in five-eighth Gary Kerkorian. They have men in Kirkland (back), Sol Naumu, Grossman and Bonetti who would grace any team in Australia right now. They had 80-minute condition.

On the debit side they carry a few football no-hopers. Their defence positioning was suicidal and their cover-defence almost non-existent. Frequently they kicked foolishly.

Referee Ballard ringmastered the show into snazzy entertainment until the Reds gradually overhauled the All Stars and finally keelhauled 'em late in the game. Full credit to the Yanks. They came again in the dying minutes with a dazzling Bonetti try. They mightn't be all stars but they're all stayers!

But listen to Queensland master-coach Duncan Thompson: 'Six weeks ago they didn't know League from bung rules. I'm staggered at their intelligence in learning the game so quickly. I shudder to think what most of our fellows would learn of gridiron in that time.'

Mike told the press: 'It was a great game and we enjoyed it. We were particularly pleased with the crowd. The better team won but I'm proud of my boys.'

His men headed to Brisbane airport for the flight to Cairns, bodies battered and bruised, egos nicely massaged.

QUEENSLAND *Rugby League winger Bob Buckley brought the spectators to their feet as he dived out of a tackle by American centre Sol Naumu to score the first of his four tries at the Brisbane Cricket Ground yesterday.*

CHAPTER 15
THE FAR NORTH

The All Stars flew into the Heart of Darkness. Far North Queensland: 1,200 miles from Sydney. The tropics. Base camp for the Great Barrier Reef. Hot, humid, sticky, suffocating air that has you sweating all over as soon as you step off the hotel veranda. Even in mid-winter.

First, a midweek game in Cairns. Then, Sunday in Townsville. This was tough rugby league country. No overseas team had ventured this far up state for a generation. The Brits won here in 1928. Few others had done so since.

One plus: Dimitro's appeal had worked. The Board of Control agreed to let George Bishop continue as assistant coach thanks to 'America's great improvement'. If Bishop could not help the All Stars, no one could.

Phillip Street also put out an encouraging statement in *RL News*: 'The NSWRL considers at this stage that the American venture has fully justified itself and will lead to bigger things... They have shown an aptitude for the code that augurs well for the future of the game in America... Big crowds, in some cases, record attendances, have seen the tourists... Harold Han and Bob Buckley are proving stars of the back division.'

CAN HANDLE THIS 'ROO

AMERICAN All Stars Mike Dimitro (left), Al D. Kirkland, and Syd Walker admire a toy Kangaroo given to Mike as a souvenir of the team's Queensland visit at their hotel at Cairns last night. The Americans play Far North Queensland at Cairns to-day.

CAIRNS

Dimitro's men checked in to Hotel Central, an art-deco gem on the corner of Lake and Spencer. It would be home for four nights.

Bishop and Latchem took their troops for two light morning practice sessions before the heat really rose, heading off for a mind-blowing boat trip to the Barrier Reef while the locals trained in the afternoon sun under the orders of their skipper, the former Kangaroo Ron Griffiths. It was not a place to lose your cool.

The All Stars now had reputations to protect and were evolving from amusing novelty act to athletic phenomenon. They had proved they could cope with the best and, heading back into the backwaters, thought they could now finish teams off.

TRY SCORED WHILE U.S TEAM ARGUED

Cairns – Wednesday – The American and Far North Queensland Rugby League teams played a torrid 17 all draw today. The Americans could easily have won, but stood arguing with the referee Renton after a penalty on their 25 had been awarded against them when they were leading 17-14. The Far North hooker Griffiths took a "dribble" penalty while the argument proceeded and sent Greenwood over for a barging try.

Newcastle Herald
25 June 1953

But Far North – with six players from the Cairns club, four from Tully Tigers, two from Innisfail and one representing Eacham – were fired up, too.

Al Abajian: 'They called a try back and we threatened to walk out! We were just tired. Harold Han scored and they called it back. So we tied. The referee bought us a couple of boxes of oranges afterwards. We asked him in the hotel: "Hey, why did you call that try back?" He says: "Well" – he was half loaded – "you guys come here, play a game and leave. I have to live here"! I wouldn't say it was illegal but that's what he said.'

Dimitro's troops had, yet again, proved themselves competitive but come away shattered, mentally and physically. They were good, very good, all things considered. But not good enough to win. Now they had to do it again, back down the coast.

Back in Sydney the NSWRL were making sure these results were being noticed. The propaganda machine was wound up again: the anonymous 'Editorial' in the next *Rugby League News* cried:

YANKS PROVE THEMSELVES

It is now becoming evident to all that the Americans are becoming established as a Rugby League team and that early predictions that they would be a force by the end of their tour will prove accurate.

TOWNSVILLE
Thursday 25 June 1953

It reported that the Americans had requested that the final fixture at the SCG on 29 July be a test match against Australia. The Board of Control had made 'no immediate decision' as 'test matches are not staged lightly'. Iron Mike was getting carried away – again.

The All Stars got off the plane in tropical Townsville, battered and bruised, and facing their seventh match in just 18 days. With only 13 fit and able players, seven games should have taken seven weeks, not two and a half. The college football players were fit fellas but this was ridiculous. Something had to give.

Townsville: 850 miles north of Brisbane, a million miles from home. A Victorian plantation port built by Chinese labourers, it is hot, sticky, green and wet. It gets so hot the roofs are white to reflect the sun. A proud little city surrounded by lush jungle on one side, sandy beaches and warm sea on the other, all drenched in sun almost every day of the year, Townsville is also rugby league mad.

The Americans were welcome visitors. Townsville was bombed three times as the Japanese attempted to destroy the US Naval Base from where the Allies headed to New Guinea, Guam, and Indonesia. The nadir came in May 1942. Five months of Japanese conquests culminated in the Battle of the Coral Sea off the coast of Townsville. USS *Lexington* and USS *Sims* were sunk, USS *Neosho* was crippled. But the Allies gutted it out to win. Dimitro probably claimed he was there. The Queenslanders' bond with America was sealed. Anyone from the other side of the Pacific that laps against its scorching sands was special in Townsville. In 1952, the US Alliance was born and thousands of Americans were still serving there.

Al D.: 'The Aussies were good guys, individualists. And they still liked us. The Americans had saved them in the war. It's hard to believe it was only eight years since the end of the war. At the reception they'd say: "500 miles north of here was the Battle of Coral Sea" – it didn't mean anything to us but, as they say, if it wasn't for our Navy, the Aussies would be speaking Japanese.'

The All Stars dumped their gear at Wirthsco Hotel Sea View on The Strand – the oceanfront promenade – and caught the ferry across to Magnetic Island, a maze of tropical wildlife with parrots, monkeys, eagles and beautiful deserted beaches. They soaked up the sun, waiting for the pounding bruises to fade and

the stinging cuts to heal. Late that night, heaven turned to hell, paradise became purgatory. Jack Bonetti fell ill.

Al Abajian: 'I was rooming with Jack that Friday night in Townsville. He said his back was hurting. I remember the moaning and groaning. I said: "Go and run a bath, lie in that and rest your muscles." We were tired and exhausted from playing and travelling and I just fell asleep.'

Jack: 'I'd played every game of the tour and I'd got real run-down without realising. I woke up with a bad back in Townsville so they took me to hospital. They thought I'd slipped a disc.'

The rest of the squad had a training run on Saturday morning at the Sports Reserve, and then paraded down Flinders Street – the main thoroughfare through town – in the sunshine. The locals finally saw these strange American footy players in the flesh and had the opportunity to show their solidarity with a nation who had saved them.

The secretary of the North Queensland RL, Mr Mitchell, had come back from Cairns warning the locals to expect a tough encounter, declaring that the Americans' handling was 'a revelation' and that they had improved 'remarkably'.

The local paper, the *Townsville Daily Bulletin*, felt the same way: 'The Americans showed brilliance in individual open play and were rugged in rucks but still lack cover defence. However, the way they have picked up the game in the short space of a few weeks amazed many spectators… with the brilliant handling and scorching pace of Albans, Kirkland, Grossman and the fast "low to the ground running" of Han… The tackling was as rugged as any seen in the North. The Americans asked for no quarter and received none. In forward exchanges they gave better than they took.'

North Queensland would take no chances, including three of the Queensland state side who had beaten the Americans the previous weekend: half-back Max Short, five-eighth Danny O'Connell and wing Bob Buckley. (Yes, there were two Bob Buckleys.)

Game day was also 25 years to the day since the first touring team's train pulled in and Townsville had since become a regular stop on overseas teams' itineraries. In 1951 Puig-Aubert's extraordinary pre-match kicking display had stunned fans at the Reserve, a green sanctuary a few blocks back from the ocean, under the shadow of Castle Hill. Despite fielding a string of international players, North Queensland had never beaten an international team.

Adverts for the game were posted in the *Townsville Daily Bulletin*, and three curtain-raisers and the now standard 'display of long passing and calisthenics' by Kerkorian and Co guaranteed a packed Sports Reserve.

NORTH QUEENSLAND 38 AMERICAN ALL STARS 17

All Stars line up with North Queensland.

North Queensland gained its first international victory in Rugby League history with a 38 points to 17 win over the American All Stars at the Townsville Sports Reserve on Sunday.

Although North Queensland won, the success was not impressive. Only a complete dominance of the set scrummages and mistakes by the Americans allowed the northerners to score several tries. The huge crowd which paid £1,553 at the gates, enjoyed the type of unorthodox football played by the Americans. The long pass was effective several times but it fell down when not executed quickly enough. Another feature was the manner in which the All Stars plucked the ball from the air and whipped it close to their bodies as they ran.

What impressed in the All Stars 13 was the glittering footwork of the backs. Change of pace took on a new meaning for northerners when the twinkle-toed Al E. Kirkland ran with the ball. He has the ability to stop almost dead in his tracks to beat a man and then swerve off at a tangent.

Although the All Stars held North Queensland to a 13-12 deficit at half-time, the visitors died away in the second half. They appeared to run out of gas in the last 20 minutes, when the home side chalked up 20 points.

With Pat Henry suffering from an infected knee, it was all Dimitro needed when Sol Naumu hobbled off five minutes from time with a damaged shoulder. And then there was Big Jack, still lying in hospital with 'a slipped disc in the vertebrae'.

Jack: 'I was in traction but when I got up to go to the bathroom in the ward, my leg gave way. Then when I got there, I couldn't urinate. It was a big worry. They examined me and said they thought I had polio.'

By Monday the doctors were sure. It was front page news.

NORTH QUEENSLAND'S FIRST INTERNATIONAL GAME WIN

North Queensland gained its first international victory in Rugby League history with a 38 points to 17 win over the American All Stars at the Townsville Sports Reserve, on Sunday.

Full back, R. Quinn; three-quarters, J. Fifield, P. Farrell, M. Webster, R. Buckley; halves, D. O'Connell, M. Short; forwards, J. Dean, T. Tavasci, A. Farquhar, K. Martin, K. O'Shea, T. Whitehead (captain).

ALL STARS

Full back, G. Kauffmann; threequarters, S. Naumu, Al E. Kirkland, H. Han, B. Buckley; halves, G. Korkorian, T. Grossman; forwards, S. Drakulvich, S. Walker, V. Jones, Al D. Kirkland, F. Mandulay, M. Dimitro (replaced in the second half by A. Abajian).

Although North Queensland won, the success was not impressive. Only a complete dominance in the set scrummages and mistakes by the Americans allowed the northerners to score several tries.

The huge crowd which paid £1,553 at the gates, enjoyed the type of unorthodox football played by the Americans.

The long pass was effective several times, but it fell down also when not executed quickly enough. The idea to beat the defence by cutting out men running with the ball is negative if the de-

River. The winners had to overcome the superiority of Herbert River's hooker, P. Castallero, but the forwards dominated play and scored three of the four tries.

With North Queensland representatives, Tavasci and O'Shea to partner Marsh and company, Ayr is going to be a hard nut for Townsville to crack in the final southern zone game of the Foley Shield early in August.

Prominent in Herbert River's 13 was centre, R. Skinner. With more support he could have given the Ayr 13 a fright.

Ayr 16 (tries, Marsh 2, Russell, Fahey; goals, Russell-Green) defeated Herbert River 8 (tries, R. Skinner, Cahill; goals, Groundwater).

In the other curtain raisers, Townsville sub-minors defeated Ayr 32-2, and Townsville Brothers defeated Mt. Carmel, 11-6.

P.T. BY ALL STARS

The North Queensland football followers caught a glimpse of the fanfare which is part of the American gridiron game at the Sports Reserve on Sunday when the All Stars began to limber up.

Prior to the start of the

Tragic circumstances now surround the recent visit of the American All Stars Rugby League players to Townsville with the admittance to hospital of one tourist as a positive polio sufferer. He is 23-year-old six-footer Jack Bonetti, who was taken to the Townsville General Hospital.

One of the American players who remained in Townsville, Ray Terry, said on Monday night that he had advised Bonetti's parents by radio-telephone in Livermore (California) of their son's illness. Bonetti's father is a service station proprietor.

"They took it quite nicely," said Terry.

Terry said that he had also seen Bonetti from a distance in hospital. "I was able to talk to him, and he is taking it fine in the circumstances," he remarked.

Terry expects to leave for Rockhampton on Thursday although his future movements will be guided by the condition of his team-mate.

Bonetti, who was until the advent of his sickness one of the most promising forwards of the team, complained late on Friday night of a sudden illness. He was admitted to hospital on Saturday, where it was first thought he had dislodged a disc in the vertebrae. However, tests taken later proved that the player was suffering from the malignant virus. It is understood that one leg has so far been affected.

On Monday the All Stars left by plane for Longreach, but two of the tourists, apart from Bonetti, remained in Townsville when seating accommodation on the plane could not be found for the entire party. R. Terry and S. Mandulay may fly to Rockhampton to rejoin the party on Thursday.

Morale of the touring party has been severely hit by the announcement of Bonetti's tragic illness. ARL liaison officer Mr J. McKenna said in Longreach last night that the players were taking the news very hard. They were worried over the effect the announcement would have on Bonetti's parents.

American consulate officials in Brisbane stated that no arrangements could be made concerning Bonetti's return to the United States until the end of the period of isolation.

Townsville Daily Bulletin
Tuesday 30 June 1953 ★ ★ ★ ★ ★ ★ ★ ★ ★ ★ ★ ★

AMERICAN FOOTBALLER IN HOSPITAL WITH POLIO

Tragic circumstances now surround the recent visit of the American All Stars Rugby League players to Townsville with the admittance to hospital of one tourist as a positive polio sufferer.

He is 22-year-old, six-footer Jack Bonetti, who was taken to the Townsville General Hospital on Saturday.

One of the American players who remained in Townsville, Ray Terry, said on Monday night that he had advised Bonetti's parents by radio-telephone in Livermore (California) of their son's illness. Bonetti's father is a service station proprietor.

"They took it quite nicely," said Terry.

Terry said that he had also seen Bonetti from a distance in hospital. "I was able to talk to him, and he is taking it fine in the circumstances," he remarked.

Terry expects to leave for Rockhampton on Thursday, although his future movements will be guided by the condition of his team-mate. He said that the period of isolation lasted up to three weeks, and then everything depended on the medical adviser.

Bonetti, who, until the advent of his sickness, was one of the most promising forwards of the team, complained late on Friday night of a sudden illness. He was admitted to hospital on Saturday, where it was first thought that he had dislodged a disc in the vertebrae.

However, tests taken later proved that the player was suffering from the malignant

Dutch Minister for N.G. Talks

SCHIPHOL (Holland), June 29.—The Dutch Foreign Affairs Minister (Professor Kernkamp) left by air last night for talks in Australia and Dutch New Guinea.

The Minister will first go to Sydney, where he will also meet the Dutch Foreign Minister (Mr. Lans) and then travel on to New Guinea.

Before leaving, the Minister said he was going to have talks in Australia with the Minister for Territories (Mr. P. M. Hasluck) "to try to achieve perfectly informal co-operation between the population of the Dutch and Australian parts of New Guinea."

He said this should take place on a local level so that no one could have any objections.

It was useful, he said, to exchange practical data about development of territory in which both Australia and Holland were interested.

Another subject of discussions between Mr. Hasluck and Mr. Kernkamp will be freer frontier traffic between Dutch and Australian New Guinea by creating a kind of ....

The story flew down the wires under the Pacific to Jack's home state:

Jack: 'I was moved into isolation in case I was contagious. I went from 210lbs to 140lbs. I was in there for about 30 days. The people in the hospital were exceptionally nice to me.'

Suddenly, the defeat in Townsville was neither here nor there. The team was rocked.

Al Abajian: 'It was our darkest moment. It was terrible, shocking.'

Al D. Kirkland: 'It scared the hell out of us. We'd all been living together for three months and we had no idea how you contracted polio. Every time we got an ache or pain we wondered "Am I getting it?" And we had that after every game. It had us terrified.'

Al Abajian: 'Earlier we'd visited a hospital in Sydney for crippled children, to the polio unit, to cheer up some young patients that were in iron lungs. We signed autographs and did our best to help in any way we could. We wondered if he picked up the virus there but, with the incubation period, maybe he didn't. We didn't know what caused it. Nobody really knows. All I know is, too many of us had to play every game, which was one of the factors that Jack got ill.'

The Townsville Daily Bulletin wrote: 'Bonetti had a great future ahead of him in the football game. In Cairns, against Far North 13, last Wednesday, he was considered one of the stars of the American team. The long grind of the League tour of Australia is beginning to tell on the tourists, who now find themselves playing up to three games a week. They have played ten games and are scheduled for nine more. Coupled with the long distances to travel and several games, is the fact that the All Stars are called upon to play a full 80 minutes of football. This is completely foreign to the tourists who are able to take rest periods during the course of the usual gridiron games.'

Abajian: 'Jack was a great athlete and had a great future in the National Football League. In gridiron, one year he played as an end, the next year he played as a guard: two very different skills, that's how good he was.'

Fate could not have been crueller to Jack. Elizabeth Kenny grew up in Townsville and became a ground-breaking nurse, devising a revolutionary treatment of polio. Her ideas were rejected by the medical industry in Australia, so she fled on the brink of the Second World War to the States. There her ideas were taken up and developed zealously. Her treatment worked. After dying in 1952, Sister Elizabeth Kenny Institutes opened all over the US.

If the All Stars returned to Townsville today, they could walk along The Strand again and sit for a while in a children's playground and gaze out over the Pacific, lapping on the shore. They would be sitting in Sister Kenny Park.

POLIO STRIKES TOURING RUGBY PLAYER BONETTI

SYDNEY, Australia, June 30 (AP)—Jack Bonetti, tackle on an all-star American Rugby team touring this continent, has suffered an attack of polio and has been isolated in the Townsville Hospital in North Queensland.

Dr. Scott Young said today that Bonetti probably will have to remain in the hospital six weeks.

Bonetti, a former Stanford University player, is from Livermore, Cal.

LA Times

July 25, 1953

ARE WE *PROUD!*

From the thousands of tailors in Australia, we—Broadway Tailors—have been chosen to fashion the sports outfits for our American cousins. Can you blame us for really feeling proud of this!

CHAPTER 16
LAST MEN STANDING

JULY, CENTRAL QUEENSLAND

The shocked and shaken party also left Sol behind with his injured shoulder and flew 500 miles south-west to Longreach. The bush, cattle country, ranch land, the outback, 700 miles from Brisbane, slap bang on the Tropic of Capricorn.

The Yanks staggered into the Imperial Hotel where they would be fully catered for, morning, noon and night, for three peaceful days. July came – it was mid-winter down under.

Dimitro received a letter from Harold Matthews in Phillip Street: he sent commiserations from the league for Jack's polio. He also acknowledged Mike's request for more suitable food: salad and fruit juice for breakfast and milk at all times; reminded him to pay Broadway Tailors their £300 bill; and announced a farewell dinner on 29 July at the Phillip Street club.

Teddy's father, Jack Grossman, wrote an open letter from Beverly Hills to the *Sydney Daily Telegraph* thanking Australia for the wonderful reception his son had enjoyed.

Rural Longreach offered another new experience.

Al D.: 'I remember Longreach had wooden sidewalks, like the Wild West – and some of it was pretty wild. Australia was probably 50 years behind us. They were still pioneers. Everything was old fashioned to us. I remember having a great time playing golf on the sand greens at Longreach though!'

Abajian: 'I remember Longreach. What an experience that was. Way out in the middle of nowhere.'

The game against Central West was less special. The home side, led by former Queensland state winger Wally McDonald, had the game won early, racking up a 13-0 lead after just 20 minutes, 21-5 at half-time. For once the All Stars staged a fine second-half comeback but they could do no better than a frustrating 26-21 defeat in front of half the town: about 1,600 bush folk, half of them women and kids. Big Al D. got a try. Dimitro got £188.

The adventure continued. They flew back out to the coast, another 400 miles, on a specially chartered plane to Rockhampton. The party shrank by one more: Pat Henry was in a Longreach hospital with a knee injury.

Saturday was 4 July – Independence Day – and few of the party could ever have felt further from home. But the sun was shining and the boys were the hottest thing in town. They got well looked after.

On Friday morning there were cameramen at the airport and a civic reception at the town hall soon after they landed. Half a dozen dignitaries made welcome speeches: men of the cloth, men of the markets, politicians. Dimitro did his best to reply. Then the whole group moved onto the local branch of Tattersall's Club for another function.

The Americans were a freak show in Rockhampton. With a population of 36,000, it was a relative city out there on the Fitzroy River. Its wide boulevards were more like LA than any other place they had been so far. But the local papers were fascinated with their fantastical guests. Xavier told reporters of his love of bull fighting, his wrestling prowess, his Spanish heritage and his training as a teacher in 'Oriental and occidental art history and architecture'; Pat Henry was joining the US Army as a Second-Lieutenant in the Chemical Corps; and Syd Walker was into economics. The local female readers were subtly informed that only Dimitro and Kauffman were married.

There was no time to rest. They trained Saturday morning, then went on a tour of American camp sites and local beaches in the afternoon before the Rockhampton Rugby League put on an Independence Day dinner on Saturday night: a four-course meal with the Deputy Mayor and several of the American servicemen who had stayed behind from the 50,000 stationed there in the war. The party continued at the School of Arts long into Saturday night.

It was not the perfect preparation for a game against a gnarled country team on a rock hard, straw-strewn field the following afternoon.

But again they competed, again they were defeated, again the game was lost early, again the All Stars made a brave comeback in adversity. This time they trailed 27-5 ten minutes into the second half, before Big Al D's goal started the comeback. Half-backs Kerkorian and Grossman got things moving with some delicious long passes, Kauffman's long kicks found touch regularly and he attacked dangerously from the back.

Centre Han and wing Abajian (on for the injured Buckley) got on the end of attacks to make some fine breaks as Dimitro, Al D. and Co in the pack – wearing long pants again to protect their knees – smashed their way forward. Six different All Stars touched down and Gary and George added to Big Al's two-pointer, but they also missed three kicks at goal. They were just 27-26 down with a couple of minutes left only to concede two late tries and lose 33-26.

They left cursing. But with over 5,000 turning up, Dimitro pocketed nearly £600 in gate money. It was a good day's work.

The tour of northern Queensland was over: four games had brought one draw, two narrow defeats, one hammering, a load of battered bodies and a skip full of heartache.

At least things would get easier now, wouldn't they? Oh no, Brisbane next.

BRISBANE

The 20 surviving players – Terry and Mandulay had rejoined the party from Townsville – only had to gingerly step down off their plane and hobble across the tarmac at Brisbane Airport for the waiting press pack to sense blood.

Unlike the ballyhoo that greeted them first time, there were few press men, and no league officials to meet them at the 'drome. The novelty had well and truly

Scoring stars to play for Yanks

By HARRY JEFFERIES

The American All Stars will play their points scoring combination in the Rugby League match against Brisbane at the Gabba tomorrow.

The combination is centre Al E. Kirkland and full-back and goalkicker Gary Kerkorian.

Between them Kerkorian and Kirkland have scored most of the Yankee points on the tour.

The Americans arrived in Brisbane by plane from North Queensland this afternoon.

There were no Q.R.L. or B.R.L. officials to greet them at the drome.

Polio victim Jack Bonetti will join the party in about five weeks time. He will be in isolation until then.

Manager M i k e Dimitro is bitterly disappointed at missing out on the Brisbane floodlight game.

He declared: "Is that game still on at the Gabba or at night time? We were told we could have anything when we first hit Brisbane and yet a request to switch the game has been refused. Is there any chance of the game being switched now?"

Told there was no chance Dimitro replied: "I might still have a go. Never say die."

The players looked tired and sore after their strenuous northern tour.

They are hoping for a big crowd tomorrow to boost along their lagging finances.

The main game starts at 3.30 p.m. Referee is Vic Lynagh.

The early curtain raiser will be between Brisbane and New South Wales schoolboys at 1.30 p.m. and the main curtain raiser at 2.20 p.m. between Murrumbah reserve and Brisbane third grade sides.

B.R.L. fixtures for Saturday are: Gabba: Wests v. South Coast; Easts v. Souths, Davies Park: Valley v. Wynnum-Manly, Oxenham Park; Norths v. Brothers.

The American All Stars Rugby League side arrived back from their North Queensland tour feeling tired and many were limping. But they are looking forward to their match against Brisbane tomorrow at the 'Gabba and are hoping for a big crowd.

The American All Stars Rugby League team arrived back from their North Queensland tour feeling tired and many were limping. The players looked sore after their strenuous northern tour. But they are looking forward to their match against Brisbane at The Gabba tomorrow and are hoping for a big crowd to boost along their lagging finances.

Brisbane Telegraph
By Harry Jefferies

★ ★ ★ ★ ★ ★ ★ ★ ★ ★ ★

worn off. They had even downgraded hotel to the National. Desperate to attract a big crowd to see them take on Brisbane, Dimitro pleaded for the game to be moved and played at night under the Exhibition Oval floodlights: 'We were told we could have anything when we hit Brisbane and yet a request to switch the game has been refused. I might still have a go. Never say die.' The cricket trust, owners of The Gabba, insisted it went ahead there on Tuesday afternoon.

Despite competing well in every game up north, the Brisbane public were not interested enough to take a day off work to see the Yanks again. And the city's

Brisbane Beats All Stars

BRISBANE, Tuesday. —The Brisbane Rugby League team to-day beat the American All Stars 39-26.

It was a drab game, but there were some bright patches, particularly the kicking exchanges between the rival full-backs, Norm Pope and George Kauttman.

American three-quarters Harold Han and Bill Albans did some excellent running.

Gary Kerkorian gave another display of accurate goal-kicking, which produced seven goals.

The Americans, weary from their strenuous tour, seemed at times unable to break out of a walk.

Some of the Brisbane players were also lethargic.

Centre Len Blaik and winger George Hayes, who scored three tries, were the brightest of the Brisbane backs.

The attendance was 7,000 and takings £1,109.

Brisbane, 39 (Hayes 3, Mundt 2, Blaik, W. Tyquin, Veivers tries; Pope 6 goals), America, 26 (A. Kirkland, Han, Abajian, Mandulay tries; Kerkorian 7 goals).

Australia players were busy elsewhere, losing the second Trans-Tasman Test 12-11 in Wellington. The Board of Control said 7,000 were scattered across the grassy hills and gabled stands but the local hacks reckoned it was less than half that.

Kerkorian had kicked the All Stars into a 6-0 lead to take his tour tally over the 100-point mark and Al E. Kirkland and Wild Bill had got the sparse crowd excited with some fine runs. But when 'ace centre' Kirkland left the field for some ambulance attention, the home side fought back to win. The game was considered 'not a patch on the Americans' spectacular game against Queensland'. Again the press seemed to overlook the extraordinary achievements of the Americans. Among the Brisbane side was one former Australian international – prop Tom Tyquin – and a future one in full-back Norm Pope, and yet still the All Stars scored nearly 30 points.

Among the crowd was a fascinated 18-year-old local league nut, Bill Abernethy, who, 50 years later still recalled: 'People were looking forward to fast, entertaining games of rugby

POOR CROWD SEES YANKS AT 'GABBA

By HARRY JEFFERIES

A poor crowd—about 3,000 at the most—saw the American All Stars meet Brisbane in the match at the 'Gabba today.

The crowd would be well below previous international touring teams for a mid-week game in Brisbane.

beauty and the Yanks led ahead 4—nil after tw minutes.

That gave Kerkorian over 100 points for the

Brisbane retaliated Full-back Pope missed a easy penalty but hal

BRISBANE 39 AMERICAN ALL STARS 26

Brisbane Rugby League team today beat the American All Stars 39 points to 26 in a drab game. There were some bright patches, particularly kicking exchanges between the rival full-backs, Norm Pope and George Kauffman. The American three-quarters, Harold Han and Bill Albans, did some excellent running and Gary Kerkorian gave another display of accurate kicking which produced seven goals. The Americans, weary from their strenuous tour, seemed at times unable to break out of a walk. Some of the Brisbane players were also lethargic.

league. The Americans had a very speedy back-line, able to pinpoint gaps, and the forwards were big, mobile men, although some lacked the rugby league tackling technique. That was the problem: they lacked knowledge and the skills of the game but that was understandable. They were always chasing possession from scrums and the Aussie hookers easily out-hooked them as the Americans had a very limited idea of a hooker's role. They had real difficulties at the play the ball and kept losing the ball.

'They had two excellent kickers though – George Kauffman and Gary Kerkorian. Both were very accurate goalkickers and possessed powerful punt kicks.

'The crowds were most appreciative of the All Stars' attempts to play fast, open football, and we were thrilled with the long, gridiron-style passes.

'But the biggest problem was the number of players who made the tour – they just didn't have sufficient reserves available.'

Abajian: 'That was Dimitro's biggest mistake: not taking enough players. We all had to play every game.'

Al D. Kirkland: 'We had to stick with the best 13 players for big games and played the rest in the midweek games, just like they do on major rugby tours. Most international tours have 30 players – we had 15 or 16. It felt like Custer at Little Big Horn at times.'

Abajian: 'Everyone got boils. The doc thought we just weren't developing the antibodies to Australian infections. I was the last player to get a boil on my knee and I think it was because I had a bacteriology class at USC and I learned that methylide was a very good disinfectant, so I took a bottle with me and every time I got a wound I soaked it with methylide. But I forgot one or two games which is why I ended up getting one eventually. It was a terrible, terrible thing. Some of them had boils so bad they could hardly walk. It was the biggest detriment to us on the tour.'

Al D.: 'The UCLA guys were really over the hill. They didn't carry their end of the bargain. Drakulvich, Mike, Mandulay and Terry embarrassed themselves:

They're Still Trying

THE ALL STARS ON THE ATTACK

POCKETED, Brisbane full-back Norm. Pope props to cut back past attacking Americans Al. D. Kirkland (15) and Gary Kerkorian (11) in the Rugby League at the Cricket Ground yesterday. Brisbane won 39 to 26.

Battered Americans

THEY'RE SORE AND TIRED

Big, burly Pat Henry is one of the battered and bruised American All Star players who are "resting up" after their strenuous northern tour. Henry, in fact, is in the Mater Hospital with a septic knee. His pal and Stanford Varsity student mate, Jack Bonetti, is in a Townsville hospital with polio.

The Yanks were so sore and tired after the northern games they have asked for a postponement of the Ipswich match which was to have been played today. They meet Toowoomba on Wednesday and Ipswich the following Saturday.

Pat Henry has probably played his last game of the tour. He will be in hospital for at least five days, depending on the improvement of his leg. He injured the leg at Cairns and it turned septic.

Henry sums up the northern tour this way: "The people meant well and so, I suppose, did the officials who planned our itinerary. The organisation was good, but heck, there were far too few players for the size of the itinerary. I'd come back next year for another tour, but with at least 28 players. With that number of players it would be lovely."

Telegraph

they couldn't move! Drakulvich and Mandulay were never in shape. And Xavier was not too good either. Syd was our only hooker and played pretty much every game, as Jack did before he was ill. There was a lot of bitching going on, rather than actual protest to Dimitro. Fortunately, Teddy was good and Kerkorian was a natural.'

Abajian: 'You know, when you put 25 men together, and you're away for that long and under stress, you know all the good comes to the surface and all the bad surfaces. In our group – I hate to say this – but some of the guys were very lonely because nobody wanted to be near them.'

After 13 games in less than six weeks – more than any had played in a four-month college football season back home – the All Stars were on their weeping knees.

The week off was a godsend. Time to party. The bedroom walls of the National were in for some sights.

Al D.: 'Al E. and I didn't know each other before the trip but we had a room together because we had the same name so it was easier just to send all the letters

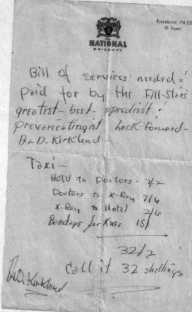

BIG, burly 26-year-old Pat Henry is one of the battered and bruised American All Star players who are "resting up" after their strenuous northern tour. Henry, in fact, is in the Mater Hospital with a septic knee. His pal and Stanford Varsity student mate, Jack Bonetti, is in a Townsville hospital with polio.

The Yanks were so sore and tired after the northern games they asked for a postponement of the Ipswich match which was to have been played today. They meet Toowoomba on Wednesday and Ipswich the following Saturday.

Pat Henry has probably played his last game of the tour. He will be in hospital for at least five days, depending on the improvement of his leg. He injured the leg at Cairns and it turned septic.

They're Sore
and Tired

Henry sums up the northern tour this way: "The people meant well and so, I suppose, did the officials who planned our itinerary. The organisation was good, but heck, there were far too few players for the size of the itinerary. I'd come back next year for another tour, but with at least 28 players. With that number of players it would be lovely.

"We were all upset when my buddy Bonetti went down with that polio. But he is a good kid and is keeping his chin up. He has a fiancee back in the States and he had planned to marry as soon as he returned home. We still reckon he will walk up that altar all right."

Good looking Bonetti

we got to our room. One night, after we'd played, I was exhausted and needed my bed. I went up to our room and the door was locked. Al E. shouted "give us a few minutes, Al". He had a girl in there, of course. So I went back down to the bar. I had a couple of drinks and went back up, really needing my bed. I knocked on the door and Al said "we're not done yet"!

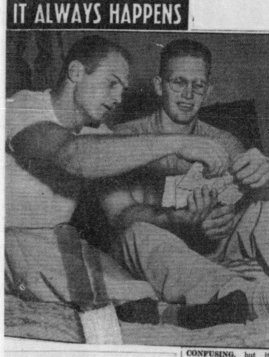

'Thirty minutes later the door was still locked so I said "I'm coming in – I'll sleep in the small bed". So I went in and tried to keep well out of the way and go to sleep. A bit later I heard "come on, let's do it again". She said: "No, Al D. is there." Then Al says to her: "Come on – he won't hear anything. It'll be more fun than eating an ice cream cone and riding a rollercoaster." With that I burst out laughing, the lights went on and she fled!

CONFUSING, but it happens all the time to Al E. (left), and Al D. Kirkland members of the All Stars' American Rugby League team, which arrived in Brisbane yesterday. They're both Al, share a common surname, but are no relation. And when the mail arrives, they've got to get together to sort out their letters.

'When I got home I got a letter from a girl – I don't know if it was that same one or another – accusing me of "trifling with her good intentions". I'd never even met her! I just thought it must've been Al E. He was like Kennedy: if he didn't have sex two to three times a week he'd get headaches. He firmly believed that.'

Dimitro received an invite from a local minister inviting the team to attend a special Footballers Service at Naremburn Congressional Church in the Northern Suburbs, followed by a short film on football tactics. The Reverend had noticed 'little room allowed for church attendance on Sundays' in the All Stars' schedule.

AUSTRALIAN RUGBY FOOTBALL LEAGUE BOARD OF CONTROL

SYDNEY
6-PM
17 JULY
1953
N S W AUST

BY AIR MAIL
PAR AVION

Mr. M. Dimitro,
Manager,
American Rugby League Touring Team,
C/- National Hotel,
BRISBANE.

IF NOT CLAIMED WITHIN 7 DAYS
PLEASE RETURN TO
BOX 4415 G.P.O., SYDNEY.

CHAPTER 17
TOMMY-ROT

The week off backfired badly. While Vince Jones went off to explore Melbourne – taking in a couple of Aussie Rules games while he was there – rumours swept Sydney that the tour was in danger of collapse.

10 JULY 1953

YANKS' TOUR MAY END EARLY
– DISSENSION WITHIN TEAM
Sydney Daily Telegraph

AMERICANS' TOUR "WILL GO AHEAD"
Sun

DENIAL ON ALL STARS
Mirror

There were three reasons why the pessimists were in clover: money worries; a massive injury list; and dissent in the ranks. Attendances had fallen away, but only to the level seen at most first grade games; of the original 20 players, only nine were fit after the Brisbane game; and the press reckoned one All Star was causing major dissent in the ranks: presumably Wild Bill.

Coach Robinson told any interested sports writer that this was a 'complete fabrication' but Harry Flegg confirmed the Ipswich game would be put back a week to give the All Stars some time to recover and Dimitro declared the show would go on.

Meanwhile, the NSWRL were at war with the *Sunday Telegraph*. The League considered themselves 'under attack'. Welcome to Propaganda City!

AMERICA GOES AHEAD

Rugby League is going to be played in America before long. The Australian Board of Control will see to that and there are many more teams coming from America to these shores in the years ahead. The present band of pioneers like the game and have quickly adapted themselves to it. Many of the tourists have sheaves of letters from home saying how popular the code has proved when screened on television in the States. Their people have made enquiries and found that the style of play is liked. That is only natural... The Board, much-criticised over this tour, has come out on top with the tour and established success.

Rugby League News
Editorial, 11 July 1953

★ ★ ★ ★ ★ ★ ★ ★ ★ ★ ★ ★

The Board also slipped in messages about the All Stars generating interest in the 13-man code in Canada and cursed Aussie Rules authorities for tempting Dimitro's gang to the south and west to play their game instead. Some of the drum-banging was justified, most of it tosh.

Dimitro took Sol, Han, Xavier and Ray Terry to lunch with *Sunday Mail* beat writer Jack Reardon – a former Kangaroo himself – to generate some positive press.

Dimitro fired out a list of changes he would make to rugby league to make it sell in the States: 60-minute games played in four quarters; injured players replaced at any time; one forward pass allowed per play and then only to a winger; wear long pants instead of shorts.

Even Ray Terry pointed out that this was basically a plan to turn league into American football.

Mike told Reardon that he planned a two-month tour of France, Italy and England with a bigger squad of players in 1954. On the same day, news broke that the British had pulled out of the World Cup series in France. Instead, the French would host incoming tours from Australia, New Zealand and, possibly, the Americans next May. It would be discussed at the International Board – but not until the New Year.

With no games to report on, smoke continued to surface. *Daily Mirror* columnist Jim Mathers thought he had got the full story:

League COULD be greatest game in the worl

BUT big bosses om "THE INSIDER" in gloom

rrent events have cast Rugby League's into abject and abysmal gloom.

...stren... defend.
...ard could be
...king that in-
...rs, most of
...living and
...for more
...ould get
...h.
...will be
...verses
...tra-
...
...as

...he
...ese
...ma-
...an over-
...

If rep...entative League s slipped, the drift is en more pronounced on dney's home front.

...emiership gates and per-ages are down, players' ...are shrinking propor-ately and worried offi-...are seeking to explain ...ng popularity.

...ey don't have to look ...The crowds have cooled ...ecause club League has is glitter.

ROAST RIVALS

...League has lost ...opularity with the r people, too.

...round-ballers have ...roasting the rival ...authorities ever since ...efused to grant Soc-...quest for three dates ...Cricket Ground, the ...the League holds the

...ward a week to July 25.

It could be coincidental, but that also is the day on which the American League team plays NSW at the SCG in a match that will mean a lot to tour finances.

Outsiders see in the move a hint of retaliation at the League for its denial of dates, but NSW Soccer As-sociation officials disclaims any such motive.

Whatever the reason, the decision is going to make a big difference to the League gate, because sport novel-ties take on these days and China-Australia Soccer Test comes under that head-ing.

Mr. Mike Dimitro won't like it.

EXPENSE PROBLEM

AN expenses slug has kept a lot of highly promising players out of the "Australian" Rugby Union team to leave for a six-match (no Tests) tour of Fiji on August 13.

The players each have to find £125 towards their indi-vidual expenses, which put Fiji out of reach for many, and illustrates the high cost of being an amateur these days.

The result is the team is hardly up to "middle grade" standard as it was flatter

WAS IT RIGHT FOR HASSETT TO RETIRE?

LONDON, Sat (Special) —Daily Express sports col-umnist queries the "retired hurt" rule in cricket and cites the case of Lindsay Hassett. He writes:

"In the Australian first innings of the second Test

The American All-Stars talk over Rugby League with Jack Reardon at The Sunday Mail office. Left to right: Sol Naumu, Harold Han,

Jack Rear and Ray T be m

All-Star Mike t

By Jack Reardon

AMERICAN All-Stars manager Mike Dimitro become the greatest game in the world if cer to the laws of the game.

The Americans are learning Rugby League the hard way from playing 13 matches in six weeks in locations from Canberra to Cairns and taking in western towns Dubbo (NSW) and Longreach (Q).

he plays at time to stay
4. Allow the a "play," to a winner HAROLD here save th

TUESDAY 14 JULY

LEAGUE ALL STARS SECRET OUT

The mystery of last night's secret meeting of the NSW members of the Australian Board of Control is OUT! "The American tour is not going bung. It will be completed and the Americans will also tour New Zealand," the chairman, Mr "Jersey" Flegg told me today. Further! A big conference between the Board of Control and the Americans will take place in Sydney on 24 July to draw up plans for establishing Rugby League with an organisation in America.

This statement will clear the air. Veiled talk about the American tour cracking up was indulged in at last night's meeting of the NSWRL. Mr Tom Brennan had applied the spark to the debate. He had seen the Americans in Brisbane last week and commented: "They looked done to a frazzle."

The Board met in an ante-room. Press men waited anxiously for the momentous announcement. After nearly an hour, the secretary emerged: "Gentlemen, we have decided to appoint Mr C. Pearce as referee of the match between the American All Stars and Riverina at Gundagai." The Board members moved around the room like Ku Klux Klanners. Everybody was convinced something startling had happened.

So I phoned Mr Flegg this morning. "Jersey" replied: "It is all tommy-rot for anyone to suggest the American tour is folding up. This has never been suggested, or implied. A week's rest from football will bring the Americans right back to the top and they will draw an enormous crowd on SCG on Saturday week."

There was certainly more going on than the Sydney press ever knew. Dimitro prepared to send a telegram home: 'Tour continued as planned. Ignore Kauffman's bologna (sic). He will take a slow boat back. Letter following, Didn't write couple days. Have cold.'

So it was the olive-skinned full-back Kauffman – a tall, dignified and respectable-looking chap, and his one-time UCLA ally – rocking the boat, not Wild Bill. And moving the Ipswich game now meant finishing the tour with six games in 15 games: a ludicrous schedule of Wednesday, Saturday, Sunday, Wednesday, Saturday, Wednesday. A killer. Something had to give. Dimitro knew it and so did the Board. The final two games on the schedule were more high profile clashes against world class opponents at the SCG: New South Wales again on Saturday 25 July and, on the Wednesday afternoon, Australia, supposedly but yet to be confirmed.

Even Iron Mike could not put his men through that. There would be no one left to board the plane to New Zealand. And Mackay Yanagisawa was still trying to arrange two football games to tag onto the end of the tour: on 30 August and 6 September – Labor Day – in Hawaii en route home. A re-think was essential.

YANKS KEEN ON REINFORCEMENTS

The Yankee All Stars are all for the suggestion that Australian "reinforcements" be used to help them finish off their Rugby League tour – but not before the completion of the Queensland itinerary. They want to see out the remaining three Queensland games. The Americans, in fact, had previously suggested the idea of a help out when casualties had begun to mount.

Brisbane Telegraph
By Harry Jefferies

15 JULY

Dimitro knew that borrowing a few star names would help bring fans through the gate and stop the slide in attendances that was threatening to leave him – and the Board of Control – in the red, let alone clearing several thousand dollars. Dimitro left it with Latchem to draft in some classy help by the time they got back to Sydney.

ALL STARS WON'T CUT TOUR

American manager Mike Dimitro last night discounted suggestions made in Sydney that the All Stars may not complete their tour of Australia.

"We are in as good shape as when we landed in Sydney," he said. "We started this tour and we'll finish it.

"We've lost Jack Bonetti, but the week's rest has helped us a lot."'

AUST V REST

NSW section of the Australian Board of Control yesterday suggested that the match in Sydney on 25 July be Kangaroos versus The Rest, with the best of the Americans included in The Rest.

QRL president (Mr Cyril Connell) replied immediately with his suggestion that four or five Queensland members of the Australian team be retained in Sydney on their return from NZ and included in the American team against NSW.

He said the Americans' coach, Norm Robinson, supported his view.

Robinson would know what Queensland players would be of greatest assistance to the Americans and should be allowed to select them.

CUT OUT NZ?

Mr Connell said he was also of the opinion that the Americans should abandon their tour of NZ and go home by ship after their last match in Sydney on 29 July.

"This way," he said, "the Americans should take some profit home with them. If they persist in their NZ tour they stand to lose any profit they made in Australia."

The Americans play Toowoomba today. Mike will play hooker as regular hooker, Sydney Walker, has withdrawn because of a sore neck. The Americans today will encounter a different type of football to any they have so far met in Australia. The Toowoomba style of backing up and continuous passing may bewilder them as it has other teams.

Jefferies, Brisbane Telegraph: The Yanks, with practically all their players recovered from injuries, boils etc., face a grim game. Toowoomba and State coach Duncan Thompson declared today: "We have trained hard for this match and there will be no easing up. This is an international game so far as we are concerned and we aim to win and in the best way possible."

The Americans should turn on their brand of spectacular football. They were a flop in their midweek match against Brisbane but when fit against Queensland had put on the best entertaining football for years.

The rejuvenated tourists were in high spirits when they boarded the train and headed out to the top of the Great Dividing Range, a couple of hours from Brisbane, to face Queensland half-back Cyril Connell and his Toowoomba boys in sky blue. Toowoomba: Queen City of the Darling Downs.

Ted: 'On the train into Toowoomba, the whole town is out on the platform to greet us. They've got the mayor, the band, the town goat. We're all leaning out of the window waving and they're clapping and cheering us. I look around and there's this hairy ass squashed up against the window: Ed's mooning them! The clapping stopped and the trumpet went "pooppp….". Unbelievable.'

Sol Naumu.

Once in the Athletic Oval, the Americans came out all guns blazing.

16 JULY 1953

Showing the benefit of their week's spell the American All Stars yesterday put more fire into their play against Toowoomba than has been previously seen from them.

Although beaten 29-15, the Americans made a good game of it. They started like winners and led 11-0 after eight minutes. The Yanks opened sensationally a minute after the start.

YANKS GO DOWN AGAIN, BUT MORE FIRE IN DISPLAY

By JACK REARDON

SHOWING the benefit of their week's spell the American All Stars yesterday put more fire into their play against Toowoomba than has been previously seen from them.

Courier Mail

George Court's
KARANGAHAPE ROAD.

INJURIES' TOLL

Forward Al D. Kirkland, who played well, also left the field in the second half with an injured knee and the Americans finished the game with 11 men. Han was injured in the first half but was replaced.

Star of the Americans was five-eighth Gary Kerkorian. He showed ability to switch play, handle and beat tacklers. He was also sound in defence.

Unfortunately Kerkorian had a day off in his goal kicking, usually most accurate, he succeeded only three times from nine attempts.

Flying winger Max Higgins scored 15 points from three tries and three goals and centre Russell Brown weaved his way to two tries.

WORTHY OF BEST

The Americans' first try scored by winger Bill Albans was worthy of the world's best winger. He took a pass from five-eighth Gary Kerkorian at half way, swerved round his opponent E. Ashman, sped along touch, then swerved again to beat fullback Bevan Hoyle and score between the posts.

Albans gave his best performance to date. He showed more inclination to tackle and ran well with the ball at all times. He left the field in the second half with badly skinned knees.

The Yanks were giving Toowoomba curry with robust tactics. Several of the Americans received cautions from Toowoomba referee Viv Vercoe, forward Fran Mandulay twice. He kicked recklessly in the rucks and it was fortunate no one was seriously injured. Cornell needed ambulance treatment while Mandulay was spoken to by referee Vercoe.

The American forwards tackled well around the rucks and bustled Toowoomba forwards off their game in the early stages as the Yanks battered the Toowoomba line...

Play was tough and hard as the Americans held on grimly to a surprisingly 13-11 half-time lead... They held on tenaciously and did not lose the lead till 15 minutes of the second half had passed. Toowoomba forwards were given a torrid time by their hefty opponents.

The country boys in sky blue were stunned. The All Stars were back – not fit but fighting.

CHAPTER 18
URGENT: HELP NEEDED

The cavalry was coming.

17 JULY 1953

Q'LD FOUR TO PLAY WITH ALL STARS IN RETURN SYDNEY GAME

Four Queensland Rugby League internationals will be included in the American All Stars team to play New South Wales at the Sydney Cricket Ground tomorrow week.

They are centre Ken McCaffery, lock Mick Crocker, second rower Brian Davis, and hooker Alan Hornery.

All are in NZ with the Australian team but they are due back in Sydney on Monday.

The Rugby League Board of Control decided in Sydney yesterday to include the Queenslanders in the All Stars team, which has been badly depleted by injuries.

It directed the All Stars coach, Norm Robinson, to select the four players, provided the American manager, Mike Dimitro, approved.

Courier Mail

The Four Horsemen: four Queensland Maroons including skipper McCaffery who had faced the NSW Blues at the SCG only a few weeks earlier. Could this be Dimitro's international rescue?

Before the big finale in Sydney, the All Stars had a week walkabout. Three games, three country towns, three teams ready to turn over these flash Yanks – and destroy what was left of them.

At the time, postponing the game at Ipswich had seemed a masterstroke. But rescheduling it for Saturday 18 July – just two days after Toowoomba and the day before playing Wide Bay – was lunacy. That meant four games in seven days, two in one weekend.

As Tiger Mike counted the bodies after the Toowoomba tussle he must have winced... then panicked. Al D. had joined the wounded list. After a week in a South Brisbane hospital, Pat Henry got straight onto a bus to head south-west to Ipswich on Saturday morning. But still Dimitro did not have a team. Refusing to face the ignominy of calling the game off, he agreed to include two ringers: local rugby union players who had to play under pseudonyms to protect their amateur status. Prop 'Jack Harald' was a 'Yankee living in Brisbane', the other a second row forward calling himself 'Pat Harvey' who ended up in hospital with a knee injury! Whoever they were, they were thrown into the bear pit.

19 JULY 1953
ALL STARS SAW STARS

Fists flew frequently in the second half of the Rugby League match between the American All Stars and Ipswich at North Ipswich Reserve this afternoon. Wild brawling tactics used by the American team showed that Australian referees had been ridiculously lenient with them.

A poor crowd of 2,500 paid £645 to see the visitors win one of the roughest games this season by 16 points to 15. There were continual fiery exchanges between forwards and fists flew freely. Team manager Mike Dimitro was spoken to by referee Les McMahon. In the second half, All Stars' winger, Albans, pushed referee McMahon aggressively, but McMahon just walked away.

TRUTH

The Greens had controlled the game at 6-0 before 'the All Stars fought back to score three good tries to lead 13-6 at the break – all three tries were the result of quick witted opportunism'. When Teddy went off injured, the All Stars brought on Sol. When Ipswich stand-off Ward left the field, the home side played with 12. And Wild Bill exploded.

YANKS WIN ROUGH GAME

Today's match was one of the dirtiest and wildest in Queensland for years. Punches and kicks were frequently made during the second half. Once the American, Albans, lost his temper and kicked Ipswich forward Rashleigh after a tackle. The incident happened in front of a linesman and Albans should have been sent off. Once Albans tried to attack the referee. Manager Mike Dimitro and winger Bob Buckley pulled Albans to the ground. Forwards also used their fists during the second half. At one stage there were groups of players exchanging punches.

Telegraph

Abajian: 'Bill had some strange ways. Some people thought he was crazy. We teased him about his stuttering. I remember against a very good team in Sydney, him hitting or kicking someone. That person got up and retaliated. A number of our team thanked them and said he deserved it!'

Pat Henry: 'I remember that game in Ipswich the most. We started with 13-a-side and ended up nine versus ten! There was what you might call a sudden disappearance. There were a lot of fights going on all over the field!'

It was a shambles. The news rapidly spread to New Zealand and scared the NZRFL.

Knowling to Dimitro: 'Some of our papers have naturally picked up on the worst reports which have come from Australia. The public in New Zealand is of a more sporting nature and are probably kinder to their visitors.'

The All Stars had only a few hours to tend their wounds and nurse their sore heads before flying up the Sunshine Coast to Maryborough, to take on Wide Bay on Sunday.

Another game: the last thing they needed.

20 JULY

CARELESSNESS COST ALL STARS LEAGUE MATCH

Carelessness cost the American All Stars their second win of the Queensland tour when they played a 33-all draw with Wide Bay at Maryborough Showgrounds yesterday. Holding a comfortable 25 to 8 lead at half time they obviously tried to coast through the second half and actually lost the match on the bell when a dropped pass in their own 25 was picked up by Faine, the Wide Bay fly half, who hurried himself across near the posts. Heidke goaled to make the match a draw.

The match produced few highlights. Late in the second half, Mike Dimitro, annoyed by a ruling by the referee, Mr N. Saunders, rushed in in a fighting attitude, but was stopped by other All Stars from creating a scene. Both sides were deplorably weak down the middle. The Americans frequently split the Wide Bay defence in the first half with Kirkland revealing himself as a class centre. Kirkland was the star player of the match but Abajian, Kerkorian, Naumu, Kauffman and Buckley revealed flashes of brilliance.

The Maryborough Herald

It was not the ideal way to finish their Queensland tour: nine games in a month, just one win, two draws and three narrow defeats to show for their huge efforts. At least the money flooded in. So did the invites: the West Australia RFL put 70 per cent of gate takings on the table to play a game in Perth and another invited the All Stars to an exhibition game of baseball in Brisbane. Neither offer was taken up, although Dimitro was still playing the hard-up card as the party flew back to Brisbane! He was already planning the next tour: to France.

The last week of the Australian tour was going to make or break them. They had one last night back in the comfort of the Prince Albert in Brisbane before the trek to the middle of nowhere: Wagga Wagga.

The *Daily Mirror* back in Sydney reported that the tour was all-square on Ray Terry's ledger – the All Stars had broken even with two to play. The Brisbane press thought otherwise.

PROFIT HERE, BUT YANKEES MAY LOSE ON AUST TOUR

American All Stars Rugby League team should make a substantial profit from their tour of Queensland for which they received about £6,000.

Mike Dimitro, who financed the tour, however, may finish 'in the red' on the whole tour of Australia due to heavy travelling expenses.

Gross 'gates' from their nine matches in Queensland were about £10,648. Receipts in NSW also compared favourably with other touring teams' 'gates'.

Estimated expenses of five weeks here are; Air travel, £1,100, hotel expenses £1,600, players expenses (£6 a week for 20) £600, incidentals £100, leaving an estimated profit of £2,600.

However, return air fares from America cost more than £10,000. The Americans have yet to complete their eight match tour of New Zealand, where the Australian team just broke even.

Mike is to have a conference with the Australian Board of Control in Sydney on Friday night regarding steps to be taken to promote League in America.

None of the Americans painted rosy pictures of League's future in America. It would have to be confined to a short season around January to March after the gridiron season is finished.

English Rugby League is interested and has asked the Australian League to procure information on the possibility of England playing in America on their way home from Australia next year.

Courier Mail

Knowling also cabled from Auckland. They would spread the New Zealand games out more, provide an experienced coach and fix ticket prices at international rates. But he reminded Dimitro that he would have to leave his slice of the pie in a Kiwi bank account.

Not that there would be much cash left anyway. There were bills to pay everywhere: hospitals, doctors, taxis. After nearly a month in Townsville, Jack Bonetti was ready to go home. It would cost nearly £200 to transfer him to Sydney: four seats for Jack on his stretcher and a return ticket for Sister Moffat to accompany him and ambulances from Mascot Airport to Sydney's Coast Hospital. Dimitro sought a sensitive nerve at Australian National Airways but found none.

Pat Henry told the Brisbane press: 'We were all upset when my buddy Bonetti went down with that polio. But he is a good kid and is keeping his chin up. He has a fiancé back in the States and he had planned to marry as soon as he returned home. We still reckon he will walk up that aisle all right.'

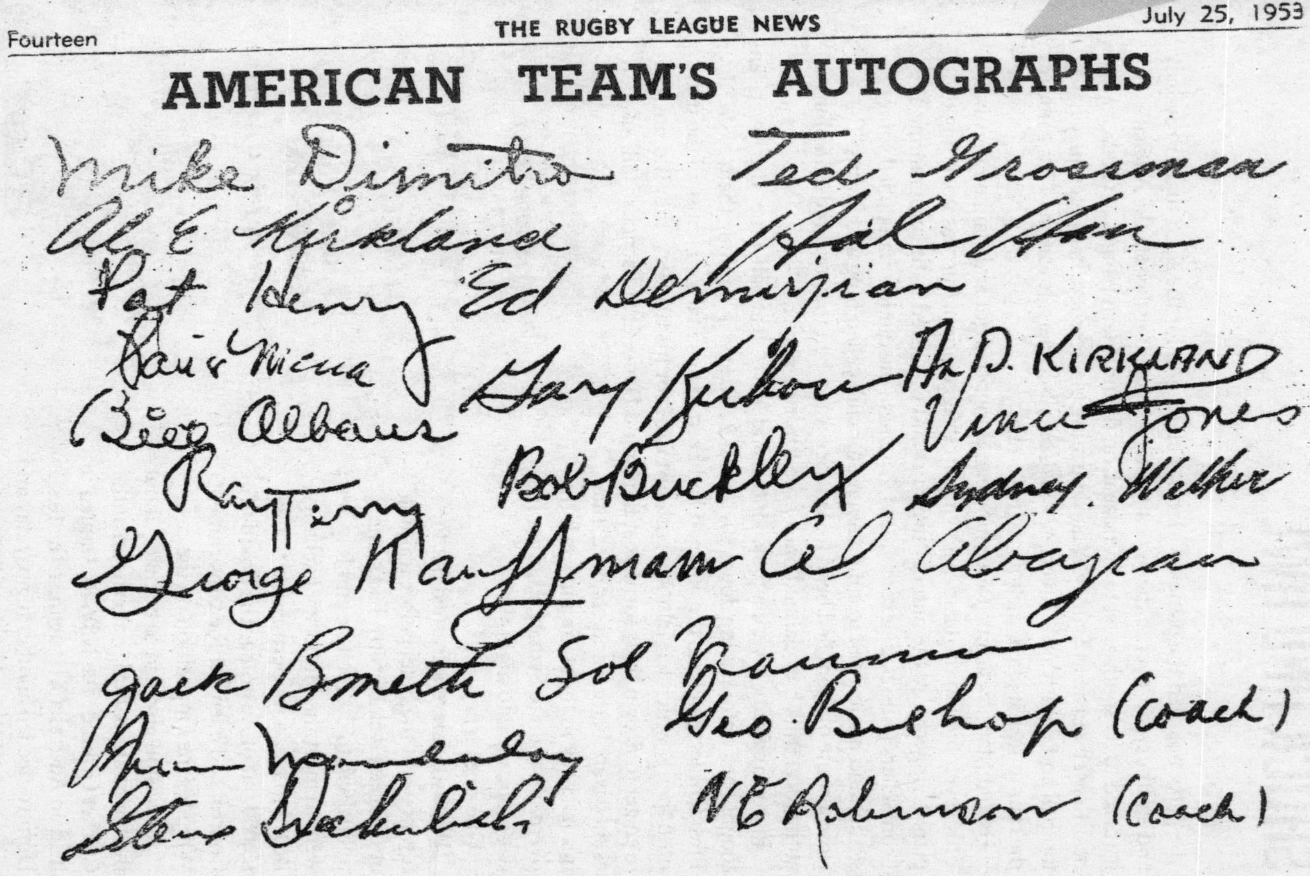

AMERICAN TEAM'S AUTOGRAPHS

Mike Dimitro

Ted Grosman

Alf Kirkland

Bob Hoffman

Pat Henry Ed Weinigrau

Louis Nieva

Gary Bukora

A.P. Kirkland

Bishop Osburn

Vince Jones

Bob Buckley

Sydney Webber

Ray Terry

George May

Norman Al Abraham

Jack Smith

Sol Rovere

Gen Bishop (coach)

Norm Vanderson

W. C. Robinson (coach)

Steve Wakulich

CHAPTER 19
SHOCK AND AWE

The party boarded the plane on Monday afternoon for the short flight to Sydney and another stop-over in the big city. After having Tuesday off, the All Stars gathered to fly south-west to Gundagai, on the northern fringes of Canberra, as near to Melbourne as Sydney. A hard farming place, where hard men play hard football and their team – Riverina – take on all-comers. It was the 17th game of the tour in just 58 days, the fourth in a week.

Harold Matthews came to see how bad things had got and claimed they had 'only seven men in the team'. Allowing for exaggeration, this was not going to plan. A ringer wore the number five shirt and was listed in the programme as Leon Sellers (who had never left LA). Latchem, the old fox, had pulled some strings and made a call to a Balmain junior club called Bing and Swing. 'The closest some of them had been to America was when they ordered a hamburger at the local milk bar,' claimed one of the Riverina players.

In pouring rain, Riverina took control and led 14-0 at half-time. The Americans fought back before going down 30-14. Just 2,560 saw it – among them NSWRL President Jersey Flegg: the old man had been in hospital for almost all the tour until then – which left Dimitro with just £281 for his troubles. They did not even get to drown their sorrows at the Grand Dance at St Patrick's Hall. As soon as they were bathed and changed, they headed back to the station to catch the overnight train to Sydney. Another long day's journey into night.

One week left.

While the players crashed out for a few hours at the hotel before training at Coogee Oval, Dimitro had some politicking to do. First he and Ray Terry went to meet the Monetary Exchange Board to plead for permission to take £3,000 out of Australia. The Board of Control had even got the Government Whip for the Opposition on the case.

A decision also had to be made about the big finale: Saturday afternoon at the Cricket Ground. The NSWRL wanted to field an Australia XIII against The Rest. Dimitro needed another big pay day and requested NSW against the All Stars (and their Queenslander guests). He got his

AMERICAN
RUGBY LEAGUE TOUR OF
AUSTRALIA

"ALL STARS"
v.
RIVERINA

Anzac Park
GUNDAGAI
Wednesday, July 22, 1953

Souvenir
Programme
1/-

wish and the Sydney public got to know about it. Friday evening and Saturday morning were spent in radio studios: ABC, 2SM and 2UW, then 2GB, 2UW again, 2CH and 2KY. Dimitro was all talked out by Saturday lunchtime but they needed bums on seats and hats on the hill after a series of reduced turn-outs had put his planned windfall in serious jeopardy.

There was no Premiership programme, but Saturday afternoon would still be a hard sell: it was the Americans' sixth game in the area (their third at the SCG); the China soccer team was in town to play Australia at the Sydney Showground; and there was the usual card of rugby union and Aussie Rules club games across the city. In the end, over 20,000 turned up: about half of what went to see the Chinese hammer the Aussies but almost twice what was expected at the big Souths-Canterbury clash at Redfern the following week.

The NSW selectors chose a 'benevolent XIII'. It still included the likes of Churchill, Wells, Pidding, Kearney and Bull but also some up and coming talent. They called up prop Jack Gibson from Easts who had started the season as a reserve in the Roosters' third grade, wore the number 55 jersey, but was now ripping it up in first grade. He was turning heads on Saturday afternoons and turning people away on Saturday night.

He worked the doors at some of the city's most intense entertainment establishments, including 'Thommo's Two-Up School' – an illegal gambling den in Surry Hills where thousands were bet on the toss of a coin. His predecessor had been shot dead. That didn't stop Gibson taking a job driving owner Joe 'The Boss' Taylor around Sydney in his black Pontiac. Gibson had seen the Americans at The Celebrity Club when they were first in town.

★ ★ ★ ★ ★ ★ ★ ★ ★ ★ ★

PIDDING'S KICKS SAVE N.S.W. AGAINST AMERICAN TOURISTS

New South Wales yesterday had to rely on winger Noel Pidding's goal-kicking to clinch a 27-18 win over a combined America-Queensland team, in a Rugby League match at Sydney Cricket Ground.

Pidding kicked three brilliant long-range goals in a crisis during the second half after America had led 18-16.

The Queenslanders – McCaffery, Crocker, Davis and Hornery – played splendidly. Their play and guidance allowed the Americans to show outstanding possibilities as League players. American half-back Teddy Grossman confessed: "I learned more playing beside those Queensland guys today than in all the rest of the tour."

By George Crawford

Clive Churchill admitted Mike's mob were much better than their first appearance at the SCG in May and credited much of that to the leadership of Crocker and McCaffery, and suggested they should have had that experience earlier in the tour.

Al D. Kirkland: 'McCaffrey would have made a great running back in football back home. Crocker was a great lineman and Hornery was a great hooker. Alan was dishonest from the word go, though!'

There was no Kauffman at full-back, no Han in the centres, no Big Al D. in the pack. The Sydney fans were impressed by the bravery the remaining Yanks showed: 'Spectators in the Members Stand, quick to acknowledge the improvement, stood and applauded the Americans off the ground after the match.'

With Sol and Mandulay joining the disabled list, NSWRFL medical officer Dr Greenberg reckoned none of the 11 Americans who played would have been passed fit to compete in a Test match. He told the *Sunday Herald*: 'Every player has some disability – influenza, boils, or some muscular or tendon trouble. Considering their injuries I thought they gave a marvellous display.'

SUNDAY 26 JULY 1953

YANKEE DOODLE DANDIES WERE REALLY DANDY

Serious criticism of yesterday's play is not warranted – it was a light-hearted blaze of popularity, crowd-pleasing and that is the finest compliment I could pay the visitors in these rock-me-to-sleep days of international sport. The crowd wanted the Americans to win, It cheered them with full-throated applause in the closing stages. When the referee awarded a penalty to America, Al E. Kirkland took up a strategic stand behind several players and ceremoniously did a salaam to the referee in grateful thanks for his benevolence. It was a neat act that took 20 seconds to perform. The crowd applause called for an encore but the game must go on. Anyway, the crowd saw more color and action in the last 20 minutes than for many a long day.

Referee Aubrey Oxford did not give the Americans any latitude. Actually he was quite harsh on them during the second-half. With a little luck the Americans could have won.

TRUTH

By Jim Mathers

★ ★ ★ ★ ★ ★ ★ ★ ★ ★ ★

Strangely, the home crowd went so far towards supporting the underdogs that they actually turned on their own side. They laughed when Oxford allowed Pidding to score from a clearly offside position in the first half, and booed Churchill for some dismal full-back play, missing attempted tackles on Albans and Davies that led to tries. Only Dimitro's lack of speed saw him bomb a try late on, laid on a plate for him by McCaffery. 'I would have needed the Grace of God to have scored that try,' Dimitro told *TRUTH*. 'I simply couldn't run the extra 20 yards with nobody in front of me.'

Geoff Allen, who called it 'a farcical match', was impressed again by Al E., who justified the hype around him with 'a smart display that might get him a game with Balmain firsts'.

Crawford was particularly excited by Wild Bill: 'Earlier in the tour, Albans had been bewildered and temperamental, often refusing to run with the ball. Now "a reformed character" Albans showed great speed and control of pace in his 40-yard run to score a really brilliant try. He first veered infield, then straightened to catch the New South Wales defence off balance. Going down the centre he beat full-back Clive Churchill with a neat change of pace. This try, and several other runs later, established Albans as the most improved player in the team.'

And yet. And yet. After 'a tame and ludicrous first half', all hell broke loose.

Geoff Allen wrote: 'Tempers frayed in two wild incidents. Albans was tackled and pushed to the ground. He lashed out wildly and kicked Bull, who retaliated. The game was held up while Albans received first aid attention and Bull was cautioned by the referee. The crowd roared "send him off" as Oxford, accompanied by a touch judge, spoke to Bull. Albans, who had shown a fiery temper earlier in the match, was then cautioned by the referee. But hoots turned to handclaps as Albans and Bull walked off the field arm-in-arm after the match, but were lucky that they had not returned to the Members' Stand earlier.

'Late in the match, Kerkorian punched NSW captain Clive Churchill after Churchill had kicked to clear his line during a wild American rally. The game went on after a touch-judge had raced to the centre of the field. Amid loud hooting from the crowd, Oxford awarded NSW a penalty kick from the spot where the ball had landed after the fracas. Again the crowd booed as Pidding took the penalty kick and missed.'

Wild Bill was on the brink.

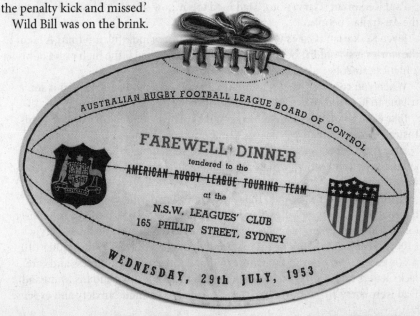

AUSTRALIAN RUGBY FOOTBALL LEAGUE BOARD OF CONTROL

FAREWELL DINNER

tendered to the

AMERICAN RUGBY LEAGUE TOURING TEAM

at the

N.S.W. LEAGUES' CLUB
165 PHILLIP STREET, SYDNEY

WEDNESDAY, 29th JULY, 1953

Jack Bonetti arrives in Sydney.

The All Stars had had enough. They could not follow that performance with another two days later. In a hastily arranged summit meeting in the Americans' dressing room after the game, Dimitro begged to scrap the final fixture at the SCG. It was a game too far. Overkill. Thankfully, the Board of Control agreed.

Dimitro hardly had a team left. Henry, Buckley, Han, Kauffman, and Abajian all had infected leg wounds; Jones had an infected face; Walker had acute dermatitis and Teddy had done his shoulder, while Gary had flu. The doctors' fees were growing.

Kerkorian's adventure was over anyway. Although he had not made it in Pittsburgh, he had another chance to crack pro football. LA Rams offered him a deal, albeit replacing the legendary Bob Waterfield as back-up quarter-back to Norm Van Brocklin. Coach Hamp Pool knew Kerkorian could play quarter-back, defensive back and kick goals, just like Waterfield, but he was hardly the glamour boy Waterfield was. Kerkorian left Sydney high on life. He took Jack Bonetti home with him.

Paul Kerkorian (Gary's son): 'Dad used to say how much fun it was. He loved the Australian people.'

Joyce Kerkorian (Gary's widow): 'He had a most wonderful, fun time. A lot of the stories just couldn't be told in public! He considered it the high point of his athletics career because it was so much fun.'

When you consider what Kerkorian achieved on a football field, that is some tribute to his team-mates and the game of rugby league.

Like Kerkorian, Jack Bonetti too should have been joining up with the Rams. Instead, he was flying home, never to play football again.

Jack: 'After a few weeks in Townsville, I was sent home to San Francisco for another month or so in a children's hospital where the polio experts were. Then I went home.'

His life was never the same. The faces on the Townsville sports scene – international swimmers, divers and entertainers – agreed to put on a fundraiser for Jack and the Board of Control launched a fund for him. The Board put in £100, NSWRL £50, South Sydney £10 and Souths supporters' club another £10.

His parents wrote from Livermore to thank Mike for his 'kindness and care'. Jack's letters home always talked of a 'swell bunch of fellows' and his Mum and Dad were sorry 'this unfortunate tragedy had caused undue anxiety and expense and had more or less dimmed the enjoyment of the entire group'. They wished the tour to continue 'as if nothing had happened': 'We feel that Jack, with his will to win, will recover from this, and will again be able to enter sports which he has always enjoyed.' His case was 'apparently mild and he will fully recover'. Reality had yet to kick in.

Jack: 'I thought "why me?" I didn't smoke or drink and I'd had no affairs and yet it was me who came down with polio. They discovered the vaccine in 1954 – a few months too late. It was very difficult to handle. I was a real son of a bitch for a couple of years. But I was so taken by the way the Aussies treated us. I made lifelong friends on that trip – it was still a truly great experience.'

Bob Buckley and Harold Han headed back to LA where their football coach at USC waited anxiously for their safe arrival. They were terrified that they would be deemed professionals and become ineligible for their senior year. They need not have worried.

After his thrilling runs and violent outbursts in the final game, Wild Bill Albans quit the tour, too.

'Dimitro promised us £12 10s a week but we only got £5,' he told the press. 'Some of us lost heavily to make this tour.' So much for the strictly amateur trip. Injured players had resorted to hawking team photo cards around the members' area at the SCG during the final game at two shillings a go. They found few takers.

The all-conquering St George club were far from happy. The state premiers had put on a Sunday morning function following the final game against NSW only for just three of the Americans to show up. Having sent a fleet of cars to the All Stars' hotel to find them still in bed, St George secretary Baden Wales was so angry he told the NSWRL that he would boycott the All Stars' farewell function put on by the Board of Control on Wednesday night.

An indignant Dimitro stood by his men. 'I told League officials several days beforehand that my boys would not attend the St George function because they wanted their last Sunday free to entertain friends they had made in Sydney,' he told the local press. 'It was not my fault that the information was not passed on to the St George club.'

Exactly who those 'friends' were is left to conjecture. A bunch of 20-something athletes, on the other side of the world from home, can hardly be faulted for wanting to indulge in some fun on their last weekend in the big city. Boys will be boys – and what goes on tour...

Al D. Kirkland: 'We didn't have much entertainment put on for us in Sydney. We had to go find it ourselves. There was a travelling production of the musical South Pacific. Somebody who knew somebody who knew somebody got us tickets. There were three American girls in the troupe. We went backstage and I said: "I just want to talk to a girl who doesn't have an Australian accent!" Somebody fixed me up with Nellie Forbush. She was the nurse. I asked her out for dinner. Vince Jones went out with a girl whose stage name was Victoria Principle. A beautiful girl. If you can't find fun in Sydney you can't find fun, period!"'

On the Monday night, Vince was an 'outstanding' guest speaker at the Australian-American Association at the Trocadero club. His team-mates had finally got their wish to replace risqué Mike with the eloquent Vince as the public voice of the tour party.

The last night brought the All Stars' farewell dinner, hosted by the Lord Mayor at the Leagues Club in Phillip Street: oysters, soup, fish, pork, ice cream, the works. And of course Jim Mathers was there to tell his *Daily Mirror* readers about when 'the curtain fell on the Greatest Show on Earth'.

Jersey Flegg gave an amusing, rambling speech: 'I really don't know where to start. So many things have happened since the American All Stars came to Australia. The All Stars have done something that will put rugby league on the map all over the world. Mike, you will find the people of Australia behind you. Australia has broken the ice.'

The Americans lined up on stage behind Flegg and Co and they all sang 'Now Is The Hour When We Must Say Good-Bye' followed by 'Auld Lang Syne'.

The only dissenting voice came from a little old man who stood up at the back of the banqueting hall: 'Well what do you all know about that? I founded the League. Without me, there would be no dinner tonight… And they didn't give me a mention in their speeches.'

'Who are you?' a stranger asked.

'Me? I'm Dally M. They call me "The Master".'

★ ★ ★ ★ ★ ★ ★ ★ ★ ★ ★

Just as the players were packing up and preparing to leave Sydney – and Australia – at midnight for what would be, for all but one, the last time, the whole shooting match blew up. Dimitro was served with a writ to stop him leaving the country. The Supreme Court of New South Wales summoned him to King Street Court House to answer charges brought by Civic Hire Service of Pott's Point. The front page of the *Daily Telegraph* announced: 'CAR FIRM SUES MIKE DIMITRO'.

The hire-car company were owed nearly £45 for cars Dimitro had rented throughout July. At 5.30pm Dimitro was in Court 2 in front of Mr Justice McClemens at a special sitting.

'I wrote out the cheque to give to the hire-car company,' the stocky

Daily Mirror billboard

wise-guy told the court, blaming the NSWRL for not passing it on. 'I have paid all my bills and I leave the country with a clean sheet. I wrote out a cheque for £500 and my cheque is just as good as any other cheque in Australia.'

Al D. Kirkland: 'Not paying for the cars and trying to flee the country? That sounds like Mike.'

Dimitro settled during an adjournment and the case was dismissed. But that wasn't the end of his troubles.

A Sydney woollen firm instructed solicitors to start proceedings to recover £83 from four members of the American team: Fran Mandulay, Steve Drakulvich and Pat Henry, who had only put a down-payment on suit lengths they had ordered from the firm. Iron Mike had not paid a penny of his £40 bill. 'Several times we have notified Dimitro that this money was still owing,' chairman of the firm, Charles Parsons, told the Sydney press. 'We notified him last by hand. It is an extraordinary thing for international sportsmen deliberately to set out to order goods and leave the country without paying for them. New Zealand should be warned.'

"Hasn't she ever heard of ODO·RO·NO?"

The nerve of some people . . . and a good thing, too!

It's no secret that people perspire. Everyone does to some degree. Yes, even you! Perspiration evaporates quickly from most of the body, but not from under the arms. So it goes stale. It soils and spoils your clothes. Worst of all, it leaves that tell-tale odour you, yourself, may not notice, but others certainly will.

A daily bath isn't enough. Talcum powder isn't enough. Perfume isn't enough. Only an effective deodorant *and* anti-perspirant like Odo-Ro-No gives you complete under-arm protection — not for seconds, not for minutes, but for the full 24 hours.

ODO-RO-NO CREAM

Make Odo-Ro-No your nicest daily habit

As the firm's solicitors applied for a writ in Auckland, they received a cheque for £55 – of the £72 still owing – signed by Dimitro and sent the previous day by the ARFL so backed off. The Americans were losing friends rapidly.

Dimitro challenged Harry Flegg's claim that they had 'cut even' on the tour. With no final game, Dimitro's financial statement to the Board of Control claimed his 60 per cent share in gate income from 18 matches was £16,376 with expenses of £16,970. Another spreadsheet claimed his share was £16,816.

He said: 'I guess it's good enough to call "cut even" but no one is taking into consideration some thousands of dollars it cost me to assemble the team. I had to mortgage everything I owned and also borrowed from the father of my assistant manager, Ray Terry, to cover the cost of assembling my team. You've got to remember that there was no rugby league organisation in America to back me. I had to stand the brunt of the lot. It's all right for Australian officials to say we "cut even" on the tour. Such statements lend the belief that the tour was more or less a success. But it seems that no one cares about the liabilities back home.'

Dimitro wouldn't disclose how much he had spent at home but claimed he was down £594 on the tour. That was a vast improvement on the £4,500 figure he had previously given. As *Rugby League Review* reported, 'he was going to make up the deficiency with seven or eight matches in New Zealand and a couple of gridiron matches in Honolulu on his way home'.

With Kerkorian and Albans gone and Vince stuck in Sydney while an abscess on his nose healed, there were just 14 Americans on board the plane, and three of them were injured: Mandulay, Mena and Walker.

Dimitro had negotiated for four different Aussie pros to accompany the All Stars to New Zealand: Kangaroo front-rower Duncan Hall as player-coach, Balmain reserve grade full-back Jim Matthews, former Balmain lock Gene Barakat – who had helped with coaching at Coogee at the start of the tour – and former South Sydney Junior Brian McKeown.

Before they headed to the gate at Mascot, there were some final words for the *Herald* hack as Dimitro suddenly admitted: 'It is nearly impossible to establish rugby league in America. The best we can do is keep in contact with the All Stars when we get home so that we can play exhibition matches if needed.'

Hardly a rallying cry.

A group of players also said they had no plans to play league again. They thought there would be no move to establish rugby league back in the States because gridiron was too popular; the All Stars lived too far apart for them to play together regularly; they did not know enough about league to coach it; they would all resume their American football careers that autumn; and some had military training while others were returning to university.

That went down like a cup of cold chowder with the now hostile Sydney press. Alan Hulls called the Board of Control 'pig-headed' for going through with the tour, the finances were 'in the mysterious class', and claimed there would be 'screams of anguish' if the NSW and Queensland Rugby Leagues have to cover any losses. He said: 'There can be no doubt that the tour has done rugby league grave harm. The tour will inevitably be known as "Flegg's Follies of 1953".'

Everyone had had enough of Dimitro's shenanigans. The Board of Control drew the line too.

That evening the ARFL told their Kiwi counterparts that no Aussies would tour with the Americans. Hall had flown down from Brisbane and checked in to a North Sydney hotel before heading for the Leagues Club. He had not appeared at the airport, presumably told to stay put at Norths.

Jim Matthews withdrew. McKeown decided to go anyway. The party boarded the plane. Harold Matthews put his foot down, insisting McKeown could not go. Matthews told the press it was the NZRL's decision: they wouldn't allow any Australian guest players. Barakat was waived: as a Kiwi by birth, who had played football in New Zealand in 1952, he could go where he liked.

For 30 minutes the rest of the bemused All Stars sat on the plane on the tarmac as McKeown's luggage was found and removed. The trip was becoming farcical.

'It would have been an ideal theme for an American fiction writer in a dime magazine, said *RL Review*. For once they were not exaggerating.

SENSATIONAL FINISH TO TOUR

– DIMITRO GOES TO COURT BUT NOT TO CLUB FUNCTION
"GRIDIRON OUR FIRST LOVE" SAY PLAYERS

The American Rugby League team's pioneering tour of Australia ended in tragedy unparalleled in the history of the game. Business firms took legal action against the Americans to recover debts, manager Mike Dimitro announced a heavy financial loss on the tour, four players withdrew from the New Zealand section of the tour and went back to America.

There was also bitter criticism in official circles of the Americans' failure to meet certain social obligations. In return for that, a member of the New South Wales Rugby League Management Committee openly announced he would personally boycott the Australian Board of Control's farewell dinner to the Americans.

But worst of all – from a football angle – the Americans, before their departure, declared that gridiron football would remain their first love and that there was little chance that rugby league would become established in America.

Back Row: BILL MOORE (Trainer), TED GROSSMAN, PAT
Middle Row: SOL NAUMU, GARY KERKORIAN, GEORGE KAUFFMANN, BI
Front Row: ED. DEMIRJIAN, JACK BONETTI, BOB BUCKLEY, MIKE DI
In Front: AL

EAGUE TOURING TEAM

LAND TOUR, 1953

ROLD HAN, AL E. KIRKLAND, LATCHEM ROBINSON (Coach).
STEVE DRAKULVICH, RAY TERRY (Assistant Manager), FRAN MANDULAY.
ger-Coach), VINCE JONES (Captain), AL. D. KIRKLAND, XAVIER MENA.
YD. WALKER.

THURSDAY 30 JULY 1953

MATCH WEARY ALL STARS LEAGUE PLAYERS HERE

Fourteen of Mike Dimitro's American All Stars Rugby League players have reached New Zealand. Of the original party of 20 that toured Australia, only 14 are left for the nine-match itinerary of New Zealand. When they arrived here by T.E.A.L. flying-boat this morning the Americans were a wiser group of men than when they spent a brief hour here on their way to Australia in May. Then they did not realise the toughness of the tour that lay ahead. But, taking it all round, Mike Dimitro is pleased with the display of his men.

Courier

★ ★ ★ ★ ★ ★ ★ ★ ★ ★ ★ ★ ★

Al D. Kirkland: 'Taking the flying boat from Australia to New Zealand was kinda exciting.'

Abajian: 'It took six hours and just after that they invented the jet and we could have done it in an hour and a half.'

Arriving by *The Aotoreoa* – a British Commonwealth Pacific Airlines flying boat – had style, though. The 'luxury' mode of transport whisked them across the Tasman and, with room for few other passengers on board, it felt like a private aircraft taking them to not just a different country but another land in another time.

The players posed for a group photo as they crouched on the tarmac at Mechanics Bay, Ray Terry looking like Mickey Cohen in wide-lapelled camel coat and trilby,

AMERICAN RUGBY LEAGUE PLAYERS ARRIVE: Members of the All Stars team after arrival by flying-boat at Mechanics Bay yesterday.

American League Players Arrive for Tour

First Game Against Auckland At Carlaw Park Tomorrow

Hard grounds, long travelling and injuries in addition to playing a new game were some of the difficulties which faced the American All Stars Rugby League team in Australia, said the manager, Mr Mike Dimitro, on the side's arrival in Auckland by air yesterday. Accompanying him were 13 equally weary players who will begin a short tour of New Zealand with a match against Auckland tomorrow at Carlaw Park.

Dimitro centre stage in a kipper tie, the others in an array of hats and trench coats and macs, over the official tour blazer. One wore a pith helmet, Big Al D. was in his Aussie army digger's hat.

Dimitro blamed bad luck, infections, diet changes and hard grounds for his depleted numbers, while claiming his team 'ran out of gas' when victory was in sight several times. There was some truth in all of this. But whose fault was it? Only Dimitro knew how many games they would play and how few players he had. Only Dimitro could know how ill-prepared his overworked men were to face top-class professionals on rock-hard ovals every couple of days.

But the Ohio big mouth was still working the bright side: Aussies would soon be trying out their crowd-pleasing gridiron passes, he claimed.

By the time they headed into downtown Auckland for a practice session with New Zealander Gene Barakat on Thursday afternoon, Dimitro did not even have a team. Just 11 Americans hobbled on to the hallowed turf of Carlaw Park. As soon as he arrived in the Kiwi capital, Syd Walker had gone straight to Lavington Hospital with an infected neck, Fran Mandulay also had an infection, and George Kauffman was injured, too. Vince Jones was still lying in a Sydney hospital getting his vicious boils treated.

The NZRFL Council agreed to cut the schedule. It would now be one midweek and one Saturday game per week. The game against South Island in the far reaches of Dunedin (next stop: South Pole) was cancelled and the fixtures with North Auckland at Whangarei and South Auckland at Huntly were 'subject to review'. But Knowling confirmed that Barakat – a former player with Richmond and South Auckland but now registered with the NSWRL – would not be allowed to play. Instead, plans were afoot to strengthen the All Stars with some local giants.

MULCARE WILL PLAY FOR AMERICANS TODAY

P.A. AUCKLAND, July 31.

Four New Zealanders, Barchard, Mulcare, Hardwick and Roff, will be included in the American All Stars Rugby League team which is to play Auckland tomorrow, in the opening match of the tour.

The teams are:

All Stars: Fullback, S. Naumu; wings, A. Abajian and E. Demirjin; centres, L. D. Kirkland and L. E. Kirkland; five-eighth, T. Crossman; halfback, N. D. Barchard; back row, F. Hardwick; second row, F. Mulcare and M. Dimitro; front row, S. Drakulovich, R. Roff and X. Mena.

Auckland: D. White; J. Edwards, T. Baxter; V. Bakalich; C. Eastlake and W. Sorenson; K. Graham; W. Goulin; D. Richards-Jolley and J. Riddell; J. Wright, G. Davidson and J. Meates.

FRIDAY 31 JULY

Four New Zealanders, Des Barchard, Fran Mulcare, Travers Hardwick and Ray Roff, will be included in the American All Stars Rugby League team which is to play Auckland tomorrow, in the opening match of the tour.

The Kiwis had saved the day – and the tour.

Mulcare, all Brylcreemed white quiff and steely glare, was rated as the best forward in the world. He had scored the Kiwis' final try in their win in Sydney which clinched their shock series victory over Australia in 1952. He was a phenomenon. Getting Mulcare on board was a marketing coup – let alone a huge addition to the team. He even missed a vital West Coast Championship game with his club side, Ngahere, to join up with the All Stars.

Fran Mulcare: 'The morale of the All Stars was at a low ebb – there had been 18 physically sapping, tough games. Dimitro indicated that they could not or would not tour New Zealand. The NZRL decided to supply four players who would provide skills in key positions, so the tourists agreed to complete the tour. I was picked as a second rower and the dummy half player for the team.'

Travers Hardwick was considered South Auckland's finest product in a decade. Typical of even the very best New Zealand players, he resisted Sydney's lure to stay in his homeland, and therefore remained an amateur player even when he captained the Kiwis to that series win over the Kangaroos. Hardwick made his living running a drapery store in Tokoroa, where he was The Man about town.

Des Barchard was a former Auckland rugby union player who switched codes and became the best stand-off in New Zealand, touring the world with the Kiwis.

Ray Roff, the craggy-faced hooker from Auckland's Mount Albert club, was quick and hard around the ruck and had represented New Zealand at home and abroad. Barchard and Roff would face up against their own mates in the Auckland team.

Mulcare: 'Hardwick was an outstanding loose forward and captain for New Zealand but on the verge of retirement. Barchard was another outstanding half-back, also about to retire. Ray Roff was one of New Zealand's most skilled hookers.'

Mulcare flew up from the South Island and joined the rest of the squad ensconced at the Station Hotel. The contrast between the Kiwis and the Californians was clear: Roff and Mulcare, uptight, anxious, nervous, always sporting their NZRL blazers, collared shirts and ties; the Americans relaxed in plaid, Mickey Cohen collars, sports coats or college baseball jackets, with pin badges on their lapels.

Hardwick and Barchard took over the coaching, starting with Friday's session on a blissfully soft Carlaw Park. They had one day to organise Dimitro's battle-scarred troops to provide some resistance against an Auckland side that featured half the New Zealand Test team. All in all, most of the Kiwi team would be at Carlaw Park, wearing Auckland's hoops or the Americans' stars and stripes.

Mulcare: 'In my first training at Carlaw I was impressed with their skills. The backs in particular were relaxed, fast runners with beautiful ball skills. Sol Naumu was a hard

ONE SHILLING

League News

AMERICAN ALL STARS v. AUCKLAND

Saturday, August 1st, 1953   CARLAW PARK, 2.30 p.m.

and fast running winger; Al Abajian an equally good centre; Teddy Grossman a quarter back in gridiron and perhaps the most deceptive carrier of the ball; Al E. Kirkland, a five-eighth – perhaps the finest player on the team. Two forwards who showed real talent were Vince Jones and the other Al Kirkland, both big powerful and fast front-rowers.'

One listings ad in the Auckland press claimed Al D. Kirkland was one of the finest forwards in American football (and came from Kansas – he did not) while Alvin Kirkland was a 'brilliant centre': 'When the Americans take the field tomorrow you will be greatly impressed by the physique of every one of the players: the lightest man is 12st 12lb and they average over 14st. They are here to show us a brand of League football that is spectacular in the extreme and we are going to enjoy it.'

Maybe it was not all hype.

Mulcare: 'The Americans were intelligent, educated men. Most of them had outstanding physiques. In the main they were highly skilled in basic football talents such as running, handling, passing and kicking – on a par with, if not higher than, international level Australian and New Zealand players playing then. But – and it was a huge but – they lacked the knowledge and positional skills on attack and defence. This was the major factor in the wins/losses. Coaches Hardwick and Barchard had to curb some of the unorthodox play, such as torpedo passes more or less the width of the field. It was a pity, but necessary. It took away a lot of the natural ebullience.'

News spread throughout New Zealand, even to isolated Greymouth, where the front page of *The Grey River Argus* told locals vital news: 'Eggs Will Be Cheaper From Next Monday'.

SATURDAY 1 AUGUST 1953, CARLAW PARK
AUCKLAND V ALL STARS

Carlaw Park: League Headquarters. Where every cup final, championship game, Test and tour match was played, set at the bottom of Dominion Hill in the heart of Auckland. Most visitors left the former market garden with nothing but bruises and humility. Players found mud in places they never knew mud could go. They would discover it days after playing there. The spiritual home of Kiwi league, it was hardly a daunting venue at first sight, not compared with the vast bowls of Stanford, Berkeley or Pasadena. A little wooden grandstand with its press box precariously mounted on the roof, smart picket fence and steep banks – too steep to stand in the corners at the Scoreboard end, where there was always 'Time for a Capstan' – it must have just looked quaint to the All Stars.

Carlaw was intimate, not intimidating. Well not until thousands of Kiwi League fans rolled down the hill and through the bright white art-deco gates to fill it. Then it was transformed into a heaving, oppressive pit where reputations were made or destroyed. The Brits and the French had both gone down to defeat there on recent tours and Australia had escaped with just a two-point win earlier that winter.

The match programme talked of spending £36,000 on Carlaw to raise the capacity to 50,000. It was big enough already. Some said 12,000 came to see the new sensations, others claimed it was more like 20,000. They were jammed shoulder to shoulder, behind the white waist-high wooden fence; all that separated them from their heroes.

★ ★ ★ ★ ★ ★ ★ ★ ★ ★ ★

ALL STARS OUTCLASSED AT AUCKLAND

A good afternoon's entertainment was provided by the American All Stars at Carlaw Park when it began its New Zealand tour by losing to Auckland 54-26. There was little doubt that Auckland could have won by a considerably greater margin than 28 points. Although the Auckland backs ran straight through the American line easily, the game did have its thrills, especially for about 15 minutes in the second half when the American backs pulled off a couple of quick scissors movements typical of the Gridiron game to reduce the deficit temporarily.

AMERICANS' FIRST TRY: A. D. Kirkland (All Stars) scoring in the first half of the Rugby League match with Auckland on Saturday. Behind him are V. Bakalich and D. White (right), both of Auckland. Auckland won, 54-26.

Auckland Outclasses U.S. And N.Z. Team at League

Auckland, with its greater skill and superior knowledge of the game, outclassed an all-nations team by 54 to 26 in a Rugby League game at Carlaw Park on Saturday. Four New Zealanders and nine members of the American All Stars team made up the all-nations side. Auckland scored 12 tries, nine of which were converted, to six tries, two converted, and two penalty goals.

The usual issues were brought up by the press: a total lack of positional play in defence, long passes that were intercepted in their own territory, a lenient and protective referee – in this case George Kelly – opposition reluctant to take full advantage, but exciting running by both Kirklands and Sol Naumu was praised for his step. It was a 12-try hiding by an Auckland rep side, 'with its greater skill and superior knowledge of the game, outclassed an all-nations team'.

But more importantly, the crowd loved it. Somehow the All Stars had turned the thrashing into a joyous experience.

'No team has ever played on Carlaw Park, probably on any other ground either, and received the ovation and appreciation that the All Stars did on Saturday,' said one paper. 'The crowd stood as one and cheered the Americans from the field of play.'

SATURDAY NIGHT

ALL STARS LOSE
– BUT IT WASN'T BAD FUN

Nine of Mike Dimitro's American All Stars, plus four New Zealanders, gave Rugby League fans a chance to laugh and cheer at Carlaw Park this afternoon. Auckland was too good but all the same it was a happy afternoon. Nobody lost their temper, nobody was hurt.... The crowd was with the Americans from the start, right from the time they took the field and indulged in their warm-up tactics – they hurled long passes over the heads of the parading Artillery Band... the tourists have several outstanding players. Winger Sol Naumu ran trickily and shoulder tackled effectively, full-back Demerjian tackled a man every time. It was not his fault that the Auckland tries mounted up... When it was all over Aucklanders gave the All Stars a cheer they will remember.

When an attendance of more than 20,000 all stay until the final bell and then accord the losing team probably the greatest ovation ever accorded a visiting side in the history of New Zealand football, there must be a reason for it. The reason was that the Americans played a brand of football that completely captivated the vast attendance.

Auckland Star Sport

The papers on Monday morning spoke of the All Stars possibly winning half of their remaining eight games.

One report read: 'The Kirklands were seen in a new light as they dummy-passed and threw the ball about. From these moves the tourists scored two tries – one, the best of the match. It was exhilarating after their previous mediocre efforts but at times quite illegal. Under the eyes of the indulgent Mr Kelly, the Americans, purposely or not, began their gridiron blocking and shielding play. The New Zealanders called it shepherding and it was certainly effective.'

THE AMERICAN ASTEROIDS

Auckland's Big Win Over Inexperience

M IKE DIMITRO'S American All Stars Rugby League team were embroiled in more muddles than huddles in the opening game of their New Zealand tour against Auckland on Saturday.

The Auckland team, which scored 54 points, contained eight New Zealand representatives; the All Stars scored 26 points, brought about by the efforts of nine Americans, four New Zealanders—T. Hardwick, D. Barchard, F. Mulcare, R. Roff—the referee (Mr G. Kelly), and the encouragement of 12,000 spectators.

The first 50 points came up in as many minutes, and thereafter the Aucklanders played out time, scoring only from loose—if spectacular—passes well wide of their 30-yard objectives.

Six tries were scored by the All Stars, three of them by Al. D. Kirkland, who showed that he, at least, has firmly grasped the principles of Rugby League football. Wing-three-quarter S. Naumu, too, played a good game (with a strapped-up hand) and his shoulder crash-tacking of V. Bakalich never once failed to spreadeagle the Aucklander. The third American who looked as if he would make an Auckland club team was E. Demirijian, the fullback; he tackled beautifully, but too often there were three and four opponents running for the goal-line when he came into the play.

The All Stars had little knowledge of positional play, either on defence or attack, and they all lacked early speed off the mark. All were suckers for the dummies C. Eastlake handed out

American All Stars team defeated by Auckland. Mike Dimitro, the American player-manager (left), caused much interest by wearing his American football attire.

gave to Eastlake, who, in a brilliant diagonal run, scored by the posts. Encouragement for the Americans came when Naumu, with his steady 3-yard approach to the placed ball, landed a second penalty, but soon afterwards Eastlake streaked away from a defensive position and, veering right, Edwards came inside for the pass to score by the posts.

This really set the seal on Auckland supremacy after 10 minutes with 13-4 on the board. However, the All Stars were keen and resourceful. The big forward Al D. Kirkland, partnering Al E. Kirkland at centre, was enterprising in possession and, stepping out of a low tackle, he scored in a handy

by Riddell. After further touchdowns by Richards-Jolley and Graham, Al E. Kirkland scored for America by darting round a breaking scrum.

It was at this 41-18 stage that the All Stars produced their long passing gridiron tricks, including dummying and reverse passes. For a while, as the Kirklands, Grossman, Abajian, Henry and the towering X. Mena (who had replaced Draknivich in the forwards) baffled Auckland, as the visitors, sometimes with the ball in one hand, criss-crossed with long throws. These interludes did not gain them much ground, for it threw their necessary Rugby combination out of gear, and the game, after several more

---

The Kiwi guest players obviously shone out but the Kirklands, with Al D. filling in at five-eighths, were 'easily the best backs' on display, their runs 'devastating'; Demirjian 'tackled well' at full-back; Naumu was 'tricky and fast'; Abajian 'the fastest back on the ground'; Pat Henry 'worked hard' and Dimitro – The Hustler – 'hustled'. Eyes were drawn to Mike as soon as he stepped onto the field in his long gridiron pants and head gear. Playing at prop, he blasted through a series of Auckland tacklers, scattering them on a downfield rampage that got the crowd roaring with delight.

At 41-18 down, the All Stars started to turn on the gridiron style, hurling long crossfield passes, dummying handoffs, and switching play with shovel passes. But without being able to throw long down field, they made little distance. It was fun though.

Dimitro, who played wearing boxing headgear with enormous padded ear protectors, was content. 'That was a hard clean game – a lot different to play than in Australia,' he admitted. 'And the fans treated us the best any crowd has yet.' The Aucklanders' White was jeered for walking the last 20 yards to score his try!

THE AMERICAN ASTEROIDS
AUCKLAND'S BIG WIN OVER INEXPERIENCE

Al D. Kirkland showed that he, at least, has firmly grasped the principles of Rugby League football. Wing-three-quarter S. Naumu, too, played a good game (with a strapped up hand) and his shoulder crash-tackling into Vern Bakalich never once failed to spreadeagle the Aucklander. The third American who looked like he would make an Auckland club team was E. Demirjian, the full-back; he tackled beautifully.

The Weekly News
by Sam Small

★ ★ ★ ★ ★ ★ ★ ★ ★ ★ ★ ★

'The Americans came to New Zealand tired of the kind of football they had played in Australia but they left for Rotorua in a very happy frame of mind and, strange to say, looking forward to the tour of New Zealand.'

The Grey River Argus

It was time to enjoy themselves again. Not that they could go too mad: public drinking was banned after 6pm. Ted Grossman could have gone to see his body double Alan Ladd at the Majestic in *Desert Legion* but the players had other entertainment in mind.

Al D. Kirkland: 'Auckland was fun. I remember drinking Scotch with the owner of a hotel there. He turned me on to Famous Grouse, which has been a lifelong relationship.'

Despite a thrashing, the buzz was back. The All Stars were loving New Zealand and New Zealand was loving the All Stars.

CHAPTER 21
NORTH ISLAND

With Dimitro cancelling the game in Hamilton, the survivors had a couple of days off to see what New Zealand was all about as they weaved their way down the North Island from the capital towards the tip of Wellington. After a night at Hamilton's Hotel Riverina, they made a trip around Waitomo Caves and spent a day marvelling at Rotorua's famous geysers and spas and experiencing Maori culture first hand.

On arrival at Rotorua's Grand Hotel, Mike was handed a telegram from Patty Dodds – aka Mrs Dimitro – in LA telling him that the hotel in New Plymouth have 'NO MONEY NEED 550 IMMEDIATELY'. Mike's reputation for being slow to pay bills was one step ahead of him. He already had a demand for £42 from a doctor in Townsville for treating Jack – he got the North Queensland RL on that case – but things were getting serious in Sydney. Charles Parsons & Sons had got a solicitor to write to him chasing the £18 they claimed was still owed for suits ordered by Dimitro, Drakulvich, Mandulay and Pat Henry.

He needed to save money and get cash quick. In New Plymouth, he checked the Americans into the flea pit Criterion Hotel. Eight rooms of bed, breakfast and evening dinner: total cost £12! He forked out £8 for just one room at the Imperial for two of the Kiwi stars, while Roff saved him a few quid by going home to Tokoroa to sleep in his own bed.

Four days of being a laid-back tourist had done the players the world of good and a couple of training sessions had enabled the Kiwis to gel far better with their American team-mates. On a Wednesday afternoon, around two thousand curious fans descended on New Plymouth's beautiful tree-lined Pukekura Park, packing the terrace down the side of the D-shaped cricket ground to see this

LEAGUE FOOTBALL

AMERICANS PLAY HAPPY GAME IN TARANAKI

Mulcare's Three Tries

P.A. NEW PLYMOUTH, August 5.

The Taranaki Rugby League team was defeated by 9 of the touring American All Stars, plus four New Zealand players by 21 points (five tries, two converted and a dropped goal to 18 (four tries, three converted), before about 3000 people at Pukekura Park, New Plymouth today. Conditions were ideal.

There were but the briefest patches of good League, but the Americans did their best to give the crowd something to remember them by.

It was obvious that the All Stars are still ignorant of many of the finer plints, but they are a happy hand and are most willing to learn. They hustled long passes almost with the speed of bullets, dummied, worked some very nice scissors, and when occasion demanded it, tackled very solidly indeed, but it was the four New Zealanders in the team, T. Hardwick, R. Roff, F. Mulcare and D. Barchard, who supplied most of the thrust and danger.

entertainment troupe. The Taranaki side included Kiwi international McKay and a wealth of rugby league experience. A couple of hours later the locals left the ground with increased respect for the men in stars and stripes.

With the outstanding Mulcare scoring a hat-trick of tries, Roff winning the majority of scrums and Barchard and Hardwick looking sharp, the All Stars triumphed in a thriller, 21-18. Roff and Hardwick also touched down as New Zealanders scored all five of the tourists' tries, fit-again George Kauffman stepping up to kicking duties with two goals and a field goal to seal victory and cap a fine display at full-back.

But the crowd favourite was Ted Grossman. With Kerkorian back in Baltimore, Ted was the playmaker, the entertainer supreme: the ringmaster. The Press Association reported: 'He was equally happy carrying the ball clasped in one hand, hidden behind a broad back, or poised ready for the throw that never came above his right shoulder. Behind his antics, there was more than a glimmering of sound common sense.'

An anonymous West Coast sports writer admitted 'their ways are strange to us – some Australian papers referred to the All Stars as an international circus. If that was correct, what international circus would not be worth seeing?'

Ray Terry gladly pocketed £166 on Mike's behalf: the share of the gate money would at least pay some hotel bills.

International Ice-Cream Eating Contest at Tip-Top.

WELLINGTON

The tour party – minus the hospitalised Walker – arrived at the southern tip of North Island on Friday evening with a booming reputation. Word of their exciting display in Auckland and victory in New Plymouth had reached the Wellington public and the *Evening Post* was preparing fans for not only entertainment but a potentially tough challenge. The previous night, cockney comic Tommy Trinder had been wowing the Wellington crowd while across at the town hall 'negro wrestling giant' Bobo 'Bearcat' Wright had lost his fight against American Don Beitelman after being 'pointlessly disqualified'. More Americans were here to conquer.

The All Stars won another international event too: a USA v New Zealand ice-cream-eating contest. The whole squad headed down to the milk bar at the Tip-Top ice cream factory in Waterloo Quay, accompanied by the local press pack. Everyone – including the reporters – had to demolish eight scoops with toppings, then the brave went back for more. It came down to a straight eat-off between Fran Mandulay and Al D., refereed by Mulcare. The title decider: eat 15 large scoops with 'extra flavourings'. Both forwards finished the lot to the owner's shock, but Al D. was declared the winner for finishing first! Not ideal pre-match preparation.

The front page of the local paper showed just how The Dominion was dominated by the mother country: stories abounded from London, an irrelevant dictator on the other side of the world. But among them were photos of a suave Teddy Grossman – 'the Wizard of the American All Stars team, known as "Danny Kaye" to his team-mates and Houdini to his opponents' – balancing a ball on his finger and Kauffman, Mandulay, Abajian, Drakulvich and Demirjian laughing as they pretend to scrum down at training in Anderson Park. With Wellington's rugby union team winning the Ranfurly Shield – the national challenge trophy – from Waikato the previous Sunday, the pressure was on their league counterparts to impress.

The All Stars were to face the pick of the local Wellington competition with players from five clubs: Miramar, St George, Randwick, Korodale and Waterside. Forwards Kreyl, English and Hurndell were all Kiwi internationals while full-back Ropata was considered one of the best kickers in the country. And Wellington's men in black and gold took the Americans more seriously than most, having a practice game against the Maoris on the Sunday.

WELLINGTON 8 AMERICAN ALL STARS 17

The venue was special too. The historic Basin Reserve, where New Zealand had beaten Australia 12-11 in a thriller just a month earlier to clinch a second straight Trans-Tasman series win, and host to many more cricket Test matches, lay in the middle of the city, oozing colonial spirit from the tall, airy stands. Their gabled roofs resembled a collection of giant parish churches gathered around an English village green; it even had a pretty gate open for the public to stroll through the ground as a short-cut home. Mount Victoria towered over the arena, watching proceedings from the heavens. This was the British Empire in full effect.

But the Basin Reserve was once an earthquake-induced swamp and almost returned to that state as rain teemed down before kick-off, keeping most fans at home and stopping the Karori Marching Band in their tracks. However, as radio reporters sent news from the stadium that the rain had stopped, thousands of fans flooded down through the gates to stand on the muddy banks that were being excavated in preparation for the imminent Royal tour.

The *Evening Post* heaped praise on almost all the All Stars, who led 12-5 at half-time and could have won by more if Sol Naumu – with his broken hand in plaster – had not missed four of his five kicks at goal.

Dimitro gave much of the credit to Hardwick, who had coached them and played a blinder, scoring one try and setting up others as the All Stars showed they could adapt their game to the sodden conditions. Dimitro told the press after the victory that he wanted Hardwick as coach, on condition: 'If his team are able to accept an invitation to compete in the "world series" rugby league tournament in France next year.'"

Wellington's Basin Reserve.

The Americans 'found the game no occasion for lighthearted mixture of league and their own gridiron football and the greasiness of the ball persuaded all but one of them that two hands were needed, and that the long throw was dangerous'. They had found a new seriousness in New Zealand – well, apart from Teddy: 'The exception was the first five-eighths, E.Grossman. While selling dummies, lofting one-handed passes and changing direction with easy grace, he still had the feeling of rugby league in everything he did. Grossman was the brightest of the Stars, and one who would twinkle prominently in New Zealand league.' Another paper called Teddy 'something out of the box, who showed enough elusiveness to indicate how difficult to catch he would be on a dry ground'.

Abajian: 'It was so muddy. I remember I swallowed some. I had a mouth full of it! We walked straight off the field into the showers with our uniforms on. Didn't bother taking anything off. The mud clogged the showers up!'

The Americans had gained a huge amount of respect. They had truly arrived in New Zealand.

The squad had Saturday night to celebrate and enjoy what the windy city of Wellington had to offer. They took full advantage.

Mulcare: 'We were at the very best hotels and were lavishly entertained: wined and dined. There was little discipline and no curfews or restrictions ever imposed. Yet I personally saw nothing but very high standards of behaviour from all the team. Perhaps the most vivid recollection I have is the number of very attractive young ladies who seemed to gather wherever we went or wherever we stayed.'

Mulcare chose his words very carefully.

Al D. Kirkland: 'Wellington was fun. All the girls wanted to… well, you know!'

And, because they were not fleeing town and heading on to the next stop straight after the game, the Americans also had a chance to talk to local fans, players and coaches about the game and read what the local sports writers thought of them in the press. It was happy reading.

Touch Of Gridiron In Their League

WIZARD of the American "All Stars" team, first five-eighth Ted Grossman, known as "Danny Kaye" to his teammates and "Houdini" to his opponents, balances a ball at Anderson Park today.

CHAPTER 22
SOUTH ISLAND

Monday morning: time for South Island. The team boarded an NAC Dakota and flew from Wellington to Hokitika – at a cost to Dimitro of £135.

Sandwiched between the Tasman and the glaciers of the Southern Alps, the West Coast is isolated. Jump in a boat here, head due west and, if you avoid the southern tip of Tasmania, the next land you see is Argentina. It is also the wettest place in New Zealand. Life is damp. And even the locals thoughts it was bitterly cold when the Americans arrived. Australia had felt far from home but they could not have felt further from Santa Monica or Hollywood Boulevard than when their bus rolled into Greymouth. Long Beach in August it was not.

Greymouth lived up to its name: a dingy, dank little town which was – regardless – the focal point for life in the rural West Coast. Once a shanty town for Australian miners hunting their fortune up the valley in the 1864 gold rush, Greymouth turned to coal-mining in the 20th century – and boomed. It had 55 hotels before depression hit and now only the beautiful art deco buildings tell of its lost power and status.

A tough town in a tough region, it was fitting that Greymouth and the West Coast should produce a string of top class forwards, afraid of nothing and ready to take on all-comers. West Coast had three Kiwi international forwards in their pack, ready to ambush the Americans: experienced skipper R. Neilson, outstanding prop W. McLennan and Charlie McBride, star of the Kiwis' 1947 tour of Britain, considered by Eddie Waring and other experts as the best second-row forward playing in England. Only five weeks earlier West Coast had pushed Australia all the way in their opening tour game at Greymouth, going down by just six points. Their fourth international forward, Fran Mulcare, had been outstanding in the battle that day. Fortunately he would be playing against his usual team-mates this time.

It was no surprise that the locals should get a little excited when a bunch of young sportsmen from the USA came to their austere post-war town, let alone these sun-tanned, quick-quipping hunks coming to play our game.

The *Grey River Argus* had been following the All Stars since they arrived in Australia, publishing reports, profiles and photos of these mythical Yankee

AMERICANS ARRIVE THIS AFTERNOON

The members of the American All Stars Rugby League team will arrive in Greymouth this afternoon and their first official call in the town will be to the Borough Council Chambers where the Mayor, Mr F. L. Turley, will tender them a civic reception on behalf of the residents of the West Coast.

The All Stars will travel from Wellington by air and arrive at Hokitika on the normal service from where they will be transported to Greymouth by bus.

After the reception, the team will retire to their hotel, but it is not known yet whether they will train this afternoon. After their fine win over Wellington on Saturday, the Americans should be in good fettle for tomorrow's match with West Coast, but they will find the opposition a different proposition. They will be meeting probably the strongest Rugby League side in New Zealand, even allowing for the fact that the second row forward will be playing against his regular team mates.

It was interesting to hear, in the review of Saturday's match, that the All Stars played really good Rugby League and did not live up to the doubtful reputation accorded them by reports which preceded their visit to this country. They have apparently learned more from their few matches in New Zealand, coupled with the fact that they are receiving excellent tuition from Travers Hardwick, Des Barchard, Roy Roff and Francis Mulcare.

Their only aim is to play good open football and their remarks on the code are certainly more than interesting to students of the game here in New Zealand.

players, and readers had received daily bulletins once they landed in the Land of the Long White Cloud. The hype was reaching boiling point: 'Each and everyone is an All Star in his particular phase of athletics…when their records are known they will astound critics… the nine Americans are at least up to Australian inter-state standard… they should fully extend any team in the Dominion… this match should be the gem of the season.'

Dimitro – as a 'champion amateur boxer' – was even asked to comment on a local headmaster's attempts to ban boxing from his college. His opinion mattered.

Excitement had gathered as the All Stars started winning games across the Tasman. Arrangements for their visit were announced in the *Argus* a week before the exotic strangers – the first American sports team ever to visit the West Coast – touched down. The West Coast Rugby League Board were busy organising suitable pomp and ceremony. The Mayor not only arranged a civic reception on them landing, but was asked to request that businesses give employees the afternoon off so they could be there at Wingham Park to see these most unusual of tourists in action.

AMERICANS ARRIVE THIS AFTERNOON

…. After the fine win in Wellington the Americans should be in good fettle for tomorrow's match with West Coast but they will find the opposition a different proposition. They will be meeting probably the strongest Rugby League side in New Zealand…

After playing and seeing Rugby League the American side has found that it really likes the game. The players agree it would be a sensation in America, but individually, some of them think it could be improved with variations.

The Grey River Argus
10 August 1953

LONG PANTS OR SHORT?

Mike Dimitro thinks the long pants which most of the players discarded after the first Sydney match are an improvement on the shorts worn by other League playing countries. "I wore long pants in Australia and I have no cuts of infected abrasions," said Mike. "But look at those other guys who played in shorts. They all had bad knees and one, Pat Henry, had to go to hospital," he added.

But while Dimitro likes the long pants, brilliant centre three-quarter Sol Naumu goes for shorts every time. "The long pans may be alright for forwards but for backs the shorts are ever so much better. You feel freer and you can run faster because there is nothing dragging your knees when you run," says Naumu.

Rugby League News

According to the *Argus*: 'The Americans have a preference for dancing as a recreation and, with this in view, an official ball will be tendered them by the West Coast Rugby League.'

Xavier Mena proposed that one forward pass should be allowed in each movement, and wanted the game played in four 15-minute quarters to ensure both teams face the same conditions. Dimitro and Mena both thought replacements should be allowed regardless of injury. But despite these suggested Americanisms, they all thought the game suited to all gridiron players, with 'more room for the backs to move in and more chances to run, and the forwards get a chance to run which is denied them in the American game,' according to Han.

At the welcoming reception, Dimitro was understandably upbeat, describing the New Zealand leg of the tour as 'wonderful'. 'Upon arrival we looked like a group of broken-down horses, but now the horses are alright,' he curiously claimed, ignoring the fact that two of his team were standing there with broken thumbs in plaster. Ray Terry provided the Coasters with some psychological ammunition by claiming the All Stars were 'very likely' to register their third straight win. As if the locals needed any more encouragement.

LEAGUE FOOTBALL

ALL STARS WERE EASY TO RECOGNISE
Unusual Attire

A splash of sartorial novelty heralded the arrival at Greymouth yesterday afternoon of the American All Stars Rugby League team. Light blue slacks, windbreakers of a design not seen locally and, above all, hats that could be only described as quaint, left the onlooker in no doubt that strangers were in town.

If prizes had been awarded for distinctive headwear they would undoubtedly have been shared by the team's two Kirklands, who incidentally are not related. Al E. Kirkland, the centre-threequarter, wore a beret which bulged in the front in the manner approved by some Continental armies, while second five-eighth, L. D. Kirkland provided apt martial competition with the traditional Australian "digger's" hat—undoubtedly obtained at some post-match function earlier in the tour.

That night the All Stars came face to face with a true global superstar. While the papers reported on McCarthy's Communist witch-hunt and the threat of war in Japan and Korea that were gripping the States, Greymouth was toasting the success of their returning son: Sir Edmund Hillary, conqueror of Everest.

Ed Demirjian: 'We went to see Edmund Hillary do a talk, just after he had climbed Everest. Vince Jones was so smart that he bought up all the climbing axes he could find in a local store and got Hillary to sign them all afterwards.'

Al Abajian: 'We called Vince "Cro-magnon" – the prehistoric man – because he had so much scar tissue over his eyebrows. But Vince was a very, very bright person, very articulate and eloquent. We wanted Vince to make all the speeches, not Mike.'

TUESDAY 11 AUGUST 1953
WEST COAST v AMERICAN ALL STARS

The cars and buses trundled across Grey River, over Cobden Hill and north on the country road to Runanga – crossing the city boundary to where the town council could not ban sport on Sundays – and coming to a halt beneath the Paparoas hills. No one wanted to miss the first international team to grace Wingham Park, the humble home of the fiercely proud West Coast Rugby League. The neat wooden stand was soon overflowing with anxious officials and over-excited spectators trying to avoid being soaked as the heavens opened once more.

The rain eventually stopped before kick-off and the covers and heaters brought in to save the field had worked, just.

It was an average crowd for a big game at Wingham: less than 2,000, officially. But that was almost half the town's population. The Americans were drawing bigger crowds in some towns than the mighty Australia had. Some 500 sat in the grandstand, 300 suffered in the open seats and the rest formed a ring around the pitch three or four deep. The cows grazing behind the posts at the far end were disturbed by the shrieks and cheers as history was made in their field.

★ ★ *Rugby League Football* ★ ★

AMERICAN
★ ALL STARS ★

V

WEST
COAST

WINGHAM PARK, GREYMOUTH,
TUESDAY, AUGUST 11,
1953 – AT 3 P.M.

OFFICIAL PROGRAMME, SIXPENCE.

★ ★ ★ ★ ★ ★ ★ ★ ★ ★

"Argus" Print

Despite the heavy defeat – the Coasters converted only two of their seven tries – this was another encouraging display from Dimitro's troops. They trailed by only a point at half-time before the injury curse struck again: Grossman had looked 'as if he had the makings of a first-class inside back' before going off while full-back George Kauffman got smashed in a tackle but refused to leave the field with ambulance men until ordered to do so by the referee.

Sol replaced Kauffman at full-back despite still having his hand in plaster and 'evoked much admiration' as 'one of the most entertaining Americans'. The Kiwi foursome drove the visitors on as the contest rose to the boil.

Mulcare: 'Even 50 years on I recall the game at Greymouth with sadness and embarrassment. This was my home town where I played club and provincial level. I'd been looking forward to the game but shortly after it commenced I found I was being subjected to what was, in those days, referred to as "a bit of a working over".

Mandulay and Mena came on as subs as the All Stars hammered the West Coast line after half-time only for Sol to miss two easy penalties. For the second successive game, the All Stars were badly missing Kerkorian's lethal boot. They saw the home side pounce to score two quick interception tries to clinch the game. The exhausted tourists had to dig deep to keep the score respectable. But for Mulcare, playing against team-mates on home soil, the red mist descended.

Page 4.   The Grey River Argus,   Wednesday, August 12, 1953.

LEAGUE FOOTBALL

WEST COAST'S BACKLINE PROVES TOO POLISHED FOR AMERICAN ALL STARS

Fast and Entertaining Play

Though better exhibitions of the Rugby League code have been seen locally, the 3000 spectators who watched West Coast beat the American All Stars team, 27-10, at Wingham Park yesterday, could not complain about any lack of incident or fast open play.

Most of the Americans obviously possessed no deep knowledge of league tactics, but they persisted with a determined passing game, and received tigerish support from the four New Zealanders, F. Mulcare, T. Hardwick, D. Barchard and R. Roff.

Two spectacular last-minute tries appeared to give the All Stars a good chance at half time, when Coast held only a one-point lead, but the home backline—which was in top form—took charge in the second spell and added 16 points.

Not Treacherous

Recent rain had made the ground heavy, but the footing never became really treacherous, and the ball apparently remained easy to handle.

The Americans were unlucky in losing their fullback, G. Kauffman, and the wing, Al D. Kirkland, through injuries, and S. Naumu evoked much admiration by playing throughout the game—mostly at fullback—with a hand in plaster. Despite handicap.

passing movement, but, with Hay unmarked, Pascoe tried to sell a dummy to Kauffman and was promptly grounded. Loose play followed, and Pascoe snapped up the ball in midfield to feed Broome, who swerved around Kauffman and scored well out. Soster's kick was just wide of a post.

As he went down on a ball Kauffman was obviously hurt, but the arguments of ambulance men proved fruitless, and it needed a direct order from the referee to make him leave the field. The ambulance men considered that

Mulcare: 'My retaliation was violent and vicious and quite out of proportion to the provocation I'd received. I know it caused pain to my family and friends and as I say still brings feeling of regret. It was the only distasteful memory I have of the tour.'

The press were sympathetic as Fran came in for 'special attention' and his retaliation late in the game was only after 'extreme provocation'. The *Argus* claimed he had merely been 'heckled for over-vigorous play' by his own crowd but still went on to knock star man McGougan down with a ferocious tackle that took the five-eighths out of the game for several minutes.

With the final whistle approaching Al D. was carried off the field on a stretcher with a torn knee ligament: his tour was over. And word came through from Greymouth Hospital that Kauffman had a broken rib.

At least the night out was a cracker. No sooner had the post-match reception and speeches concluded than what was left of the team headed off to St Columba Hall for the Long Night Dance in their honour. They partied from 9pm until the

Vince Jones (18) supports Pat Henry (7).

Rene Jacobs Orchestra stopped playing at 1am. It was long after that before some crawled back into their beds at the Albion Hotel.

Anyone still capable must have done a rain dance as the heavens opened and Wednesday's planned training session was washed away in a monsoon. The boys stayed tucked up in the hotel and abandoned the scheduled afternoon sight-seeing trip to Punakaiki. Instead they rolled up at Mawhera Quay to catch the Tranz-Alpine train to Christchurch that evening.

CHRISTCHURCH

The train journey across the Southern Alps from the West Coast to Christchurch, cutting through the spectacular mountains, hurtling along the valley bottoms, is one of the greats. Al Abajian remembers it for something else.

Abajian: 'We were playing charades on the train across the New Zealand Alps to Christchurch. Mike says: "Four words, movie." The answer was *The Express Pony*, the new Charlton Heston movie. He thought Express was two words! That was what Mike was like.'

The decision to cancel the Dunedin game – originally scheduled for 13 August – was a godsend, saving money on flights and protecting the few remaining bodies. With a clash against the Canterbury province beckoning on Saturday, the players desperately needed the three days off to recover from the games – and the partying.

The city of Christchurch spreads from its appealing, genteel centre out to the plain. With

provincial charm, picturesque squares and colonial buildings, it was as foreign as anywhere on the tour for these young Americans.

Big Al D.: 'The difference between New Zealand and Australia was like night and day. Australia was like the wild west… with wooden sidewalks and sand golf courses! But I really wanted to go to New Zealand – I'd never been before, of course. It was lovely, with the Alps, the inlets and real nice people. New Zealand was a calmer pace, not further behind Australia, just more sedate, more British. They didn't have TV in Australia or New Zealand – or Polaroid cameras! Vince had a Polaroid he was quite proud of.'

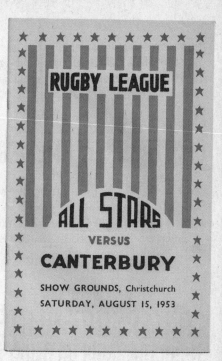

RUGBY LEAGUE

ALL STARS

VERSUS

CANTERBURY

SHOW GROUNDS, Christchurch
SATURDAY, AUGUST 15, 1953

> *There's many ways to catch a possum*
> *But only one way to dispose of the skin…*
> *Send it to Wright, Stephenson and Co Ltd, Dunedin*
> *– for expert grading and highest price at auction.*

These were things of wonder indeed for the good folk of Christchurch. The match programme editor claimed: 'One way the Americans are more fortunate than us; they have television to sell anything new to their public.' He was not alone in being blown away by Vince's instamatic snapper: 'While watching New South Wales play Queensland in Sydney a few days after their arrival they were taking photos of some of the moves with a camera which photographed the shot, developed and printed it within ten seconds. A few seconds after the move was finished they were studying it and discussing its capabilities. Even we, who are supposed to take our football so seriously, don't seem as keen as that.'

The editor summed up the local spirit though: 'Our soldiers, sailors and airmen fought side by side with the sons of the United States, and it is indeed a great pleasure that they can now play competitively against each other in the one game. We hope this is only the forerunner of many more games between us and these boys of Uncle Sam.'

Having trained well on Thursday, two inches of rain on Friday almost put paid to the game. Hitched up in their Christchurch hotel on a rainy Friday afternoon, the players were visited by match referee Mr Wilkinson. As always, the cameras were there. Syd Walker sat there wearing a bow tie and Vince Jones, like Des Barchard, immaculately turned out in jacket, slacks, pullover, collar and tie. The Yanks were trying too hard to fit in.

SATURDAY 15 AUGUST 1953
CANTERBURY V AMERICAN ALL STARS

Lying low in the inner city suburb of Addington, the Canterbury Agricultural and Pastoral Association's Show Grounds was a dull, uninspiring, horseshoe-shaped arena next door to the horse track. It was also a graveyard for touring teams.

Canterbury had their best team for years, led by a fearsome forward pack with Butterfield, Atkinson and Blanchard. The locals turned up en masse, packing five deep around the railings, to see another culling of foreign meat by their men in red and black.

CANTERBURY BEATS AMERICANS
31-POINT MARGIN ON HEAVY GROUND

Although they were beaten by 39 points to 8, the American All Stars were warm favourites with the crowd. On a ground that had one end churned into a sea of mud they never forsook their open style of play. The passing and handling in the conditions were at times brilliant and were well appreciated by the crowd. They showed they would be able to play very spectacularly on a dry ground. Still learning the finer points of the game they nevertheless offered a few lessons to local sides....

The handling of Grossman, the first five-eighth, was the finest seen at the Show Grounds for a very long time. No matter where the ball came from, or how it came, he took it without blemish. His passing was also both crisp and well-directed...

For all the over-generous plaudits, the All Stars were still well beaten before the break, going into the locker rooms down 20-2. For once, they improved after half-time but still conceded a second-half hat-trick by Atkinson and were heading for an embarrassing thrashing. They belatedly showed both pride and ability to reduce the deficit as Ted got over the line and Vince finished off a fine move under the posts, only for Sol to miss a sitter with his kick. It was the only time in the New Zealand leg of the tour that Americans got all the points. And at least Al E. was back.

Among the Canterbury team was John Bond, who had just made his debut for New Zealand. He said: 'They were just an amateur team trying to learn the game. They should have been playing country sides or something like that, instead of metropolitan teams. The worst thing they did was going to Australia first. The

Australians just hammered them and when they got here they had no players left. It could have got going in the States if the Aussies hadn't killed them.'

That was the South Island done. Monday 17 August: fly back north. Three days off. Three games to go. Three in six days. The end was nigh.

CHAPTER 23
THE FINAL STRAIGHT

From the South Island to the top of the North. To Whangerei, the Bay of Islands. Maori country.

Dimitro got news from Harold Matthews in Phillip Street: it was not good. The federal authorities in Canberra still had not sanctioned his request for Mike to take even £3,000 in dollars to the States. This was a disaster. The mood in The Settlers Hotel was bleak.

Yet the sun shone on the All Stars at last at Jubilee Park on Wednesday afternoon.

Northland Rugby League (Inc.)

Proudly Presents the

American All Star Team

At Jubilee Park, Whangarei,
Wednesday, August 19th, 1953.

ALL STARS V. NORTHLAND

at 2.15 p.m.

Price 6d.

WEDNESDAY 19 AUGUST 1953
NORTHLAND v ALL STARS

Northland Rugby League were clearly not best prepared: they took to the muddy field wearing royal blue and gold jerseys – UCLA colours – almost exactly the same tone as the All Stars' star-shouldered shirts. It was as baffling for the players as the fans, until Northland switched to red shirts at half-time.

With Barchard, Mulcare and Roff joined by another Kiwi – Mt Albert and Auckland full-back Roy Moore – the All Stars had guile to add to their natural speed and strength and it was too much for Northland. Sol Naumu was unstoppable on the wing as the visitors won 25-6, Moore converting all four tries and adding three penalties. Even Iron Mike scored a try, his first since Rockhampton.

The paper claimed 1,500 were there. The turnstiles reported less than 900. The takings were just £127. The Americans' share hardly covered the hotel bill. They even had £1 15s deducted for damage to the changing room door.

Back in Auckland, *City Beneath The Sea* was playing in Technicolor while the All Stars were supposed to be playing the City, beneath the city: against Auckland at Carlaw Park – again. There was no point in that. Instead the Auckland RL agreed to field a Maori XIII instead, selected from the best Maoris and Polynesians at Auckland's clubs.

The Maoris had fuelled the growth of rugby league in Auckland before the war: the Manukau club drew big crowds to Carlaw as the indigenous people saw their own take on all-comers. That movement collapsed but there was still passion and players among the Maori.

Selector Ernie Asher put together a side dominated by the Point Chevalier club, who provided six players, alongside Maoris from Otahuhu, North Shore, Mount Albert and Ponsonby. They had already beaten South Auckland, Waikato Maoris, and Auckland at Carlaw before the Kiwis v Kangaroos Test match. Their five-eighths Bill Sorensen was the Kiwi stand-off. This combination would draw the crowds back into Carlaw: one final big pay day for the Auckland RL – and Dimitro. Down the hills they came again in their thousands.

SATURDAY 22 AUGUST 1953
AMERICAN ALL STARS v MAORIS

The Yankee ranks were shrinking by the day. Dimitro fielded five Kiwis and sent Sol out again with his broken hand. The North Shore club were furious with the NZRFL that Ray Roff appeared in the All Stars team. The NZRFL blamed Roff himself for not clearing it with his club first.

The international All Stars looked capable of beating the Auckland Maoris, leading 15-10 at one stage. But the indigenous side, resplendent in all-white shirts and shorts, roared back, scoring 15 points in five minutes to take control, star half-back Sorensen at the helm. But it was with the boot that the game was lost. Maori full-back Haggie kicked eight goals to go with his try: Roy Moore missed nine kicks at goal, several of them sitters as the Maoris won 40-23.

Again the American backs Grossman, Abajian and Al D. impressed the journalists, as did Sol Naumu before being replaced by Fran Mandulay. They liked the effort of Mike, Pat Henry and Vince Jones up front but it was Des Barchard who pulled the strings at half-back. All the All Stars' points were scored by guest Kiwis.

AMERICAN ALL STARS v. MAORIS
Saturday, August 22nd, 1953 CARLAW PARK, 2.30 p.m.

D.B. LAGER and WAITEMATA
Today's Best Sellers
Brewed at the WAITEMATA BREWERY, Otahuhu

THE BEST CYCLES on THE BEST TERMS!
FROM ONLY 5/- DEPOSIT WEEKLY 3/9
CLARKES CYCLE WORKS L^td.
NEWMARKET   267 KARANGAHAPE RD · OTAHUHU

Ray Terry feverishly jotted down the ticket sales and gate figures. The Americans would leave with their share of £1,368 takings.

The remaining rump of Americans had one last Saturday night out in Auckland: one to remember at the Maori Community Centre with a concert and dance. Most would never be back. Most would never forget.

MONDAY 24 AUGUST 1953
AMERICA v SOUTH AUCKLAND

The finale: against a South Auckland representative XIII in the rugby union stronghold of Hamilton. The rules were explained to 'Rugby' fans new to watching 'League' via the programme, just as they had been to the All Stars three months earlier when they landed in Sydney. This was not going to be a grand farewell. Just 97 tickets had been sold in advance. This in a city planning to build a new 70,000-capacity stadium.

On the day, nearly 2,500 turned up at the home of Hamilton Rugby Union, to see South Auckland take on these strangers in a strange game. Resplendent in black and gold, South Auckland fielded two Kiwi internationals in skipper Burgoyne in the second row and young wing Berryman. The All Stars neither knew who they were nor cared. They just wanted to survive.

Ted: 'We're playing the last game, near Auckland, and before the game we'd said to each other: "This is the last game, whatever you do, don't get injured." We had two weeks in Hawaii coming next. So I find myself at full-back and this huge Tongan guy – I forget his name – is running at me. I look around and there's no one there but me. I saw the beaches of Honolulu, the sun, the girls... in fact my whole life flashed before me – so just as he got to me I did a matador and waved him through. The crowd went wild, shouting "ole"!

Al D. Kirkland: 'The crowd loved Teddy and so did the press. He deserved it. He was fantastic.'

Miraculously, the All Stars managed a 'well-deserved win', 22-19 in a 'hard, fast game played in fine spirit'. The crowd were thrilled by the powerful rushes of the fast-running American backs.

Kirkland: 'We survived – and that was an accomplishment.'

It was time to go home.

PRO TEM: T. Hardwick, the former Kiwi, scoring a try for All ...ting the League match with Auckland Maoris at Carlaw Park on Saturday. G. Turner just misses him.

Maoris Win Spectacular League Match

1 a spectacular Rugby League match the Auckland Maoris ...ted the American All Stars team by 40 points to 23 at w Park on Saturday. The entire 23 points of the American were scored by the New Zealanders. Five New Zealanders in the side.

The total takings through the turnstiles in New Zealand was £6,437. Mike's 60 per cent share came to less than four thousand.

Ray Terry calculated the costs in Australian pounds:

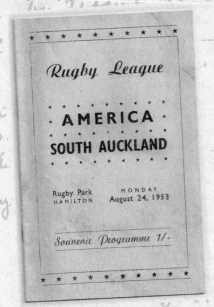

Accommodation	3,312
Travel	
* US to Australia	
* New Zealand to US	11,200
Internal travel	2,156
Players' allowance	1,320
Blazers	340
Trainers	200
Outfits	850
Sundries	500
Extra meals	300
Pictures	350
Insurance	600
Medical	250
Phone	200
Dry cleaning	100
Laundry	50
TOTAL	21,778

Not included were Jack Bonetti's private care or flight, or the hire of training grounds such as Coogee Oval – Ray crossed his fingers and hoped no bill would ever arrive for those.

Abajian: 'The big question we have – not that it makes any difference 50 years later – how much money did Dimitro really make? Nobody knows.'

Al D. Kirkland: 'It must have cost a fortune flying everyone down there, hotel rooms, meals, transportation there, paying the Australian coaches. There were pretty good crowds at some games but I don't know how much the admission was. It didn't bother or affect me. We were down there to have some fun, play some games. It wasn't about money.'

Mulcare: 'Whilst a member of the touring party I gained the impression that basically the tour was a commercial enterprise with any financial benefits accrued going to Mike Dimitro and Ray Terry.'

Dimitro said the tour cost over £22,000 (that's Australian $750,000 in 2018). He was not lying. But that's half of the £2,000 per player Dimitro originally claimed. Only giving them around £70 each in total 'allowance' – when he had first promised £12 a day – helped trim the fat.

Dimitro had told the players they could holiday with their wives after the tour and buy clothes with the profits made. What wives? What profits?

Abajian: 'When we were trying to leave New Zealand to go to Honolulu, they wouldn't let Mike on the plane. They had five or six big security of some kind – federal agents or something – surrounding him. They wouldn't let him leave the country until he'd paid the bills. He usually talked his way out of everything but they wouldn't let him talk his way out of this. I don't know how he paid them. We laughed! That was just the way he was. He was a scoundrel. He embarrassed us. I'll never forget that. There's only one Mike Dimitro in this world. There couldn't be another one.'

Al D. Kirkland: 'We were pioneers I guess, even if unwilling ones! We filled in so many forms and I'd written "Student" so many times [under Occupation] that when we were leaving Sydney for Hawaii I wrote "white slaver". I thought nothing more of it until we were leaving New Zealand to come home and the guy at immigration said: "Ah, Mr Kirkland, Al D., may I see some of your wares?". I said: "What do you mean?" He said: "Can I see some of your wares?" "What?" "It says here: Occupation – white slaver." He had me!'

Mulcare: 'They were due to play an exhibition game in Hawaii on their way home to the States. Mike had discussed this with me and asked if I wanted to travel with them and play there. I readily assented. However the NZRL had differing views and to my great regret I found myself winging my way to home and farm work while the American All Stars winged the other way. I was left with many memories of one of the more interesting and certainly the most amusing tours I have ever experienced.'

Mike's ambitious plan to play in Hawaii fell by the wayside. With few fit players and even less goodwill, there was no chance of a game of football or rugby league.

When Dimitro got to Honolulu he picked up a telegram from Matthews: 'Government approval granted to forward $6,711 leaving £130 in Australia to meet debt.' Once the bills were paid there, Commonwealth Bank transferred £3,004 – around US$5,000 – into Dimitro's US bank. In 2018 that would be around US$46,000.

Al D. Kirkland: 'Mike arranged for us all to have first-class tickets from Honolulu to the States on the way home. I stayed in Hawaii with an old frat friend for a couple of weeks on vacation. When I went to pick up my first class ticket, it had gone. Mike's wife had used it! I had all the restrictions on mine. That was typical of Mike.'

When Dimitro got home to Ceilhunt Avenue, he opened a letter from Bill Fallowfield. Fallowfield was proposing that Mike hosted Great Britain the following summer for two exhibition games under floodlights on their return from touring Australia, via San Francisco. It would 'establish the practice'. Australia and New Zealand could do the same en route to or from Britain and France. A natural new stop on the international circuit was there for the taking.

Iron Mike bit his hand off and suggested the US team go to France and the UK in spring or summer of 1954. France confirmed they would pay for the All Stars to go to the World Cup now confirmed for October that year and if the income was over 48m francs, the competing nations would split the surplus. Mike's dreams were coming true. He even told Fallowfield that he had held exhibition games in

Hawaii 'which the fans had loved'. Vince Jones wrote to Harold Matthews of 'the first rugby league game ever played in Hawaii'.

Al Abajian: 'We never played in Hawaii. Who would we have played against anyways?!'

Al D: 'You've got to give him credit for putting it together, give him respect for what he did. It was an adventure. If we could do it all again, I would.'

But would the other All Stars? Even those who made it all the way to the end and were back in the States starting the next chapters of their lives?

And was it a success? Quarter of a million people saw them play. They paid around £35,000 to do so. The host teams made well over £10,000 for their troubles.

Jersey Flegg wrote to Mike in LA: 'You did what no other fellow did in America – you brought an inexperienced lot of players and created great interest in Australia and New Zealand. I'm pleased to say you made a financial success of the tour.'

'This was a genuine attempt to expand our code,' said Matthews in his end of year report to the Board of Control.

As September came, Latchem Robinson was rushed off to hospital for a major operation and Clive Churchill's Souths beat Noel Pidding's St George at the SCG in the first grade final.

Back in California, Jack Bonetti's fiancée could not face life caring for a polio victim and broke off the engagement, his offer from the Rams now worthless. In November his father died of a brain haemorrhage. By then, Vince Jones had crossed the Atlantic from New York on the *Queen Mary,* and was enjoying the first few weeks of life as a Rhodes Scholars at Oxford University.

Al D. Kirkland: 'I actually graduated while I was in Australia, which came as something of a surprise as I thought I still had classes left. I'd still applied to graduate and they agreed! I got a letter from my parents saying I'd got a diploma in the post. I thought: "That's nice!" So I went to Business School at Stanford in the fall of 1953 and coach Chuck Taylor got me a job as assistant coach of freshmen.'

The next time Al D played rugby was as goal-kicking full-back for Stanford. He was still there in 1956.

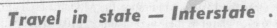

CHAPTER 24
THE FRENCH TRIP

Back in LA, Dimitro could run but he couldn't hide. Townsville Hospital was still chasing him for more money for Jack Bonetti's treatment. Luckily he had allies: the North Queensland RFL dismissed the charges, and the Minister for Health and Home Affairs waived the statutory £1 a day charge to foreign patients.

Dimitro's life was peripatetic. He had left Andrew Jackson High to go to Australia and when he returned got a job teaching Social Studies and English at Virgil Junior High, (whose pre-war pupils included a Norma Jeane Baker, aka Marilyn Monroe). Surely, there were more suitable candidates.

Despite the scrapes, the scraps, the arrests and the arguments, Iron Mike still had the tour bug. He had to get away again. He searched for another destination and a new market.

Rugby league was booming in France. Crushed by the fascist Vichy regime during the war, it was now resurgent at club and international level. Everywhere he had been in Australia, the locals had crowed about Puig-Aubert's wonderful French team which had stunned the Aussies two years before and proved it was no fluke by doing it again in the return series in France. Having just completed the European Championship, the French Federation were free to welcome a touring team over Christmas and New Year 1954.

Dimitro negotiated with Antoine Blain, secretary general of *Federation Francaise de Jeu a XIII*. Blain, a bushy-browed former rugby union international, wrote to Dimitro in LA from his office in Rue Marbeuf in Paris. It was mid-November 1953. He suggested the All Stars come over for five games. Dimitro proposed seven. With the help of a translator, on 8 December Mike accepted his offer: he needed 20 return plane tickets and $2,533 to cover uniforms, practice equipment, insurance, baggage and postage.

Mike and Ray Terry had the financial breakdown from the Kangaroos' European tour in 1952. From the 13 games in France, the ARFL made a £21,000 profit, paying out £333 to each player as their part of almost £10,000 in bonuses. Around 35,000 watched the Test matches in Lyon and Paris.

The All Stars would play three warm-up games, then finish with two Tests against France in Lyon and Paris. Blain expected the big game in Paris to bring in 4m francs, 2.5m in Lyon, Perpignan 2m, Albi 1.5m, Carcassonne 800,000. There could be as much as 12m francs up for grabs.

Mike had two weeks to get a team together. It was Mission Impossible II.

A NEW TEAM
The majority of the original All Stars either castigated Dimitro, wanting nothing more to do with him, or they were ensconced in the next stage of their lives. Some were back at college, others had jobs, a couple were pursuing pro football careers.

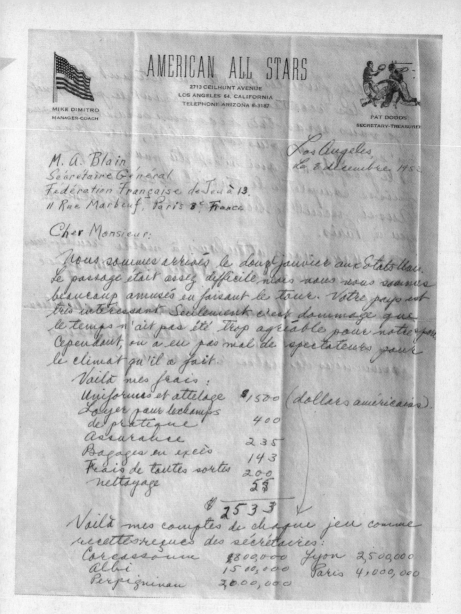

Big Al was elsewhere.

Al D. Kirkland: 'I didn't want to be drafted and I knew the Army wouldn't draft me because I couldn't see! Then at the draft, I took one step forward, raised my right hand and the next morning I woke up in Fort Ord near Monterey! That was 18 January 1954 and I was in the Army for nearly two years, in Counter Intelligence. I was sent to Fort Holabird in Baltimore and then on assignment in Washington, DC.'

Al Abajian: 'I got asked to go to France – Mike was even going to pay me more money, that's how sneaky he was – but I had to finish my teaching course. My college schedule was too heavy. I'd been back to SC to take my finals so I could start teaching. I was graduating with a BS and later acquired an MA at Oxford.'

Vince Jones: 'I went to Brasenose College straight after we got back from New Zealand. They wanted me to play rugby [union] there but I told them there may be a problem with that as I'd played League and just got back from captaining the US team in New Zealand. But the captain of Brasenose was a guy called Alec Ramsey whose father was very influential in the RFU. Alec himself was later president. He told his father and his father replied: "If he wasn't paid and didn't know he was playing a professional game, maybe we can get a waiver." They knew all about it! That's the way I got to play against Cambridge at Twickenham in the Varsity Match. The Twickenham people knew all about it when I took my son and grandson there a few years ago. Their comment was that I must be one of very few players to have played American football, rugby league and rugby union.'

Dimitro finally found one or two tour veterans who were willing to give it another go. Xavier Mena came on board again. Ray Terry would carry the bags. And there was another surprise returnee.

Teddy: 'I'd been to Europe in the Services and thought five weeks in France, with seven games on soft fields, would be great. I begged with the others to go but they thought I was nuts. They wouldn't have crossed the road again with Dimitro, let alone the Atlantic. I told my Dad about it, that no one wanted to go because they can't stand the manager. He said: "Take the opportunity – these things happen once in a lifetime." He was so right.'

Dimitro needed another 20 novices to put their bodies on the line in exchange for an adventure in Europe. He tried the same recruitment policy: hit the campus trail at LA's universities. With the tour taking place during the Christmas and New Year holidays, he could sell it as a winter vacation to current college players.

Word had got round UCLA about his antics down under. Despite X. Mena helping out, few were singing Mike's praises to prospective recruits. They did sign up a law student from UCLA: Larry Moreno would leave Sunset Boulevard to spend his Christmas vacation playing a new football code in frozen Europe.

Dimitro returned to the well at USC. He again approached the Trojans' Canadian full-back Leon Sellers – who so nearly went to Australia – and his mate, USC's third-choice quarter back Landon Exley. Exley had a couple of opportunities at QB for the Trojans in 1951 and 1953 but his only action in 1952 was in defence. He had also punted so had the skill set needed for rugby league.

Ted Grossman.

Landon Exley: 'We were high profile after getting to the Rose Bowl but the next year we lost all that great defensive team as they graduated, and we had to start over again. In 1953 we ended six and four, I think. The NFL Chicago Cardinals wanted me to try out as a free agent as I hadn't been drafted, but I probably wasn't good enough. Anyways, I didn't want to play pro football. I was done with my eligibility in football at USC and I had six months more at school to finish off before I had to go into the Air Force. They put all the football players in the ROTC – the Reserve Officers Training Corp – so we didn't have to go to Korea in the war. They wanted the football players to stay behind.

'I was looking for something to replace the thrill of college football. I had to wait nine months before active duty so I had this free time and I heard about this deal.

'They were practising at Dorsey High School, about ten minutes from the USC campus. So Leon Sellers and I said: "Let's go out and see what this was all about."

'I knew some of those guys: Al [E] Kirkland, Buckley, they were all my teammates at USC. They came back from Australia and said they had a pretty good time but it was really rough and they all had knees and elbows infected because they played on dirt fields, I guess, or because they'd played too many games – almost every other day. It damn near killed them.

'The players came back very, very disillusioned. Dimitro was, by today's standards, almost a crook. He was really a tough guy. When Leon and I went out there to practise people said: "Be careful of Dimitro: he'll steal the fillings out of your teeth!"

'So Leon and I went out there with scepticism to see what it was all about. But Mike said we'd only play seven games in France in about 30 days or something so we decided to try out for it because Leon was in the same boat as me.'

Another USC man trying out at Dorsey was Tony Rappa.

Tony Rappa: 'Mine is a kinda sad story. I went to Southern Cal as a linebacker and I was not very big but I was quick. I played my freshman year there – it was 1952. I did well and I was supposed to be a starter on the defense as a sophomore. I have a clipping somewhere where coach Jess Hill said that. I was doing "too well". Then in the spring of that year they changed the rules of football. You couldn't just play defense or offense: for a period of time you had to do both – which messed me up completely. The rule change meant that fewer players got involved in a game so I was very discouraged.'

The notion of 'two platoon' football, where separate teams ran on to play defence and offence, was an anathema to rugby league folk. But it was introduced when the doomed AAFC pro league lifted the limit on substitutions, followed by the NFL doing likewise in 1950. College football was undecided: when the Army used this tactic to thrash Stanford 43-0 at Yankee Stadium two years earlier, they had been booed throughout. For now, the NCAA insisted on limited substitutions and players staying on to play defence and offence.

Rappa: 'I had great hopes of doing well so that second year in college I was transferred to guard, which I'd never played before. I was disillusioned. So when I heard about this trip I decided I would try out for that team and afterward join the service because you could volunteer for the draft. I was going to leave college for a time and go back – and I did go back.

'I wasn't a letterman on the Varsity. In those days freshmen didn't play on the Varsity team. In those days they wouldn't play you unless you were going to play enough because you'd lose a year of eligibility and you only had three in those days. So we had Freshman teams and played UCLA, Stanford and Cal.

'So anyway, I tried out for the rugby team and I made the squad. I don't know how many tried out: not a lot of people.'

Landon Exley found an old room-mate from USC among the guys working out at Dorsey: Norm Stocks, a world champion sprinter. Stocks had broken the 800 yard relay world record running for USC at the 1949 Coliseum Relays. It helped that one of his team-mates was reigning Olympic sprint champion Mel Patton. A California State 400m champion while at San Diego High School, Stocks, too, was lightning fast but had next to no rugby experience.

Dimitro approached another of USC's track and field Olympic champions. Parry O'Brien had decent oval ball pedigree: he had led Santa Monica High School to a state football championship and won a football scholarship to USC. But when he got blind-sided in a freshman game, O'Brien lost his love of gridiron and focussed on field events instead. In the summer of 1952, O'Brien, only weeks out of his teens, won shot put gold at the Helsinki Olympics, setting an Olympic record along the way. A few months before Dimitro's tour proposal, he had broken the world record – the first of 16 such feats.

But Dimitro tempted O'Brien, just 21, to join his old pals on a trip back to Europe to try this new football code. At 6ft 3in and 240lbs, he had the size and quick feet to be a destroyer in the pack of any rugby league team. O'Brien also asked along his pal Erkie Cheldin.

Erkie Cheldin: 'Parry, Landon Exley and I played together at Santa Monica High School and freshmen football at USC. Parry got me to come along to the try-outs at Dorsey. Mike D. got the other guys like X Mena to do the brain work, but he was the main promoter.'

Harry Taylor was dragged out of Exley's frat house to become the sixth Trojan on the tour – he would play in the second row.

They would trail through their old boys' network again, starting with a former UCLA freshman football player: Don Lent.

Don Lent: 'My father worked at the Hollywood Palladium Dance Hall as a maitre d' during and after World War II. He met many of the great college and professional athletes around Southern California and the rest of the US because they had banquets at the Palladium. That's how he got to know Mike. When I played freshman football at UCLA in 1948, Mike was on the Varsity team. We became good friends.'

Unable to crack the Varsity squad at UCLA, Lent transferred to George Pepperdine College, a small Christian liberal arts college in Vermont Knolls. Pepperdine had an impressive new football programme, humbling plenty of visiting teams at Sentinel Field in Inglewood in the post-war years.

By the time 1953 came around, Lent had used up his college football eligibility and instead turned to coaching. Not only was he desperate to play some more football, he also had some influence over the whole team. Dimitro had his 'in'.

Lent: 'I couldn't go on the trip to Australia as I only got married the year before, and had to work. However, Mike invited me to come to France and it was a shorter trip over Christmas vacation, so I made it.'

Lent recruited five of his Pepperdine Waves team-mates: Bob Lampshire, who was also with him at UCLA; pole-vaulter Bob Ferguson; linebacker Virgil Elwess, a record-setting punter and points-scorer at San Jacinto High who had specialised in shot put at college; 192 lbs guard Pat Bandy, and running back Don Webster. Lent had coached all five in the 1953 season and Pepperdine's end of season trip became a tour of France, playing rugby league football.

Virgil Elwess.

Ferguson: 'I didn't know Mike Dimitro before he recruited me, Bob, Virgil and Don following the end of college football. But I knew his reputation!'

Rappa: 'I didn't know much about Dimitro. I knew he might've been an ex-boxer and was also a manager of boxers.'

Dimitro was not their biggest problem. That was how to play rugby league.

Cheldin: 'Most of us had never played before, however we did have football experience.'

Rappa: 'I don't think any of these people had seen a game of rugby before in their lives. I hadn't. I just loved the idea of going to Europe! That's why I tried out for the team. All we could do from our experiences of football was block – or rather, tackle – but it was pretty sketchy. I don't know how they picked up anyone who was any good as no one had played before. We were American football players so we had a knowledge of – and liked – physical contact. When we first got together there was an explanation of the rules but we still had no idea of what the game was. The first game of rugby that I saw was the one in which I first played!'

Ferguson: 'I'd never seen a rugby game. I knew little about rugby, including the difference in union and league. Nor did most of us. So we had several practice sessions to learn a little about the game but it was a real challenge to try to learn the basics in a short period of time.'

Exley: 'We practised three or four days a week in the evening for an hour or two at Dorsey. Dimitro and Xavier Mena taught us what to do and we had Teddy Grossman, who had played before. I guess we had about 25 or 30 training and they took about 20. Not everyone got to go.'

Along with the USC and UCLA crowd, Dimitro turned again to his old 'Bama sidekick Ray Terry for help. With Dimitro forced to play most of the games down under, Terry had been the de-facto manager – and was more use at that than playing. But he was up for another adventure.

Rappa: 'I remember Mike's assistant – Ray Terry – was a nice guy. I made a point of hitting him, on every play, so he remembered me. I think maybe that helped me be picked! I was really happy about being picked. I think it was all paid for – I don't remember paying for anything. I might have, because I loved the opportunity of going there.'

Joining them for the trip of their young lives, was the full-back from the College of the Pacific – a red-headed tearaway called Willie Richardson. But when Parry O'Brien pulled out, afraid he might lose his amateur status for track – and with it his Olympic dream – the squad was looking worrying small. Teddy

Grossman was not going to let that happen again. He put in a call to his brother Sam, who had studied at both UCLA and Stanford. He had played football for the Navy but had excelled most at skiing.

Sam: 'I got involved because Parry O'Brien couldn't make the trip and my brother got me on it as his replacement. I'd had no practice sessions in LA. We didn't know what the hell we were doing. We didn't know the difference between rugby league and rugby union. This was a Dimitro promotion and hustle and we were all faking it!'

Unlike the Australian adventure, there were no other illustrious college football names or NFL stars primed to tour France. They were a bunch of oddballs and no-marks, rejects and wannabes. There was one other American on the roster. The French papers called him Hildenberg, Hildengberg, Helteberg, Hildenger and even Calvine. A tall, slim, serious-looking athlete, no one knew who Calvin Hilgenberg was. The 21-year-old from Chicago was the mystery man of the tour.

Don Lent: 'I somewhat remember the name Hilgenberg, but I guess I didn't get to know him very well. I don't remember him playing much.'

The new team was ready to go. But even some of those who had attended practice and seemed certainties still had their doubts, Exley among them.

Exley: 'My only hesitancy about that last day was… well, first of all, I didn't have any money, which made me nervous – although they said you get all your expenses paid and don't have to pay for any meals and accommodation, which was true. But inside I just didn't trust Dimitro, you know. You're 22 years old: you don't know what's going on.

'I had a girlfriend and we were supposed to be getting married in April 1954. About two or three days before we were due to leave, Leon and I decided to go. But we were very cautious.

'So this is the day of our departure: we're supposed to be at Los Angeles Airport at five o'clock. I'm at the fraternity house and I have no money and I don't even have a suitcase. So I was with my room-mate who, today, is still my best friend. He said: "You have to go." He went around the fraternity house and collected 100 dollars for me – we had no dough in those days – then I borrowed my friend's suitcase and threw all my clothes in. I still wasn't sure but they said: "You have to." At least I had my passport: that was the one thing I did go do!

'Anyway, I phoned my parents and said: "I'm going." They said: "You are?!" and I said: "Yes, I'm going." So off I went, with just 100 dollars for a month, and one suitcase: that's all I had. My parents drove up to LA Airport and I got to see them for a few minutes just before we went. As I boarded the plane, I still wasn't sure.'

He wasn't alone.

CHAPTER 25
ALLEZ WILLIE!

Erkie: 'We flew to New York from the old Los Angeles Airport on a four-engine super-constellation plane. Man, did that plane vibrate and make some noise! We spent a few hours in New York, went up the Empire State Building and took a cab back to the La Guardia Airport.'

The intrepid explorers then boarded an Aer Lingus flight to Ireland and then on to Paris.

Landon: 'We had a good time. We just went from town to town on our bus. Sometimes we took the train. We took the train from Paris down to Carcassonne, then came back by train from south to north: to Perpignan, Avignon, Albi, Lyon and eventually Paris. The Rugby League of France handled it all – Dimitro had nothing to do with the scheduling.'

Don Lent: 'My bags got lost on the plane going to France. I know that they ended up in South America and we didn't get them back until we reached Paris.'

Ted: 'I'd had to persuade Sam to come. His bags went to South America. They had a better trip than he did.'

Don: 'I borrowed clothes from the other guys and washed my clothes every night in the sink so I could be clean. Fortunately I had my overcoat with me as it was real cold most of the trip.'

Landon: 'They took us to the best places. Carcassonne, Perpignan and Avignon were just sensational. They were all walled cities. Of course, we'd never seen anything like this in our lives before. It was truly beautiful and very interesting.'

Aux cotés de MM. Paul BARRIE RE, Antoine BLAIN et Georges RAMOND, les joueurs americains qui devaient se produire à Carcassonne, ont été abondamment fleuris dès leurs premiers pas dans notre ville.

Tony Rappa: 'We took nylons and cigarettes, which was a big deal – after all, it was only six or seven years after the war. Everything there was so inexpensive: that's certainly changed! The French people were so wonderful to us (that's also changed!) In every city, of course, they had a reception and that was always very nice.'

It was a long trek south overnight from Paris. Arriving late on Monday morning into the famous medieval southern city of Carcassonne, they checked in to Hotel de Ville then headed off to the town hall to meet Antoine Blain and his fellow French Federation bigwig Paul Barriere, the president of AS Carcassonne, the mayor of Carcassonne, the cabinet chief of Aude prefecture, the director of sporting education, the consular general – among others! Rugby league was big business in Carcassonne and the 'Americains Eleves' were front as well as back page news. Toasts were made, drinks were taken, speeches made, hands shaken.

Dimitro has rarely looked so awkward – or mentally fragile – as he did on the town hall steps clinging to a gigantic floral display. What would this adventure hold? Would he get away with it again? At his first meeting with the press he spun the usual lines: he had fallen in love with rugby league watching Welsh immigrants at the steelworks in West Virginia, he had been on a clandestine trip to the Sydney Cricket Ground, and he had gone to Alabama University in 1941... a couple of years later than what he had claimed down under.

The party retired to their hotel for a siesta before their first training session at Stade Albert-Domec.

The All Stars used Carcassonne to acclimatise. They had nearly a week to get used to the change in culture, climate and code: they had to learn how to play

Landon Exley.

rugby league. They also had time to learn about Carcassonne. They had a tour around La Citie's stunning medieval walls, towers and turrets, acquiring berets en route – they clashed incongruously with the UCLA baseball jackets and leather bombers. They were always cold, even in the winter sunshine. Some resorted to training in their berets along with their standard sweatpants and sweatshirts.

At La Citie.

Tony: 'We were all surprised at the facilities. None of the rooms had toilets or showers – you had to go down the hall. That was very new to us. It made us realise how prosperous southern California was: we felt very lucky. I was only 19 so I probably didn't take it all in but we were kind of a curiosity. When we stopped at a place there'd be people gathered to look at us. I just loved being there.'

Don: 'I also remember us all lined up at the latrines in the men's toilet once when these women walked in! We all jumped and realised we must be pretty shy in America. They were just the waitresses coming in to get the linen off the shelves in there.'

Not everyone was shy in the presence of French women, however.

Landon: 'One of our team was found in a house of ill repute. He'd fallen in love with a prostitute and he wouldn't leave. We had to go and get him out one morning before a game! Oh my, we had some fun! But we were only 22 years old.'

All Stars in Carcassonne: Xavier Mena (13), Ted Grossman 9), Leon Sellers (20), Virgil Elwess (4), Landon Exley (22), Larry Moreno (9), Bob Lampshire (6), Bob Ferguson (1), Willie Richardson (27), Harry Taylor (19), Tony Rappa (7), Calvin Hilgenberg (11), Pat Bandy (15).

Don: 'One thing we did notice in France was the lack of young men our age. They lost over a million young men in World War II and it was obvious that a generation of young men was missing. It was very disturbing.'

Eventually, after six days of preparation, it was time for business.

SUNDAY 20 DECEMBER 1953

LANGUEDOC XIII v AMERICAN ALL STARS

Stade Albert-Domec, Carcassonne

Stade Albert-Domec sits between the train tracks and the river that runs around the foot of La Citie, a spectacular and beautiful setting for any football game. Not that the All Stars could spend long admiring the view. They had been thrown into the lion's den.

Just like his headlong launch into the deep end in Sydney, Dimitro had agreed to

a fearsome opening challenge in France: a select XIII from the Languedoc region. This was Carcassonne, the reigning French champions and holders of the Lord Derby Cup, giants of the game, plus two guests from Perpignan (second rower Gacia and hooker Moulis) and one from Toulouse (Poletti).

The rookie Americans were to play their first ever game against a team directed by the star players from the best team on earth: 'Les Canaries' of Carcassonne had an all-international half-back pairing of Claude Teisseire and Gilbert Benausse, with national hero Louis 'Lolo' Mazon in the centres. Mazon's teenage years had been somewhat different to most of the Americans: twice he had escaped imprisonment by the Nazis and helped liberate Carcassonne from the Germans. Beating up some young Americans would be a walk in the park.

Through the art deco arch and out into the modern concrete velodrome – their very own coliseum – the hopeful Americans lined up beside the Languedoc XIII for the national anthems. The Americans wore their royal blue shirts with red stars decorating the white shoulder panels, white rugby shorts and hooped socks. Their uniform was fabulous.

Their body language was less imposing. Captain Xavier Mena stood tall and barrel-chested beside the match officials, resplendent in their long-collared white shirts and black blazers. The other side of Mena was little Teddy Grossman, hands behind his back, looking impish and mischievous: the naughty schoolboy up to see the Principal, failing to hide his guilt. Those two knew what was coming.

The others appeared suitably terrified. Hands limp by their sides, most stood shoulder to shoulder. There was a gaping hole between Moreno and Lampshire and another between Rappa and Hilgenberg while Bandy loitered alone at the end, hands cusped in front of him, a vision of discomfort.

Torrential rain caused the championship match between Catalans and Toulouse to be called off down in Perpignan that day but freezing Carcassonne was spared the monsoon. Instead this historic encounter got a flood of points for more than 5,000 locals to enjoy.

Landon Exley.

The strange young American bucks were blown away in the first 40 torturous minutes. The All Stars trailed by five tries to one at the break. Moreno had intercepted a pass and raced past Poletti to make it 8-3 and Rappa had been held up a couple of inches short of the line just before half-time as the Americans 'executed audacious combinations' according to the local press. They had shown some promise in attack and a second half comeback suggested good things to come.

Willie Richardson clashed with thrilling stand-off Benausse before Xavier – one of the few Americans to have ever played the game – blasted over for two tries, sandwiching Lessalle's hat-trick try. The All Stars tried to haul themselves back in to the game. Willie the redhead and barrel-chested Rappa scored. But there was to be no 'coup de theatre' as Teisseire scored to complete a 30-22 win for 'Les Audois'.

Conceding nine tries was not part of the plan, but with 11,000 kilometres to clear from their exhausted bodies, it was hugely impressive to score six of their own.

Landon: 'In that first game in Carcassonne we did some real infractions and people booed but we picked it up. They were ahead of us 19-3 and then we started to figure it out. It was a baptism of fire but by the end of that first game we pretty much understood.'

Don: 'When we first started playing, we had a problem understanding what the refs were saying in French. It really was a problem to know what was going on. To solve that, Dimitro and the French Federation decided to send to England to get a referee that could speak English and French. So Mr Appleton came, and went to all the games with us and officiated them. That way, at least we had someone that understood our complaints.'

Bilingual Appleton, a 45-year-old former player from Liverpool who managed an entertainment club in Warrington, had refereed the England-France amateur international the previous year and was sent on tour by Bill Fallowfield and the International Board to help, save (or spy on) the Americans.

He was to be their saviour.

Landon: 'The referee from England – Charlie – travelled with us and he was great. He'd come to practice and show us some techniques, some gimmicky plays or something. He was a very nice guy. But you can only be taught so much about a game without having seen it.'

Sam: 'Charlie was really great to us.'

Don: 'He was a real nice guy and we talked with him a lot about rugby and England.'

The All Stars had four days to prepare for their next test: against Albi on Friday: Christmas Day. They practised all week, trying to grasp the techniques of rugby league in a crash-course led by Teddy and Charlie as much as Dimitro, Terry and Mena.

Landon: 'What we didn't understand was that when we were down we had to kick that ball back pretty much immediately. We would take our time and line up and Charlie kept saying: "No, no, no." What do you call it? Play the ball? Yes, "play the ball". A couple of times early on the fans were hissing.'

It was soon decided by the French Federation that the game in Lyon would be against an International XIII, not all Americans. The Federation couldn't risk two one-way processions in the final week of the tour. No one would turn up to see these innocents get stuffed in Paris if the same had happened the week before in Lyon. No matter that the France v USA posters were already printed.

What the All Stars had to do was use their own particular skills from American football to their advantage.

Landon: 'They brought me because I was a quarter back. This is how crazy they were, this was Dimitro's idea: instead of short passes we were going to throw the ball a long way. So they wanted me out there on the wing. They were going to pass the ball out to me real quick and, because I was left-handed, I was to stop and throw it all the way back across the field to the other side where someone would be. That way, Dimitro in his demented mind, had it figured out that that guy would run unscathed all the way to the end zone.

'We tried it several times but the problem is that the damn ball was too big! I could throw a football, you know, forever, but it was kind of hard to throw a rugby ball, what with the cold weather and the wind. It worked a couple of times but we soon played in the normal way with short, lateral passes. We were always doing something crazy.'

Some gridiron traits were tough to erase, though.

Rappa: 'Leon Sellers loved to put his head down and bowl people over. The first game he did a lot of damage. He was very good but maybe too big. All he really knew what to do was to carry the ball forward and put his head down. Leon beat the hell out of those guys. He'd just run right over them until they figured out to just let him run, let him past, then grab his leg. Which they did, and that changed the whole thing. They would let him have one or two more yards but then they'd grab his foot and flip him. He did real well for a long time.'

Landon: 'The basic problem was that when Leon got the ball he didn't want to give it to anyone else. He just kept running and would bang into them and hit

RUGBY à XIII INTERNATIONAL

DIMANCHE
20
DÉCEMBRE
à 15ʰ

CARCASSONNE

STADE
ALBERT DOMEC

LANGUEDOC
U.S.A

HAR
FORT

"Location: CAFÉ CONTINENTAL"

PERNOD 45

Imp. HARFORT 58 r. du Temple-Paris

Leon Sellers (20) and Landon Exley (22) break away.

heads. He and Willie Richardson just liked to run into people and not pass so we sort of defeated ourselves in that respect. When he got near the goal-line, boy he'd just butt his head at them.'

Rappa: 'Leon – like the rest of us – learned then that we had to be a little more sophisticated in our approach to the game, if we were to be successful. We learned as we went along.'

Landon: 'We got to understand the rules pretty quick. It didn't take me very long to remember I didn't have a helmet on so not to tackle with my head… but it did Willie Richardson! He was a wild man and he kept putting his head in there. After a while they would see him coming and they would throw the ball away because they didn't want to get hit by him. He was just a complete killer. He was the hooker but on defence he was all over the place. He was just running around hitting people. He had bright red hair and they loved him! They were always shouting "Allez Willie".'

ALBI

Albi lies beneath the Black Mountain, an hour or two north of Toulouse. Its beautiful narrow cobbled streets and tall red-brick medieval walls make it a magnet for tourists and a town the locals do not want to leave. The enormous stone bridges that span the River Tarn are dramatic; the gargantuan Sainte-Cecile, the largest brick cathedral on the planet, towers over 'The Red City'. Beneath its shadows once wandered an artistic local boy: Henri Toulouse-Lautrec.

The All Stars soon realised they were visiting some of the most attractive places in France. But they were not here to just sight-see. 'Rugby a XIII' was the

RUGBY A XIII INTERNATIONAL
VENDREDI
25
DÉCEMBRE
à 15H
ALBI
STADE
MAURICE RIGAUD
ALBI
U.S.A
HARFORT
"Location : HOTEL du VIGAN"
PERNOD 45

dominant code in Albi before the war. The Vichy regime's ban had forced the league club to merge with their union rivals. Albi XIII was having to find its feet again. They did so quickly, winning the French title by 1956. 'Rugby a XIII' was the dominant code in Albi before the war. The Vichy regime's ban had forced the rugby league club to merge with their union rivals and now Albi XIII was having to find its feet again.

For most of the Americans, it was their first Christmas away from home. What better way to forget what they were missing in California than to go head to head with a leading French team on Christmas Day?

25 DECEMBER
ALBI v AMERICAN ALL STARS
Stade Maurice Rigaud

Ferguson: 'That was the first and only time I have been away from my family at Christmas time.'

Lent: 'Playing on Christmas didn't amount to much. In those days they didn't celebrate Christmas in France like they do now or like we do here in the USA. There were very few decorations and not much in the stores.'

Exley: 'I don't recall phoning home on Christmas Day but there was a large reception put on by the French after the match.'

A mile west of Albi's bustling alleys and squares stood the humble Stade Maurice Rigaud. It may have been Christmas Day in a Catholic cathedral city but the ground was overflowing. The tiny terraces were packed with French fans who had come to see Les Americains.

Desperate ticketless lads hung to the leafless branches of trees overlooking the field, others formed

All in at Albi.

a precarious line along the rooftops of the neighbouring bank and boulangerie that lined the main road, motionless silhouettes with hands thrust deep in trench-coat pockets like human targets on a shooting range.

Landon: 'Another new creation of Mike Dimitro's was that we were going to out-fox them and wear our football pants!'

Little did Landon know that Mike had tried this before down under with little but embarrassment ensuing. However, for once, the long pants tucked into knee-high socks, were ideal protection on a frozen field.

The 'Yankees' scrambled heroically in defence and, when they got the ball, scampered downfield and battered away at the Albi line. 'Les Albigeois' didn't play as well as Carcassonne had but led 8-0 at half-time. They could only score once more after the break as the tourists put in a heroic performance as they lost by just 11-5.

Willie Richardson at hooker v Albi.

Admiration poured from the packed terraces and stand. It was a performance to be proud of. Be-quiffed centre Sellers, 'le talenneur' Richardson, 'l'ailier' Ferguson and 'bulldozer' Dimitro were all feted by the press, the Americans being 'excessivement rapide' and gaining great territory.

Lent: 'I think I scored in Albi {he did}. I had a good game anyway. I was given the game ball for outstanding play so I must have done something right. I still have it in my trophy case at home. The local newspaper called me Leigth instead of Lent.

'Exley: 'All I remember of the game was that the field was frozen and it was so cold. We beat them up physically but they scored more points than us, again!'

Erkie: 'That night in Albi, Ted Grossman got very sick from drinking milk and threw up in the bidet. He couldn't get out of bed to make the game the next day, so we left him in his room, he couldn't move. When the maid came in to make up the room she didn't notice Ted. Then she saw the barf in the bidet, then looked at the bed. Ted was so weak he couldn't move anything but his big eyes. The maid screamed bloody murder and ran out of the room. We all said Teddy died that day in Albi!'

Spending Christmas with a gang of young athletes from California was hardly a grind. Although, by this stage, most of the group were starting to suss Dimitro out. He had told the French press he was only 28 when he was nearer 32, and claimed he had played rugby league for five years, rather than

Calvin Hilgenberg (11) and Don Lent (17).

Guy...
Studio Guy
ALBI

five months. But that was a minor blemish on his character. Despite his credit from UCLA in public speaking, Mike needed to be kept away from the microphone.

Tony: 'Dimitro was not very polished, he was very crude. I don't know if he was a crook but he was on the make, taking advantage of whatever he could. We kind of laughed at him because he was a very crude guy. He always said 'futch' – I think was that it. He used to say 'futch 'em' so he didn't say fuck. He said it a lot! He wanted me to be a boxer. He really was kinda punch drunk. He was a real boxer. He looked like he had been through that whole thing. Nice enough guy. He was only after what he could get. He didn't care about anything else. No one blamed him for that.'

The fellas certainly looked like they had a good time that Christmas night. Out in Albi, resplendent in leather jackets, tartan scarves, blazers, macs and SC varsity jackets, they have a blast, and even befriend a mystified dog. Centre of the entertainment was usually Teddy.

Landon: 'Ted was just so laid back – it didn't really matter to him whether we won or lost. He was just there for the fun. And we had a lot of fun.'

G. BONNE...MAISON

Plus entraînés, mieux adaptés
les AMÉRICAINS ont tenu tête aux ALBIGEOIS
Mais ils ont encore beaucoup à apprendre
(De notre envoyé spécial J. BOUDEY)

A ALBI : Albi XIII bat U.S.A. XIII par 11 points (trois essais de Balent, Corduries (2), une transformation de Rives) à 5 points (un essai de Lani, une transformation). Temps couvert, terrain gras. Recette : 1.858.000 francs pour 5.808 spectateurs payants. Arbitrage de M. Fabre, d'Albi.

CHAPTER 26
THE DOUCHE BOWL

Le XIII des U.S.A. à la Préfecture

Durant l'allocution de M. le Préfet (à l'extrême droite) on reconnait MM. Antoine Blain, secrétaire général de la F.F.J. XIII. Chamut, chef de Cabinet, Dimitro, manager et capitaine de l'équipe des U.S.A. Maria, président du XIII Catalan et, en partie masqué, à droite Paul Barrière, président de la F.F. XIII.

LA VIE SYNDICALE

PERPIGNAN

After two surprisingly narrow defeats, and practice every day under Teddy's instruction, Dimitro's crew were gaining in confidence. But Dimitro had done it again: the schedule was ludicrous. With just Saturday off – most of which would be spent travelling south across the Corbieres – the All Stars had no recovery time from the Albi dogfight before being sent out to confront a different, but equally daunting, challenge: Les Espoirs de France, the best young talent in France.

The fact the game was taking place in another lovely medieval city was a mixed blessing. Perpignan, capital of the Catalan region and home to much of the best rugby league talent in the country, was a delight, but the Californian college football players had little time to enjoy it.

On arrival that evening, they headed for a reception at the Prefecture with another clutch of movers and shakers, including the FFJXIII supremos Blain and Barriere, and the manager, president, coach and several players from XIII Catalan. There were more toasts in the Americans' honour. And they were late again.

SUNDAY 27 DECEMBER 1953
ESPOIRS DE FRANCE v AMERICAN ALL STARS
Stade Jean-Laffon, Perpignan

The sun was out as the crowd packed into Stade Jean-Laffon, filling the tiny stands and piling up six deep against the pitch-side walls in the shallow paddocks, but the game was up by the break as the home side led 23-8. It was no contest. The French kids were untouchable from the kick-off, racing out for a point a minute lead. Bob Lampshire hit back with a try and a goal but the French rattled in five first half tries to two, Larry Marino touching down for 15-8. The likes of Descous, Garcia, Bessieres, Delhoste, Save, Carmouze and goalkicker Guiraud were too hot for the Selection Americaine to handle.

The French eased up after the break but still scored four more tries, allowing 'les Yankees' to score three. When Don Lent went over to make it 37-21 with five

LES AMERICANS OUT BEAUCOUP A APPRENDRE!

L'Independant

PROFITANT DES ERRUERS DE LEURS NOVICES RIVAUX
LES ESPOIRS DE FRANCE DISPOSENT DES USA 37 A 21

Pat Bandy (15) in Avignon.

minutes left, referee Monsieur Jaubert blew time early, with the score-line respectable to both parties.

Landon: 'The French players didn't like the way we played. We didn't have the finesse that they had. We would beat the heck out of them physically because in America we tackle very, very hard and they more kinda grab. We'd be in the game, in the game and then all of a sudden they'd score and we didn't know how they did it. It happened so quickly: we'd literally be saying: "How'd they do that?" They had some quick players, you know.'

In the French championship that afternoon, XIII Catalans drew 0-0 with leaders Villeneuve enabling Bordeaux to go top after battering Toulouse, 31-5.

Finally, after three defeats and an awful lot of learning, the lads had a few days off before the New Year's Day game in Avignon. There was one trip down to the Spanish border to a Pyrenees mountain village, while others carried on to Barcelona for a day in the city.

It was no Rose Bowl Game but at least they still had a game of football on New Year's Day to look forward to. Don Lent and his pals christened it the Douche Bowl in honour of the French toilets which they had never seen before – and didn't know what they were for!

Vendredi 1ᵉʳ Janvier
Amérique contre Provence

Composition des équipes

AMERIQUE XIII

LAMPSHIRE (6)
MARINO (9) FERGUSON (1)   SELLERS (20) EXLEY (22)
o. : CALVINE (11)   m. : GROSSMAN (8)
BENDEY (15)
RAPPA (7)   TAYLOR (19)
MENNA (13)   WILLIE (27)   VIRGIL (4)

BERAUD (Av.) CARBONA (Carp.) FERRERO (Mars.)
BALDASSIN (Carp.)   LOPEZ (Cav.)
PEREZ (Marseille)
o. : GERMANO (Cav.)   m. : DOP (Marseille)
MAIGRE (Carp.) GRANGEON (Av.) PAGNETTI (Cav.) GAYE (Cav.)
PEREZ (Carp.)

PROVENCE XIII

Arbitre : M. BOUDON
Ligue Méditerranée - Provence

N. B. – *Nous nous excusons pour les erreurs ou omissions certains éléments nous ayant fait défaut en dernière minute.*

New Year's Day football was traditional in rugby league too. And in Sporting Olympique Avignonnais XIII, the city had one of the best clubs in the Championnat. Led by France prop Andre Beraud, SOA were top of the league and the town of 60,000 was dreaming of upsetting the big city clubs of Marseilles, Lyon, Carcassonne and Toulouse – 'who have not even heard of Avignon and it's tiny little Stade de Ruf', according to the home town programme – to win the national title.

The All Stars were up against a team representing the Provence region, featuring players from SOA alongside those from Carpentras, Marseilles (originally supposed to be the wonderful Dop but in the event not) and Cavaillon. It included SOA's talismanic Beraud but not their prolific try-scorer Savonne.

FRIDAY 1 JANUARY
PROVENCE v AMERICAN ALL STARS
Stade de Ruf, Avignon

As usual, the USA made the worst possible start: conceding a try after just four minutes and losing Virgil Elwess to a reoccurrence of an old football injury to his shoulder. His tour was over. The lanky Bandy came on at loose forward and Taylor, who had moved into the second row, went over for a try almost immediately. Maigre then scored twice but Provence missed all three conversion attempts to lead

FIRST VICTORY FOR USA 13 – MIKE DIMITRO'S STARS MAKE GREAT PROGRESS IN 15 DAYS

just 9-3. The crowd huddled under the deep pitched roof must still have expected a French procession.

Instead, they got 'an exhibition of eccentric play by the visitors, much to their delight'. On 25 minutes, Granite Mike touched down and Lampshire converted. Six minutes before the break, they were ahead.

Andre Alauzen wrote: 'In the 34th minute of the USA-Provence match, the press box in the Stade de Saint-Ruf in Avignon was awoken from its stupor and alive with joy. Hildengberg scored a try that put the Americans up 11-9. It was the first moment since their tour of France began that the Americans were ahead!'

Teddy Grossman's try and Lampshire's conversion made it 16-9 after the break and, driven on by the 'inspirational' Dimitro, the All Stars were not going to let this go. Lampshire got over the line for 19-9 and when a second interception by the slender crew-cutted young winger Exley led to another try for the tall, brooding Hilgenberg on 65 minutes, the game was won. Grangeon's late try was no consolation for a humiliated Provence XIII.

There was a mixed reaction to the shock victory. Sellers, Lampshire, Exley, Teddy Grossman, Mena and Richardson were all lauded in the papers, who dissected why the Americans, with unorthodox methods but brute strength, great size and speed, had managed to beat the hugely-experienced Provence. Some thought the visitors were given a helping hand:

Sam: 'They had to throw the game in Avignon to make us win, otherwise nobody would have shown up in Paris.'

Don: 'I think we were able to score so many points because of the excellent individual athletic ability in our team. Most were hard running players. We were used to running in a low position with our heads and shoulders low so that we broke through many tackles. We also ran some unusual plays like running cross-backs – that's where one player hands it off to another or fakes a hand-off. They couldn't see where the ball went. But the main reason we competed was that we caught on to rugby very fast and we really enjoyed the game.'

Bob Lampshire was also becoming a star of the tour.

Don: 'Lampshire was a great quarter back at Pepperdine but he was also a great kicker. He scored the most points on tour from his kicks. In one game, he kicked a drop kick for about 50 yards over the goal posts and the crowd roared. Then he had to kick it properly – a place kick – from a sharp angle. It was another 50 yarder and he made it again! The crowd roared even more: they loved it.'

Lampshire wasn't the only American gaining respect from opponents and a following in the stands.

Landon: 'The French fans loved us – they were just wonderful. They did boo us and hiss us a few times in the first and second game but I don't ever recall anyone being nasty or anything to us.'

Erkie: 'The crowds liked watching Landon pass the ball all the way across the field and the way Leon ran.'

Don: 'Although most of us had no rugby experience, we learned the game fast and even used some innovations from football. Like we threw the ball overhand and they didn't know what to think, but ruled as long as it was to a player behind us, it was legal. The French players then wanted to learn from us how to throw it overhand but they were terrible!'

Landon: 'Teddy and those guys got us coming along pretty good. We got used to playing without pads but it hurt more when you hit the ground. We played two or three games when it was very cold, like in the 20s, Fahrenheit. And falling on the frozen fields hurt. I can remember that. It was cold, so cold the whole time. We were freezing to death and playing on those cold fields was awful.'

Erkie: 'The field was frozen and there we were in our shorts, some beach boys from Southern California.'

Ferguson: 'It was so very cold! We didn't have the appropriate clothing. But we survived. I remember the hot tea and rum that was served at intermission. We were happy to see that!'

Erkie: 'Man it sure hurt went we hit the turf. We were used to head and shoulder tackling and with no pads or helmets we were taking some hits that hurt. We didn't have a Band-Aid, we didn't have a trainer, so there were some guys walking with pain between matches. Some guys really had their bells rung and were a bit punchy for some time.'

Neither Sam Grossman nor Erkie Cheldin had played much. They were there mainly for the ride. Neither was chosen to play Provence. So off they went on their own adventure.

Erkie: 'We had a break of about five or six days so Sam and I took a train from Avignon down to the French Riviera. I don't think we had twenty bucks between us. Our first stop by train was Cannes. We got off the train and started to walk through the station and saw what looked like American sailors. I went up to the first one and said: "Hi, we're from California. Where are you from?" What I heard was unknown to me so I asked Sam: "What did he say?" Sam didn't know so I asked again. It took a little time to understand his strong accent but we finally got it. He was from Brooklyn!

'From there we went to Nice and Monte Carlo. No bags, no toothbrushes, no anything. Just the clothes on our backs. We were a mess but we had some laughs. I don't remember how we got back but somehow the train did alright for us. Is youth crazy or what?'

CHAPTER 27
BIRD'S HEAD'S
BANQUET

Landon Exley and Leon Sellers.

The tour party headed north, a few hours from Avignon in the south-east
to the big city – Lyon – close to the Swiss border. There was a week until the
international against France in Paris but the American players were on stand-by
for the 'Selection Internationale' who were taking on France in a prestigious game
to mark the 30th anniversary of the Federation. 'Selection Internationale' would
see the best Americans join a team of star players from around the world and
almost all of them playing in England.

The 'rugbymen Americains' were indulged at a formal afternoon reception at
the Hotel de Ville, with all Lyon's great and good present and ready to pronounce
their delight at such distinguished guests from across the Atlantic.

Lyon was a booming Treize city: the Lyon club were on a run that saw them win
or be runners-up in the French Championship and the national cup seven times
in six years. They supplied half of the France squad: Rey, Lecuyer, Crespo, Duffort,
Audoubert, Krawzyk, Bastianelli, and Vanel.

Among the American party was one of the leading players and personalities
in the world game: Great Britain and Bradford star Ernest Ward. Ward spent the
days before the game in Lyon with the Americans and helped Charlie Appleton
and Teddy with the coaching.

With the Americans being the only foreign team touring France, Dimitro
nominated seven of his men to be available for selection: Lampshire, Sellers, Exley,
Marino, Rappa, Richardson and Mena. Come game day, Lampshire, Sellers and
Richardson were named in the starting XIII, and were in illustrious company. Ward
took the number one shirt; Lampshire and the Canadian Sellers formed an All

Stars partnership on the right wing with two Australians on the left: Leeds's big money recruit from Eastern Suburbs rugby union, Keith McLellan, and Huddersfield's awesome try machine Lionel Cooper.

The half-back pairing was Welsh stand-off Billy Banks, who arrived from Huddersfield to partner Warrington's pocket rocket Gerry Helme. It was a fitting start to a life-defining year for Helme in which the floppy-fringed scrum-half would score the winning try in both the Challenge Cup and World Cup finals.

Amazingly the selectors agreed to give Willie the hooking responsibilities despite his lack of experience. He might not win many scrums but he would blast holes. Alongside him in the front row were Welshman Owen Phillips and Northern Irish-born, Scottish-raised prop Tom McKinney, who could also play hooker. The second row consisted of Welshman Bernard McNally and Italian star Giovanni Vigna; Scottish talisman Dave Valentine locked the scrum. As if being a ginger American did not make him stand out enough, Richardson wore his navy football pants with his white shirt (and traditional rugby league V) and socks. His team-mates wore shorts.

The neo-classical Stade Gerland must have felt a little more familiar to the All Stars: it had echoes of the huge stadiums of California, with steps leading from the street up grassy banks to palatial archways, fans entering the arena via dozens of grand concrete tunnels, emerging on to huge sweeping stands that curved up beyond the running track. This was more Rose Bowl or Coliseum than the local park feel of Longreach, Greymouth or Albi.

This bunch of talented multi-national strangers were up against arguably the best national team in the world.

Willie Richardson v France.

France were led from the back by the majestic Puig-Aubert and featuring the star wingers Raymond 'Bird's Head' Contrastin and Vincent Cantoni, a half-back pairing of Jiminez and Joseph Crespo with Rene Duffort at hooker, and Lyonnais hero Jean 'Don Don' Audobert – a 210lbs 5ft 9in human beer barrel – barging his way forward at prop. It was the heart and soul of a French side that had stunned the Aussies home and away, a team that shocked world rugby and introduced a new brand of the handling game.

Predictably, France beat the scratch Internationale XIII, but only 19-15. Banks, McKinney and the outstanding Vigna touched down for the internationalists and Ward kicked three goals. The Stade Gerland crowd got what they wanted: a close game, plenty of entertainment and a French win. Everyone was happy. Especially Don Lent.

Don: 'Dimitro chose me to be an alternate and I suited up for the game along with Lampshire, Sellers and Richardson. As far as I can remember, I believe I got in a little at the end. The rest of the team watched from the stands without suiting up. It was a very impressive game with some high-powered athletes.'

That evening the whole party were invited to the XX Anniversaire Jeu a XIII dinner at Restaurant Nandron in Lyon. For starter: caviar. Then cocou de soie escargot. Then fromages. Then soufflé. And to cleanse the palate? Vermouth, cassis, 1947 champagne and liquers de France. Nine courses. The Americans slept well – when they eventually found their beds.

Ferguson: 'The banquet in Lyon stands out. It was outstanding… even though none of us spoke French and couldn't understand most of what was occurring!'

THE FRENCH RUGBY LEAGUE TEAM WHICH TOURED AUSTRALIA IN 1951

Back Row—P. Bartholetti, O. Lespes, V. Cantoni, R. Benausse, G. Comes, F. Rinaldi, L. Mazon, R. Caillou, J. Adouberr, F. Montrucolis, M. Martin
Middle Row—M. Andre, E. Poncinet, R. Perez, M. Lopez, G. Delaye, E. Brousse, G. Calixte, A. Beraud, R. Duffort, R. Contrastin
Front Row—C. Teisseire, J. Merquey, J. Don, A. Puig-Aubert, G. Geroud, J. Crespo

INSTALLATIONS SPORTIVES de GERLAND
Stade Municipal, Palais des Sports, et Piscine.

LYON

Landon: 'There must have been 500 people there. All of the French players would come and talk to us – we couldn't communicate at all but they would say: "You guys are very fast and very strong." They kept telling us: "Rugby league as a game is not boom, boom but finesse, finesse." They would always preach that to us but then the next game we would just go out and bang the hell out of them again and… lose! We were always in the game but then all of a sudden they would just go racing past us.

'But we hadn't even seen a game before and to have those guys pull off some of that really slick stuff that they did… But apart from not knowing all the nuances of the game, we thought we could beat them because we were better athletes, or at least we thought we were.'

Monday morning and those who could make it out of bed headed on another excursion, east through the Alps across the Swiss border to Geneva.

Bob: 'The bus to Geneva had no heat, so we'd take turns putting our hands and feet on the towelling that covered the drive shaft. That was the only thing that was warm!'

Sam: 'We weren't dressed properly. We were from southern California, this was January in France. We all froze our collective asses off. We'd go on these bus tours with no heat, we'd stay in hotel rooms with no heat, there were no hot showers. This was early on. Out of the 21 or 22 guys on the trip, 18 of us had bronchitis, a couple of guys had pneumonia. It was a real screw-up in terms of organisation.'

Landon: 'To me, Dimitro was well-organised – we made all our trains and all our buses and all of our games and the accommodation was okay. We don't know

Les rugbymen des U.S.A. ne craignent pas le froid. Avant de se rendre à l'Hôtel de Ville où une réception était organisée en leur honneur, ils ont fait une courte promenade sur la place Carnot. Notre reporter photographe a saisi l'entraîneur Mike Dimitro, entouré, de gauche à droite, par ses cinq vedettes : Jaossman, Salers, Lamshire, Richardson et Exley.

all the gory details of what problems there were but he seemed okay. Everyone was as nice as they could be. After every game there was a reception with wine and Pernod and cookies. The mayor would come and salute us and thank us for coming.'

The All Stars were even snapped for the local paper strolling the Place Carnot: Teddy, Sellers, Dimitro, Lampshire, Willie and Landon, all wearing such lightweight gear the caption claimed they didn't feel the cold. How wrong they were.

CHAPTER 28
SERIOUS AND SOBER?

After four games – five for some – in three weeks and a whistle-stop jaunt around the south of France, the banged-up but elated All Stars returned to Paris for the finale. With the terrifying prospect of an inaugural full international fixture against the mighty France at Parc de Princes rapidly approaching, the young 'Yankees' had a few days to explore one of the  world's great cities. They checked into their hotel on Haussmann Boulevard then set out to enjoy themselves.

It was time to party in post-war Paris.

There were visits to the Eiffel Tower, the Arc De Triomphe, and the markets of Montmartre. Exley donned a black beret and pipette for a photo on the Champs Elysses. They shivered along the Seine, towering Larry Taylor wearing only a light blouson, Tony Rappa, Sam Grossman and Exley wrapped up in trench-coats.

The Americans dined out at Lido Theatre-Restaurant on the Champs Elysees and made a celebrity visit to the Bazar shops at the Hotel de Ville – and handed out free tickets for Saturday's match at Parc de Princes to the first 200 of a fervent mob of young Parisian boys to visit the shop, all captured on the back page of *Le Parisien*.

They bought gabardine coats and berets to finally keep out the bitter winter winds; were special guests at the opening of an art exhibition where the wine and women were of more interest than the paintings; and crammed into 'les salons Pernod Fils' on Rue Bassano for a special night on the local spirit. The tourists squeezed up against the bar where the Pernod shot glasses were lined up while a giant bottle of the stuff is passed overhead. Their grins are ear to ear. A fine time was had.

Mena took command, conducting a chant of 'for he's a jolly good fellow' and compering the orchestra. He told the reporter Andre Bozon, who shadowed their every step: 'J'adore le Pernod Fils!' X claimed he had a bottle with his own name on it in his jazz club in LA!

Lent: 'All I can remember about Paris is that it was fun. We didn't have much money so we mostly just did some sightseeing, which was great. We saw the Eiffel Tower, Notre Dame, the Champs Eli-whatever, the museums, and I bought my wife some Chanel No. 5.'

Exley: 'I spent one day walking the streets of Paris looking for gloves for my mother. I found some and she loved them! We had some fun nights out in Paris, though, just prowling around.'

Ferguson: 'Paris was great: the Eiffel Tower, the Louvre, and the general beauty was an awesome sight, especially to me as a young man who had never travelled.'

Lent: 'I remember we had the Head Waiter at our hotel – the Commodre – bring all our dinners in one course instead of about six courses so we could hurry out to see everything. We also asked for no snails or snail sauce on our steaks. The waiter thought we were nuts! Oh well, we probably were.'

Sam: 'In Paris, like all the other places we went, they'd give us these monstrous seven, eight or nine course banquets. We didn't understand any of it, nor did we like it. We were looking for hamburgers and milkshakes! We just didn't get it.'

The media spotlight was back on the All Stars. They did the press circuit: Dimitro and Antoine Blain were interviewed on Radio

Les joueurs américains ont présidé hier, au B. H. V. à la remise des billets gratuits pour France-Amérique

HIER après-midi, au Bazar de l'Hôtel-de-Ville, bien avant l'arrivée des joueurs américains de rugby à XIII, de nombreux enfants parisiens occupaient les locaux du grand magasin. Ils attendaient avec impatience les fameux Yankees, lorsque ceux-ci apparurent ils furent aussitôt entourés et fêtés. Pour recevoir les deux cents billets accordés par le B. H. V. et LE PARISIEN libéré il y eut beaucoup plus de candidats que d'élus et c'est pourquoi on vit les enfants se livrer à une petite bousculade digne des meilleures mêlées pour recevoir le précieux papier qui leur permettra d'aller au Parc, samedi après-midi. Sur notre document on reconnaît, au premier plan à gauche, l'entraîneur américain, Mike Dimitro en droite et au fond, certains de ses équipiers sont, eux aussi, assaillis par une meute joyeuse.

Monte-Carlo; Willie, Mike and Ray Terry visited the offices of sports paper *L'Equipe* with Blain. And *L'Equipe* responded by following the Americans step by step around Paris: on Tuesday night at Folies-Bergere nightclub, where they were VIP guests. The 'tres sexy cette Yvonne Menard' had dressed 'rouquin' redhead Willie Richardson in a brown wig and danced for him. Landon Exley was the lucky recipient of a dancer's bracelet. This was not a Christmas vacation they would soon forget.

Bob Ferguson chose to drink a 'curious mix of coca-cola and milk' much to the hosts' bemusement. *France Soir* devoted half a page to these bizarre visitors.

Dimitro, 'Le Professeur de Los Angeles', said his men had seen the 'gay Paris' but now were ready for the 'serious and sober' side. He meant Arc de Triomphe, Tour Eiffel and Invalides but he could just as well have meant playing Puig-Aubert and Co at Parc de Princes.

LE XIII DES U.S.A. CHEZ PERNOD

Après leur dur « training » d'hier matin au cynodrome de Courbevoie, le XIII des U.S.A., au grand complet, a été reçu par le Comité France-Amérique dans les salons Pernod Fils. Les rugbymen d'outre Atlantique n'ont pas caché leur satisfaction en dégustant ce fameux produit français. Sur notre document, on reconnaît, avec l'arbitre anglais M. Appleton, le solide capitaine manager et pilier de l'équipe, Mike Dimitro, dit « Granite », et les vedettes américaines, Mena, Sellers, Exley, Fergusson, Bandy, etc.

The next day *L'Equipe* ran a full-page feature showing the squad pretending to start a gallop across Cynodrome de Courbevoie, the race course where they were training on a soccer field, wearing their trademark pale grey college sweatsuits. Another shot had a group of ten players, some wearing gloves, another a beret, piling on top of each other, having a ball. They were freezing but happy. The track had a huge totaliser board behind one goal: racetrack guru Ray Terry must have felt at home.

Erkie: 'It was snowing and the press came out for our practice session and took pictures. For some reason my picture showed up on the sports page of *L'aurore* the day after the game. My French stinks but the caption said something like: "Is this a man equipped for a polar expedition or simply Erkie Cheldin, an American rugby player?" When I got off the plane at LA my father and brother handed me a copy of *Newsweek* and there I was again.'

Cheldin is there in the mass circulation American mag, hamming it up in a woollen jump suit and balaclava but there is no explanation of what these 'rugby' players were doing in Paris in the first place.

Landon: 'Back home they didn't know what we were doing – didn't know and didn't care! One of those photos ended up in the *New York Herald Tribune* too. I still buy it when I'm in France to see the football scores.'

Don Lent: 'It was so cold in Paris that when we practised, the air would freeze our throats, so we had to quit.'

They could mess around no longer. They had to enter the lions' den. The decision to play France was wildly ambitious. It may have been over two years since the Chanticleers had stunned Australia with a magnificent display of free, attacking 'champagne rugby' to clinch the series at the SCG; but in the winter of 1953/54, France were still as good as any national team in

the world, arguably the best. There was little between the big four: in the previous two years, Britain, New Zealand and Australia had all won a series against each other. France had beaten Australia home and away, and put 42 points on England in Marseilles, but in the last few weeks had lost by two points

FOLIES-BERGÈRE

MARDI SOIRÉE
Fauteuil de Balcon
1re Série

PRIX 703.00
Timbre en compte avec le Trésor .. 7.00
TOTAL 710.00

Prière de conserver ce ticket pour être présenté à toute réquisition.
N° 105983

VILLENEUVE REFUSE
de céder Jimenez
au XIII de France

pour jouer samedi
au Parc
contre les Américains !

(De notre correspondant particulier René VERDIER)

VILLENEUVE-SUR-LOT. — Le treize villeneuvois n'a pas obtenu les résultats que ses dirigeants étaient en droit d'attendre, en raison même des individualités de valeur qui la composent. L'équipe au nom brillant cherche actuellement à cela r le grand nombre de blessés enregistré depuis septembre provoque des changements trop fréquents. Elle veut, pourtant, bien se comporter à Avignon, dimanche, face au leader, et la commission de rugby travaille minutieusement cette expédition en pesant le pour et le contre. (Lire la suite p. 7, rub. Rugby XIII).

ANTOINE BLAIN A MONTRÉ LA « BOTTE » DE PIPETTE AUX AMÉRICAINS !

Dès leur arrivée à Paris, les rugbymen américains sont venus nous rendre visite, à « L'Equipe » avec leur conseiller technique, l'arbitre anglais M. Appleton, et Antoine Blain, secrétaire général de la FFJ XIII. Devant notre vitrine des trophées, ils ont été vivement intéressés par la chaussure avec laquelle Puig-Aubert battit le record des buteurs lors de la tournée en Australie en 1951. Mike Dimitro et le talonneur rouquin Willie Richardson manifestèrent le désir d'examiner de près la fameuse botte de Puig-Aubert. Antoine Blain leur montra lui-même la botte qu'ils redoutent tant. De gauche à droite : Antoine Blain, Willie Richardson, Mike Dimitro et le secrétaire de la tournée américaine.

Les rugbymen américains après le « gay » ont visité le « serious and sober Paris »

Si d'aventure vous croisez dans Paris une petite troupe d'athlétiques et joyeux garçons, il se pourrait que ce soient les treizistes américains qui, samedi, affronteront au Parc des Princes l'équipe de France.

Genre très étudiants en vacances, les Sellers, Exley, Mena, Rappa, Grossman, se reconnaissent d'ailleure facilement à leur tenue vestimentaire. Venus de leur chaude Californie, les boys de Mike Dimitro devaient ignorer que la France était un pays où sévissait l'hiver. Aussi tous ces sportifs sont-ils équipés de vestes ou pantalons type « tropical » qui les défendent très peu des morsures du froid...

Voilà pourquoi hier matin ce collège ès rugby est allé s'équiper en achetant gabardines et bérets, ce couvre-chef dont ils avaient eu la révélation lors de leur bref passage à Perpignan.

Les premières vingt-quatre heures parisiennes des Américains ont d'ailleurs été bien employées.

Yvonne Ménard
a séduit Richarson

D'abord une tournée aux Folles...

Aujourd'hui, à 16 heures, les joueurs des U.S.A. visiteront les grands magasins du Bazar de l'Hôtel-de-Ville.
A cette occasion, la sportive direction du magasin offrira une invitation pour le match de samedi, au Parc des Princes, aux 200 premiers enfants qui se présenteront à cette réception.

...TIS HIER

in England and squeezed past Wales by just a single point in Marseilles.

Half the France side were legends in the making: lethal wingers Constrastin and Cantoni; Gilbert Benausse, the Carcassonne stand-off, on his way to 49 caps, and near immortality. They were joined by a swathe of young talent – and France's greatest-ever rugby-a-treize star, Puig-Aubert.

Aubert had torn the Australians to shreds in 1951, his beautiful attacking lines, passing, tricks and speed bewildering the nation that thought it had seen it all. The fact that he did it with a smile on his face and, occasionally, a cigarette in his mouth was the icing on the cake. Known by his thousands of fans as 'Pipette' – The Little Chimney – Aubert would cheekily nip off from his fullback duties to share a smoke with a spectator during a stoppage in play. He was not much off a last line of defence anyway: tackling was not his job. Pipette was there to weave magic and he did so gloriously.

The big clubs in Sydney had offered Aubert a fortune to stay in Australia after the French triumph but his love of pastis and Gitanes was too strong

Winter in Europe: this Rugby player tried to keep warm in icy Paris . . .

to leave behind. Bizarrely, Aubert was now playing for both Paris in the second division and top club Carcassonne, spending much of his week trekking the 300 miles between the two. The only thing he practised was his goal-kicking – otherwise he did not train!

Villeneuve were furious that Jiminez had been selected as it would mean he missed their crucial championship game against league leaders Avignon. They spent much of the week refusing to release him before relenting under pressure from the French Federation.

**LES AMERICAINS
SE SONT ENTRAINÉS
AU GRAND GALOP**

*Malgré le froid très vif qui ré-
gnait hier sur Paris, les Américains n'ont pas hésité à se lever
de bon matin pour aller s'en-
trainer deux heures durant au
cynodrome de Courbevoie. Voici
le départ de ce « training » au
grand galop.*

The Americans had already tried and failed to stop these stars inflict major damage, either in Lyon or in the other tour games. This was the tallest of tall orders.

Lent: 'We were basically playing the world champions. They showed us the World Cup at a get-together before the game and it was the biggest trophy I have ever seen. It was at least five or six feet tall.'

Dimitro could not bluff his way out of this one: his men knew what was in store. If Dimitro thought taking on New South Wales at the SCG was a tough assignment, this was mission impossible. Or utter madness. He had once again put them in the line of fire. At least he joined them.

Around 20,000 Parisians turned up at the famous Parc de Princes stadium, a bastion of French sporting pride: be it football, Jeu a XIII, rugby union or Le Tour. They packed the stands down to the edge of the cycle track to see the demolition.

9 JANUARY 1954

It was so cold that not only were the All Stars covered from neck to feet by their stars and stripes jerseys, gridiron pants and striped socks, but Dimitro wore gloves.

Rappa: 'It was awful. It had rained heavily before the game and then it started to snow. The field was muddy, it was cold. I don't believe anyone of us had ever been so miserable. We sloshed around the whole game in cold mud which covered our whole bodies. California boys had real trouble with that kind of environment, so we lost badly.'

Blaine, *Miroir des Sports*: 'Of course the French were also handicapped by conditions but less so than the American novices. They are used to running around under serene Californian sun on dry surfaces that nonetheless take a stud: sodden turf and slippery ball were not just things they hadn't come across, they were more like insuperable obstacles.'

FRANCE-SOIR

orts - France-soir *Sports* - Fran

PAR − 5° LES AMÉRICAINS SE SONT ENTRAINÉS A COURBEVOIE

L'entraîneur Dimitro jouera samedi pilier contre la France

ARRIVES hier soir à Paris, où ils se sont installés dans un hôtel du boulevard Haussmann, les rugbymen américains se sont dirigés à la fin de la matinée vers le stade municipal de Courbevoie pour un premier entraînement en vue de leur match contre le XIII de France samedi au Parc des Princes.

Après s'être livrés à des exercices d'assouplissement dans leurs vestiaires, cependant que leur coach Dimitro, qui fut un excellent boxeur, s'échangeait (pour s'amuser bien entendu) quelques rounds avec le « rouquin » Wille Richarson, les joueurs sont allés sur le terrain, où la thermomètre marquait moins 5 degrés. Ils avaient pris soin de se couvrir d'épais survêtements en laine, les jambes bien protégées, et l'on pouvait même voir Kyle Cheldin, la tête enveloppée d'un capuchon, comme en portent les écoliers. Mais au moment de commencer l'entraînement, on s'est aperçu qu'il n'y avait pas de ballon et en hâte on est allé en chercher, ce qui a retardé le commencement du training.

M. Appleton, l'arbitre anglais, s'est surtout efforcé d'apprendre aux joueurs américains la position à adopter sur le terrain, position d'attaque et position défensive. On sait que cette dernière ne leur est guère familière et que c'est surtout pour cette raison qu'ils ont essuyé de nettes défaites au début de leur tournée en France.

Dimitro pilier

A l'issue de l'entraînement qui s'est terminé un peu avant 13 h., Dimitro a formé comme suit l'équipe américaine dans laquelle il jouera lui-même pilier :

Arrière : Lampshire (6); Trois-quarts : Ferguson (1), Lent (17), Sellers (20), Marino (9), ou Helfenberg (11) ; Demis : (o) Exley (22), (m) T. Grossman (8) ; Avants : (3° ligne) Bandy (15) ; (2° ligne) Taylor (19); Rappe (7);

(1re ligne) Mena (13); Richardson (talonneur), (12) ; Dimitro (27).

Un nouvel entraînement aura lieu demain matin, à la même heure et sur le même terrain.

Pierre GROSMOLARD

Jimenez jouera

VILLENEUVE-SUR-LOT, 6 janvier. — La sélection de Jimenez dans le « treize » de France, qui jouera samedi à Paris contre les Américains, n'enchante pas évidemment les dirigeants de Villeneuve 13.

Le club lot-et-garonnais a en effet le lendemain un match très important à jouer en Avignon et il semble donc normal que les responsables du comité villeneuvois soient attachés au résultat du championnat de France, qui les concerne, qu'à celui du treize tricolore. Ils ont donc essayé de faire « dédouaner » à leur meilleur élément des lignes arrières

Jimenez pour cette rencontre internationale, afin d'avoir ce joueur en possession de tous ses moyens pour Avignon. Mais ils se sont heurtés au refu de la Ligue Française de jeu à treize et se trouvent donc dans l'obligation de faire contre mauvaise fortune bon cœur.

Jimenez, de ce fait, remplira ses engagements. Il sera à Paris samedi et après une nuit passée en chemin de fer, il rejoindra ses co-équipiers de Villeneuve 13 à Avignon pour jouer l'après-midi du dimanche, à moins (pas sûr qu'il ait été victime de blessures contre les Américains).

Roger RUSS.

Dimitro, l'entraîneur du XIII américain (à gauche), a pris part ce matin à l'entraînement de son équipe. Il jouera samedi contre la France.

Rappa: 'We'd fall and slide in this ice cold mud: it was miserable. I wished we had played on a better field on a warmer day. I'm sure they would have still beaten us but it would have been closer. None of us even tried that game. They would give us the ball and say "take it" but none of us wanted to play. I don't know if anyone else will admit that. They tried to make it look like a game but we'd had it. That was the big game but nobody wanted to be there.'

Blaine, *Miroir des Sports*: 'All the tourists come from an American football background. Some of them wanted to believe this was an advantage but all it did was cause them to react in ways which didn't suit rugby, certainly not rugby league.'

Exley: 'We sure didn't know what was going on. I just remember playing against Puig-Aubert and those guys and they were just laughing at us.'

Ferguson: 'It was no contest.'

Lent: 'Those guys were out of our league, they were real pros and very tough. That is why we didn't score any points.'

FRANCE 31 – US ALL STARS 0

France destroyed Mike Dimitro's claims for his American tyros against our national team. While we hadn't gone all the way in agreeing with the optimism of the St Andrew's College coach, we did, however, think that the American All Stars would have fared better, despite France's undeniable strength. The Parc de Princes pitch was a major influence with it having been transformed into a skating rink after several days' snowfalls and rain which froze.

Miroir des Sports,
French secretary general Antoine Blain,
11 January 1954

L'ailier Ferguson, par un crochet, vient de déborder Contrastin. Le ... de mêlée français ... se replie et va le ...

Blain, *Miroir des Sports*: 'As for athleticism, these Americans lack nothing in comparison, far from it. But it will be no use unless they rid themselves of the tendencies. It isn't impossible but the speed of transformation will vary from individual to individual: Richardson, Lampshire and especially Sellers showed in Lyon that they are real international quality.'

Cheldin: 'Leon Sellers was the greatest. One tough guy.'

At times, Dimitro's men also impressed Puig-Aubert, who kicked five conversions from seven nonchalant attempts. In his column in *Miroir des Sports*, he praised the All Stars' handling skills – 'some of their takes are quite unbelievable' – and admired their explosive strength but admitted they could not sustain it over two 40-minute halves.

Puig-Aubert: 'When I think back to those opening minutes, I'm still shaking. They were constantly on our line and kept possession brilliantly. We got the impression all 13 were packed into the same space, their attacks kept coming relentlessly. Blue jerseys were popping up everywhere. They shouted encouragement to each other which lifted them. I was very worried indeed.'

But in the All Stars defence, the holes were way too big to plug.

Lent: 'At the end of the first half, I was tackled as I was carrying the ball and hit the ground very hard. It was frozen solid and had no grass. I separated three cartilage in my chest and broke a couple of ribs. I was supposed to go to hospital but I wanted to fly home with the team so I endured the pain until I got home and went to our team physician at Pepperdine.'

Blain, *Miroir des Sports*: 'As you read this, Mike Dimitro's men will have returned to their Californian home and be applying themselves to the tasks in hand for they are desperate to take part in October's World Cup here in France. A decision will be taken on their entry in May, after France have played over there to gauge their progress.'

Le centre américain Sellers s'est infiltré dans la défense française. Benausse l'a rejoint et l'a plaqué. Jimenez, Guilhem et Pambrun accourent en soutien. De g. à dr. : Jimenez, Cantoni (de dos), Richardson (12), Benausse, Sellers (à terre), Guilhem et Pambrun.

Ferguson: 'The entire trip was a great experience. We were treated very well, the food was good. Lots of fun and laughs. I don't think the French thought much of our rugby skills – obviously, we were unable to read the newspapers – but they seemed impressed with our physical strength and conditioning.'

J'AI ATTAQUE PARCE QUE... J'AVAIS FROID!
[ATTACKED BECAUSE I WAS COLD]

'They hate to defend. They are not keen to move up on the ball-carrier and put him down – they are very naïve defensively. After we'd settled down, I knew we would win comfortably and that's when I decided to make my contribution. I think I surprised the Parc de Princes crowd who had rarely seen me attack so much: however, that was because standing all by myself at full-back, I was frozen!'

by Puig-Aubert

Landon: 'France was just wonderful and we had a pretty good time because there was enough space between the games.'

Lent: 'Flying home in agony was a chore. It took about 18 hours. The good news was the airline stewardess took exceptional care of me, changing my bandages etc – it made the others guys jealous!

'All the team got up and ran to one side of the plane to look out at the scenery as we came back to the States. The pilot said over the intercom: "Would the rugby team please return to your seats: you're making the plane tip to one side!"'

Rappa: 'The fella I miss most was Ted Grossman. After the tour was over we went together for a week or two to Monte Carlo and some other place – I don't remember where we went. He's a very funny guy and we had a good time. We got

Le centre américain Lent s'est échappé, mais il est rejoint par le Français Benausse qui l'a plaqué. A g. : Cantoni se replie.

Le talonneur yankee Richardson fonce, dans une rush impressionnante, vers nos buts, poursuivi par Bernard et Guilhem.

BROUSSE ET PONSINET ONT TROUVÉ LEURS SUCCESSEURS : PAMBRUN ET SAVE

par Antoine BLAIN

PAR 31 points à 0, l'équipe de France n'a réduit à rien les prétentions formulées par Mike Dimitro sur le comportement de ses étudiants américains face à notre représentation nationale. Sans partager exactement l'optimisme du « Coach » du Collège de Saint-Andrew, nous pensions cependant que les « American All Stars » constitueraient un sort meilleur malgré la valeur incontestée de l'équipe de France.

La raison majeure en est, à notre sens, l'état de la pelouse du Parc des Princes, transformée en véritable patinoire par la neige fondue et la pluie succédant au gel des jours précédents.

QUE D'EAU ! QUE D'EAU !

Certes l'inconvénient était le même, pour les Français chevronnés, mais à un degré moindre que pour les néophytes Américains. Ceux-ci ont l'habitude d'évoluer sous le ciel perpétuellement serein de la Californie, sur des terrains à la fois souples et secs ; la pelouse détrempée et le ballon glissant étaient pour eux, en plus du manque d'expérience, d'insurmontables obstacles.

Ce handicap signalé, il restait bien peu de choses, techniquement parlant à nos néophytes qui n'ont que six mois de pratique du jeu à Treize, mais qui auraient mérité, malgré la sévérité du score de sauver au moins l'honneur.

DEFAUTS ET QUALITES

Cette première tournée américaine terminée, le moment est sans doute propice pour effectuer un bilan des qualités et défauts des poulains de Mike Dimitro, pour essayer de déterminer leurs chances futures dans la carrière internationale.

Tous les joueurs qui opérèrent au cours de cette tournée viennent du Football américain, où malgré ce que certains voudraient bien en dire, provoque des réflexes absolument opposés à ceux que réclame le rugby et notamment le rugby à Treize. Le Football américain fait appel davantage à la force destructrice qu'à l'intelligence constructive, par ailleurs le porteur du ballon protégé par obstruction y joue un rôle simpliste qui consiste à courir sur le chemin déblayé par les partenaires, d'où une tendance au jeu individuel ; enfin le porteur du ballon, qui réceptionne en un profond retrait, attend que ses coéquipiers aient commencé leur travail de destruction avant de démarrer, d'où des départs arrêtés qui nuisent à l'efficacité de l'attaque.

Par contre du point de vue athlétique : souffle, souplesse, vitesse d'exécution (encore qu'en vitesse pure ils auraient intérêt à troquer leurs longs travers contre nos shorts) les Américains n'ont rien à nous envier, au contraire.

Ces qualités sont une bonne base pour la pratique du jeu à Treize qui réclame des qualités athlétiques supérieures, mais elles ne seraient d'aucune utilité si les pratiquants américains ne se dépouillaient des réflexes que nous énumérions plus haut. La chose n'est pas impossible, elle sera l'aboutissement d'une pratique plus ou moins longue selon les individus : Richardson, Lampshire et surtout Sellers démontrèrent l'autre dimanche à Lyon qu'ils étaient à même de s'intégrer dans une solide Sélection internationale.

LA VICTOIRE TRICOLORE

Quand ces lignes paraîtront, les joueurs de Mike Dimitro auront rejoint leur Californie natale et ils se mettront à l'ouvrage, car leur désir serait grand de participer, à la Coupe du Monde qui se déroulera en France en octobre ; la décision de cette participation sera prise en mai, après que l'équipe de France aura été en Californie jauger les progrès accomplis.

On se réterdra pas davantage sur la confortable victoire du Treize tricolore : Puig-Aubert mit 19 points à son actif en transformant cinq essais sur sept que Cantoni, Teisseire, Save, Benausse et Pambrun s'attribuèrent. Aussi bien nous n'attacherons qu'une importance relative tant au score qu'à la victoire pour nous réjouir de l'incorporation dans notre représentation nationale d'éléments nouveaux qui se sont hissés au niveau de leurs prédécesseurs.

La meilleure acquisition sans doute de l'équipe de France est sans doute la deuxième ligne Pambrun-Save, qui se montrèrent de la confiance internationale aura poli leurs qualités ; de plus Bernard à démontré qu'il pouvait être aussi bon que pilier que brillant deuxième ligne. Par ailleurs les Benausse, les Teisseire, les Rey auxquels pourront s'ajouter les Vignier, Alberti, Lassalle, Boutonnet (qui peut prétendre à la succession de Puig-Aubert quand il aura vaincu une certaine timidité) tous fraîchement émoulus du service militaire ont devant eux, grande ouverte, une brillante carrière qui permet de bien augurer de l'avenir.

Un avenir qui ne manquera pas de piquant avec la prochaine tournée aux Antipodes et surtout la Coupe du Monde, dans laquelle les adversaires les plus coriaces seront peut-être — sait-on jamais ? — les Américains...

LES EQUIPES

France : Puig-Aubert ; Cantoni, Jimenez ; Rey, Contrastin ; Benausse (o), Teisseire (m) ; Guilhem, Save, Pambrun ; Bernard, Audoubert, Rinaldi.

Etats-Unis : Lampshire ; Ferguson, Lent, Sellers, Marino ; Exley (o), Crussmann (m) ; Bandy, Rappa, Taylor ; Dimitro, Richardson, Menn.

along real well. I ran out of money and I borrowed I think $200 from Ted – a lot of money – but I paid it back right away.'

Ted Grossman: 'Me and Rappa went to the Riviera and then to Rome by train, then we flew to Madrid. Tony was in awe of the Vatican: he thought he'd been born again!'

Landon: 'Tony Rappa took to rugby league like anything – he loved it.'

Rappa: 'I never played or saw a rugby league game again. But about 20 years later I spent some time in Paris. I was in Harry's American Bar, right by the Ritz. I'm talking around 1972 or so. I recognised this guy in there and he recognised me. It was Puig-Aubert! He'd

Typical Puig-Aubert in '54: laughing, smoking, winning.

given me his jersey on the field after the game in Paris. I brought it back with me but I don't remember what happened to it. I don't speak any French and he didn't speak any English but we said hello and patted each other on the back.'

It was a trip none of the Americans would ever forget.

CHAPTER 29
INVITE RESCINDED

While Dimitro was in Paris, the battle to control rugby league's expansion to the States continued – in the north of England.

Harry Sunderland scribbled a frantic plan and sent it from his Manchester home to the RFL: the All Stars could leave Paris after the game and head up to England for an exhibition match under the new floodlights at Leigh, the rugby-mad mining town north-west of Manchester. Leigh were enterprising enough to be only the second club in England to install lights and Sunderland thought a visit from the glamorous American tourists, with possibly 'another Galia amongst' them, would be just the ticket to help Leigh start recouping their outlay at Hilton Park.

By his calculations, the extra game in Leigh, a tour of London and visits to Leeds' Headingley ground and Bradford's Odsal would cost £429. Leigh players were to get a fiver each for playing and every spectator – Sunderland hoped for 14,000, more than Leigh had got for the floodlights opener a few weeks earlier – would get a souvenir card to say 'I was there' when the first American team played in Britain. Floodlights were a new development in British sport: it was only a few weeks since the first international match had taken place under lights, at Odsal, screened live on BBC TV.

Sunderland's letter arrived just in time for an RFL council meeting the next day. The suggestion was rejected outright. Fallowfield wrote to Dimitro back in LA to explain why: the approaches to play in Leigh were 'quite unofficial and regrettable', arranging a match at a few days' notice was 'thoroughly impracticable', the game would clash with the televised Challenge Cup draw and 'winter has set in and I assure you very few fans, ardent though they may be, would like to sit out on a cold winter's night watching a rugby league floodlit game'.

Fallowfield hoped Dimitro would 'not feel slighted': 'Mr Sunderland should, of course, have put his suggestions to us before making any approach to you and then this slight contretemps would not have arisen.'

Fallowfield did have the grace to praise the performances of the Americans who played against France in Lyon and suggested the Americans could one day be invited to England.

Sunderland called it a slap in the face for US rugby league. But even he must have known five days was farcically short notice to arrange an international trip. Not that all of the Americans could have stayed in Europe any longer anyway – some of them had to be back in college classes at the start of the spring term.

Fallowfield, the game's leader, and Sunderland, a far bigger voice than just being the *Sunday Dispatch* reporter, were clearly in a power struggle, sitting in their northern English cities, staring out at sheeting rain and charcoal skies, dreaming of sun-kissed California. Fallowfield was a control freak, Sunderland was ego-tripping. And both were upwardly mobile, transforming their own lives from humble backgrounds to positions of power and influence.

Just as he would eventually see potential with television, Fallowfield had a vision for rugby league in the States. But only if *he* controlled its development. He wrote to Dimitro back home in Ceilhunt Avenue, and invited the Americans over to play Great Britain. It was the start of years of negotiating and bartering over thin air. Mike wanted to take the All Stars to England and favoured a tour in April 1954 or perhaps a series of floodlit games in June. Rugby league on summer nights? A ludicrous suggestion: it was the closed season and clubs re-seeded their fields in summer. Fallowfield turned him down. Perhaps Great Britain could play the US in the LA Coliseum in May en route to Australia, then have two games in Hawaii on their way home? Fallowfield seemed keen on the California idea. But he was scrambling for delaying tactics and excuses to put the French – and anyone else – off the Americans' scent. Realising what potential lay across the pond, he wanted to get his own hands on it. Meanwhile, he was negotiating on the quiet with a rival set of Americans led by Dimitro's original PR guy Ward Nash.

Nash had supplied Jersey Flegg at the NSWRL with a list of sports promoters in California. Dimitro's name was not on it. Flegg informed his man: 'Mr Nash appears to have an axe to grind.' Dimitro and Nash had gone their separate ways before the Australia tour and never reconciled their differences.

Iron Mike was on the move again anyway. He tried to get a coaching gig at the Ohio football factory of Massillon High School near home, where legendary coach Paul Brown had churned out a series of future top coaches, but there were no openings. Instead he left Virgil Junior High and moved on to San Fernando High, where he taught the kids how to drive (a far more suitable role).

Moments after Sunderland's Leigh plan was rejected, Nash's report *The Establishment of the Code in America* was read out to the RFL hierarchy. Nash would use his business partner and fellow sportswriter Maxwell Stiles to sell the league code to LA sports fans. He knew international competition was hot: Davis Cup tennis, Ryder Cup golf and the 1948 Olympics had gone down a storm with the patriotic Americans. Baseball and football could not compete with that. With transatlantic flights now affordable, Europe was open to American sports teams: they just had to play the same game.

Nash's main route to take off was international football. 'If rugby league is ever established in America – even in a few well-chosen centres – the financial returns with international competition could run in a few years to thousands of dollars,' he told the RFL committee.

The inaugural World Cup in France was looming. The International Board sent Knowling on a fact-finding mission to the States. He liked what he saw: or what Ward Nash told him. On his return, the French Federation invited the States to join themselves, Great Britain, Australia and New Zealand at the World Cup in November 1954.

The invite angered Fallowfield, the International Board secretary. He wrote to Blain, complaining that the Americans' 'standard may in no way compare with that of our own, in which case it would not be a practicable proposition to include the US team. If the team from the US is to be included, there appears to be no reason why a team from Canada should not also be invited.'

Fallowfield had never seen the All Stars play. And yet he vetoed the International Board's invite. He did not invite the Canadians either. Nor the Italians, nor the Yugoslavs, both of whom had club competitions and could have travelled to France with ease.

FEBRUARY 1954

Exley: 'Dimitro was trying to get us into the World Cup. I remember him saying there would be the best players there from Australia and France. Dimitro and Mena definitely had intentions to take this game, form a league and get more people involved. In his mind, by going to the World Cup that's how we'd have got started. But looking back I think it's a blessing in disguise that we didn't go as us Americans would have got obliterated. Or maybe not. Maybe by then we'd have learned some more style and technique.'

Rappa: 'There's no doubt in my mind that if we had an All Stars team from the United States we'd beat everybody. The form of the game was not so unfamiliar to us. There were rules that we didn't know, but you take the ball and you run: what else did they do that we couldn't do? Kicking, maybe. But in those days we had

FRANCE GUARANTEE WORLD CUP COMPETITION

…France has guaranteed £2,000 by way of expenses and the cost of air travel to each competitor, plus a share of the profits, if any. They were desirous of including AMERICA, but they will be wise to change their minds in view of the fact that the younger players from the States are still immature. It would have been an excellent idea had the United States been able to put a team in the field capable of holding its own in the stern competition it surely will be: but not as they proved themselves to be on their Christmas visit to Europe. They are still apprentices.

Rugby League and Soccer Monthly
By Jack Kennedy

such a base of thousands and thousands of football players and I don't think Europe had that kind of base. If the US took rugby seriously, the specialities are not so different that they couldn't do it.'

Al D. Kirkland: 'After a while we realised that if the US took up rugby league seriously, we would've been dominant. Jim Brown would have been a huge star – no one would be able to stop him. Football is over in November or December at college and until spring practice we needed something to do. There was no weight training in those days, so we played rugby. I can understand the reluctance of the authorities to allow us to play in the 1954 World Cup. That was a fiasco but we would have been too good for England and Australia if we had really gotten going.'

Harry Sunderland.

There was still enthusiasm among the American players. Pat Henry met Ray Terry at a UCLA rugby union game against Stanford and was told that Mike was planning trips to Europe later that year. Terry even wrote to Dimitro to thank him for the ride and apologise for his moaning: 'I sure bitched as much or more than anyone but always I took advantage of the tours so many thanks. I also straightened the rugby union heads in San Francisco on our trip. I showed them the good side of our publicity – what union players sent back – so that kind of shook them a little.'

Exley: 'I think most of us would've done it again, done another trip, but it never happened. I never played rugby ever again. Never before and never after. When I came back I finished off my college credits, graduated, got married and went into the Air Force. I did three years. I went to Sheppard Air Force Base at Wichita Falls, Texas. Wichita Falls is the worst place you've ever seen in your life. It was

RUGBY LEAGUE EMPIRE IS GROWING

I think America will be the next to join up provided they are encouraged. If they are bold enough to send teams to Australia and France I feel sure that it will not be long before they organise competitions among themselves. It is to be regretted that the contingent which recently visited France were unable to have one or two matches in England.

For years there has been talk about British teams returning from Australia tours via the States and playing a couple of exhibition matches in San Francisco. Australia, too, has indulged in similar imaginations. Australia is better situated to do the propaganda work in America. But nothing practical has ever been done. Now is the time to think deeper and "strike while the iron is hot."

Says Jack Kennedy

horrible. I just wanted out of there. They had a football team there and everyone wanted me to play but I got orders to go to Callous Air Force Base, Sacramento. It was kinda a rinky-dink deal. We had a team up at Callous too, but it was like eight-man football, not regular. I played on that for two years but it was nothing exceptional.

"There were a lot of success stories among us after the trip which makes it all the more crazy that the rugby league people never kept in touch with us."

Ferguson: 'I did watch one game of rugby union a few years after our trip because my junior partner was playing at the time. No other time was I involved with rugby.'

Sam Grossman: 'I never did play rugby league again, although I really enjoyed the game much more than football. I haven't seen a match since.'

Tony Rappa swears he hasn't seen another game of rugby since either.

Rappa: 'France was the last time most of us played football or rugby. No one ever tried to get me to play, that I remember. I think I did pretty well. I was in the scrum, in the second row. I got the ball a lot. After the trip I did two years in the Army. I did my basic training here, then I went to Virginia for training, back here to the Presidio in San Francisco, and then Kaiserslautern in Germany for a year. Then I came home. My parents had already opened the snack bar in Monterey, on the wharf. It was small and really seasonal: you'd have a few months then really struggle the rest of the time when it was quiet. I worked there but my parents tried to make it like they couldn't manage without me, so I felt guilty the whole time!'

There were no more games and just a single member of the squad remained involved with rugby league.

The exception was Don Lent. Having graduated from Pepperdine with a teaching degree, Lent spent a summer practising with the LA Rams before heading up to Canada with Bob Lampshire to try to get a contract in the Western Interprovincial Football Union. Lent headed to Winnipeg Blue Bombers before joining Lampshire at the new BC Lions franchise. With only nine import deals up for grabs to Americans, it proved a fruitless trip.

Lent: 'I played full-back and linebacker and Bob played quarter back. We only stayed one year and then both went into coaching. We were both married and had kids and the pay was poor.'

Returning to Southern California, Lent and Lampshire both headed into teaching, coaching high school and college football for years. They even coached together at an All Star game. Meanwhile, rugby started at Pepperdine.

Lent: 'After the trip to France, some of the other guys formed a rugby club at Pepperdine. I wasn't involved as I was coaching then, but it was definitely as a direct result of the All Stars trip. They played rugby union in a Southern California League against other rugby clubs such as Eagle Rock and Long Beach, I think, in the off-season of football.'

But Lent kept the rugby league flame flickering in the most unlikely places. While his team-mates gave up the game immediately on their return from France, Lent decided his school football players could learn from the game – and enjoy it.

Lent: 'The rugby experience influenced all of us very much. Mike was a real character. We became good friends after France and we coached together at Elsinore High School in Wildomara for two years. Rugby league was a tough sport and I never liked rugby union. So Mike and I incorporated some of the rugby league plays into our football programme at Elsinore.

'Later, when I was head coach in high schools and college I had all my football teams learn to play rugby league in the off-season. I taught rugby league at Elsinore, Anaheim High, Magnolia High in Anaheim, Newport Harbor High and at Cal Poly University at Pomona. It was good for keeping our players in good condition and in competition, as well as toughening them up without pads.'

No one in Australia, New Zealand, France or England knew that a couple of All Stars were keeping rugby league alive in Southern Californian schools. No one would have believed it anyway.

Nothing could be finer

CHAPTER 30
NASH, NIXON, ROZELLE AND THE RAMS

JANUARY 1954

Ward Nash's plan for American rugby league was to find influential people who would bite. He claimed friends in very high places. He would need them if rugby league football was to get on the runway in the States, let alone take off. He would approach NFL franchise-owners, suggesting rugby league as a way of paying their players in the off-season and promoting their franchise to the public.

While the second All Stars team were still in France, he sent a report to the International Board suggesting the Australian RFL leader should meet an illustrious neighbour of his from Whittier, who had played football at the local college and would soon be visiting Australia: the new vice-president of the United States, Richard Nixon. As Hunter S. Thompson put it, Nixon was 'a complete football freak'. Like Dimitro and thousands of others, he had spent time in 1943 fighting alongside Brits and Aussies in the Solomon Islands where he must have been exposed to rugby. 'I am positive that he would like to meet briefly with you,' Nash claimed. If Nash was true to his word, this was a huge opening.

With or without Richard Nixon's help, Nash knew that his only chance of a breakthrough in the States was to bring the game to America. He had to get two top teams to show the US public what they were missing. To do that, he needed money, influence and a stadium.

Nash headed straight to Tex Schramm, assistant to the president at LA Rams. He wanted to use the Coliseum, which the Rams hired from the Coliseum Commission, for an international exhibition game. Incredibly, not only was Schramm interested in the plan, he even offered to pay $3,000 to a world-class team to perform there.

FOOTBALL-COLISEUM, LOS ANGELES

Reeling with a head full of possibilities, Nash put the suggestion to Fallowfield at the RFL in Leeds: surely the RFL would bite Schramm's hand off? Be paid to send two teams over to play in LA and spread the league gospel? But no. The RFL wanted a $6,000 guarantee. The deal collapsed. For the sake of a thousand pounds sterling, Fallowfield had snubbed one of the most progressive men in the NFL. Big mistake.

Nash turned to the other side of the world. Even if the USA were no longer invited to the World Cup Nash realised it was still a golden opportunity: both Australia and New Zealand would be passing through America on their way home from France. All he had to do was convince them to play a couple of exhibition games against each other in California.

Veterans Stadium Long Beach.

Interested in the idea, the Australian Board of Control commissioned their own report on league's prospects in the States by the legendary journalist Ernie Christensen, a powerful voice in Sydney sport. Christensen, a league icon, had helped Dimitro with some advance press for the All Stars tour before moving to LA himself. He had authority and the ear of rugby league's decision-makers.

He told the Board: 'The Americans are great believers in publicity, ballyhoo, public relations or whatever it may be called. I found the sports writers eager to assist rugby league but I also learned they will not go out of their way to chase news about our game.'

US pro teams would employ several press officers to feed the media 'reams of stories' from which to pitch their angles, even during games. Rugby league had to be seen, either via exhibition games or by getting on TV. There was one other way: piggy-backing the major football franchises.

Crucially, Christensen was impressed with the wheeler-dealer Nash, especially by his contacts on the LA sports scene. 'His reputation is very high in Los Angeles,' he reported to Australian supremo Harold Matthews. When they attended a football game at the Coliseum together, Nash introduced Christensen to a bunch of top sports writers, telling the Australian how enthusiastic they all were about promoting the prospective Australia v New Zealand game.

The Board of Control were sold on the idea and the New Zealanders voted 'yes' too. So long as it did not cost them a penny, they were prepared to put their men on display to sell the game to LA.

After more than two decades of failed attempts, rugby league was coming to America.

Nash persuaded local newspaper mogul Dave Lewis to back the first of the two games, to be held at Long Beach, 15 miles south of central LA. They budgeted for a 10,000 crowd in the 12,500-capacity Veterans Stadium with tickets priced at $2 so as 'not to cheapen the show by selling it at bargain rates'. Nash wanted to play on Thanksgiving Day and televise it to 'thousands of sportsmen who spend the day at home'.

He beavered away with negotiations to stage the second game at the Coliseum, possibly as a curtain-raiser to the Rams v Baltimore Colts NFL clash. Nash was

Eddie Waring gets rugby league at the forefront of British TV.

planning ahead, thinking big. He began talks with the Rams and 49ers about providing football players for a US league team to take on France as they came through America en route to Australia in 1955.

Tex Schramm put Nash on to his PR chief, a talented local boy: Pete Rozelle. After serving with the Navy in the Pacific, Rozelle enrolled at Compton Junior College, where the Rams held their training camp in the summer of 1946. He offered his services to the Rams' publicity boss Maxwell Stiles, who got him some weekend work on the sports desk at the *Long Beach Press-Telegram*, while Schramm hired him to help produce the Rams' game-day programmes.

The following year, Stiles was sacked by the Rams for leaking stories to his mates at the *Press-Telegram*. When Schramm was promoted to general manager, he recruited Rozelle to become the Rams' PR chief.

Stiles was back on the beat with the *LA Mirror-News, Oakland Tribune* and *Press-Telegram*. Using him to promote rugby league was hardly going to impress the Rams' hierarchy.

However, Nash told Christensen that 'both teams are prepared to release their players and if necessary have an Australian or New Zealander coach them for several months'. The 49ers had an annual wage bill of $750,000 and were looking at any way of sharing that burden.

Astonishingly, the LA Rams and San Francisco 49ers wanted to get involved with rugby league. The pair were building a pro football rivalry to challenge those that drove the college game. When the teams met in the Coliseum in 1952, 77,000 were there to see it. In 1953 there were 86,000. In 1954, over 93,000. Crowds were booming in the NFL – the average doubling in a decade to nearly 44,000 – but this rivalry was getting huge by any standards.

With Cliff Evans having moved back to the UK to coach Swinton, Harry Sunderland was central to Nash's plans. He had made such an impression with

LA's sports writers that Christensen implored the Australian Board of Control to employ Sunderland to 'sell the game to America using Nash's contacts', despite the Queenslander being based in Manchester.

Christensen also suggested the Australians try to get sponsorship from airlines to fund their flights, and target Hollywood film studios for support, particularly Bob Hope's Paramount. Hope, the Rams shareholder, had watched League in Australia and met up with Eddie Waring in LA. He was still a target.

Although the only UCLA Bruins games to have been shown live on TV were two derbies with USC, televised football was about to explode in the States. Yet back in England, rugby league fans were protesting that the BBC didn't even read out the results on national radio and the RFL refused the BBC permission to show the 1953 Challenge Cup Final to protect ticket sales. They would soon try to ban the televising of all league games too.

American pro sports had already been through this. In 1950, with television sets already in 7.5m American homes, Tex Schramm cut a deal with Admiral TV to show Rams home games in exchange for $307,000 compensation. He sat back waiting for attendances to rocket on the back of the new publicity and a superb season. Instead, average gates at the Coliseum crashed from 50,000 to 27,000. The following season, with a league-wide TV blackout within a 75-mile radius of each stadium, crowds shot back up.

Now 25m American homes had TV. Minor league attendances had crashed. The future was TV. The future had arrived.

Tex Schramm: 'The 1950s was a decade in which everybody became watchers instead of do-ers. Television meant the end of the minor leagues as we had known it. It also signalled the end of regionalism. People started to think on a national scale.'

Not in rugby league they didn't. The NFL was still operating on a par with the RFL and Australian RFL in some ways. Their provincial Philadelphia offices were around the corner from commissioner Bert Bell's home. They had no receptionist or secretary and Bell's son did the admin. Fallowfield and Matthews could relate to that. But pro team sports were about to take off in the States, leaving Britain and Australia way behind.

Gary Kerkorian signs for the Colts.

No one got as far as telling the All Stars about the 49ers and Rams plans. Landon Exley had 'zero knowledge' of the proposal and dismisses any suggestion of the Rams' interest in rugby league; Big Al D. Kirkland 'didn't know anything about it' despite being an acquaintance of 49ers' star quarter back Gordie Soltau; it was news to Erkie Cheldin, too. None of the All Stars knew Nash, Christensen or Sunderland either.

Ironically, the one player at the Rams who could have led their rugby league franchise was on his way out of LA. Gary Kerkorian just could not get a game in the NFL. He needed a change.

Joyce Kerkorian: 'At that time in his life, Gary just didn't know what to do. He was floundering. His uncle wanted him to get out of football and go sell used cars!'

Instead he got a move across the country to Baltimore Colts, a new team in only their second year. Their young coach Weeb Ewbank could not prevent the Colts from having a dreadful 1954 season, losing nine of their 12 games and finishing last in NFL West. Kerkorian, their third-choice QB, survived the cull and hung around for another two seasons.

Joyce Kerkorian: 'There was no money in football or rugby then. In those days it wasn't considered smart to stay in pro football. He made far more as a lawyer. Gary made $12,000 a year at the Colts and they told us all he was the highest paid player on the team.'

He probably was. NFL players were paid little more than the man in the street. Most were getting anything from $4,000 (£1,111) to $20,000 (£5,555) per season. A standard offer was $5,000: little more than you could make in a factory and a few dollars less than what Rozelle was getting as the Rams' PR man. Players had to decide between the security of a day job or an adventure in the volatile world of pro football, where contracts meant little and the sack was just a day away.

In 1953, Bert Bell estimated what it would cost Baltimore to bring pro football to the city: $210,000 in players' wages, $27,000 for coaches and $2,000 for the doctors' fees. The American economy was soaring compared to the British Empire.

Most NFL players played full-time in the five-month season but took another job from New Year to late summer. In his rookie season of 1956, Colts quarterback Johnny Unitas worked as an ironworker before going to practice. The following year – when he was the NFL's Most Valuable Player – he worked as a salesman for a corrugated cardboard company. In 1957 he sold paint.

'Professional' rugby league players in England and Australia played part-time and worked full-time all year round, apart from the summer holidays. They only trained two or three times a week and got paid a pittance. In New Zealand, no rugby players got paid – they were still amateurs. The stars of Sydney's Premiership were getting little more than expenses. In 1953, Harry Wells played 28 competitive games for South Sydney, City and Queensland and pocketed just £245 ($500) for his efforts. He took home just £10 each week for his 18 Premiership games for Souths. Most young first-graders in the Sydney comp were getting just £7 ($15) a game. Wells got nothing at all for seven games for Australia on their tour of New Zealand. And he had to take six weeks off work to go, usually unpaid leave. Wearing the green and gold jumper was deemed honour enough.

The official wage limit in England was £6 a game plus £2 for winning: so even the first-team regulars would be getting paid just £8 ($29) a week. Some clubs broke the wage cap but even Great Britain stars would go home with less than £4 for losing an away game. The most a top player might ever earn from a big game was £20, the only major pay day when they signed for a new club: £500 was the going rate for a real talent.

Many league players would also be on £8 for a week of manual labour in a shipyard or down a mine. So going on tour for months was a costly business unless the ticket money produced a handsome profit. After the Ashes tour in '54, the RFL gave each Great Britain player £400 as their slice of the pie.

But rugby league players rarely complained. Like their football counterparts in the States, almost all had emerged from the working classes to earn a living in a game of controlled violence and skill that they loved. Some found fame and glamour, very few found fortunes.

Ward Nash had to come up with the best deal to keep the Rams and 49ers on track. The answer was obvious: bung the Board of Control and Kiwis a couple of thousand bucks to bring their own teams over to put on an exhibition – they could pay their players a retainer and the crowds would flock in.

As Christensen declared: 'There is so much money to be made in America.'

AMERICAN RUGBY LEAGUE FOOTBALL

A new governing body. No Dimitro. No Sunderland. No Nixon. No Hope? Between them Nash and Rosey Gilhousen – a face on the LA sports scene who seemed to know everyone – would put on their first event, one that could change the rugby league world: Australia v New Zealand in Long Beach and Los Angeles.

AMERICAN RUGBY LEAGUE FOOTBALL

(A Non-profit Organization)

Promotion of International Football for American Youth
818 Santee Street
Los Angeles, California

Chairman
ROSS "ROSEY" GILHOUSEN

Secretary
WARD B. NASH

Publicity
MATT GALLAGHER

Dear Friend:

This little note is to announce that the American Rugby League
Football Association is sponsoring a World Cup match between the
Internationalist teams from Australia and New Zealand on November
28, in the Los Angeles Memorial Coliseum.

We solicit your attendance to this fine Rugby contest which will
be the only time two teams of this caliber have met in the United
States.

There will be a preliminary game of Soccer between the Los Angeles
All Stars and the Latin All Stars just prior to the Rugby match.

We are also pleased to announce that the Australian, New Zealand,
Canadian and British Consulates will be present along with our
own Mayor Norris Poulson.

Tickets can be secured at the Southern California Music Company
or any of the Mutual agencies.

Price . . . $ 1.50 - General Admission
2.50 - Reserved Seats

Will you please put this date on your calendar or your notice
boards.

We will look forward to seeing you November 28.

Thanking you sincerely,

Rosey Gilhousen

Ross (Rosey) Gilhousen
"Chairman"

Affiliated with Rugby League Councils in France · England · Australia · New Zealand

CHAPTER 31
CALIFORNIA DREAMING

The World Cup dreams of Australia and New Zealand were broken on 11 November when they were beaten by Great Britain and France, respectively. Ten days later, after GB had beaten the hosts to lift the new trophy, the Kangaroos and Kiwis were accompanied across the Atlantic by the top table of international rugby league officials.

The Kangaroos would make a six-nation hop to play two exhibition games. After the final in Paris, they headed to London and joined Bill Fallowfield on the New York flight. Fallowfield was there to oversee the whole adventure and report back to the RFL and the International Board.

The fuel stop at Prestwick Airport on the west coast of Scotland turned into an overnight stay because of foul weather. The Kiwis boarded there and the whole party endured another landing in Iceland and then Newfoundland before arriving in New York City at 2am Tuesday morning. After a day exploring the Big Apple, a plane full of international rugby league talent flew west from La Guardia Airport, finally arriving in Los Angeles at 8am, Wednesday 24 November. It had taken four days. And they were only half way home. It was still quicker than the boat.

The exhausted party – including top English referee Ron Gelder – were met at LAX by not only Nash, Sunderland and Rosey Gilhousen but also American Rugby League Football's PR man – Harry Lee – and 'publicity' officer Matt Gallagher. Nash and Sunderland were flustered already. They thought the teams were late. Fallowfield assured them they had arrived as per schedule. The hosts immediately complained about the lack of publicity material sent to them: nothing about the teams, no photos from the World Cup. It was not a good start. Fallowfield took four players with him to the TV studios to set the ball rolling. It could have been the jet lag. It was probably his negativity overload but Fallowfield was not happy. He was taking notes: 'First impressions: Like French – 95% fancy; Long distances impair efficiency; Extremely difficult to get at facts; Hampered by Sunderland.' The teams had only two days to recover from the epic journey before playing the first match on Friday night at Long Beach Stadium. The papers – who had been told this was a World Cup game, not an exhibition – were at the Coliseum for the first practice session. The

RUGBY—Here are three members of the Australian rugby team working out at the Coliseum yesterday in preparation for Sunday's contest against the New Zealand team. Left to right, players are Gregg Hawick, Harry Wells, Alec Watson. —Los Angeles Examiner photo.

LA Examiner carried a photo of Gregg Hawick, Harry Wells and Alec Watson in full flow ahead of 'Sunday's Soccer-Rugby spectacle'. The radio and TV seemed genuinely interested. Maxwell Stiles was delivering the goods in his *LA Mirror* column: 'Films of Rugby League games, such as you may see tomorrow at Long Beach and Sunday afternoon

AUSSIES DRILL FOR BIG GAME
By Frank Percy

Two important steps closer to Sunday's Soccer-Rugby spectacle at the Coliseum were completed yesterday. The New Zealand and Australian professional rugby squads completed their first workout in Califor

at the Coliseum, are sufficient to convince me that Ward Nash is not far off the beam in his evaluation – "Rugby League gives you the fastest action of any running game being played today. Professional rugby league has very little semblance of the Rugby we have seen played in this country."

It was vital that American sports fans realised this was not the rambling, pedestrian, social game that was rugby union in the US: it was a far more exciting, quicker and explosive one.

'Harry Sunderland visions the game as an international sport in which players of the Los Angeles Rams, the 49ers and other pro clubs in this country could tour the world in the spring, thus giving players full-time employment rather than five months as now. The games at Long Beach and the Coliseum are NOT exhibitions. They are being played to decide the down under championship.'

The Mirror by Maxwell Stiles ★ ★ ★ ★ ★ ★ ★ ★ ★ ★ ★ ★ ★ ★ ★ ★

A falsehood but still, things were looking up. Then the great man in the sky intervened. Between previews of the games on local radio were warnings about the night fogs that were descending on the City of Angels every evening. Listeners were constantly urged to stay at home unless absolutely necessary: there had been over 300 traffic accidents in the city the previous week when fog made driving lethal. Three of the All Stars were among the victims this time.

Abajian: 'Teddy and I and Demirjian went together to see the Australia-New Zealand game. We were on our way to Long Beach to the night game and the fog got so bad we had to give up. It was terrible.'

Grossman: 'It was so bad we almost couldn't find our way home!'

With about 1,500 people somehow making it to the stadium – a hulking concrete shelf out by the airport, above the city – the game kicked off. No one could see a damned thing. Six minutes later, the farcical episode was abandoned. Fans were offered tickets for the second attempt, the following afternoon, or refunds. Only 500 asked for their money back.

'The effect of the weather on the attendances was disastrous,' admitted Fallowfield.

With no time to promote the new kick-off time, it was a pleasant surprise when 1,500 again turned up on Saturday afternoon. Among them was the Vice-Mayor of Long Beach, who reminisced about playing 'rugger' in the early 1900s and assured Fallowfield that older men remembered the game fondly. Australia won a decent contest, 30-13.

AUSTRALIAN RUGBY TEAM WINS 30-13

Southern California athletic history was made in Long Beach Memorial Stadium when the Australian Kangaroos defeated the New Zealand Kiwis, 30-13. It was the first game of 13-man Rugby League football played upon American soil. The second will be played this afternoon in the Coliseum (kick-off 2.45pm) between the same colorful great international teams. Harry Wells and Brian Davies scored two tries each for the winners and Norm Proven and Ken Kearney each added a try, the equivalent of an American touchdown. Noel Pidding kicked all six conversions after the tries, one from 35 yards out next to the sideline. Neville Denton, John Yates, and Cyril Eastlake scored tries for the New Zealanders. Eastlake added a 2-point conversion and a two-point 30-yard penalty kick as he proved the individual all-round star of the day.

LA Times by Dick Hyland

★ ★ ★ ★ ★ ★ ★ ★ ★ ★ ★ ★ ★ ★ ★

Just when rugby league needed a massive lift-off, it was a damp squib. Told all about the style and panache of game-day presentation at gridiron games in LA, Fallowfield had been preparing to have his socks blown off. Instead he got little more than the dour and spartan experience he would get in England. There were no programmes – Gilhousen claimed Nash, who worked in the magazine print business, did not have time to produce them – and the pitch was a mere 56 yards wide when there was room to expand beyond the gridiron sidelines to regulation width. Worst of all, just when they needed razzmatazz, old man Nash was the voice of the event, hogging the microphone to commentate. Fallowfield's notes continued: 'No propaganda. Presentation of the game – poor – principally because of Nash on loudspeaker and lack of organisation.'

Nash made rallying cries for volunteers and enthusiasts over the PA system. When he announced the wrong teams, an exasperated Fallowfield snapped and declared himself PA announcer for the game at the Coliseum the next day.

RUGBY DEBUT DOMINATED BY AUSSIES

Rugby League made a speedy and spirited Los Angeles debut before 4,554 fog-bound spectators at the Coliseum yesterday as the Australian Kangaroos completed their conquest of the New Zealand Kiwis by the score of 28-18. The victory, which followed by one day on Australia's 30-13 win over the New Zealanders at Long Beach, was emblematic of the Down Under championship in a game which has become tremendously popular in Australia, New Zealand, France and Great Britain. The two games played here over the weekend were the first ever staged in the United States, Rugby League differing from the old-time Rugby in several interesting aspects and being considerably faster. Here is a sport that could become a springtime interlude of considerable stature in this country if it were spiced up with something which was lacking yesterday – local teams capable of holding their own with the national teams of other countries and for whom American crowds could root. An Australian half-back named Keith Holman was the game's outstanding player. The Aussies led at half-time 12-0. Here's how they scored: Australia: Tries (touchdowns to you) by Pidding, Holman, Flannery (2), Diversi, Kearney. Conversions by Pidding (3), Field goals by Pidding (40 yards) and Churchill (30 yards). New Zealand: Tries by Johnson, Austin, Yates and Atkinson. Conversions by Bond (3). (Note: Tries count three points, conversions and field goals each count two).

LA Examiner by Maxwell Stiles

However, the locals 'seemed very appreciative in spite of the ignorance of the laws', admitted Fallowfield. Finally, after 22 years of trying, a rugby league match had taken place in the US of A.

★ ★ ★ ★ ★ ★ ★ ★ ★ ★ ★ ★ ★ ★ ★ ★

The next day the teams met again at the gargantuan Coliseum. Despite Kangaroos skipper Clive Churchill – The Little Master – being handed the keys to the city and then given the full horns-blaring police escort to the stadium, less than 5,000 intrigued Angelinos turned up, leaving 100,000 empty spaces in the giant Olympic bowl. Among the spectators again were Al Abajian and his pals, knowing they were probably watching some of their opponents from a few months earlier. In the booth, Nash and Fallowfield fought over the microphone. Bill called Nash uncooperative. Still, it was progress. After an All Stars soccer game opened proceedings, Australia completed a series win.

Although Fallowfield vowed to approach the New Zealand team management and players about the Kiwis 'irritating high tackling' ahead of their next series against Great Britain, head-high shots went down a storm with the football fans of southern Cal. The more biff the better. No helmets required or allowed here. Another of Fallowfield's notes was: 'The crowds evidently found the open nature

Hollywood Stars Hollywood Baseball Association

December 9, 1954

Mr. William Fallowfield
Honorable Secretary
The Rugby Football League
180 Chapeltown Road
Leeds, England

Dear Sir:

Attached herewith you will find a notarized account of the expenses and revenue for the Rugby League game played in the Los Angeles Coliseum November 28, 1954.

The game played at Long Beach was handled by Mr. Dave Lewis of that city and he assumed one-half of the guarantee of 1,000 pounds. I have noted this under item one.

Item two, under Coliseum expenses, represents the rental, staffing, clean-up, dressing rooms, ticket taking and auditing plus all expenses incurred at the Coliseum the day of the game.

As the representatives of your team and Mr. Fallowfield know, I originally had to post a guarantee of $2,500 for the use of the field. Members of the commission who control the rental of the Coliseum met and decided as this was a pioneering game for Rugby that they would only charge me $1,591.30, which was the absolute expenses.

Under Publicity, I hired three men to handle newspaper, radio, television and public relation work. In my contract with them I allowed them 10¢ a mile for their automobile expense plus their parking and entertainment expenses. The postage and printing was for letters, posters and pamphlets that were mailed or distributed throughout Southern California.

As we did not receive any publicity photos that were clear or pertained to the actual teams that were to

---

of the game and its continuity a pleasing contrast to American football.' And that was that.

A cuckolded Dimitro turned up to take the teams out on the town in LA and took his chance to mock Nash's efforts: 'Mr Nash was a very poor hoster. He didn't even see the both teams off or even drop by to see the boys. It was a big joke. Trying to play rugby during our football season which they lost money.' Once the teams had headed off home across the Pacific, Fallowfield continued his one-man mission to destroy Nash and take over whatever remained of American rugby league. Before he left LA, Fallowfield sat down face to face with Nash, Sunderland and half a dozen colleagues. Sunderland made a brief speech and then retired. Fallowfield noticed immediately that Gilhousen was absent. He leant over and whispered to O'Neill about his whereabouts. Gilhousen was sent for. Nash, meanwhile, made a 'rambling report' on the previous visits of Sharpe, Knowling and Christensen. Fallowfield's notes revealed: 'In his report during which it became increasingly evident that he had no regard for the truth Nash said among other things: 17 colleges were going to play RL next spring – later denied; Sharpe wanted $20,000 for Australian game; Not much lost at Long Beach – although Lewis lost £1,000 plus; No publicity at all before arrival of teams.

'I cut off rambling and fired questions.

Fallowfield: Can a US team be raised to play France?

Nash: Yes.

Fallowfield: How much will it cost?

Nash: $2,500. This answer is unreliable because he obviously had no knowledge of guarantee required.

Fallowfield: Who will promote it?

Nash: The Rams. Later backed down when Gilhousen was present.

Fallowfield: What can be done about coaching?

Nash: English coach required. Wages $500-750 a month – rather vague as to how this money can be found. Possibility of getting American football players to play France but Gilhousen says off-season activities are controlled although payments made from 1 Aug to 1 Jan.

Fallowfield: Why can't RU teams change over to League?

Nash: Northern California Union very anti-RL. About 12 teams in N California – 1 or 2 in S. California.' Against Fallowfield's advice, a committee was formed comprising of: Nash, Evans, Schroeder, Donald, Beck, and Edmundson. What about the money? Dave Lewis stumped up $500 of the $1,000 given to the two teams in Long Beach and Fallowfield predicted that he must have lost at least $1,500 on the game. The Coliseum game brought in $6,077, most of it from ticket sales (at $1.50, $2.50 for reserved seats), and programme sales. Expenses were $9,267. This totalled a loss of $3,190 (£878). As well as the usual costs – stadium hire, ticket agency, tax, printing costs and rebates – was a series of expenses new to Fallowfield. Three media men had been paid $400 each: Gallagher to secure newspaper coverage; Lee for PR; and a Leonard Cummings for getting the games

promoted on TV and on the radio. Another $350 went to the local media to buy good coverage. Fallowfield noticed that *LA Times* hack Dick Hyland (not to be confused with the former Australian forward of the same name, who had died while the All Stars were down under) was knocking the game throughout but miraculously wrote a positive piece. It turns out he was 'bribed to write well': Nash had bunged him $200 and called the MVP Award the Dick Hyland Trophy. Hyland was worth trying to convert. He had starred for Stanford's football team that won the Rose

Bowl back in the 1920s and for the gold-medal winning US rugby union team in the 1924 Olympics. He knew his stuff. Another $700 went on wining and dining the decision-makers. Gilhousen knew money had to be spent to give rugby league a chance. 'All of this money was spent to give us an "in" with these men and it certainly paid off and will be of value for future games,' reported Gilhousen. The games had received 37 radio plugs and 19 TV shots, 'including three coast to coast telecasts which reached into the millions of viewers'. For this, Gilhousen paid himself $500 plus expenses

OFFICIAL PROGRAM

AUSTRALIA vs. NEW ZEALAND

PRICE **25¢**

WORLD CUP RUGBY LEAGUE FOOTBALL
VETERANS MEMORIAL STADIUM
Long Beach, California

– Fallowfield was flabbergasted that the agreed 5c a mile gas deal had become 10c – and over $300 was put down for printing and postage. A defiant Gilhousen was unswayed: 'If we had not run into the nasty weather that we did, I believe the results could have been easily reversed. I am not discouraged in the least. I have already started plans to organise both American and Negro teams which we hope in the future will build to a strength to where we will be able to compete with your fine teams.' Fallowfield was actually not despondent. 'Bad organisation and publicity can be improved', he noted. Lessons learnt – first time ever. He did have one new policy though: Future games – contact man Rosey. Ignore Nash. 'It would appear that Mr R. Gilhousen is the only person willing to accept the responsibility of organising the game. I recommend he is recognised as the Organiser and correspondence from the four countries should be addressed to him.

'Our contact over the years in California (Nash) most certainly wishes the game well but apparently has done nothing practical other than find two promoters for the games. Nor does it appear that he will be of any practical value in the future. The only "man of action" on the scene is Gilhousen, who was originally brought in as a promoter solely but has since expressed a determination to establish the game if only he can be "shown the way"'. Gilhousen knew LA sport inside out. An occasional football referee and former baseball coach, Gilhousen was a man of connections. He scouted for Hollywood Stars, who played minor league baseball to packed crowds at Gilmore Field, where Erkie Cheldin used to play football, right next to CBS Television City studios. The Stars were owned and supported by the people who made Hollywood sparkle. Robert H. Cobb, not only inventor of the Cobb salad but owner of the painfully hip Brown Derby restaurant, and

Fans flock to watch Hollywood Stars baseball at Gilmore Field.

Oscar-winning film director Cecil B DeMille, held the purse-strings. Cobb wanted the Stars to belong to Hollywood and so create perpetual self-publicity: 'The Hollywood Stars baseball team, owned by the Hollywood stars.' With celebrities walking in from CBS next door, the Stars were unique. Bing Crosby conducted the opening ceremony; singer Rosemary Clooney, screen heroes Spencer Tracy, George Burns and Jack Benny mingled in the stands with gangsters Bugsy Siegel and Mickey 'The Misanthropic Mickster' Cohen and his henchman Johnny Stompanato; a teenage Elizabeth Taylor was a bat girl; 'Miss Hollywood Stars' was Jayne Mansfield. The Stars, who fed into Brooklyn Dodgers, were hugely successful on the field too and were the first to broadcast home games live on TV. Landon Exley was usually there at Gilmore Field with his father, and Al Abajian rarely missed a game. Gilhousen was at the heart of all this. He knew how a minor league sport could flourish in LA.

All these opportunities were staring American rugby league in the face. At least Fallowfield knew that Rosey was his man: 'Mr Ward B. Nash, whilst undoubtedly displaying a great interest in the game, lacks those practical qualities which are necessary in an organiser. It would appear to me that we must rely for further initiative and action on Mr R. Gilhousen, assisted by Mr Charles Edmundson, a former Bradford man, whose realistic views on the position in California and whose voluntary assistance were invaluable.' Fallowfield was so smitten by Rosey the baseball guru that he suspended his usual Yorkshire tight-fistedness to get him on the International Board's payroll 'to keep Gilhousen 'sweet'. Despite the supposed interest from the Rams, the city's media, various sports administrators and promoters in Long Beach and LA, and Gilhousen's contacts, Fallowfield was cautious about the Californian dream. But was there really a line of millionaires waiting to give the ARLF what they needed to get up and running?

★ ★ ★ ★ ★ ★ ★ ★ ★ ★ ★ ★ ★ ★ ★ ★ ★

CHAPTER 32
PLOTTING IN THE WEE SMALL HOURS

MARCH '55

Frank Sinatra wrapped up recording 'In The Wee Small Hours' at KHS Studios in Hollywood. It had taken a year. In that time, since the All Stars returned from France, American rugby league had staged two international games and nothing else. It had ambitious plans for more but no one could decide who should tour, where or when. Each party seemed obsessed with playing high profile international fixtures and making money, rather than starting a league and developing players.

On his return to England – via a survey of Canadian rugby league which depressed him even more – Fallowfield reported back to the International Board. He suggested each country send coaches and players to the US to teach them the game, invite American teams to tour, send teams over there and generally welcome them to the rugby league community.

Although he respected the power of football in the States, Fallowfield thought its players could be tempted by the all-action nature of rugby league compared to the specific roles each player had in gridiron.

Fallowfield reported to the RLIB: 'From the player's point of view American football can hardly be called a game. The player's activities may consist solely of kicking at goal! If no kicks are taken he will remain on the bench. The only attraction to the player appears to be the attendant publicity and ballyhoo which is his lot if he becomes a star.'

When to tour was a major issue. The American football players were free between February and June but the RFL wanted them at the start of the British season in August and September, the Australians wanted them over in April, May or June. No one suggested the Americans may be better off coming when they wanted and playing far less daunting club sides on midweek evenings rather than risky international fixtures.

Ward Nash was desperate for France to tour the States in May '55. By late March he was still making plans for their arrival with no sign of them actually confirming their trip. He proposed a back-up plan for New Zealand to come over in February '56. And he made outlandish claims as to who he had contracted to play for the US.

In a post-script to a letter to Harold Matthews in Sydney about France's non-communication, Nash wrote: 'The following players have been alerted and are ready for practice: Frank Gifford (New York Giants); Duane Putnam (Los Angeles Rams); Johnny Williams (San Francisco); Gary Kerkorian (Baltimore Colts); Primo Villanueva (Vancouver Lions); Jim Sears (Chicago Cardinals); Paul Cameron (Pittsburgh Steelers); Bob Heydenfeld (Edmonton, Canada); Volney

Peters (Green Bay Packers); Art Battle (USC Trojans); Ted Grossman (Los Angeles); Bob Buckley (Los Angeles); Don Doll (LA Rams); Chuck Doud (U of Cal. LA); (Six or seven others from local Universities that have played R. Union).'

It was an eye-watering list. Nash had seen Dimitro's plan work and was following it to a tee: targeting tough, top quality SoCal football players who would play rugby with their pals. He had got Grossman, Buckley and Kerkorian to signal their intent. Then he had supposedly lined up a who's who of USC and UCLA alumni, some of whom were now starring in the NFL, such as Frank Gifford, fast becoming a legend at New York Giants, and Green Bay's Volney Peters. Bob Heydenfeldt and Primo Villanueva had just helped the Bruins clinch the National Championship by beating USC in front of 102,000 at the Coliseum before heading to Canada's Western Interprovincial Football Union. And Art Battle was also president of the Trojans Alumni club – a worthy contact.

In short, a team of USC and UCLA football lettermen was supposedly primed to play rugby league.

If this was true, Nash had lined up some world class athletes to take on the best France or New Zealand had to offer. A big if.

A familiar face at UCLA was Mike Dimitro, who was telling an intrigued Bruins assistant coach George Dickerson – a football and rugby letterman in the 1930s – how he had introduced a 'rugby offense' to the football playbook at Elsinore Union High School in Riverside, CA. Elsinore was Mike's latest stop on the merry-go-round of LA schools, his sixth in six years. He was taking home $357 a month, wife Maryon $260. His assistant coach was All Stars veteran Don Lent.

AUGUST '55

New Zealand rep TF Mackenzie convinced the International Board that Nash and Gilhousen had 21 pro football players interested in playing league and whose clubs would release them, and Nash told Fallowfield that five junior colleges in Southern California were playing rugby to '90 per cent league rules'. Mackenzie reckoned 17 colleges had agreed to start playing league in 1956. Discussions were also supposedly on-going with UCLA about use of the Rose Bowl rather than the Coliseum. Suggestions that the ARLF build their own stadium were soon silenced when Fallowfield mentioned it would cost $5m.

Nash and Co were also going to approach the Helms Athletic Foundation to see if they were still interested in investing in American Rugby League Football.

The Kiwis had little interest in mentoring the Americans, however. 'I am convinced that whilst Australia, New Zealand and France can play their part to the full, England is in a far better position to carry on the organisation, appointment of coaches and supervise the effort,' said Mackenzie. Geography was clearly not his forte.

Fallowfield had been given free reign. But could he make it work? And did he really want it to?

SEPTEMBER '55

President Eisenhower suffered a heart attack. Vice-President Nixon took the reins. Helping American rugby league was not on his To Do list.

NOVEMBER '55

New Zealand secretary Knowling turned down Nash's invite for the Kiwis to tour America en route to the UK but he did offer to play games in Vancouver, San Francisco, Los Angeles, Long Beach and San Diego on the way home in January and February 1956 if all expenses were paid – plus $7,200.

Nash had just two months' notice to put the tour together and lodge a bond in a San Francisco bank. Knowling had learnt from experience: the money needed to be seen in advance.

Meanwhile, Nash's main contact at the Rams – impressive PR manager Pete Rozelle – had left the club to work on marketing for the 1956 Olympic Games in Melbourne; and in Baltimore, Gary Kerkorian was reaching the end of the road. After spending the season as back-up quarter-back, Kerkorian quit the Colts and went off to LA to study full-time at Loyola Law School. Colts coach Weeb Ewbank replaced him with a kid who was building roads in the day and playing sand-lot football in Pittsburgh on Thursday nights for $6 a game. His name was Johnny Unitas.

Joyce Kerkorian: 'Gary called that his "greatest contribution to pro football": going full-time so they called Unitas!'

1956

There was a familiar face back in Sydney. His football career seemingly over, Al E. Kirkland had flown 8,000 miles from Bakersfield to Sydney to see if he could make it in rugby league. Kirkland's magnificent performances in the centres for the All Stars had left a reputation in New South Wales and Queensland that was worth exploiting. Less than three years after leaving Australia, Kirkland was back, courtesy of the Parramatta club.

Parramatta had been in the Sydney Premiership less than a decade and as the invincible mantle passed from South Sydney to St George, Parramatta were the worst team in the league. The Fruit Pickers needed to try something different. Al E. was certainly that. They invited him back to New South Wales, west along the Parramatta River from Sydney. He got a job in the munitions factory at St Mary's, training with the reserve grade several evenings a week throughout pre-season.

By the time the opening games of the season came around, Kirkland had done enough to get a start in first grade. New coach Cec Fifield put

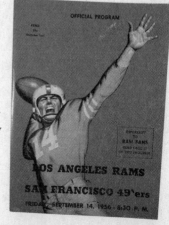

him on the wing so he could watch what it was all about from near the touchline.

He did just fine. He was soon moved inside to play at centre. The kid could handle it, no problem. Each game came and went. Most games Parramatta lost. But each week Al E. got better and better.

Eventually, his was one of the first names on the team sheet. By the end of the season, with the Eels rock bottom of the Premiership table, Kirkland was playing at five-eighths, given a central role to create openings at second receiver. He was a class act. Ever-present in all 18 games, Kirkland scored four tries and was lauded by all who saw his remarkable

Al E. Kirkland training at Parramatta.

performances for a guy playing only his second season of rugby league.

Meanwhile, Dimitro was on the move again, heading up to Canada to try out with Edmonton Eskimos. Back in the States, Elvis Presley was debuting on the *Ed Sullivan Show,* watched by 80 per cent of America's TV audience. He would earn a million dollars by the end of the year. The days of Johnnie Ray, Doris Day and Ted Heath's Band were numbered. Teenagers were coming. Times were a-changing.

In America's fall, Kerkorian's sporting adventure got a post-script. With leading QB George Shaw injured, Johnny Unitas came on for his NFL debut away to Chicago Bears. His first throw was intercepted for a Bears touchdown as the Colts were thrashed 58-27. The next day, with Baltimore now 1-4 and desperate, GM Don Kellett tried to drag Kerkorian out of Law School on the other side of the country to provide cover for Unitas.

Don Kellett: What can I offer Kerkorian?

Coach Ewbank: Money.

Don Kellett: No, seriously. What can I promise him?

Coach Ewbank: Money.

Gary took the bait. Unitas, under sudden severe pressure, responded with match-winning performances, leaving Kerkorian to play bit-parts in just three games. He only threw two passes – both connected, one for a touchdown – and kicked an extra point, before returning to Loyola and a new life as a lawyer. He was a class act.

JANUARY '57

Dimitro attended a Bruins Coaching Clinic at Spaulding Field run by UCLA head coach Red Sanders and Rams head coach Sid Gilman, a bow-tied, crew-cut visionary who revolutionised the NFL with his use of film analysis and the forward pass.

FEBRUARY '57

Major League Baseball was coming to the Golden State. The Brooklyn Dodgers and New York Giants baseball teams were moving to the west coast. California's sporting landscape was changing forever.

MARCH '57

Bill Fallowfield talked about arranging Great Britain v France exhibition games in Canada en route home from the World Cup down under but soon gave up when 'no suitable contact' could be found. Instead they went via South Africa.

APRIL '57

Back home after his year with Parramatta, Al E. Kirkland wrote to Fallowfield hoping to get a move to the UK: 'My ultimate goal in mind is to play in England. I feel I have a firm grasp on the game now and would like a chance to try out for one of your teams. The ban on Australian players, of course, does not affect me because I am an American.'

Thomas Griffiths ran the Bay Area operation from his house in Millbrae.

The nature of the overseas players ban was unclear: re-imposed in 1947, English clubs had instead started signing Antipodean rugby union stars instead until that loophole was closed in 1951.

Kirkland enclosed a reference from Australian RFL boss Harold Matthews, who wrote to Fallowfield: 'Mr Al Kirkland during the past season has been a member of our Parramatta DRLF Club and as a centre three-quarter and wing showed great promise and we feel that we can confidently recommend him to any of your clubs that need his services. Mr Kirkland was one of the few members of the American All-Stars that did have a rugby knowledge and the experience he gained on that tour, plus the playing with one of our District Clubs during the past season has brought the best out of him. Commending this matter to your most favourite consideration.'

MAY '57

Fallowfield, to his credit, got on the case and Kirkland paid his own air fare to England to take up an offer from Leeds RLFC, on the RFL's doorstep. Leeds had won the Challenge Cup Final and were narrowly beaten by eventual champions Oldham in the semi-final of the Championship play-offs. Al E. was going in at the top.

JUNE '57

Dimitro quit his post at Elsinore Union High. He would start the next school year with yet another job, at Huntingdon Beach Union High School.

JULY '57

Tex Schramm left the Rams for CBS TV in New York. Co-owner Ed Pauley refused all the suggested replacements until Bert Bell recalled the dynamic PR man who used to work there: Pete Rozelle returned to the Rams as general manager.

17 AUGUST 1957

KIRKLAND TO PLAY IN FIRST TEAM

A crowd of 4,208 at Headingley last night were highly delighted with the form of Al Kirkland, Leeds Rugby League Club's new American winger in a 31-3 victory over Featherstone Rovers A. Kirkland scored two tries and will play in Leeds' first team against Blackpool Borough at Headingley on Monday evening.

Yorkshire Post

Al had hit the ground running. The following afternoon, Leeds' first team opened the season with a 41-25 hammering at Hull, conceding nine tries in their first game since winning at Wembley in May. With their second match coming on the Monday evening, they decided to give Al a chance against the minnows from Blackpool.

20 AUGUST 1957

LEEDS 68 BLACKPOOL 6

Lewis Jones broke the Leeds Rugby League Club goalkicking record in a runaway victory over Blackpool at Headingley last night and but for the friendly gesture towards Al Kirkland, the new American winger, he would have broken the club's points-scoring record for one match as well.

Jones broke clear of his own 25 and had the Blackpool line at his mercy but instead of trotting over himself he slowed down and unselfishly provided Kirkland with his first League try.

Leeds played with a daring unorthodox style which bewildered Blackpool. The opposition was only a minor nuisance. Al Kirkland in his first senior game showed praiseworthy handling ability. Judgement on whether he has enough speed and enough ability to beat a man to hold his place in the first team must be postponed.

Yorkshire Post
By Alfred Drewry

A crowd of 11,000 had seen Jones kick 13 of his 17 attempts at goal for 29 points, just short of his own record of 30 in a game. It was Leeds' highest score since the 1936/37 season and they did it all with only 11 men after losing two players to injury for much of the game. Blackpool were woeful.

Sadly the Leeds public and English rugby league did not get to see Al prove he had what it takes. He was left out of the XIII as Leeds went with a full-strength side at Barrow on the Saturday, winning 52-12, probably playing for the A team in their Yorkshire Senior Cup win at Dewsbury instead. Nor did he play on the following Wednesday when Leeds lost at Huddersfield. A week later he had gone.

4 SEPTEMBER 1957

KIRKLAND TO GO BACK TO U.S.
AL KIRKLAND, THE AMERICAN WINGER, IS GOING HOME TO CALIFORNIA NEXT WEEK

Yorkshire Post

He had been refused a work permit by the Ministry of Labour and was unable to turn professional. It was a complex affair, not simply down to him being from overseas: the following day Hull signed a South African centre!

Devastated, Kirkland headed home to Bakersfield, his rugby league dreams in tatters over red tape.

Al Abajian: 'He told me he couldn't get a work permit at Leeds: boy did they miss out. I tell you, Al was a great athlete. He wasn't used that often at USC – I don't know why because he was a great, great runner. He was sensational at rugby league.'

SEPTEMBER '57

The last Hollywood Stars baseball game was played at Gilmore Field. Jayne Mansfield presented Bob Cobb with a new car before the game as fans gave him a standing ovation. Minor league sport was dead in LA as the majors were on the rise.

Pete Rozelle was already revolutionising the Rams. They started to fill the Coliseum, with a record 102,368 heading to the game against the 49ers. TV and radio was awash with national broadcasts of pro football and Major League Baseball. Fans could support who they like, wherever they lived. It was the dawning of a new era for pro sports.

Meanwhile, Dimitro was doing some moonlighting as a private detective for the LAPD. His contact was the top forensic scientist, Leland V Jones. Jones' career changed forever one night in January 1947 when he was called to Norton and 39th – not far from Dorsey High, near the Coliseum – where cops had found a horrifically mutilated female body. It was Elizabeth Short, a Veronica Lake lookalike. She was christened 'The Black Dahlia' by the press. Jones would become 'Sergeant Leland Blanchard' in James Ellroy's classic novel about the case that has yet to be solved.

CHAPTER 33
L.A. CONFIDENTIAL

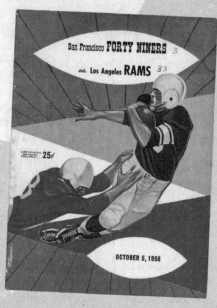

San Francisco FORTY NINERS 3

vis. Los Angeles RAMS 33

25¢

OCTOBER 5, 1958

APRIL '58

Back in Bakersfield, Al E. Kirkland – on behalf of the suitably-titled Optimists Club – was liaising with Harold Matthews in Sydney to bring the Kangaroos to play in the Municipal Stadium there, either en route to Europe in October or on their return journey in January 1959. Like Nash, Kirkland – who had shown League films to the Optimists members – was going to do a Dimitro: form a team from American college rugby union players and try to get an English coach to teach them the game (in this case, legendary player Arthur Clues). Matthews suggested England may stop off on their way home from Australia in late August.

Meanwhile, 400 miles north, one of the biggest names in pro football was keen to launch the new football in the Bay Area. Gordie Soltau, a San Francisco 49ers icon, was about to commence his ninth and final season in the NFL. The wide receiver or tight end had missed just one game in his 49ers career, and was a three-time Pro Bowler. Facing retirement, Soltau was looking for a new challenge. He was sold the idea of rugby league by a Mr Thomas Griffiths in neighbouring Millbrae who, seemingly independent of Dimitro, Nash or Kirkland, wanted New South Wales to send a team to San Francisco at the end of June to play against a

49er's

Gordon Soltau
END   SAN FRANCISCO 49ers

team of NFL pro players who Griffiths claimed had 'formed a rugby team'. Griffiths would pay all costs and would like the Americans to tour Australia in July in exchange.

Soltau had spoken to enough 49ers team-mates to think a rugby league team was viable. If the LA Rams plan could be resurrected, American rugby league could be on to something.

Dimitro and Nash were conspicuously absent from discussions. Dimitro was working as an extra on TV shows like *Bodyguard* and Sam Peckinpah's *Gunsmoke*.

Fallowfield to Matthews: 'Ward B. Nash seems to have completely disappeared from the scene. He was never of great practical

American Rugby League Football
818 Santee St
Los Angeles

Secretary: Ward B Nash

28 August 1958

To the International Board

The following may be of interest to you....
The owners of the National Football League of America have given permission to any of their players to join with or play Rugby League football in the months of June to July of any year. In San Francisco, they have already formed a complete team. In Los Angeles, the basis of the team has already been started and will probably be complete within a very few days. In addition to the American teams, the British Colombia Lions of the Canadian Football League have also indicated that they might like to join the American teams in a series of games later on.

The tentative schedule would start with games in San Francisco on 25 January 1959, and would run through the month of March. This would allow three or four games in Kezar Stadium (65,000 cap.) and the same number in Los Angeles Coliseum (100,000 cap.) and in Vancouver City Stadium (35,000 cap.).

Mr Derek Gardener who has been, for the past four years, Secretary of the Southern California Rugby Football Union, has resigned from that position and has accepted the position of Organizing Secretary of the American Rugby Football League [sic]. As mentioned at the start of this letter, this information is merely to keep you informed as to the progress of our organization here, and undoubtedly, Mr Gardener may be writing you more fully shortly.

Yours very sincerely,

Ward B. Nash

value in any case, although he was definitely interested in our game.'

Wishful thinking. Griffiths was just Nash's man in San Fran.

The Rams and 49ers rivalry was hotting up. Their annual meeting at the Coliseum had broken pro football attendance records year on year. How many would turn up to see them play rugby league in the sunshine? Surely enough to make the show pay. It sounded too good to be true.

It was.

The 49ers were not keen to let their employees play rugby in the spring rather than take other temporary jobs – but the players certainly were. With most pro football players on around $5,000 for a season, the ARLF's offer of $300 a night was not to be sniffed at. Griffiths, living in a quiet crescent tucked behind the train line, freeway and SF airport car park, claimed he had lined up Stanford Stadium for the 49ers' opening rugby league game, with the Olympic Club playing a union game as a curtain-raiser. The *San Francisco Examiner* was supposedly keen on sponsoring a charity game and he was trying to recruit players for a second team from players around Northern California. All he needed now from Nash was a rugby league rule book, an Australian coach and 'maybe a player or two'.

On 29 October 1958, Gardener wrote to Fallowfield: 'We have a verbal commitment from the Los Angeles Rams football team to lend players to ARLF and allow us to use their name. San Francisco are not getting the same commitment from the 49ers.'

If this was true it was the opportunity of a lifetime. International rugby league was facing an open goal, staring a gift horse in the mouth. Now was the time to act.

An NFL franchise was not only offering up their players but also the chance to market rugby league under the LA Rams name.

Frantic letters began to frantically criss-cross the Atlantic every few days. The subterranean phone lines started to ring. It was getting serious.

NOVEMBER '58

In Los Angeles, the ARLF had a former Australian league player called Clive Spilsted chasing the Rams. Spilsted, now in his 50s, had crossed the

Bill Fallowfield.

AMERICAN RUGBY LEAGUE FOOTBALL

(A Non-profit Organization)

Promotion of International Football for American Youth
818 Santee Street
Los Angeles, California

etary
. NASH

November 25, 1958

Mr. W. Fallowfield
180 Chapeltown Road
Leeds 7
ENGLAND

Dear Mr. Fallowfield:

Since I last wrote to you certain problems have made themselves very clear on the promotion of Rugby League in this country. I am writing this letter to you as a confidential explanation of some of our problems with regards to raising the finances and I hope you will keep the contents of this letter as confidential as you possibly can. There are no copies going to any of the other Leagues.

Rugby League in this country will not be as easy to promote as the overseas Leagues seem to think. The game, although fast, is not spectacular in the American sense and the American people will have to go through a period of education to the game. Due to this, we cannot promise any investors a return on their money for a very considerable period of time. This, then, reduces the type of man we can approach almost entirely to the millionaire philanthropist type of person.

Another approach has been suggested from the strictly social aspect of the game. I feel that if one of these millionaires was approached by someone of high standing in both Rugby League and society it would be of very great benefit to us and probably open doors in this very highly protected level of American society that cannot be opened in any other way. We would then be able to offer them the post of Patron of the American Rugby League which, in their minds, would place them on a level with the patrons of the four other Leagues. This would be a very considerable lever that we could use and, in the opinion of the two experts whom I have consulted on this subject, the only practical way of attempting to start the game in this country.

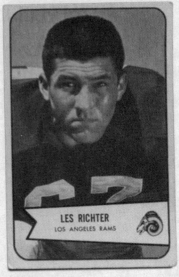

LES RICHTER
LOS ANGELES RAMS

Pacific from Sydney to California. When his work took him to Vancouver, Spilsted handed over the LA business to an Englishman from Devon called Derek Gardener. Gardener arrived in LA in 1952 and played rugby union for South California RFU before becoming their secretary. He was based at Lexington Avenue, right at the heart of Hollywood and Southern Cal sport.

Spilsted put Gardener in touch with Griffiths in San Francisco, and Ian Hamilton in the NZ Consul's office. Hamilton was tasked with trying to raise the cash to launch the new league, which would be packed with NFL stars: 'The idea of proprietary clubs studded with "name" gridiron stars seems to me to be the only method of establishing a pro game as RL in the USA and Canada and it is on these lines that those concerned are working both in Frisco and Los Angeles. This will be the dominant factor in establishing the code as gridiron stars like Les Richter and John Annette [sic, USC captain Jon Arnett] in Los Angeles [Rams] and Hugh McElhenny [49ers running back] and Gordie Soltau in Frisco [49ers] will cost money to buy.'

Spilsted continued working for ARLF from Vancouver. He told Fallowfield that two friends – former Great Britain locks Dave Valentine of Huddersfield and Wakefield Trinity's Ken Traill – may be interested in coming to Canada to coach. He also suggested some other familiar names from the All Stars tours as potential coaches: guest All Star Travers Hardwick, Vic Hey or Ray Stehr. He claimed some of the American players had been excellent rugby union players in college, particularly Les Richter.

Spilsted abandoned plans for a 'four-club semi-amateur competition' in Vancouver and set his mind to forming 'Vancouver Tigers' and hosting a Canada v the US international game at the city's new Empire Stadium in early April 1959 instead, with Canada heading to LA and San Fran for return legs three weeks later: 'This is tentative only. The experience each team will gain will be most valuable and later with England, NZ, French and Australian teams passing through it is anticipated that in two or three years a team can be sent overseas to recover the prestige lost by Mike Dimitro and his non-entities.'

Spilsted was dreaming of a rugby league circuit packed with major NFL stars alongside their league equivalents in England. But Gardener was concerned by the whole project. Would the American public watch a new code of football just because they knew some of the players? How would the players learn to play a game they had never seen? Where was the money going to appear from to finance a professional rugby league circuit packed with football stars?

Derek Gardener suggested requesting the assistance of the Earl of Derby, on the board of the RFL at the time: 'This may seem to you a very devious way of trying to promote this game. Please rest assured that having lived 23 years in England and 6 years in this country and after consulting some very successful promotional men in Los Angeles, I have come to the conclusion that this is the most practical approach.

'The man we have in mind is Mr Ed Pauley, who is a multi-millionaire, and will be very approachable from the strictly social angle. Money, as such, is no concern to him. He is an extremely well-known sportsman in this country and one of the co-owners of the Los Angeles Rams Football Team. Please give this whole question your urgent consideration and ask the Earl of Derby if they would not consider writing a letter to Mr Pauley on this subject.'

Ed Pauley Jr was an ex-UCLA man, a bigwig in the Democrat party, an oil magnate and major player in American sports expansion. President and quarter-owner of the Rams he, like Richard Nixon, had a dubious past. In 1946, his pal President Truman put him forward as Under Secretary of the Navy only for the Navy to reject Pauley believing it to be a sap to his oil muscle. Instead he was made Assistant to the Secretary of the US Army. It was a big controversy at the time.

The ARLF were not the only ambitious men hoping Pauley would help them get their foot in pro football's door. Just as Nash, Spilsted and Co were trying to get the 49ers and Rams to launch their own spring rugby league football teams, two young southern businessmen wanted the NFL to expand into Texas. Pauley told them that no NFL owner would share their wealth with new kids on the block and pointed them in the direction of his PR man, Pete Rozelle. NFL commissioner Bert Bell confirmed there would be no expansion. So, like Spilsted, Lamar Hunt and Bud Adams planned their own football league. Unlike Spilsted, they had the money to do it.

28 NOVEMBER 1958

Rugby Leaguer
newspaper, England

RL TEAMS IN U.S.A.
– TEAMS BEING FORMED NOW

Spilsted told Fallowfield that each ARLF franchise would need about $100,000 capital. That ruled out any RFL investment immediately. They were struggling to break even. While NBC were paying the NFL $100,000 for exclusive television rights to screen the Championship Game, the RFL banked just £2,000 from the BBC to show the Challenge Cup Final. The ARLF needed the NFL's money as well as their players.

★ ★ ★ ★ ★ ★ ★ ★ ★ ★ ★ ★ ★

No one had mentioned Rosey Gilhousen. His year had been beset by tragic family bereavement. He was understandably emotional when he sent a passionate four-page letter to the International Board:

To
Mr William Fallowfield (Leeds, England)
Mr Harold Matthews (Sydney, Australia)
Mr JE Knowling (Auckland, New Zealand)
Monseiur Antoine Blain (Paris, France)

8258 E.Bevan Street, San Gabriel, California
U.S.A.

11 December, 1958

Gentlemen:

It has been four years since I have written to you people; however, you have been on my mind completely. Why haven't I written you? There is no need to arouse the hopes of Rugby League officers until some light of hope springs into view. It is easy to sit aside and dream of what might be accomplished, but the fact remains that there can be no Rugby League in America without many hours and years of solid, step-by-step organization.

I have read several letters that have been sent on to you people telling of the wondrous progress that has been made, of the plans to play Canada in April 1959, etc., etc. Hogwash!! The fact remains, gentlemen, that there is not a single Rugby League team organized in the United States. If you were to ask anyone connected with the so-called Nash regime where they could find a ball to play with, you might, and then again you might not, get an answer. Who is going to coach the team? There again there is no one person connected with the League who can coach the game… Words written in letter after letter are not the basis of foundation for a solid house. They are the results of dreamers on both sides of the issue.

Up to now everything looks bitter, dismal and hopeless. What can be done to overcome this listless mess? Here and only here can you men from Rugby League help us.

Rosey said he wanted their experience, not money, to make America an international contender. He insisted that they must build from the roots up, instilling the game in schools and working with colleges who played rugby union. Gilhousen, who had spent his life in pro sport, was taking the exact opposite stand-point to his franchise-driven colleagues. He wanted a ten-year plan, not a series of high-profile, cash-sapping exhibition games: 'We must build a solid base, not one that will topple over as it did in 1954, when one fogged out game sent all parties to the showers.'

He paid tribute to Nash as 'one of the finest men you could wish to meet in a lifetime' and 'the ramrod for rugby in America', adding: 'Sure we need Ward's great burning desire and advice... the organisers of American rugby league should be young men acting on the advice of you people.

Please take some of your time to write to me. Don't pull your punches. Get rough with the cold facts, and give it to me straight from the shoulder.

Sincerely yours,
Ross "Rosey" Gilhousen

★ ★ ★ ★ ★ ★ ★ ★ ★ ★ ★ ★

28 DECEMBER 1958

In the NFL Championship game, Baltimore Colts beat New York Giants with a touchdown in sudden-death overtime. They were driven down the field in the dying seconds by a masterclass of quarterback leadership by Johnny Unitas. It was described as the greatest game in NFL history, the game that took American football to a whole new level. Televised across the nation, it brought pro football to the people.

On the sidelines, an unrequired third-string quarter back, was Gary Kerkorian. Called back yet again by Weeb Ewbank that fall, Kerkorian arranged a transfer from Loyola to Georgetown, about an hour from Baltimore, and signed up for the Colts as a part-time player, in case of emergencies. There were none, but that did not stop Kerkorian becoming the only student at Georgetown with an NFL Championship ring. And the only one of Mike Dimitro's American All Stars to win the National Football League.

Gary Kerkorian, Baltimore Colts.

CHAPTER 34
OPPORTUNITY LOST

MEETING THIS WEEK

Rler 9 Jan 1959

MAY we be pardoned in paraphrasing a famous journal's old-time slogan and say—"IF YOU SEE IT IN "RUGBY LEAGUER" IT IS SO"? The reason for our modesty being of all Rugby League publications we told you more about developments in the United States and warned you that big moves were afoot across the Atlantic.

This paper was alone in giving readers details of the 1952 Tour of Mike Dimitrio's "American All-Stars" R.L. team to Australia, and in both 1957 and 1958 we have recorded with much interest the extension moves being made in the State of California. Now the daily and weekly press are sitting up and taking notice of these moves too, so we'll tell you of the latest developments.

Readers will recall in our feature "R.L. IN U.S.A.—TEAMS BEING FORMED NOW" in our issue of 28th November last we reported that moves were being made to form an American Rugby League, and that permission had been given by the National Football League of America for any of their players to join with or to play in R.L. football in the months of June and July in any year—i.e., in their off season. The moving spirits behind this potential extension on the Pacific Coast of the U.S.A. were Mr. Ward Nash of Los Angeles and Mr. Ray Norman the famous Australian R.L. coach. What now then?

By the time these lines appear in print a meeting will have been held in San Francisco to investigate the full possibilities of organised Rugby League football.

It is getting ample press publicity in the Los Angeles papers, and of course R.L.

headquarters in Leeds are fully aware of what is happening. Our headquarters presumably wish to see the outcome of this week's meeting before extending their contacts with the United States—a wise procedure in my opinion, for with the best will in the world one must "go steady" in such matters and cut one's coat according to one's cloth.

The Italian developments are likely to be of more immediate concern to our home Headquarters, whilst the American venture (if it matures in any positive way) could well be nurtured by the Australian R.L. administrators who are nearer geographically than we are. Any "missionary games" or Schoolboy and Youth Tours such as we described in an earlier feature ("A GREAT CHANCE IN AMERICA"—6th September 1957 issue) would have to be fostered by the Australian and/or New Zealand

league bodies until such time as the R.L. International Board will again foregather when there should be much of interest to discuss both as regards Italy and America.

Is all this too optimistic? Would we (press and administrators) be better serving the game by concentrating upon curing some of the ills the game at home seems still to be suffering from? We can hear some readers voicing those thoughts already.

We can only say that IF Rugby League does get a hold in the States (and the Californian Coast seems to be a reasonably fertile ground) then it will be launched in a characteristically BIG American way.

Therefore it behoves our authorities in both hemispheres to not only hold their watching brief, but to see that the arrangements whenever and wherever made, conform to standard practice in all respects. That way, and that way only, will lead to real progress and the avoidance of misunderstandings and incorrect practices.

But things seem to be moving! Already a Los Angeles newspaper has been talking of such things as "the organisation . . . and perhaps a few games in 1959"; ". . . . in 1960 Rugby League would be under way on the Pacific Coast as Australia comes through on tour to Europe"; and the possibilities of R.L. President The Earl of Derby attending a match at Los Angeles Coliseum between their local team and England!

Well,—don't say we didn't tell you so! Further than that we will keep you informed of any major moves that might arise in the near future.

9 JANUARY 1959
Rugby Leaguer

1959 All the big player wannabes and grafters were finally brought together around a table at the Plaza Hotel in San Francisco: Ward Nash, Spilsted, Gardener, Soltau, Hamilton, Fitzgerald, and Gilhousen, along with three or four others. The only notable name missing was Dimitro. The fact that most had travelled around 500 miles to be there, from Vancouver or LA, showed that this was a serious meeting.

Charles Edmundson, an English expat from Bradford, was elected chairman of the new organisation and Gardener remained secretary. The group unanimously decided to call the league the 'North American Rugby Football League'.

Three franchises were granted: Vancouver (to Spilsted and a GA Hunt); San Francisco (to Soltau and Ian Hamilton); and Los Angeles (to Edmundson, Nash, Gardener and Gilhousen).

They were valid until 1 January 1960 when they would be confirmed or cancelled by the NARFL Board of Control. No one had put any money into the organisation: they had simply been given the task of getting a team up and running. They had a year to make it work.

AMERICAN SIDE TO TOUR BRITAIN?

GUS RISMAN on Rugby League

FOLLOWING my recent note that Rugby League interest in America was developing, it now appears that Vancouver, Los Angeles and San Francisco are all keenly interested in starting a league.

The outcome of a meeting in San Francisco this week is awaited with interest by R.L. headquarters in this country, who up to now have been holding only a watching brief.

The American team which toured Australia a few years ago showed little idea but plenty of enthusiasm. If anything comes of the American discussion, can we expect a repeat tour of Gt. Britain towards the end of the season? I suggest R.L. headquarters get cracking on this possibility immediately.

● GUS RISMAN . . . would the Americans send a Rugby League side to tour Britain towards the end of the season?

B.C. LIONS

11 JANUARY 1959
Empire News and
Sunday Chronicle

The Vancouver press proclaimed 'FIRST PRO RUGBY GAME NEXT APRIL', with 'city accountant' Spilsted predicting Bakersfield, Houston and Seattle would also join to make a six-team league. The Vancouver team would be a joint venture with the BC Lions: Spilsted had talked with their GM Herb Capozzi and claimed Lions stars Primo Villaneuva, Sonny Homer, Ted Hunt and Gordie Mitchell had all played rugby so 'could soon acclimatise' to rugby league.

Most Canadian football clubs had been around since forming as rugby clubs when Queen Victoria ruled, just as many were doing in northern England. But small-town teams like Sarnia Imperials and Kitchener-Waterloo Dutchmen would no longer get a crack at the big boys. Instead, there was a coast-to-coast professional eight-team Canadian Football League.

But there was no history of pro football in Vancouver, the vibrant port at the foot of the Rocky Mountains, closer to Seattle than any of Canada's other cities. Only when the mayor was persuaded to bid for the 1954 British Empire Games did Vancouver FC get the stadium they needed for a franchise, as an old golf course in East Hastings evolved into the 25,000-capacity Empire Stadium, the largest in Canada.

The renamed BC Lions drew the biggest crowds in the league despite shocking results thanks to an unprecedented entertainment budget which worked a treat. General Manager Capozzi – a Rhodes scholar, like All Star Vince Jones – arrived from the lakeside town of Kelowna and his marketing soon filled Empire almost every game. He was potentially a fine ally for Spilsted, who was planning to share Empire Stadium with the Lions.

Another potential benefit was brewing. Clubs in the rival two leagues were at loggerheads over a proposal that all citizens of British Commonwealth countries be regarded as non-imports, enabling Canadian pro football to recruit top British, Australian and Kiwi rugby players without affecting their import quotas.

Such a move would give rugby league a massive boost. Canadian football had evolved from rugby over the first half of the century to become a distinctly different sport but with many transferrable skills. If dozens of rugby players were already at these clubs, encouraging them to play League in the football off-season – with the clubs' support – would be far easier.

RECEIVED
21 APR 1959
RUGBY FOOTBALL LEAGUE

FOUNDED 1959

F 219

British Columbia "Tigers"
RUGBY LEAGUE FOOTBALL CLUB
VANCOUVER, B.C.

AFFILIATED WITH THE
NORTH AMERICAN
RUGBY LEAGUE

April 15th, 1959:

Messrs. Fallowfield, Matthews, & Gardener.

Please be advised that as from the above date the franchise for Vancouver in respect to the North American Rugby League has been transferred to Mr. William E. Dunbar of 748 Handsworth Avenue, North Vancouver, B. C. Canada. Phone No. Yukon 7-4182 who is the President of the British Columbia Rugby Union Referee's Association (or was) and was an outstanding Rugby Player at the University of British Columbia.

The co-holder of the franchise with Mr. Dunbar is Mr. George Ferguson, well known Vancouver financier and also an outstanding Rugby Union player at the University of British Columbia. Mr. Ferguson resides at 1132 West 23rd. Street, North Vancouver, B. C. Canada. Phone No. Yukon 7-9137

Both of these gentlemen are well known and have been most helpful in the establishment of Rugby League, and Mr. Ferguson assures me that he has all the finance necessary to proceed on a high professional level. All my other associates in Vancouver together with the press, radio, and television are most happy with Ferguson and Dunbar and have assured me of their utmost co-operation. It is therfore considered that any plan that I have had in promoting Rugby League in Vancouver will not suffer due to the fact that as Canadians will be watching Rugby League, playing Rugby League on Canadian soil it is most appropriate that it be promoted and financed by these two Canadian gentlemen.

, It would be appreciated therefore if any future correspondence pertaining to Rugby League in Canada be addressed to Mr. Ferguson at the address quoted above.

Thanking you.for your assistance in the past and assuring you that anything I am able to do to establish the game of Rugby League in North America whilst in Washington D. C., I will be only too happy to render any further assistance within my capabilities.

With kindest regards.

Yours sincerely,

APRIL '59

A six-team North American Rugby Football League was looking possible. While LA's backers had pulled out, their franchise was replaced by Seattle who, along with San Francisco and Vancouver, were 'ready to go'. Portland, Bakersfield, Phoenix and Houston were also keen on a NARL franchise.

Spilsted, now working at the Australian Embassy in Washington, DC, told Matthews and Fallowfield that the league would 'be underway in January 1960' with coaches appointed at in each city. Spilsted had transferred his Vancouver Tigers franchise to two former University of British Columbia rugby union players, Bill Dunbar and George Ferguson, but claimed it would not threaten its financial or media backing:

'As Canadians will be watching rugby league, playing rugby league on Canadian soil it is most appropriate that it will be promoted and financed by these two Canadian gentlemen. The big factor is that there is NO pro outdoor sport on the Pacific Coast from Jan 1st to May in any year – the season is therefore made to order. Dimitro's fiasco in Sydney should be forgotten.' He had even lined up a referee – Queenslander Vince Fitzgerald, now a bank teller in Vancouver – to take charge of games.

Spilsted pleaded with Fallowfield to encourage the Kangaroos to play in the States en route home from France: 'With ex-players of the calibre of Eric Day and Bob Nielsen on hand plus personal offers by my sincere friends Ray Stehr and

Travers Hardwick to come over and coach for plane fares only, pro sport permitted on Sunday afternoons, grounds available and Fitzgerald to referee, there can be no logical reason to refuse our offer to play here.'

Fallowfield agreed and claimed Spilsted only had to guarantee that the Australians would not lose money and the fixture would be sealed. He even suggested an English team would go if the Kangaroos would not. Bill was warming to the American dream.

If they went, the Australian RFL budgeted to pay each player US$200 per game plus a $15 a day allowance. With ticket prices between US$1 and $3, players would be getting 200 times the cheapest ticket price. Nice work if you can get it.

FOUNDED 1959

MAY '59

Spilsted admitted to Fallowfield that only Seattle, Portland, San Francisco and Los Angeles were likely to be ready to launch the first NARL.

He still wanted Great Britain to play two games in Vancouver one weekend in the following spring – and predicted average takings of US$20,000 plus TV rights. And yet he still didn't even have a copy of the play-the-ball rule for prospective clubs or players.

JULY '59

Tex Schramm quit the Rams to work for NFL newcomers the Dallas Cowboys. The NFL had expanded into Texas after all, but not via Lamar Hunt or Bud Adams, who instead announced the formation of the American Football League. It would begin in 1960 with franchises in Los Angeles, New York, Denver, Minneapolis, Dallas and Houston. Each owner lodges a $25,000 bond with the league. The City of Angels would again have a second pro football franchise – the Chargers, owned by hotel magnate Barron Hilton, and playing at the Coliseum.

Hilton was not only Elizabeth Taylor's brother-in-law and stepson of Zsa Zsa Gabor but a USC old boy: he was the kind of figure rugby league needed. The NFL's battle with the AFL was about to commence. Rugby league football was no longer on their agenda.

Meanwhile, Dimitro was accused of 'intimacy' with a student at Huntington Beach High, where he taught. The girl later claimed that the statements she made were 'under duress and completely incorrect and erroneous'. He moved to Westminster High in Santa Ana to coach football: his tenth job in ten years. He still would not give up on his rugby league dream and told the Australian RFL he could take another team down under.

SEPTEMBER '59

Clive Spilsted, now posted at the Australian Consulate General in San Francisco, replaced Gardener as NARL secretary. Gardener was still trying to secure a backer for the LA franchise, yet was claiming they would play in the Rose Bowl. With BC Tigers set to be based at Empire Stadium and San Francisco at Kezar Stadium in Golden Gate Park, no franchise could be accused of setting their sights too low. Rosey Gilhousen was no longer working with Nash on the LA project.

OCTOBER '59

Spilsted told Fallowfield that a group of players from each of the three franchises would meet in LA in the New Year to be coached for six days a week and then return to spread what they had learned to their new team-mates. The plan was looking thin.

Barron Hilton threatened to withdraw his LA Chargers unless the AFL provided them with a West Coast rival. Suddenly, Oakland Senors were born. They would share Kezar Stadium with the 49ers. There would be pro football there every week from September to Christmas – and then, supposedly, rugby league in spring.

NOVEMBER '59

The AFL began recruiting. A bidding war soon broke out as they offered top college stars double the money the NFL did. The new boys were outbidding the establishment left, right and centre. It was crazy. The Rams sacked innovative coach Sid Gillman and he was immediately snapped up by Hilton to bring some entertainment to the Chargers. Gillman would provide him with a glamorous, thrilling, attacking team. The AFL breathed new life into pro football. Rugby league had no chance.

CHAPTER 35
A SIXTIES REVOLUTION

1960 While Ward Nash continued to plan and dream, Spilsted was getting frustrated. Every time he tried to organise a breakthrough event, something or someone let him down.

First it was the Australians. Spilsted had the Coliseum lined up and had seen TV executives about broadcasting the game. He had backers committed to provide the Aussies with $600 a day and a budget of $20,000 to pay for a team of local gridiron stars to learn to play league from an imported coach. He even had an appointment booked with Bob Hope. But the Board of Control would not commit to a date to play in the States that summer.

On 6 January, Spilsted wrote to Matthews:

'Well all the effort has been in vain as far as the Kangaroos coming here in 1960 is concerned.

'Rugby League is a game that will appeal to the American public. Due to Rugby League being an unknown quantity, some big backers are reluctant to lend their name to something which they consider could be a failure.

'The only way to get people introduced to the game is to have a team of grid-iron stars extensively coached for at least six weeks – these players must have played at University or be exceedingly adaptable and they must be in the public eye. I am supported by Ed Pauley (multi-millionaire oil magnate) in this respect.

'Secondly a professional promoter who is a skilled public relations man and can obtain unlimited space in sports pages, television and radio must handle all publicity to put the first games over. The NARL franchise holders in each city must have the backing and support of reputable citizens in sports organisations.'

Spilsted knew he needed a Pete Rozelle, or the Rams or 49ers onside, or even Canadian pro football teams if this was going to work. Rozelle had just been elected commissioner of the NFL – at just 33 – and would transform pro football from a working-class game played by miners, steelworkers and mill men – America's rugby league – into a glamorous and luxurious strategic battle played out by millionaires on TV screens across the world.

Spilsted to Matthews: 'I have several big shots interested but being just before Christmas and right at the tail end of the gridiron season when all the Div 1 games are in the headlines they all said "see me in the New Year". Rugby league could not fail if introduced and promoted scientifically, as top pro sports seem to be in the USA. There can be no half measures. People like Bob Hope cannot be associated with half-baked affairs. I feel sure when I see him to discuss the whole matter in detail that he will insist (if he backs it) that the highest possible promotion be the order of the day. I have received some expert advice and

American Rugby League Football

818 SANTEE STREET · LOS ANGELES 14, CALIFORNIA, U.S.A.

Telephone: MAdison 2-2061

January 25th, 1960.

Commissioner
& Organizing Secretary

Mr. W. Fallowfield,
182 Chapeltown Road,
Leed 7, England.

Dear Mr. Fallowfield,

Many thanks for yours of January IIth, and your comments as well as the dates arranged for the world cup.

As you are no doubt aware August to December each year is the period covering American grid-iron season. We do not wish to start our introduction in opposition to the American game particularly as we intend using several grid-iron stars. It would therefore appear unwise to have Australia or New Zealand play here in October. However we will discuss it at the next meeting of the N. A. R. L. which is scheduled for Saturday February I3th, I960.

Considering the publicity we have had in the last I2 months we are most anxious for at least one exhibition game this year and Ward Nash has written the cultural attache at the French Embassy, in Washington D. C. and Colonel Eagan has also written a similar letter asking for the French team to visit the Pacific Coast on a short tour from April 23rd to May I2th which would entail them playing 3 easy games all on three successive Sundays as we consider they would not entertain a short strenuous tour before visiting Australia.

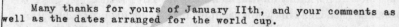

Our proposition is not involved as Air France commence a weekly flight direct from Paris to Los Angeles on April 2nd, 1960. Our idea is for them to play in Los Angeles on Sunday the 24th April, San Francisco, on Sunday May Ist, and Vancouver, Canada on Sunday May 8th. With regards to finance we are prepared to offer a flat guarantee of six hundred dollars per day and free transport from Los. Angeles to San Francisco and San Francisco to Vancouver, as well as free transport to and from each of the grounds from their hotels. Also every effort will be made for them to see as much of the United States as possible and reception committees would be set up to cope with this aspect. Will you please relay the foregoing to Mr. Blaine and point out to him that the living expenses for a party of 30 would be only 300 dollars per day, and as our financial backers are taking the risk on this introductory game they are therefore not willing to offer gate per centages but rather they have doubled the actual expense(viz. 600 dollars per day). I know you personally appreciate the position and if we are to get the game off the ground and big finance behind it we first of all must let the backers have a sample of what the game is, and naturally they are reluctant to envest big money until they have seen the public's response and sports writers attitude etc.

guidance from men like Larry Crosby (Bing's brother) and sports writers such as Maxwell Stiles, and when they are convinced we are organised then the support and interest will be forthcoming.'

Larry Crosby was a top Hollywood PR man. Bing Crosby and Bob Hope were close mates, and had just starred in *Alias Jesse James* together. Hope knew about rugby league from his time in Australia and, ten years earlier, had met English svengali Eddie Waring. Stiles was still a big influence at the *LA Examiner*. He was trying to use President Eisenhower's People to People programme to make the connections: Pakistan's national cricket team had visited the USA so why not the Aussie rugby league team?

The People to People Sports Committee included Hope, Olympic legend Jesse Owens, baseball superstar Joe DiMaggio, former world heavyweight boxing champ Jack Dempsey and TV star-maker Ed Sullivan. Spilsted was soon invited to join them but he needed help from Leeds and Sydney. People to People had a 60 minute slot on national TV – Spilsted hoped to get the film *This Is RL* broadcast to 80 million potential viewers. 'The men associated with the introduction of the game here are sincerely keen – all they need is encouragement from Bill Fallowfield and yourself – they are not asking for help financially but only patience.'

A furious Spilsted chose his words carefully, anxious not to burn his bridges. That would be fatal. But he told Fallowfield what he really thought: 'This has caused much embarrassment to us all. We now have a lot of important people interested. Ward Nash, Ross Gilhousen and Derek Gardener are still actively interested in Los Angeles and Ian Hamilton and Gordie Soltau are the power in San Francisco. My 12 months' work in Vancouver may be in vain if I am not able to do something in the USA in the next two months. It has been a hard road to hoe but I feel the ground is softening at last.'

At 'considerable expense' the North American Rugby Football League became a legally constituted organisation. Gary Kerkorian was back on the scene as lawyer and 'took care of the incorporation'. Nash, Gardener and acting secretary Spilsted declared themselves 'the founders to promote and control rugby league on the North American continent and Hawaii'.

Fallowfield suggested the Americans try to get either the Kangaroos or Kiwis or both to stop over en route to or from the next World Cup in England in October. There was no invite for the US to join the party. Spilsted was disappointed but said the US would aim to be at the 1964 World Cup.

Playing rugby league in the American football season was a non-starter. Instead they invited France over on Air France's new Paris-LA route for 'three easy games' on successive Sundays in April in LA, San Francisco and Vancouver. Again the Americans offered $600 per day with free transport for the party of 30.

But the French domestic season was coming to a climax in April. Instead, they suggested coming in August and playing night games to avoid the searing LA heat. A plan was hatched: they would arrive on a Pan Am flight from Auckland into LA on 8 August, play in the Coliseum on the Friday night with sponsors donating all profits to leading charities. Spilsted promised to lodge $8,000 with the French Consul General in Los Angeles.

As spring went by, there was no confirmation from the French Federation until, in July, a cable arrived in LA: France had cancelled the tour. Spilsted was understandably distraught and dismayed.

He resorted to asking if England would consider playing in the States on their way to Australia in 1962. Then he pleaded that the US be granted a place in the 1960 World Cup after all. They had arranged for Australian forward Ray Stehr to spend two months converting a group of union and gridiron players and would be funded by the People to People programme.

Fallowfield said no. One man, the man supposedly responsible for developing rugby league as a sport, had strangled it at birth in the greatest sporting nation in the world. Fallowfield had gazed down the mouth of probably A the biggest gift-horse ever to offer itself to a minor sport. An enormous opportunity had been missed in excruciating fashion.

That summer, any football player looking for work was heading towards the AFL. They came from all corners: college, Canada, rugby union, the Army, the Navy. Hundreds turned up to try-out at each of the eight teams that summer, and one in ten were signed. The Rams and 49ers had a fight on their hands and had better things to do than negotiate with a bunch of amateur speculators trying to launch a strange and fanciful spring rugby football league.

Late July and Spilsted is speaking at a Los Angeles Chamber of Commerce Sports Promotion Committee luncheon about a visit by New Zealand on their way home from the World Cup.

But the Kiwis didn't come. In fact, no one ever came.

The renegade American Football League kicked off on 9 September 1960: Boston Patriots, playing on Friday nights to avoid clashing with college football, hosted Denver Broncos. The first ever points in the AFL were kicked by the Patriots' Gino Cappelletti: a year earlier he had been playing touch football for a Detroit bar team; the year before, he was a part-timer in the Ontario Rugby Football Union. He would have been an ideal recruit for the North American Rugby League. The next day saw LA Chargers play Dallas Texans at the Coliseum. A terrified Lamar Hunt spent $10,000 to broadcast the game back to Dallas, where it went head to head with Miss America. Few saw the football, but at least it was on TV.

Barron Hilton spent a fortune on his Chargers team – they did everything with style while the other teams operated on the breadline, to ensure the players stayed loyal despite crowds of just 15,000 at the Coliseum. That was more than Oakland got over the Bay at Kezar Stadium. They were crowd figures the NARL would have been thrilled with, but they damn near killed the AFL.

In November, John F. Kennedy beat Richard Nixon in the Presidential election by 0.2 per cent of the vote. Nixon's eight-year spell as Vice-President was over.

Ward Nash died, aged 71, following a heart attack in Arcadia, California. That afternoon, Spilsted wrote to inform Fallowfield of the passing of 'a great worker to try to establish Rugby League in the USA'. Fallowfield wrote a letter of condolence to Mrs Nash. A month later Spilsted told Fallowfield that Nash had achieved 'nothing constructive' and that 'everyone on meeting Ward would quietly steer away from interest and support. I could say more but under the circumstances I think it best to look to the future and forget the past. If we start on the village green, that is where we will finish.'

Ironically, that was just what Spilsted was now proposing. After six years of posturing and planning, he had abandoned the pursuit of NFL stars and was now suggesting community projects, converting American rugby union players to league.

No one was listening. Rugby league's American dream was over.

21

CHAPTER 36
DIMITRO'S WORLD CUP

There was one more fling, a last throw of the dice – and it came from Dimitro. Iron Mike just would not let it lie. His life remained one of continual change. He switched towns, states, jobs changed, his age, his wives, his name. By 1963 he was coaching football and teaching history and science at Compton High School in South Central LA. He was living in Huntington Beach with his third wife, Maryon Gazarian.

Dimitro re-launched the 'AMERICAN ALL STARS TOURING TEAM'. The headed paper had him as manager and coach, Maryon as secretary-treasurer, and a publicity director called 'Johnny Mack', based at 49 South Grand Oaks, Pasadena 10.

At Compton High he met an old friend of Patty Dodds from UCLA – Alma Mae Fisher Marx – who was teaching home economics. She soon became his fourth and final wife. The couple moved to Laguna Beach and had a daughter, Michelle. By this time, Mike had slashed five years off his age on application forms and was calling himself Mike D. Fisher, when it suited. Court appearances were more regular than desired.

In the spring of '65, Mike was back in the headlines, telling the *San Diego Union* that he 'and nine or ten businessman backers' from California and Illinois were interested in buying Barron Hilton's majority share in the Chargers, who had moved from the Coliseum down to San Diego. There was talk of a new stadium in Mission Bay and 'bringing several outstanding foreign rugby teams to San Diego for games during the spring season'. Whatever Dimitro had to say would be 'of benefit to the Chargers'.

Dimitro and Xavier Mena – by then also a teacher at Kearny High School in San Diego – were setting up a meeting to 'bargain' with Hilton who was reportedly willing to sell, but only for $7m. Dimitro believed that included an initial 30 per cent payment – around $2.5m – which his group was 'willing to meet.'

Hilton saw through the charlatan and by September, Mike was being pursued by lawyers seeking unpaid surveyors bills of $45. In October, Dimitro was in Santa Ana's Municipal Court on trial over unpaid bills of $600 for property surveying at Laguna Beach. His defence attorney was a Lawrence J. Moreno, Attorney at Law, 315 South Beverly Drive, Beverly Hills – aka All Star Larry Moreno.

Moreno's services were required again in December '65 when 'Michael M. Dimitro aka Mike Machnov Dimitro' had his teaching credentials revoked by California's State Board of Education. He appealed, successfully, and the accusation was eventually dismissed.

Dimitro changed tack again, trading beans and corn in Illinois while living with Alma and baby Michelle and running the Laguna Terrace Motel and Apartments at 2200 South Coast Highway. But he never gave up on his dreams of being a big-time sports promoter. At Christmas 1968, living in Las Vegas as Michael Fisher, he worked with Moreno and Fran Mandulay (now known as Mike!) to produce a proposal for the Mayor of Dallas to host a charity All Star College Football Game on Easter Sunday at the Cotton Bowl.

That spring, Dimitro reopened communications with the Australian RFL and Fallowfield in Leeds. He pronounced himself 'sole controller' of the new United States American All Stars Rugby Football League (headquarters in Las Vegas, in his house!) and claimed that there was more rugby league being played in the States than ever before. The Australians called his bluff and offered to visit to assess the situation.

Fallowfield was eager again: he suggested Dimitro invite Antipodean teams to the States early in 1970 and offered to send the England and Wales national teams over in early summer.

Moreno visited Mike at yet another new Dimitro home – in Neoga, Illinois – to put a new plan into action: the tautologically-named American Rugby Football League of the United States. They planned to play games at Florida State's stadium in Tallahassee, at Jacksonville's Gator Bowl and in the Tangerine Bowl, Orlando. The games never happened, of course. Nothing happened.

Dimitro began negotiating with new Australian RFL secretary Ken Stevens and Fallowfield to host games in June 1970. Then Maurice Tardy, by now president of the French Federation, invited him to send a USA team to the 1970 World Championship, hosted by England and France. Dimitro accepted. 'We will be there with our best American team,' he replied. After 15 barren years, international rugby league suddenly wanted the USA on board.

While he traded ideas with Fallowfield about British teams playing in the States, Dimitro had his eyes on a bigger prize: hosting the 1970 World Cup. He asked Stevens to canvas the International Board about moving their tournament to the States. Fallowfield told Dimitro that it would cost approximately £60,000 plus stadium hire.

'Personally I would welcome transferring this competition to the States if it can be sponsored and if a suitable time, acceptable to all the competing countries, could be found,' wrote Fallowfield. Astonishing: the World Cup was up for grabs and it was Dimitro's, if he could afford it.

By October '69, the Kiwis, French and Australians were all in favour of going to the States if the money was right and Fallowfield was prepared to postpone Great Britain's Antipodean tour to play the World Cup in America in May 1970 instead.

Fallowfield wanted a seven-match, month-long, four-team event with no room for a US team. Iron Mike was defiant. 'I will also have an American team in the Series,' he replied. It would be in Florida from 15 May to 15 June... and return each year to a different part of the United States. He could never be accused of lacking ambition.

A month later Fallowfield was pouring cold water on the plan and the saga dragged on throughout the winter. Of course, Dimitro could not get the money in and no one could agree when to play. By March 1970, the project was shelved and the World Cup was to take place in England.

Fallowfield was still keen to get his American adventure and suggested Dimitro bid to host another World Cup in 1971, even though one wasn't due until 1974 or 1975. But with neither Australia nor New Zealand willing to cross the Pacific in the middle of their season, it would have to go ahead as a northern hemisphere event. Fallowfield, Tardy and Dimitro agreed to a 'World Championship Rugby League' in May and June 1971, featuring England, Wales and France. Not a full World Cup but the sort of terrific launch event American rugby league has sought since 1954.

In the meantime, from his latest winter bolt-hole in Palm Springs, Dimitro also offered Tardy an end-of-season quadrangular tournament in June 1970: USA, France, England and Wales playing over three weeks in Houston, LA, San Francisco and New Orleans, with the Liberty Bowl in Memphis hosting the opening game and final. He promised TV deals to finance the whole affair and sold it as a World Cup warm-up.

Tardy bit, announced that France would fly out on 27 May, and planned to play against Great Britain in Montreal on the way home to promote the code to the Bretons and Basques who had emigrated there. A game in New York was also being considered. The

RUGBY XIII

Le XIII de France invité en Amérique

Par l'intermédiaire d'Antoine Blain, ancien secrétaire général de la F.F.J. XIII, le président Maurice Tardy a reçu une invitation pour une tournée du XIII de France en Amérique. Cette invitation est envoyée par Mike Dimitro, dirigeant du football américain, qui, il y a quelques années, vint en France avec une sélection des Etats-Unis qui tentait une première expérience treiziste.

Il est proposé à l'équipe de France de se produire outre-Atlantique pendant trois semaines en Arizona, en Californie et au Canada, à Vancouver. Maurice Tardy est d'accord sur le principe, reste à trouver la période idéale. Mike Dimitro propose septembre 1969 ou février-mars 1970, c'est-à-dire avant et après la saison de football américain, ce qui soulève certains problèmes. Il serait en effet difficile de bien préparer une équipe nationale pour la fin du présent été et, en revanche, une tournée en plein cœur de la saison risquerait de perturber sérieusement le calendrier du Championnat de France.

Le Comité directeur va étudier à fond cette intéressante proposition d'étendre l'influence du rugby à XIII outre-Atlantique où les efforts des pionniers du néo-rugby ont abouti à la création de l'American Rugby League.

journal l'Équipe 30-5-69

NEW ZEALAND RUGBY FOOTBALL LEAGUE
(INCORPORATED)

Treasurer

HON. SECRETARY J. E. KNOWLING, F.C.I.S.
PHONE

C.P.O. BOX 712
AUCKLAND, C.1

6th October, 1969.

Mr. Mike Dimitro,
P.O. Box 12131,
Las Vegas,
Nevada,
U.S.A., 89112.

Dear Mike,

Your letter, which was delayed through short postage, has at long last come to hand and it was pleasing to hear from you again and know that things are going well with you.

I have mentioned your proposals to the Council of Management of the New Zealand Rugby League and we hope that it will be possible to co-operate with you. However, as we lost considerable money in the last visit to America, the Council is not prepared to meet the costs of sending a team unless some firm arrangements can be made. Your organization would have to be responsible for return fares, suitable accommodation for players and a guaranteed amount to each player to cover his expenses. This would run into a substantial sum of money and would need to be available before the tour took place.

There will be no difficulty in getting a good team together to give an excellent exhibition but the financing and promotion problems would, of course, be yours. You can rely on us for all the help we can give you but we are not in a position to contribute financially to this venture. There are many players in New Zealand who would love a visit to your country for a short time and many of them would be star players of considerable ability.

I reciprocate your good wishes and hope everything is going well with you.

Yours faithfully,

Ted Knowling

FÉDÉRATION FRANÇAISE DE JEU A TREIZE

AGRÉÉE SOUS LE No 2401 DU 8 MARS 1948

•

400, RUE SAINT-HONORÉ - PARIS (1ᵉʳ)

TÉL. 073.76.37

ressez votre correspondance à:
siteur Raymond FORGES
e-Président de la F.F.J. XIII
rue de la République

- Carcassonne

         FRANCE

f : RF/SG

Carcassonne, le 8 Octobre 1969

Monsieur Mike DIMITRO
AMERICAN ALL STARS
P.O BOX 12 131

LAS VEGAS
           NEVADA
U.S.A. 89.112

Cher Ami,

      Je pense que vous comprenez le français ou que vous aurez tout moyen pour vous faire traduire cette lettre.

      Vous pouvez de toute façon me répondre en anglais car je parle couramment votre langue, mais malheureusement ma secrétaire ne comprends pas l'anglais et de ce fait je ne peux vous écrire qu'en français.

      Je suis à l'heure actuelle un des Vices-Présidents de la Fédération Française de Rugby à XIII et Président de la Division des Relations Internationales, raison pour laquelle notre secrétaire général de notre Fédération m'a fait suivre le double de la lettre que vous avez envoyée à Monsieur KEN STEPHEN secrétaire de la Fédération Australienne de Rugby à XIII.

      J'ai pris connaissance de cette lettre et je peux vous dire personnellement je suis favorable à votre projet en ce qui concerne la possibilité de disputer les les prochains championnats du monde de Rugby à XIII aux U.S.A. en 1970.

      Je dois rencontrer mes amis britanniques du 22 au 26 Octobre courant et je profiterai de l'occasion qui m'est offerte pour connaître leur point de vue à ce sujet. Entre temps j'aurais soumis votre proposition aux Membres du Comité de Direction de la Fédération Française du Rugby à XIII et je pense avoir toutes les

               .../..

AMERICAN ALL STARS

XXXXXXXXXXXXXXXX
XXXXXXXXXXXXXXXXX
XXXXXXXXXXXXXXXXX

P. O. BOX 12131,
LAS VEGAS, NEVADA
U.S.A., 89112

PAT DODDS
SECRETARY-TREASURER

MIKE DIMITRO
MANAGER-COACH

October 16, 1969

W. Fallowfield, Secretary
The Rugby Football League,
180, Chapeltown Road,
Leeds, 7
England

Dear Mr. Fallowfield,

Thank you for your letter of the 7th October.
I know time is getting short, but there is plenty of time
to put the World Championship Series here.

I would appreciate your sending me the list of
details that must be done to make this concrete.

I would like to have a contract made out with
all the participating countries in the World Championship
Series. I want to make this an Annual Affair. Each year
we can put it on in a different part of the United States.

This World Championship Series will be played in
the Southern part of the United States, mainly in the
State of Florida.

I will also have an American team in the Series.

The best days to play the series in the States is
Friday, Saturday, Sunday, and Wednesdays.

How many men will be representing each country?
I will need to know, so I can make my hotel reservations
four months in advance.

This is all that I can think of at the present.

Until I hear from you again soon.

I remain,

Sincerely yours,

Mike Dimitro

Mike Dimitro

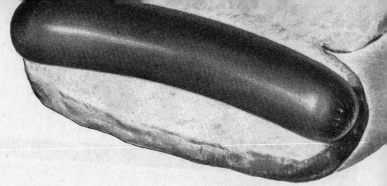

Dimitro in the sixties.

French were on board, then Fallowfield gave the RFL's green light: all Dimitro had to do was put down a £40,000 advance to cover the costs for France, Wales and England for a three-week trip to LA. Dimitro promised to have the money in place and their plane tickets booked by 5 May. It sounded just too good to be true. It was. He did not.

On 8 November in Leeds, Australia won a vicious game against Great Britain in 'The Battle of Headingley' to lift the World Cup. Rugby league never heard from Mike Dimitro again.

165 PHILLIP STREET, SYDNEY • BOX 4415, G.P.O., SYDNEY, AUSTRALIA 2001 • P

PRESIDENT   W. G. BUCKLEY
HON. SECRETARY   K. G. STEPHEN

5th February, 1970

KGS:RW

Mr. M. Dimitro,
P.O. Box 12131,
LAS VEGAS NEVADA U.S.W. 89112

Dear Mike,

Many thanks for your letter of 21st January last which was discussed at our meeting held on even date. As far as our fellows are concerned the month of October would be most suitable to this League for the staging of a World Championship Series in your country.

We are very interested as you can well imagine in your proposition but feel that it would be preferable if the situation was investigated from your end instead of you coming out here. We feel that should you be able to guarantee the travelling expenses for two representatives to visit America I am sure that the selected representatives could get together with you at a very early date.

We would be pleased to have your comments on this suggestion.

Kind regards from all members of the League.

Yours sincerely,

HON. SECRETARY

THE RUGBY FOOTBALL LEAGUE

FOUNDED 1895

Patron: HER MAJESTY THE QUEEN

President
THE RIGHT HONOURABLE
THE EARL OF DERBY

Secretary
W. FALLOWFIELD, O.B.E., M.A.

180, CHAPELTOWN ROAD
LEEDS, 7

Telephone 624637
Telegrams "Norfu," Leeds 7

WF/SJ.

20th February, 1970.

M. Dimitro Esq.,
American All Stars,
P.O. Box 12131,
LAS VAGAS,
Nevada,
U.S.A. 89112.

Dear Mr. Dimitro,

Thank you for your further letter of the 14th February. As pressure has been building up for us to stage a World Championship in Europe in October 1970, this League has now proposed to Australia, France and New Zealand that the Championship be promoted by the English League in England. Previously we were considering making it a joint promotion between France and England but this, we feel, is impractical.

It would be a little too late to consider transferring this to the United States for this year but I think we would all be prepared to consider staging a World Cup Competition or World Championship, whichever word is preferred, in the States. Could we not set a target date as October 1971? Say the last two weeks in October and the first week in November. This should enable you to give us a little more detail than we have been able to obtain hitherto. You will be able to investigate to see if Stadiums are available and give us some concrete proposition.

Although it is essential for us to meet at some time in the future I think it would be better first to have in writing some concrete details regarding the arrangements you can make in America before we meet, because obviously we over here cannot advise you of conditions in America and these can only be sorted out by yourself and other associates, if any.

You should be able to work something out provided you could obtain the necessary grounds, on the details we have already given you. If you assume that four teams will take part; France, Australia, New Zealand and Great Britain and that they will each play each other once, making a total of six matches and then a final game is played for the Trophy between the two teams having the best records, this Competition being based on the £65,000 estimate previously sent to you.

If necessary we could double up on the matches so that each team played each other twice and the Final is still between the two teams with the best playing record. This would involve a lengthier stay in the States and, of course, more expensive. It would be up to you to state which of the two schemes you prefer.

/Continued...

From Bill Fallowfield.

EPILOGUE

Al D. Kirkland in his digger's hat, 2003.

Mike Dimitro kept moving and re-inventing himself. He joined the California State Sheriffs' Association and became acquainted with members of the Secret Service's Presidential Protection Unit. Dimitro made homes in San Francisco, in Temecula, and finally in San Diego.

Michelle Dimitro: 'I remember Dad leaving to go on a business meeting to try to get the American All Stars rugby league off the ground again when we were living in Las Vegas and later in Palm Springs and Mattoon, Illinois. He never gave up trying, even when we were in Indio and Escondido, California. My Dad's attitude stayed positive, even though all the feedback coming back was not. He always hoped the Americans would learn to love the sport which Dad felt was one of the best in the world. My father lived and breathed the game. He would sit around coming up with plays and always wanted the sport to take off. He especially wanted TV to get ahold of it because then he felt the American population would get to see what a wonderful game it truly is.'

He died in Riverside, California on 18 December 2002, aged 80 (probably) or 72 (unlikely).

Al Abajian, Gary Kerkorian, Bob Buckley and Ed Demirjian at a reunion.

Al D. Kirkland spent two years in the forces, where he did not play football or rugby, but did play rugby union for five years at the Bay Area's Olympic Club while working in sales. Living in Santa Cruz, Al became Assistant Dean of Engineers at Stanford for 12 years and then went into construction and engineering. Al was married to Jeanne for nearly 50 years and they had five children. They lived in Southern California and Tucson, Arizona, before retiring back in Palo Alto. Al continued to support Stanford's male and female rugby teams passionately until he passed away in August 2012.

Gary Kerkorian completed his law degree at Georgetown and became an attorney. He had six children with his wife, Joyce, and moved to her home town of Fresno, Ca, where Gary became a judge at the County Superior Court. The panoramic photo of the All Stars and Sydney teams lining up for the national anthem inside an absolutely rammed SCG held pride of place above his desk in his chambers until the day he retired in 2000. He died just four months later. 'Al Abajian, Jack Bonetti, Ed Demirjian and the guys came up to see him when he was ill,' said Joyce. 'They talked about old times and had a good old laugh. He liked that. They were special to him.' Joyce still has Gary's NFL championship ring. She sees it every day. It hangs around her neck on a gold chain.

Vince Jones, 2003.

Vince Jones spent two years studying jurisprudence at Oxford: 'We were real playboys so when we got called in to college at the end, there were six professors sitting there and I was sure we'd failed. But I got a second and the other American got a first!' Vince also won a half-blue at basketball and travelled behind the Iron Curtain to play in Hungary and Romania. He returned to Stanford and finished law school, and played some rugby union for the Olympic Club. Vince practised law in LA and latterly Chicago, where he worked for Sears. He returned to Northern California in 1991 to live with his son. They have a construction and a mini-storage business. Outside their plot, at the end of a cul-de-sac in a small town, stands a replica Gypsy Moth plane on a totem pole.

'I learned to fly at Dartmouth so when we were in Australia we rented some Gypsy Moths. Then, when I went to England, one of my class-mates at Oxford – Frank Wells – was the son of the Governor of Kenya. He said his father would set us up with a hunt on the Serengeti Plain as long as we could get there ourselves. He said we could spend three or four days there doing "game management". We wanted

Ed Demirjian, Al Abajian and Ted Grossman at USC, 2007.

to borrow some of our scholarship funds to buy a little three-seater aircraft so we went to see the Dean of Brasenose. He eventually agreed, as long as we were insured. It's a good job we were. We flew across the Med to Cairo and up the Nile and crash-landed in a field outside Nairobi! We were okay but the plane was a write-off. We had to catch a flight home with a plane load of construction workers who said we could catch a ride as long as we served their drinks. So we did. Frank went on to become a vice-president of Disney. He died in a helicopter crash.' Jones came back to Stanford and played scrum half for the first XV.

Al Abajian finished at USC and went on to teach PE and Biology, becoming a vice-principal in junior and senior high schools in LA County. He was a junior high principal for 19 years. He never played rugby again but did see a few games.

'I have to tell you a funny story. Dimitro worked in the Huntingdon Beach Union High School District. But he had some problems here and was dismissed as a teacher. A few years later I was refereeing a football game at Compton College. I was aware of someone on the sidelines shouting stuff at me. I just ignored him.

Al Abajian, 2007.

'He finally said something like "hey rabbit"! He called me "Rabbit" in Australia because of the way I ran. It dawned on me who it was. I turned to see Mike there, teaching at Compton College. It was really ironic. This was immediately after the Watts riots and we didn't feel comfortable refereeing a game there, but everything went well. The youngsters playing for Compton High School were the politest, most well-behaved kids I ever refereed. They were gentlemen – I was really proud of them. The Watts riots was one of the tragedies of Los Angeles. Dimitro was whining and I just told him to shut up and he laughed.'

Retired and still living in Huntington Beach, Al remains friends with the surviving All Stars and a fan of USC Trojans.

Jack Bonetti recovered sufficiently from his polio to take over his father's oil delivery business. 'I did the paperwork and PR for six years. I coached football to little kids in Livermore for a while but I couldn't do it properly because of my leg brace. I did a bit of recruiting for Stanford and stayed close. I still see the guys now and then.'

After selling the business, Jack went into life insurance in Oakland. He was very successful and became a senior vice-president of marketing in Sacramento before retiring in 1992. He became a more than useful golfer and still enjoys regular rounds near his home north-east of the Bay Area. 'Jack called himself "the one-legged kangaroo"', recalled Abajian. 'He's a very, very precious person. We still keep in touch.'

Ed Demirjian became a successful businessman in sales, living in Monterey Park. He retired in a beautiful house in Rancho Palo Verdes overlooking the ocean and golf course. He is a huge supporter of Trojan football, a neighbour of USC coach Pete Carroll, and proudly saw his grand-daughter enrol at USC.

Ted Grossman returned to Los Angeles and the movies, becoming a top-rated stuntman and occasional actor in Hollywood. He dated Goldie Hawn after working with her in Steven Spielberg's *Sugarland Express* and a year later worked with Spielberg again. When Ed Demirjian asked him what he was doing, Ted replied: 'Some crappy B-movie with a rubber shark.' Teddy is now best known as 'Estuary Victim', snatched from his rowing boat by Jaws! He can also be seen in *Dallas, ET*,

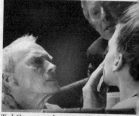

Ted Grossman between Clint Eastwood and Hilary Swank in Million Dollar Bab

the Indiana Jones films, *The Goonies*, a couple of *Naked Gun* movies, *Starsky and Hutch* and the Oscar-winning *Million Dollar Baby*. He lives in Beverly Hills and remains good friends with several of the All Stars.

THE REST OF THE 1953 ALL STARS

Bill Albans became a popular model on TV commercials for Salem cigarettes and in the likes of *Sports Illustrated* magazine advertising American Airlines and Arrow shirts while living at Village Inn on Sepulveda Blvd in Westwood, LA. As a severe stutterer, he could only get non-speaking parts. 'The only time I ever saw Bill Albans again was in a TV commercial jumping over some sand dunes!' recalled Jack Bonetti. 'When he had a few drinks he was always in trouble.

I heard he was killed by some Samoans in a bar off Malibu.' Al Abajian said: 'He wasn't killed but it's my understanding that he got into a feud and got cut up real bad. We had no contact with him when we came back to the States.' Bill actually made it to 64, before dying in Puerto Rico in 1990.

Bob Buckley remained very active with USC football. He ran a national printing company in Encino, north-east of Los Angeles, where he retired.

Steve Drakulvich moved from LA's Wilshire Boulevard to Alabama, where he suffered a leg amputation due to diabetes. He then moved to his wife's home state of Montana.

Harold Han went back home to Hawaii and worked in sales in Honolulu.

Tony Rappa outside his restaurant, Monterey, 2007

Pat Henry spent two more years on the Stanford rugby union team and played for the Northern California rep side against the touring All Blacks in San Francisco in 1954. After graduating, he played for the Olympic Club and then San Francisco Bald Eagles seniors team – even touring Canada and New Zealand. 'I played rugby union for 40 years! But 1953 was the most memorable year: I played union against Ireland, league against the Kangaroos in Sydney and Kiwis in Auckland and then the All Blacks in San Francisco! I was fortunate to play with and against many great athletes. We played hard and with total respect for each other.' Pat lived in Fremont where he worked for Amchem Products Inc. He died in 2006 after suffering from Parkinson's disease.

George Kauffman lived in San Diego, where he worked for the National Cash Register Company. He missed the 1963 reunion because he was selling 'several million dollars of cash registers' to a client in Dallas.

Al E. Kirkland returned from Leeds to Bakersfield, where he ran a very successful import-export business, including rugby equipment. He had a patent on Velcro equipment which you could remove from football pads when the pads needed cleaning. He died in his 70s after a heart attack while riding his bike along Long Beach. His close friend Al Abajian spoke at his funeral.

A couple of years after his All Stars adventure, **Michael F. Mandulay** founded a car dealership in Ojai Valley, California, and was very successful. He died in Ojai in 2003, aged 78.

Xavier Mena returned to education, got a PhD and later became assistant head of health education in the state of California. He lived in Point Loma, CA, but retired to Falls Church, Virginia.

Sol Naumu also returned to Hawaii, living in Pearl City and worked for the postal service.

Ray Terry became a teacher in Orange County, lived in La Jolla, CA, and later Corona Del Mar in Oregon. He remained a big sports fan. Before the 1963 All Stars reunion he was in Vegas watching Cassius Clay train for his fight with Sonny Liston.

Syd Walker became an MD and then a psychiatrist. He moved to the east coast and worked at Boston Medical School.

The 1953 All Stars had regular reunions, in ever decreasing numbers. It was almost a full house when Bob Buckley organised a ten-year 'Hot Meat Pie Reunion'. Gary Kerkorian claimed he and his wife would be there in their headgear, Al E. Kirkland promised his 'cobber' he would bring his 'bloody schooner glass and a penny hapenny'. 'Good on ya mate!' Even Wild Bill turned up.

In later years the reunions were held in Fresno to be near an ailing Gary and closer to Jack and the other boys in the Bay Area. Michelle Dimitro even attended to represent her Dad. In 2009, the surviving All Stars had another reunion, this time with Jack in Sacramento, to celebrate football and life.

THE 1954 ALL STARS

Landon Exley spent 30 years building houses in Southern California, retired for a year, then found a real estate deal in Boise, Idaho. He bought a farm there and travels up from his Laguna Beach base 'for the gorgeous fresh air'. Landon and second wife Debbie, a fellow USC alumni whose father played USC football, are avid members of Cardinal and Gold, raising money for the football programme and volunteering. A season ticket-holder since 1960, Landon still goes to two away games a year. 'I'm a football freak,' he admits.

Tony Rappa returned to Monterey in Northern California after his national service and worked at his parents' fish restaurant, eventually taking over Rappa's Harbor View restaurant on the pier.

Sam Grossman became a hugely-successful real estate developer, building hotels, shopping centres and office buildings with his Grossman Company Properties based in Phoenix. He also lectured around the world on real estate, health and nutrition, writing several dietary books, and being a competitive white-water kayaker. Sam is still a football fan and said: 'I tried to buy the Redskins but it did not work out, much to my chagrin; I would have loved to have had that deal.' He still enjoys skiing, windsurfing and surfing. 'Every once in a while when we run into some of the guys we have a lot of laughs.'

Erkie Cheldin continued to grow his Cheldin Insurance Agency, now known as Crusader Insurance Company Inc. He is actively involved in the day-to-day operations as chairman of the board. Also renowned for inventing the 'Erkie' staple remover, Erwin is 'very busy with work, a young daughter and a wife' in Woodland Hills.

Bob Ferguson finished his post-graduate work at USC and became good friends with Landon Exley, who he still sees occasionally in Southern California, often at Trojans football events. He lives in Fullerton, California.

Don Lent became a football coach and college professor. He converted to Christianity after a near-death experience following a car crash, joined the ministry and became Rev Donald J. Lent. He formed the Timothy II church and changed his name to Timothy II.

Bob Lampshire coached high school football and college football in Southern California. He coached with and against Don Lent and was converted by him to Christianity. Rev Lent conducted Bob's funeral.

Don Webster coached football for 30 years in Southern California, **Pat Brandy** lives in Orange County, California, **Virgil Elwiss** in Riverside, California and **Calvin Hilgenberg** died in Oakley, Contra Costa, California in 1997, aged 64.

Larry Moreno became an attorney and a member of the exclusive Bel Air Country Club with many of Hollywood's big hitters. He defended Mike Dimitro in several court cases.

THE REST OF THE CAST

RFL supremo **Bill Fallowfield** remained secretary of the International Board until his death in 1985. Only one country joined the world circuit during that time – Papua New Guinea. Ten years after his reign ended, rugby league's international scene had expanded by a dozen more countries including the USA.

League svengali **Harry Sunderland** died in Manchester in 1964. The Man of the Match award in the RFL Championship Final was named after him. The star man of the Super League Grand Final now receives the Harry Sunderland Medal.

Australia superstar **Clive Churchill** died in 1985, aged just 58, of cancer. A huge new stand at the Sydney Cricket Ground was named after him.

Cliff Evans had a magnificent 20-year coaching career in England after leaving his restaurant and car-washing businesses in LA to become a teacher in Lancashire. He is still the only man to coach three different clubs to RFL championship triumphs: Swinton in 1963 and 1964, St Helens in 1970 and Salford in 1974.

Kiwi guest players **Travers Hardwick** and **Des Barchard** both went on to coach the New Zealand national team, Hardwick in 1959/60, and Barchard in the 1968 and 1972 World Cup tournaments, which could have taken place in the US if Dimitro had pulled it off. The Kiwis lost all six games under Barchard's charge.

LA promoter **Rosey Gilhousen** spent the rest of his life in pro baseball. One of the LA Angels' original employees, he was a successful MLB scout for Kansas City Royals and the Angels. He died, aged 84, in 1997 in Rancho Mirage, where the Dimitros lived.

Eddie Waring became a huge TV celebrity in the UK, fronting primetime Saturday night entertainment shows, as well as being the BBC's voice of rugby league. His catchphrases and increasingly extreme accent was much impersonated and eventually mocked. He died in 1986.

The author with Ed Demirjian and Ted Grossman at LA Coliseum, 2007.

BOOK LAUNCHES

No Helmets Required was launched in the United States in 2014 with events at Stanford University and the University of Southern California, and then in Australia in 2017 in Cairns and Townsville, where the All Stars played in 1953.

1 *All Stars Don Lent, Al Abajian, Landon Exley, Ed Demirjian and Bob Ferguson with the USC Rugby team of 2014.*
2 *Current Stanford Rugby coaches and an All Stars team-mate with the author at the Stanford launch, 2014.*
3 *No Helmets in illustrious company on the shelves of Australian bookshops.*
4 *USA team train at Townsville Sports Reserve, where the All Stars played, before playing Italy at the 2017 World Cup.*
5 *Players and staff from the USA's RLWC2017 squad learn about the pioneering All Stars at the Townsville launch.*
6 *ABC Radio Far North feature No Helmets Required and the All Stars visit to Cairns.*

APPENDIX 1
AUSTRALIA AND NEW ZEALAND TOUR

American All Stars squad: Al Abajian – wing/half-back; Bill Albans – wing/full-back; Jack Bonetti – second row/lock; Bob Buckley – wing/centre; Ed Demirjian - wing; Mike Dimitro – second row; Steve Drakulvich – utility forward; Ted Grossman - half-back; Harold Han – centre/wing; Pat Henry – prop/hooker; Vince Jones - prop; George Kauffman – full-back; Gary Kerkorian – five-eighths/centre; Alfred D Kirkland – lock; Alvin E Kirkland – centre/five-eighths; Fran Mandulay - prop; Sol Naumu - full-back/wing/centre; Xavier Mena - prop; Ray Terry - forward; Sidney Walker - hooker.

Guest Queensland players against New South Wales: Harold 'Mick' Crocker; Brian Davies; Alan Hornery; Ken McCaffery.

Guest Kiwi players in New Zealand: Travers Hardwick; Ray Roff; Des Barchard; Fran Mulcare; Roy Moore.

AUSTRALIAN LEG
Wednesday 27 May 1953
v SOUTHERN DIVISIONS*
Mankua Oval, Canberra
Won 34-25
Attendance: 4,827
* Also referred to as 'Southern Districts & Monaro', 'Canberra', 'Monaro', and 'Southern and Monaro Districts'.

Saturday 30 May
v SYDNEY
Sydney Cricket Ground
Lost 52-25
Attendance: 65,453

Tuesday 2 June
v NEW SOUTH WALES
Sydney Cricket Ground
Lost 62-41
Attendance: 32,554

Sunday 7 June
v COMBINED COUNTRY
Showgrounds, Wollongong
Lost 35-9
Attendance: 11,787

Wednesday 10 June
v WESTERN DIVISION
No 1 Oval, Dubbo
Lost 24-21
Attendance: 4,717

Saturday 13 June
v NEWCASTLE
Sports Ground, Newcastle
Won 19-10
Attendance: 14,160

Wednesday 17 June
v NORTH COAST*
Coffs Harbour
Lost 26-18
Attendance: 5,400
* Also referred to as 'North & North Coast Division' and as 'Northern Districts'.

Saturday 20 June
v QUEENSLAND
The Gabba, Brisbane
Lost 39-36
Attendance: 24,397

Wednesday 24 June
v FAR NORTH QUEENSLAND
Parramatta Park, Cairns
Drew 17-17
Attendance: 6,042

Sunday 28 June
v NORTH QUEENSLAND
Sports Reserve, Townsville
Lost 38-17
Attendance: 7,808

Wednesday 1 July
v CENTRAL WEST QUEENSLAND
Longreach
Lost 26-21
Attendance: 1,635

Sunday 5 July
v CENTRAL QUEENSLAND COAST
Murray St Ground, Rockhampton
Lost 33-26
Attendance: 5,332

Tuesday 7 July
v BRISBANE
The Gabba
Lost 39-26
Attendance: 7,000

Wednesday 15 July
v TOOWOOMBA
Athletic Oval, Toowoomba
Lost 29-15
Attendance: 5,778

Saturday 18 July
v IPSWICH
North Ipswich Reserve
Won 16-15
Attendance: 3,155

Sunday 19 July
v WIDE BAY
Maryborough Showgrounds
Drew 33-33
Attendance: 6,166

Wednesday 22 July
v RIVERINA
Anzac Park, Gundagai
Lost 30-14
Attendance: 2,560

Saturday 25 July
v NEW SOUTH WALES
Sydney Cricket Ground
Lost 27-18
Attendance: 19,686

ALL STARS' RECORD IN AUSTRALIA

Played	18
Won	3
Drew	2
Lost	13
Points for	400
Against	560

Try-scorers: Al E. Kirkland 11; Abajian 8; Bonetti 7, Han 7, Al D. Kirkland 7; Grossman 6; Kerkorian 5, Albans 5; Buckley 3; Demirjian 2, Jones 2, Mena 2; Buckley 1, Davies 1, Dimitro 1, Drakulvich 1, Henry 1, Kauffman 1, Mandulay 1, McCaffery 1, Naumu 1, Walker 1.

Goals: Kerkorian 74, Kauffman 5, Al D. Kirkland 1.
Field goal: Kauffman 1.

The figures do not include a try for an unspecified Kirkland v Brisbane and Wide Bay, and do not include the game against Riverina as scoring information was not available.

NEW ZEALAND LEG

Saturday 1 August
v AUCKLAND
Carlaw Park
Lost 54-26
Attendance: 12,377

Wednesday 5 August
v TARANAKI
Pukekura Park, New Plymouth
Won 21-18
Attendance: 1,971

Saturday 8 August
v WELLINGTON
Basin Reserve
Won 17-8
Attendance: Unknown

Tuesday 11 August
v WEST COAST
Wingham Park, Greymouth
Lost 27-10
Attendance: 1,913

Saturday 15 August
v CANTERBURY
Addington Showgrounds, Christchurch
Lost 39-8
Attendance: 4,273

Wednesday 19 August
v NORTHLAND
Jubilee Park, Whangarei
Won 26-5
Attendance: 867

Saturday 22 August
v MAORIS
Carlaw Park, Auckland
Lost 40-23
Attendance: 6,673

Monday 24 August
v SOUTH AUCKLAND
Rugby Park, Hamilton
Won 22-19
Attendance: 2,496

ALL STARS' RECORD IN NEW ZEALAND

Played	8
Won	4
Drew	0
Lost	4
For	157
Against	211

Try-scorers: Mulcare 8; Hardwick 5; Roff 4; Al E. Kirkland 3; Barchard 2, Grossman 2, Al D. Kirkland 2; Dimitro 1, Jones 1, Moore 1.

Goals: Moore 11, Naumu 8, Kauffman 2.
Field goal: Kauffman 1.

These figures do not include the game v South Auckland, for which the scoring details were unavailable.

ALL STARS' TOTAL PLAYING RECORD DOWN UNDER

Played	26
Won	7
Drew	2
Lost	17
For	557
Against	771

Try-scorers: Al E. Kirkland 14; Al D. Kirkland 9; Abajian 8, Grossman 8, Mulcare 8; Bonetti 7,
Han 7; Albans 5, Hardwick 5, Kerkorian 5; Roff 4; Buckley 3, Jones 3; Barchard 2, Demirjian 2, Dimitro 2, Mena 2; Buckley 1, Davies 1, Drakulvich 1, Henry 1, Kauffman 1, Mandulay 1, McCaffery 1, Moore 1, Naumu 1, Walker 1.

Goals: Kerkorian 74, Moore 11, Naumu 8, Kauffman 7, Al D. Kirkland 1.
Field goals: Kauffman 2.

APPENDIX 2
FRANCE TOUR

American All Stars squad: Bob Ferguson; Virgil Elwess; Bob Lampshire; Tony Rappa; Ted Grossman; Larry Moreno; Calvin Hilgenberg; Willie Richardson; Xavier Mena; Pat Bandy; Don Lent; Harry Taylor; Leon Sellers; Landon Exley; Mike Dimitro; Norm Stocks; Sam Grossman; Erwin Cheldin; Don Webster.
Manager: Ray Terry.

Sunday 20 December 1953
v LANGUEDOC XIII
Stade Albert-Domec, Carcassonne
Lost 30-22
Attendance: 5,000

Friday 25 December
v ALBI
Stade Maurice Rigaud, Albi
Lost 11-5
Attendance: 5,800

Sunday 27 December
v ESPOIRS DE FRANCE
Stade Jean-Laffon, Perpignan
Lost 37-21
Attendance: Unknown

Friday 1 January 1954
v SELECTION de PROVENCE
Stade de Saint-Ruf, Avignon
Won 22-12
Attendance: 3,000

Sunday 3 January
France 19 Selection Internationale 15
Stade Gerland, Lyon

Saturday 9 January
v FRANCE
Parc de Princes, Paris
Lost 31-0
Attendance: 20,000

Played	5
Won	1
Lost	4
For	70
Against	121

Try-scorers: Lampshire 3; Hilgenberg 2, Lent 2, Moreno 2, Mena 2, Rappa 2, Richardson 2; Dimitro 1, T Grossman 1, Taylor 1.

Goals: Lampshire 7, Richardson 1..

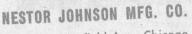

THE AUTHOR

Gavin Willacy has been a sportswriter since putting together a newsletter for his Subbuteo club when he was seven years old (all four members). He was a fanzine-writing student in St Albans and Salford which lead to him getting his first job as a staff writer at *Shoot!* football magazine, before joining the launch team of Football365.com.

Having been taken to rugby league once a year throughout his football-obsessed childhood, his interest in the 13-man code was rekindled when he found himself living above a London pub that had Sky Sports. Thus began an infatuation with rugby league fuelled by the missionary zealousness of the convert. His interest in American football, hatched in the early 1980s, also continues.

As a freelancer, Gavin has written features for *FourFourTwo*, *World Soccer* and *Esquire* magazines, reported for *The Times*, *Independent* and *Observer*, and been a regular contributor to *Forty-20*, *League Express* and *Rugby League World*. Since the publication of this, his fourth sports book, he writes the successful *No Helmets Required* blog for *The Guardian* website.

He is a fanatical follower of Preston North End Football Club, and a loyal supporter of Lancashire County Cricket Club, while his club rugby league affiliations lie with London Broncos and London Skolars, and internationally he follows Scotland (for whom he was press officer for many years), Italy, and, of course, the USA.

Gavin lives in Hertfordshire, England with his long-suffering wife and oblivious cat.

Gavin after being interviewed on ABC Radio Far North in Cairns, 2017.